ELIZABETH BARRETT BROWNING

broadview editions
series editor: L.W. Conolly

ELIZABETH BARRETT BROWNING

SELECTED POEMS

edited by Marjorie Stone and Beverly Taylor

broadview editions

Library and Archives Canada Cataloguing in Publication

Browning, Elizabeth Barrett, 1806-1861
[Poems. Selections]
    Elizabeth Barrett Browning : selected poems / edited
by Marjorie Stone and Beverly Taylor.

Poems.
ISBN 978-1-55111-482-8

    1. Browning, Elizabeth Barrett, 1806-1861—Criticism and interpretation.
I. Stone, Marjorie I., 1951- II. Taylor, Beverly, 1947- III. Title. IV. Title:
Poems. Selections.

PR4182.S76 2009   821.8   C2009-901711-3

Broadview Editions

The Broadview Editions series represents the ever-changing canon of literature by bringing together texts long regarded as classics with valuable lesser-known works.

Advisory editor for this volume: Betsy Struthers

Broadview Press is an independent, international publishing house, incorporated in 1985. Broadview believes in shared ownership, both with its employees and with the general public; since the year 2000 Broadview shares have traded publicly on the Toronto Venture Exchange under the symbol BDP.

We welcome comments and suggestions regarding any aspect of our publications—please feel free to contact us at the addresses below or at broadview@broadviewpress.com.

North America
PO Box 1243, Peterborough, Ontario, Canada K9J 7H5
2215 Kenmore Ave., Buffalo, New York, USA 14207
Tel: (705) 743-8990; Fax: (705) 743-8353
email: customerservice@broadviewpress.com

UK, Ireland, and continental Europe
NBN International, Estover Road, Plymouth, UK PL6 7PY
Tel: 44 (0) 1752 202300; Fax: 44 (0) 1752 202330
email: enquiries@nbninternational.com

Australia and New Zealand
UNIREPS, University of New South Wales
Sydney, NSW, Australia 2052
Tel: 61 (0) 2 9385 0150; Fax: 61 (0) 2 9385 0155
email: info@unireps.com.au

www.broadviewpress.com

Broadview Press gratefully acknowledges the financial support of the Government of Canada through the Book Publishing Industry Development Program (BPIDP) for our publishing activities.

The interior on this book is printed on paper containing 100% post-consumer fibre.

PRINTED IN CANADA

Contents

Acknowledgements

Our Introduction, headnotes, footnotes, and Select Bibliography record our great indebtedness to previous editors of Elizabeth Barrett Browning's poems, prose, and letters, and to many scholar-critics past and present. All students of EBB are profoundly indebted to Philip Kelley, who as a collector, editor, and publisher has made essential materials available in superb editions; to Betty A. Coley Fredeman, with him co-author of *The Browning Collections: A Reconstruction*, which by locating and describing the Browning possessions dispersed at auction in 1913 made it possible to study EBB manuscripts; to Scott Lewis, Kelley's co-editor of *The Brownings' Correspondence* (following the death of Ronald Hudson) and editor of newly available material in EBB's *Letters to Her Sister Arabella*; to Edward Hagan, co-editor with Kelley and Lewis of Volumes 15 and 16; and to Meredith B. Raymond and Mary Rose Sullivan, whose excellent edition of EBB's correspondence with Mary Russell Mitford initiated the remarkable series of indispensable Brownings' correspondence from the Wedgestone Press. All scholars of EBB in our generation are indebted to path-breaking full-length studies by Dorothy Mermin, Angela Leighton, Helen Cooper, and Glennis (Stephenson) Byron. Sandra Donaldson, Simon Avery, Clara Drummond, Rowena Fowler, Tricia Lootens, and Elizabeth Woodworth have generously shared information and their expertise. The liberal assistance of librarians at the Berg Collection of the New York Public Library, the British Library, the Huntington Library, the Ransome Center at the University of Texas, Wellesley College Library, and particularly Cynthia Burgess and Rita S. Patteson at the Armstrong Browning Library of Baylor University deserve warm thanks. We are indebted to Lesley Newhook, Barbara Kanellakos, David Anderson, and Ryan van Huijstee at Dalhousie University and to Jennifer Cadwallader, Meagan Foster, Beverly Pearson, Natalie Phillips, and Cheryl Thayer at the University of North Carolina—Chapel Hill for valuable research assistance. The Social Sciences and Humanities Research Council of Canada, through its Standard Grants Program, Dalhousie University, and, at the University of North Carolina—Chapel

Hill, William Andrews and James Thompson as Chairs and the Kenan Fund of the Department of English, provided generous funding for research travel. Thanks are due to the Armstrong Browning Library; the Rare Book Collection, The University of North Carolina, Chapel Hill; and the Yale Art Museum for permission to reproduce images. For permission to reproduce or cite manuscript materials, we gratefully acknowledge the Annenberg Rare Book and Manuscript Library, University of Pennsylvania; the Berg Collection of the New York Public Library; the Huntington Library; and the Wellesley College Library. Finally, we would like to thank Julia Gaunce, Marjorie Mather, Leonard Conolly, Betsy Struthers, and Piper-Lee Blackey of Broadview Press for their expert advice, assistance, and patience.

Abbreviations, Primary Sources, and Website

ABL   Armstrong Browning Library, Baylor University, Waco, Texas.

AL   Elizabeth Barrett Browning, *Aurora Leigh,* ed. Margaret Reynolds (New York and London: W.W. Norton, 1996).

AL (Ohio)   Elizabeth Barrett Browning, *Aurora Leigh,* ed. Margaret Reynolds (Athens, OH: Ohio UP, 1992).

BC   *The Brownings' Correspondence,* ed. Philip Kelley, Ronald Hudson, Scott Lewis, and Edward Hagan, 16 vols. to date (Winfield, KS: Wedgestone Press, 1984–).

CGW   Elizabeth Barrett Browning, *Casa Guidi Windows,* ed. Julia Markus (NY: The Browning Institute, 1977).

CW   *The Complete Works of Elizabeth Barrett Browning,* ed. Charlotte Porter and Helen A. Clarke (NY: Thomas Y. Crowell, 1900; rpt. NY: AMS Press, 1973).

Diary   *Diary by E.B.B.: The Unpublished Diary of Elizabeth Barrett Barrett, 1831-1832,* ed. Philip Kelley and Ronald Hudson (Athens, OH: Ohio UP, 1969).

EBB   Elizabeth Barrett Barrett, prior to her marriage in 1846, and Elizabeth Barrett Browning subsequently.

HUPS   *Elizabeth Barrett Browning: Hitherto Unpublished Poems and Stories with an Inedited Autobiography,* ed. H. Buxton Forman (Boston: Bibliophile Society, 1914).

LEBB   *The Letters of Elizabeth Barrett Browning,* ed. Frederic G. Kenyon, 2 vols. (London: Macmillan, 1897).

LTA   *The Letters of Elizabeth Barrett Browning to Her Sister Arabella,* ed. Scott Lewis, 2 vols. (Waco, TX: Wedgestone Press, 2002).

LTH   *Elizabeth Barrett Browning: Letters to Her Sister [Henrietta], 1846-1859,* ed. Leonard Huxley (London: John Murray, 1929).

LTM   *The Letters of Elizabeth Barrett Browning to Mary Russell Mitford, 1836-1854,* ed. Meredith B. Raymond and Mary Rose Sullivan, 3 vols. (Winfield, KS: Armstrong Browning Library of Baylor University,

The Browning Institute, Wedgestone Press, and Wellesley College, 1983).

R   Philip Kelley and Betty A. Coley, *The Browning Collections: A Reconstruction with Other Memorabilia. The Library, First Works, Presentation Volumes, Manuscripts, Likenesses, Works of Art, Household and Personal Effects, and Other Association Items of Robert and Elizabeth Barrett Browning* (Winfield, KS: Armstrong Browning Library of Baylor University, The Browning Institute, Mansell Publishing, Wedgestone Press, 1984). An updated version is now available at http://www.browningguide.org.

RB   Robert Browning

SBHC   *Studies in Browning and His Circle*

VP   *Victorian Poetry* (the journal of that title)

Supplementary Website: http://www.ebbarchive.org

Note on Citation Practices and EBB's Punctuation

With the exception of primary sources included in the list of abbreviations, works in the Select Bibliography (pp. 357–68) are cited throughout this edition by the author's last name and date of publication; for other sources, full information is provided. When quoting from EBB's published writings, we reproduce the punctuation used in the edition we cite. In most instances, these editions record her practice of using two dots that may sometimes represent an ellipsis, but often indicate the kind of pause more conventionally suggested by a dash; we also reproduce her occasional use of doubled punctuation, such as a comma followed by a dash.

Illustrations

Preface: About this Edition

Range and Selection of Texts

With the exception of critical editions of her major long works *Aurora Leigh* and *Casa Guidi Windows*, and variorum and facsimile editions of the *Sonnets from the Portuguese*, there is no scholarly modern annotated edition of Elizabeth Barrett Browning's poetry that incorporates research into textual history, manuscript sources, and recently published correspondence. The last ostensibly "complete" scholarly edition of her poetry appeared in 1900;[1] more recent, relatively comprehensive editions reproduce suspect texts and include little or no annotation.[2] Even recent paperback selected editions provide unacceptably limited offerings, lack adequate annotation, and, in some cases, include inaccurate notes along with unreliable texts.[3] A complete scholarly edition of EBB's work, including textual variants as well as the large body of juvenilia and numerous unpublished works and fragments, is in progress by a team including the editors of this volume, headed by Sandra Donaldson, to be published by Pickering and Chatto in 2009.

This annotated critical edition offers a representative selection of work from EBB's earliest recorded poem to works posthumously published by Robert Browning after her death fifty years later. The selections reflect the range of poetic forms that distinguishes her output as well as her unusually extensive range of subjects. We include in full or in substantial excerpts many works that played a prominent role in nineteenth-century literary history, among them *Sonnets from the Portuguese* (1850), *Casa Guidi Windows* (1851), several

---

1 See *CW* in the "Abbreviations" list, which includes some helpful annotation and a critical introduction.

2 The other fullest available editions are *The Cambridge Edition* (Boston: Houghton Mifflin, 1974), a reprint of the 1900 volume edited by Harriet Waters Preston, which provides very limited notes, and the volume issued by the Wordsworth Poetry Library 1994, which follows an unspecified source and lacks notes altogether. Neither includes poems from EBB's 1826 collection, *An Essay on Mind, With Other Poems,* that she subsequently excluded from her *Poems* (1850), as Sandra Donaldson notes (2002, 49). Frederic G. Kenyon's *The Poetical Works of Elizabeth Barrett Browning* (London: Smith, Elder, 1897) is available only in research libraries.

3 See Stone 1997 for a survey of several selected editions.

of EBB's ballads, her anti-slavery poems, and her more influential political poems such as "The Cry of the Children." In addition, readers will find here poems never before printed in collections of EBB's works: her earliest known poem "On the Cruelty of Forcement to Man"; the "Fragment of an 'Essay on Woman,'" reflecting her reading of Mary Wollstonecraft's *A Vindication of the Rights of Women* (1792); and, most notably, a monologue depicting her favorite Greek dramatist, Aeschylus, just before his death, previously included only in editions of Robert Browning's poetry. Known as "[Aeschylus' Soliloquy]"—but here, using the term by which EBB referred to it, called "[Aeschylus's Monodrama]"—this work points to the difficulties that have beset editors dealing with the dismembered manuscript remains of EBB's large corpus of poetry. Until 1982 the Aeschylus monologue was attributed to her husband—indeed saluted as one of the best dramatic monologues he had left unpublished—until discovery of EBB's rough draft conclusively identified it as her work. The major omission from this volume is *Aurora Leigh*, readily available in Margaret Reynolds's excellent edition.[1] This Broadview Edition focuses instead on the works written before and after *Aurora Leigh* that made EBB one of the most influential poets of the nineteenth-century in the English-speaking world.

Textual Revisions and Choice of Copy-Texts

Earlier selected and "complete" editions of EBB's poetry do not note the substantial textual revisions she made in many works after their initial publication. In initially collecting her poetry in *Poems* (1844), she heavily revised works such as "The Romaunt of the Page" (1839) and "Catarina to Camoens" (1843) that had earlier appeared in periodicals or annuals. Moreover, in preparing her expanded 1850 collection, she comprehensively revised the texts of many earlier poems. "I took great pains with the whole, & made considerable portions, new" (*LTM* 3:310), she said of works in the 1838 collection included in *Poems* (1850). In 1850, she also revised—

---

1 Available in both a variorum edition (*AL* Ohio) and a Norton Critical paperback (*AL*).

though to a lesser degree—works first published in *Poems* (1844), continuing to make changes up until *Poems* (1856).

Whenever possible, we have reproduced her poetical texts as they appear in *Poems* (1856), the last edition of her collected works to appear under her attentive eye, in order to respect the artistic integrity and purpose that led her to revise so many of her poems. As with Tennyson's revisions of works in his *Poems* (1832) for *Poems* (1842), the changes that EBB made in her earlier poems demonstrate her artistic maturation, her attention to readers' and critics' assessments of her work, and her reactions to events of her day. Moreover, the 1856 texts of her poems generally form the basis for the more reliable editions published thereafter, such as the fifth Chapman and Hall edition of *Poems* (1862) supervised by Robert Browning. These are the texts, in other words, that influenced readers and writers through the generations. For earlier published poems that EBB did not reprint in 1856, we have followed the latest version she published. For works published after 1856—those from *Poems before Congress* (1860) and *Last Poems* (1862)—we follow the first British editions, overseen in the first instance by EBB herself and in the second by her husband Robert, who indicated that he followed her plans for a future volume in publishing the posthumous collection. For poems in manuscript, we indicate our copy text and its state of finish. In all cases, we provide the earliest known publication date, as well as the date (if it differs) of its first appearance in a poetry collection.

Annotations and Contextual Material

In the case of contextual materials editors face a daunting wealth of information. EBB's correspondence is voluminous; the poems themselves often teem with allusions to events, figures, and debates, as well as to other literary works; and the body of reviews and critical work is enormous. We have given priority in this edition to providing a guide through this embarrassment of riches for students, scholars, and interested general readers, not to packing in the maximum number of poems by EBB possible within constraints on length (we provide annotated texts of a number of additional poems on a supplementary website, http://www.ebbarchive.org).

Our annotations draw on the multiple selected earlier editions of her letters (especially her lively letters to Mary Mitford, *LTM*); the recently published *Letters* to her sister Arabella (*LTA*), which includes many new details about the years following her marriage; and the progressively appearing volumes of *The Brownings' Correspondence* (*BC*)—an invaluable, comprehensive resource still too little used by students and scholars. The Introduction and the notes to each poem provide information on its contexts, composition, form, and reception, demonstrating how intensively EBB engaged with important social, political, religious, and artistic developments of the early to mid-nineteenth century, as well as with the literary traditions she invokes, echoes, challenges, and modifies.

Our appendices—another resource absent from earlier selected editions of EBB's poetry—provide important contexts for the poems. Appendix A concentrates on reviews and criticism that appeared after 1850 (earlier reviews are reproduced in full in appendices to *The Brownings' Correspondence*). Many Victorian reviews illustrate how the period's gender stereotypes shaped critical response to EBB's work. Among historical contexts we include mid-Victorian religious discourses, the industrialization of England, the trans-Atlantic anti-slavery movement, and the struggle for Italian liberation and nationhood that engaged EBB so passionately following her marriage in 1846. We also include in Appendix C the original, uncancelled opening of "The Runaway Slave at Pilgrim's Point" (featuring a male, not a female speaker). EBB's manuscript remains are rich in examples of "poems in process" that space constraints prevent our including here. This example may at least begin to suggest the dynamic qualities of EBB's works and career as she mastered her craft.

While *Aurora Leigh* has hitherto dominated the critical recovery of EBB's works in our own time, many of her other works also entered in far-reaching ways into nineteenth-century literary, social, and political developments. The growing number of books and articles on EBB (see the Introduction and Selected Bibliography) suggests that, after suffering neglect through three-quarters of the twentieth century, she is reclaiming her prominence in literary history. We hope that this Broadview Edition will contribute to this ongoing reclamation by giving readers ready access to poems and poetic contexts effectively lost for too long.

Elizabeth Barrett Browning: A Brief Chronology

1806   Elizabeth Barrett Moulton Barrett born 6 March, at Coxhoe Hall near Durham, first child of Edward Barrett Moulton Barrett (1785-1857) and Mary Graham-Clarke (1781-1828).

1809   Family moves to Hope End, an estate in Herefordshire.

1812   Robert Browning born at Camberwell, 7 May.

1817   Begins studying Greek with her brother Edward's tutor, Daniel McSwiney.

1818   Writes short autobiographical essay "My Own Character" (*BC* 1:347-48).

1820   Her epic *The Battle of Marathon* privately printed, 50 copies at her father's expense. Formal tuition in Greek ends when Edward ("Bro") leaves for boarding school.

1820-21 Writes autobiographical sketch, "Glimpses into My Own Life and Literary Character" (*BC* 1:348-56).

1821   Writes essay, "My Character and Bro's Compared" (*BC* 1:357-58). "Stanzas, excited by some reflections on the present state of Greece" published in *The New Monthly Magazine*, May. Seriously ill, she goes to Gloucester Spa for treatment, June.

1822   Returns to Hope End from Gloucester, May.

1826   *An Essay on Mind, with Other Poems* published.

1828   Begins studying Greek with Hugh Stuart Boyd, who began a correspondence with her in February 1827. Her mother dies, October 7.

1830   Her paternal grandmother Elizabeth Moulton dies, leaving EBB £4,000.

1831-32 Keeps a diary, June 1831-April 1832. (See *Diary* in "List of Abbreviations.")

1832   Father sells Hope End and moves family to Sidmouth.

1833   *Prometheus Bound, Translated from the Greek of Aeschylus, and Miscellaneous Poems* published.

1835   Barrett family moves to London, December.

1836   Meets writers William Wordsworth and Mary Russell Mitford, May.

1837	Queen Victoria ascends to throne, June. EBB's favorite uncle Samuel Barrett Moulton Barrett dies in Jamaica; his bequest makes EBB financially independent.
1838	*The Seraphim, and Other Poems* published. Barrett family moves to 50 Wimpole Street in London. EBB relocates to Torquay for health, August.
1840	Brother Sam dies in Jamaica, February. Favorite brother Edward ("Bro") drowns at Torquay, July, precipitating a prolonged, near-fatal illness.
1841	Receives spaniel Flush from Mitford, January. Returns to London, September.
1842	Prose work "Some Account of the Greek Christian Poets" published in *The Athenaeum*, February–March; "The Book of the Poets," a survey of British literature since Chaucer, published in *The Athenaeum*, June–August.
1843	"The Cry of the Children" published in *Blackwood's Magazine*, August. Begins collaborating with R.H. Horne on *A New Spirit of the Age* (published March 1844).
1844	*Poems* (2 volumes) published; EBB widely reviewed as a major poet.
1845	EBB-RB correspondence begins (first letter from RB 10 January; first meeting 20 May). Begins writing *Sonnets from the Portuguese*.
1846	EBB and RB marry, 12 September, and leave a week later for Italy, first pausing in Paris and arriving in Pisa on 14 October.
1847	Brownings move to Florence, April. EBB begins writing "A Meditation in Tuscany" (Part I of *Casa Guidi Windows*). "The Runaway Slave at Pilgrim's Point" published in the Boston anti-slavery annual *The Liberty Bell* (dated 1848), in December.
1849	Brownings' son Robert Wiedeman Barrett Browning ("Pen") born, 9 March. EBB reveals to RB the completed text of *Sonnets from the Portuguese*, July.
1850	*The Athenaeum* proposes EBB for Poet Laureate (June) when Wordsworth dies (Alfred Tennyson named to the

post). Expanded edition of *Poems*, including *Sonnets from the Portuguese* and additional new works, published in November.

1851   *Casa Guidi Windows* published, May. Brownings travel to Venice, Paris, and London, where they stay from July to September and attend the Great Exhibition. In Paris, fall and winter, when a coup d'état elevates Louis Napoleon Bonaparte from President to Emperor, December.

1852   Brownings meet George Sand in Paris, February. They return to England in July, back to Paris in October, and to Florence in November.

1853   New, revised edition of *Poems* published, October.

1854   EBB's "Plea for the Ragged Schools of London" published with RB's "The Twins" for sale at a charity bazaar, April--their only joint publication.

1855   Brownings travel to Paris in June, then on to London in July. Return to Paris, October to June 1856. RB's *Men and Women* published, November. EBB's "A Curse for a Nation" published in the 1856 issue of the *Liberty Bell*, December.

1856   Brownings return to England, June, then home to Florence, October. EBB's new further revised edition of *Poems* and *Aurora Leigh* published, November. Death of the Brownings' beloved friend John Kenyon, who leaves them £11,000.

1857   Second and third impressions (called second and third editions) of *Aurora Leigh*, January, March. Death of EBB's father, April.

1858   Brownings holiday in northern France with both their families, July, then move to Paris until October. Winter in Rome, November to May 1859.

1859   Brownings return to Florence in May. Fourth (revised) edition of *Aurora Leigh* published, June. EBB seriously ill, July. Brownings in Siena, July to October, in Rome, November to June 1860.

1860   Tuscany becomes part of the new kingdom of Italy. *Poems before Congress* published, March. Brownings

	return to Florence in June, summer in Siena, July to October, then move to Rome, November to June 1861. EBB's sister Henrietta dies, late November.
1861	EBB confined to room by ill health. Brownings return to Florence in June, where EBB dies, 29 June. Buried in Protestant cemetery, 1 July. RB and Pen move to London, August.
1862	*Last Poems* published. Florentine government erects a plaque on Casa Guidi to honor EBB's support of Italian unification.

Introduction[1]

Elizabeth Barrett Browning and Literary History: A Poet Gained, Lost, and Recovered

"England has given to the world one great poetess—Elizabeth Barrett Browning." This opening salvo of the 1888 essay "English Poetesses" by poet, dramatist, and critic Oscar Wilde pays tribute to the woman poet who, in his view, was "the only one that we could name in any possible or remote conjunction with Sappho."[2] In comparing EBB[3] to the most famous woman poet in Western history, the ancient whose reputation lingered while nearly all her work was lost to posterity, Wilde unknowingly anticipated the nineteenth-century poet's fate. In the century following her death in 1861, the writer whose works were widely known and cited not only in England but also in North America and in Europe would increasingly be remembered more for the romance of her life than for her poetry itself or its historical influence. For Wilde in 1888, however, EBB was "an imperishable glory of our literature" because of the social and political import, variety, scope, and cultural impact of her poetry. She "heard the cry of the children from dark mine and crowded factory ... in the feigned sonnets from the Portug[u]ese, sang of the spiritual mystery of Love, ... wrote the 'Vision of Poets,' and 'Casa Guidi Windows,' and 'Aurora Leigh.'" She lived "not alone in the heart of Shakespeare's England, but in the heart of Dante's Italy," where her "human passion for Liberty" was "to a certain extent a real factor in bringing about that unity of Italy that was Dante's dream." Wilde also emphasized her crucial role

---

1   See the "Note on Citation Practices," p. xiii.

2   Although the poetry of the early Greek poet Sappho (born c. mid-seventh century BCE) survives only in scant fragments, her reputation as the greatest woman poet in European history persisted. Poetic representations of her mythologized life abounded in the nineteenth century. See Yopie Prins, *Victorian Sappho* (Princeton: Princeton UP, 1999), and Margaret Reynolds, *The Sappho History* (NY: Palgrave Macmillan, 2003).

3   See p. 9, note 2 below for an explanation of our using "EBB" instead of the more usual "Barrett Browning."

in advancing women writers: "To her influence, almost as much as to the higher education of women, I would be inclined to attribute the really remarkable awakening of women's song that characterizes the latter half of our century in England."[1]

Wilde's emphasis on the social, political, and philosophical functions of poetry—especially notable in an author himself known as an apostle of aestheticism or "art for art's sake"—resonates with EBB's own sense of her mission as a poet. "I never mistook pleasure for the final cause of poetry; nor leisure, for the hour of the poet," she stated in the "Preface" to *Poems* (1844), the collection that established her international reputation in the English-speaking world. Referring to the political throes of Italy, the subject of much of her later poetry, she declared, "if, while such things are done and suffered, the poet's business is to rhyme the stars and walk apart, *I* say ... that the world requires more earnest workers than such dreamers can be.... I don't dream and make a poem of it. Art is not either all beauty or all use, it is essential truth which makes its way through beauty into use" (*LEBB* 2:382-83). The testimony of nineteenth-century readers and critics makes it clear that EBB's poetry made its way into "use," while the complex debates it stimulated underscore the difficulties inherent in defining what is beautiful. How do we determine "essential truth"? Who decides, based on which criteria?

Despite the diverging responses to EBB's poetry, she was clearly rated by many of her contemporaries among the leading poets—female or male—writing in English from the 1840s to 1900. Like Byron in the previous generation, with whom she was sometimes compared, she achieved a reputation that was international and cosmopolitan. Her work was discussed in France, was especially popular in North America, and was translated into Italian as well as into Russian.[2] Poe dedicated *The Raven and Other Poems* (1845)

---

1   Wilde, "English Poetesses," *Queen* (8 December 1888), 742-43; for excerpts from this essay, see the supplementary website to this edition <<www.ebbarchive.org>>.

2   EBB's Poems (1844) "had a more general and hearty welcome in the United States than any English poet since the time of Byron and company," stated her obituary in *Harper's Magazine* 23 (1861): 555. On the Russian translation of "The Cry of the Children," see Waddington. In France, EBB's works were treated by the critic Joseph Milsand, among others (*LTM* 3:336n6; *LTA* 1:424n15), as well as by Joseph Texte and Hippolyte Taine (Stone 1995, 201). On the Italian reception of her works, see Bisignano.

to "Miss Elizabeth Barrett Barrett," the "Noblest of Her Sex," an honor which prompted her to quip to her cousin John Kenyon, "What is to be said, I wonder, when a man calls you the 'noblest of your sex' ... 'Sir, you are the most discerning of yours'" (*BC* 12:164-65). She had achieved sufficient distinction by 1850 that a reviewer for the influential periodical *The Athenaeum* proposed that she should succeed William Wordsworth as Poet Laureate.[1] Writers such as John Ruskin, George Eliot, and Edgar Allan Poe heralded the importance of her poetry.[2] The works of the next generation of English, American, and Canadian poets, including Christina Rossetti, Dante Gabriel Rossetti, A.C. Swinburne, Emily Dickinson, and Isabella Valancy Crawford, attest to her impact on their development.[3] One index of her influence is the number of tribute poems written to her before and after her death, many of them by women writers, bearing out Wilde's view of EBB's role in the "remarkable awakening" of women's poetic activity in the nineteenth century.[4] By 1900, however, a dramatic reversal in her reputation had occurred. In Amy Lowell's "The Sisters" (1925), it is difficult to recognize the woman poet whose works led Emily Dickinson to experience "Conversion of the Mind" in "I think I was enchanted," one of the three or more poems she wrote about

---

1　Despite Margaret Forster's suggestion to the contrary (245), the nomination was entirely serious. "There is no living poet of either sex who can prefer a higher claim than Mrs. Elizabeth Barrett Browning," the *Athenaeum* observed in the column "Our Weekly Gossip"(1 June 1850): 584. Though EBB inferred that the nomination was made by the *Athenaeum's* literary critic, H.F. Chorley, it was in fact made by its editor, T.K. Hervey (see *LTA* 1:320, 325n6, also *LTM* 3:413). Alfred Tennyson won the post after the 1850 publication of *In Memoriam*.

2　On Ruskin, influential Victorian aesthetic and social critic, see Stone 1995, 32, 84, 222; on George Eliot, see below, p. 6; on Poe, see Appendix A2.

3　Christina Rossetti doubted "whether the woman is born, or for many a long day, if ever, will be born, who will balance not to say outweigh Mrs. Browning"; Mackenzie Bell, *Christina Rossetti* (1898), 101, 103; on her response to EBB, see Harrison 1990 and Stone 1994, 1999. On D.G. Rossetti's many echoes of EBB, see Appendix A and Florence Boos, *The Poetry of Dante Gabriel Rossetti: A Critical Reading and Source Study* (The Hague: Mouton, 1976), 279-81. Swinburne praised EBB's work for its "moral ardour," "ethical energy," and genius (Prefatory note to Smith, Elder edition of *Aurora Leigh*, 1898). On Emily Dickinson, see Swyderski 2000, 2003; on Isabella Valancy Crawford, see Campbell 1991.

4　For the texts of many of these tribute poems, see the supplementary website: www.ebbarchive.org.

EBB. For Lowell the poetry was completely overshadowed by the legendary image of Mrs. Browning "[s]tretched out on a sofa," her heart "squeezed in stiff conventions," waiting for the "escape" through Robert to "freedom and another motherhood / Than that of poems."

EBB's critical fortunes declined so precipitously in part because modernist tastes devalued the work of many Victorian poets.[1] In her case, though, the reaction was more extreme, given her outspoken contributions to Victorian debates over the "woman question," the overtly political stance she took in her later poetry, and the stylistic registers of her work—all features at odds with the values privileged by the formalist "New Criticism" of the 1930s, 1940s, and 1950s. Her translation into the passive "Mrs. Browning" of Lowell's poem also reflects gendered segregations that were even more constricting in modernist than in Victorian criticism. While Harriet Waters Preston remarked that, as late as the 1880s, a "well-connected and presumably well-instructed Englishman" could "stoutly deny that there were *two* poets of the name of Browning,—a man as well as a woman!," twentieth-century critics increasingly represented her as an ancillary figure to Robert Browning or categorized her as one of a group of minor Victorian "poetesses."[2] By the 1950s she was represented in anthologies, literary histories, and scholarly studies almost entirely by *Sonnets from the Portuguese* (1850), approached within the sentimentalized context of a mythic love story epitomized in Rudolf Besier's play *The Barretts of Wimpole Street* (1930), which was translated into a Hollywood film (1934) viewed by millions. It was a story that cast EBB not as the most famous woman poet of her age in the English-speaking world, but as the daughter of one man (the tyrannical Mr. Barrett of Wimpole Street, a type of the Victorian patriarch) and the wife of another (the younger poet Robert Browning, whom EBB secretly married

---

1 For an analysis of this modernist reaction, see Chapter 1 in Armstrong 1993 and Kathy Psomiades's "'The Lady of Shalott' and the Critical Fortunes of Victorian Poetry," in *The Cambridge Companion to Victorian Poetry*, ed. Joseph Bristow (Cambridge: Cambridge UP, 2000), 25-45.

2 Cited by Stone 1995, 208, who also notes (209) that Hugh Walker's *The Literature of the Victorian Era* (1910) casts Tennyson and Robert Browning as the "two kings" of Victorian poetry, relegating EBB to the seventh subsection of a chapter on "The Minor Poets," among the "poetesses."

in September 1846). In Tricia Lootens's apt terms, EBB became a "lost saint," venerated as an exemplar of femininity while her work fell from view.[1] By 1908, John W. Cunliffe had converted her from a leading poet into a mere muse and handmaiden to Browning's genius, arguing that her "most enduring contributions" to litera- ture lay in her influence on her husband (cited by Stone 1995, 208). Cunliffe made this claim even though EBB's poems were re-issued in edition after edition in the later nineteenth century (see Barnes 1967); indeed, they continued to be appreciated in the twentieth century by writers such as T.S. Eliot (see Cuda 2004) and Virginia Woolf, who stated in 1931 that EBB's poetry "still commands our interest and inspires our respect" (1986, 208). As Woolf recognized, however, her claim ran against the critical currents of her era. She satirically summed up the dramatic decline in EBB's reputation by picturing her assigned to "the servants' quarters" in the "mansion of literature," where, in company with other forgotten Victorian poets, "she bangs the crockery about and eats vast handfuls of peas on the point of her knife" (Woolf 1986, 203).[2] G.K. Chesterton was one of the few exceptions to such views, defending the "manly" lines in EBB's poetry, her epigrammatic wit, her cosmopolitanism, and her originality: "As to the critic who thinks her poetry owed anything to the great poet who was her husband, he can go and live in the same hotel with the man who can believe that George Eliot owed anything to the extravagant imagination of George Henry Lewes," Chesterton saltily observed (see Appendix A9).

In the 1970s feminist scholars began to remedy this collective cultural amnesia by producing new editions of *Casa Guidi Windows* (1851) and the novel-epic *Aurora Leigh* (1856).[3] As the first extended poetic portrait of the woman writer in English literature, *Aurora Leigh* dominated the critical recovery of EBB's achievement in the 1980s and 1990s. Wilde's tribute reminds us, however, that the

---

1   On the virtual erasure of EBB's poetic achievement, see the annotated bibliography by Donaldson 1993; Chapter 5 in Stone 1995; Chapter 4 in Lootens 1996; and the "Introduction" in Avery and Stott 2003.

2   Simon Avery notes that, while Robert Browning was saluted as a "key progenitor of literary modernism," EBB became either a "fairy-tale princess or madwoman in the basement" (2004, xxiii).

3   See *CGW* and *AL* in "List of Abbreviations, Primary Sources, and Website," and Kaplan 1978 in the Select Bibliography.

poet's fame and cultural influence arose from a wide range of works aside from this novel-epic. In recent years, scholars have increasingly turned to investigating works written throughout her career, variously considering not only her gender politics but also issues of nation, race, and religion in her poetry, her experiments with form and genre, and the intricate connections between her poetics, her poetic identity, and her politics.[1] Today readers find EBB's poetry exciting in its bold perspectives and psychological astuteness, its range of subject matter, its formal experimentation, and its political critique—characteristics that manifest a general transgressiveness that often unsettled readers of her own time. Victorian critics expressed conventional gender categories by praising women writers for their depth of feeling and men for their intellectual power, and by categorizing women as "poetesses" rarely compared to the great male poets largely because women's "appropriate" subject matter and tone were considered to be limited to the personal and domestic sphere. While some critics celebrated the spirituality, sentiment, or even the political agenda of EBB's various works, others carped about her unfeminine erudition, particularly her command of classical languages and thought, and her temerity in speaking on sacred or political subjects. The responses to her poetry over several decades thus offer a revealing record of Victorian struggles with gender stereotypes and debates over what Victorians termed the "woman question." Like numerous reviewers, the novelist George Eliot suggested that EBB appealed to Victorian readers precisely because she defies the stereotypes; indeed, she is a "woman of genius" because she "superadds to masculine vigour, breadth, and culture, feminine subtlety of perception, feminine quickness of sensibility, and feminine tenderness."[2] Resisting limitations implied by the label "poetess," even as she learned from the example of Romantic precursors such as Felicia Hemans and Letitia Landon and searched throughout the English tradition for

---

1   Full-length studies include those by Leighton 1986, Cooper 1988, Mermin 1989, Glennis Stephenson 1989, Stone 1995, and Lewis 1998, and a book co-authored by Avery and Stott 2003. For essays and articles, see the Select Bibliography to this volume.

2   "Belles Lettres," *Westminster Review* 67, no. 131, n.s. 11 (January 1857). Eliot's judgment echoes EBB's own assessment of the French novelist George Sand; see the sonnets "To George Sand" in this edition.

what she called poetic "grandmothers"—"I look everywhere for Grandmothers & see none," she commented (*BC* 10: 14)—EBB self-consciously joined the European and predominantly male poetic tradition tracing back to classical antiquity. In "A Vision of Poets" (1844), for example, she obliquely manifests her own powerful desire to enter the ranks of the immortals by invoking the entire European tradition of "king-poets"—with Sappho the only woman among its ranks. In the same phase of her career, in a letter, she associated both her appearance and thirst for poetic fame with this acclaimed female forerunner—"I am 'little and black' like Sappho, en attendant[1] the immortality" (*BC* 8:128)—although she never openly courted such comparisons in her poetry.

In seeking to join the English and European poetic traditions, EBB emulated, while adapting to her own ends, genres and forms such as epic, tragedy, verse drama, didactic couplet, sonnet, ballad, lyric, ode, and epigram—defining herself with and against antecedents including Homer, Aeschylus, Dante, Petrarch, Milton, and Pope. Simultaneously, though more ambitiously and confidently in her more mature works, she engaged with Romantic and Victorian precursors and contemporaries such as Byron, Keats, Wordsworth, Blake, Hemans, and Landon through intertextual allusions she embedded in her poems. Her themes range from the intensely personal to affairs of state— from grief, religious doubt, loss, and love to the victimization of factory children, the struggle to abolish slavery, the laws affecting the status of women, the 1851 Great Exhibition, Greek and Italian liberation, and the politics of nation-states. In the latter instances, EBB's poetry speaks most vitally to modern readers through its historical embeddedness, its engagement with issues specific to her moment. Rather than inhabiting a "Palace of Art"[2] or aloof realm of transcendent aestheticism, many of her works reflect her participation in key nineteenth-century movements, debates, and controversies, extending to both Europe and North America. Her most intense and long-lasting engagement, reflected in *Casa Guidi Windows* (1851), *Poems Before Congress* (1860), and many of the

---

1 en attendant: (French) while waiting for.

2 Cf. Tennyson's 1832 poem, "The Palace of Art," on a poetic soul's aesthetic isolation from humankind.

works posthumously published in *Last Poems* (1862), was with the *Risorgimento,* the political and philosophical rebirth that led to the creation of Italy as a modern nation and its liberation from despotic rulers controlled by the old monarchies of Austria and Spain. Writing with incisive intelligence, energy, wit, and a capacious human- ism, she embraced aspects of the cultures she encountered in her wide and eclectic reading in several different languages and in the European travels she experienced after her marriage, eventually defining herself as a "citizeness of the world" (*LEBB* 2:13). She also articulated, in the "Preface" to *Poems before Congress* (1860), a transnationalist vision of special relevance to our own period of globalization, when children in "Third World" countries continue to be exploited, race relations shaped by the slave trade remain a challenge, and the politics of intervention across national borders are, if anything, more fraught with complexities than ever.

Romantic Beginnings: Family Origins, Colonialism, Hellenism, Prometheanism, Nature, and the Sublime

Born 6 March 1806—only eleven years after Keats and four years after Landon—EBB responded passionately to the Romantic poets as members of her own generation: "Byron, Coleridge .. how many more? .. were contemporaries of mine without my having approached them near enough to look reverently in their faces" (*BC* 7:319). She is less often treated as a Romantic poet than Landon or Hemans, the poets she regarded as her principal female rivals in her apprenticeship years. Yet her earlier works resonate with the themes and historical movements characteristic of English Romanticism: colonial expansion, the upheaval of the Napoleonic wars, Romantic Hellenism (the emulation of ancient Greek culture inspired in part by the modern Greek struggle for liberation), the rebellious spirit that found voice in Romantic representations of the classical Titan Prometheus, the Romantic aesthetic of the sub- lime, and the vision of a beneficent Nature found in the poetry of Wordsworth and others. Moreover, many of the literary forms she adapts—the ballad, the dream vision, the ode, the sonnet, and the lyrical drama—were genres especially important to Romanticism.

As Joseph Bristow observes, we need to question "the inflexible narratives" associated with oppositions between "Romanticism" and "Victorianism" if we are to understand how poetic genres came into circulation in a period when neither term had yet developed its regulative meaning (2004, 90).

EBB's life reflects the expansion of the British Empire more directly than those of some other nineteenth-century poets because she was born into wealth resulting from the Atlantic trade in slaves, sugar, and British manufactured goods that fuelled the Industrial Revolution. Her father, Edward Barrett Moulton Barrett, came from a long line of successively wealthier Jamaican plantation owners; her mother, Mary Graham-Clarke, came from a Newcastle family who owned Jamaican sugar plantations, shipping interests, mills, and a brewery.[1] Unlike her siblings, EBB did not normally use the compound surname Moulton Barrett, preferring to identify herself as Elizabeth Barrett Barrett before marriage, and Elizabeth Barrett Browning after it, or often simply as EBB.[2] She explained her complicated name and ancestry to Browning during their courtship: "our family-name is *Moulton Barrett*, & my brothers reproach me sometimes for sacrificing the governorship of an old town in Norfolk with a little honorable verdigris from the Heralds' Office.... Nevertheless it is true that I would give ten towns in Norfolk (if I had them) to own some purer lineage than that of the blood of the slave!—Cursed we are from generation to generation!" (*BC* 11:252). This passage has provoked repeated speculations about her ancestry, revived by biographer Julia Markus in 1995, who argued that EBB "believed she had African blood through her grandfather Charles Moulton" (106). Although there were racially mixed branches of EBB's father's family, genealogical research does

---

1 EBB's family origins are documented in Marks 1938, Barrett 2000, and the "Introduction" to Vol. I of *BC*. See Barrett (p. x) on the hyphenation of her surname Moulton Barrett.

2 EBB published her earliest work anonymously or signed by her initials; she also often used her initials in signing unpublished manuscripts and in her correspondence, although in letters to family and close friends, she also sometimes used her family's pet name for her, "Ba" (on its pronunciation, see Tucker 2006a, 464n14). After she married Robert Browning in 1846, she maintained her characteristic signature initials, a continuity that pleased him (*BC* 11:248-49). To honor her authorial self-designation, and to avoid the confusion of using both her maiden and married names, we usually identify her as EBB.

not indicate African blood in her lineage, and Markus's speculative claims have been critiqued on various grounds.[1] In light of EBB's strong anti-slavery sentiments by the time she shared her family history with Browning and the fact that he had similar sentiments derived from his own Jamaican connections, she was more probably alluding to the Barrett family's complicity in the "curse" of profiting from the blood of slaves.[2] Nevertheless, she accepted the legacies from her paternal grandmother Elizabeth Moulton and her paternal uncle Sam (approximately £4,000 from each), that derived indirectly from the family's colonial roots.

From 1809 until she was past twenty, EBB lived at Hope End, an estate in the Malvern Hills, Herefordshire, in a mansion of Turkish design built by her father. By virtue of her seniority, force of character, and intelligence, she reigned over her ten younger surviving siblings, enjoying a physically robust girlhood up to 1821, when she fell ill along with her sisters Henrietta and Arabella. While her sisters recovered quickly, she did not. At a Gloucester spa, she was tentatively treated for spine disease (*BC* 1:325-27), although there is no support for the reiterated story that she injured her back while impatiently trying to saddle her pony Moses. Prescribed opiates, sometimes in the form of laudanum (opium powder dissolved in alcohol), she was subjected to treatments that included cupping, the use of setons (thread passed through folds of skin with a needle), and suspension in a spine crib, which may well have increased her physical debility.[3] The barriers to opportunity that illness underscored were accentuated by the departure of her closest and dearest brother Edward, or

---

1 See Kennedy 2000 and Phelan 2003, and the *New Dictionary of National Biography* essay by Stone 2004.

2 This sense of complicity may be obliquely conveyed in "The Runaway Slave at Pilgrim's Point." RB's father, Robert Browning senior (1782-1866), appalled by what he witnessed when sent to Jamaica to participate in running plantations in his mother's family, rejected the wealth to be made through enslaved labor and returned to England to a bank clerk's modest income (BC 13:299). Whereas RB's father earned £300 a year, the year following EBB's birth her father's income was £4,000 (Barrett 2000, 55).

3 See Forster 1988, 25 for an account of these treatments. The illness EBB suffered at this time seems to have differed from the bronchial or pulmonary disorder she suffered from in later years, beginning in 1838 (see below, pp. 20-21).

"Bro," who was fifteen months younger than she, for boarding school and the formal education denied to girls of the period.

In EBB's memoir "Glimpses into My Own Life and Literary Character," begun when she was fourteen (*BC* 1:348-56), she recalls that at six she began reading novels, at eight she was enraptured by Pope's translations of Homer, and at ten she began to study Greek with Bro's tutor, even though classical study was generally considered a male preserve. Almost entirely self-educated after her girlhood, she also studied languages, including Hebrew, German, French, and Italian, as well as the major English and continental writers. She was similarly precocious in writing poetry. With her mother "publishing" many of her early compositions by transcribing them into notebooks, she produced one of the largest bodies of juvenilia left by any English writer, much of it still unpublished (see Taylor 2005a). Her earliest extant poem, written at six ("On the Cruelty of Forcement to Man," 1812), laments the impressment of civilians into the navy, while at eleven she drafted a letter to a neighboring aristocrat to protest his support of suspending citizens' right of *habeas corpus* (*BC* 1:41-43). At eleven, EBB also ambitiously began the 1,462-line Homeric epic *The Battle of Marathon* (1820), inspired by Pope's translation of Homer, which her father paid to have privately published when she was fourteen. Celebrating an important Athenian victory, *The Battle of Marathon* reflects the Romantic passion for Greek culture she shared with Byron, Shelley, and Keats, as well as the ardent political Republicanism she associated both with ancient Athens and with Byron's and Hemans's support of the contemporary Greek revolt against Turkish rule.[1] Especially inspired, as the young Tennyson was, by Byron, she wrote three poems mourning his death in 1824 in Greece, where he was supporting armed rebellion against the Turks.

Like *The Battle of Marathon*, "An Essay on Mind" (1826), a philosophical verse essay of 1,262 lines, is influenced by Pope in its style (heroic couplets) and its epigrammatic wit (see Tucker 2006a). Yet in its focus on the powers of the human mind and its Byronic Hellenism it is similarly inspired by Romantic themes. "An Essay on Mind" reflects EBB's intensive reading program recorded in

---

1 See Avery and Stott 2003, 50-52; Stone 1995, 59-61; and Mermin 1989, 23-25.

1824–26 in an unpublished notebook of analytical comments on literary, philosophical, political, and historical works by an eclectic range of writers, including Locke, Hume, Hobbes, Berkeley, Kant, Byron, Southey, Mary Shelley, Maria Edgeworth, Hemans, and Landon, among many others. The notebook shows that she read Landon's poetry with a particularly keen eye, and that she could be satiric even of her idol Byron, noting in her "Remarks on L^d. Byron's 'Island'" that he was "derogatory to the sex!" and exclaiming, "I never knew that woman was an *animal* or peculiar to the summer season."[1] Critical response to *An Essay on Mind, with Other Poems* emphasized, as later criticism would do, EBB's "unwomanly" erudition; one reviewer commended its "metaphysical acumen," but deemed it "too learned."[2] Publication of the volume expanded EBB's intellectual horizons by prompting correspondence from two classical scholars who lived near Hope End, Sir Uvedale Price and H.S. Boyd. With Price, she carried on a discussion of the technicalities of classical meter; with Boyd, who was blind, she read Greek, working as his amanuensis and recording her complicated feelings for him and his "empty minded wife" in her 1831–32 diary (*Diary* 48). Her diary also records her conflicts with her aunt Arabella Graham-Clarke or "Bummy," who became a mother-surrogate after EBB's mother died in 1828, and her continuing self-education in Greek drama (she read "every play of Æschylus Sophocles & Euripides"), as well as her responses to Romantic writers and works, including Joanna Baillie; the "genius" of Mary Shelley's *Frankenstein*; "Colleridge's [sic] Ancient Mariner"; Keats's *Lamia, Isabella, The Eve of St. Agnes, and Other Poems*; several works by Shelley (including *Adonais,* his "perfectly exquisite" elegy for Keats); and of course her beloved Byron (*Diary* 54, 58, 83, 85, 93, 102, 138).

Despite Byron's attitudes towards the female "sex," EBB was particularly drawn to his representations of the poet as a Promethean rebel, as her *Prometheus Bound, ... And Miscellaneous Poems* (1833) makes clear. A Titan of classical mythology credited with inventing domestic and fine arts and with stealing fire from the gods

---

1   1824–26 Notebook (R D1405, 43, 51–52), Wellesley College Library.

2   *The Literary Gazette* 495 (15 July 1826), 436.

to share with humankind, Prometheus was frequently used by Romantic writers to represent the Poet's altruism, aspiration, rebellion against authority, and capacity to produce radical transformations in society and politics. Translating Aeschylus's *Prometheus Bound* in only twelve days, EBB later repudiated this translation as a "frigid, rigid exercise," as "flat as Salisbury plain" (*BC* 10:105, 66).[1] Yet the production of an accurate translation of Aeschylus by a young woman with no university training was a significant feat. One reviewer exclaimed, "Æschylus presents difficulties to the manliest Greek scholar—think of these rugged obstacles to a woman's mind!" (*BC* 4:390). Prometheus's disobedient theft of fire from the gods no doubt exerted strong symbolic appeal to the aspiring young woman poet who had defiantly described her own "early association with '*Fire-thieves!*'" (*BC* 4:34). In 1845, EBB wrote a second, much improved translation of *Prometheus Bound*, publishing it in *Poems* (1850). While poetry written throughout her career celebrates the Promethean rebel against social oppression, she also interrogated the destructive potential of the Promethean over-reacher, as Mary Shelley had done in *Frankenstein: The Modern Prometheus* (1818). In the "Preface" to her 1833 collection, EBB develops a systematic contrast between Prometheus and Satan, questioning Milton's confounding of the two.

Like Byron and Shelley, EBB drew on the repertoire of the sublime in representing Promethean rebels as well as human relationships with Nature and the divine. Edmund Burke's *A Philosophical Enquiry into the Origin of Our Ideas of the Sublime and the Beautiful* (1757) had defined the aesthetic category of the sublime in opposition to the beautiful, delineating the former in masculine terms of vastness, ruggedness, power, darkness, solitude, vacancy, and terror, and the latter in terms of the smoothness, delicacy, smallness, brightness, light, and weakness associated with the feminine. EBB energetically invokes the masculine rhetoric of the sublime in poems such as "A Sea-Side Meditation" (1833), where she uses Nature's vastness to signify the limitless capacities

---

1   She also translated Johann von Goëthe's dramatic monologue "Prometheus" (1773) (*R* D750).

of the human mind. In contrast, "A Sea-Side Walk" (1836) is Wordsworthian in its quiet evocation of the fusion of mind and nature, reflecting EBB's divided attraction to two of her most powerful Romantic precursors, as well as her debt to Landon.[1] As her invocation of Byron in "A Vision of Poets" (1844) suggests (see ll. 412-14), she resisted the mid-Victorian reaction against him—what she described in 1842 as "the present fashion of decrying Byron"—and continued to defend him as "a great & wonderful poet"; at the same time, she held Wordsworth to be "the greater poet" because he was "the profounder thinker, the nearer to the poetic secrets of nature," and the "more influential for good" (BC 6:171).

EBB's attraction to both Byron and the rebellious figure of Prometheus related directly to her liberal Whig politics, reinforced by her family networks.[2] In 1832 she exulted that the First Reform Bill, extending the franchise beyond the landed classes, made the English "a freer people" (BC 3:25). However, the year 1832 was a time of dramatic change for her family as well as the nation. Financial difficulties aggravated by her father's labyrinthine legal disputes over his colonial assets led to the sale of her childhood home at Hope End, her temporary fear that the family might have to leave England for Jamaica (BC 2:307), and their move to Sidmouth, where they lived from August 1832 to December 1835, before moving to London and a permanent home on Wimpole Street. The Emancipation Act of 1833, initiating the process of abolishing slavery in British colonies, compounded her father's financial reverses. Yet in keeping with her reading of Byron, her support of Greek liberation, and her Promethean sympathies, she declared that she was "glad" that "the negroes" were "virtually—free!" (BC 3:86).

---

1   See the supplementary website for texts of "A Sea-Side Meditation" and "A Sea-Side Walk": www.ebbarchive.org.

2   See Avery 2006 and Avery and Stott 2003, 34-36. Whigs elevated the civil, religious, and legal rights of the individual above the power of the monarch or state. The opposing party, the Tories, essentially supported the monarchy. EBB's Uncle Sam was a Whig Member of Parliament representing Yorkshire from 1820-28.

Religion, Gender, and Spiritual Questioning: *The Seraphim* (1838) and Questions of Faith

Early in her publishing career, EBB's religious poetry won her a reputation for feminine spirituality, though some reviewers found even her most pious verse troubled by a transgressive boldness of thought. The title poem of her 1838 collection, *The Seraphim, and Other Poems* (the first to be published under her own name), is a lyrical drama conceived as a contrasting companion to *Prometheus Bound,* the drama by Aeschylus she had translated in 1833. Somewhat audaciously, her drama portrays two angels as they witness and discuss the high subject of the Crucifixion, leading one Victorian critic to comment, "[w]e are not at home in speculating on the minds of angels" (*BC* 5:388). EBB's theology was shaped by her Dissenting[1] background and, more particularly, by her family's affiliation with the Congregationalists, who invested authority in individual congregations rather than in a central hierarchical authority as the established Anglican Church did. In her early years, she recalled that she was "in great danger of becoming the founder of a religion of [her] own," in revolt against "the idea of an established religion" (*BC* 1:351). In the last year of her life she commented, "I have been called orthodox by infidels, and heterodox by church-people" (*LEBB* 2:420)—an observation capturing the paradoxes of a religious position that grew increasingly iconoclastic as she matured.[2] As a Dissenter shaped by the Evangelical movement[3] that swept through England in the late eighteenth and early nineteenth centuries, she felt that individuals should experience unmediated connection to the divine: "why should not *we*, for whom Christ died, & in whom the spirit 'maketh intercession,'—speak to God out of the fulness of our hearts?" (*BC* 8:150). While she criticized Roman Catholics for "being born in their creed instead of choosing it," and thus being "put in irons

---

1   Dissenters rejected the doctrines of the Anglican Church, the official Church of England.

2   On EBB's religious beliefs, see Lewis 1998, 1–15; Scheinberg 2002; Wörn 2004; and Stone 2005.

3   In this context, the Evangelical movement refers to a religious revival originating in the preaching of John Wesley (1703–91) and George Whitefield (1714–70) in the mid-eighteenth century, which emphasized individual conversion.

by other men under the name of 'Church' & 'Tradition'" (*LTA* 1:79), she also defended them against other Dissenters (*BC* 10:193). She was equally critical of the Methodists' "strange contractive opinions" and their mistrust of literature and art (*BC* 5:278). In response to those who chided her for making religion "subservient to poetry" or for daring to treat sacred subjects in "The Seraphim," she observed that "[a]ll truth, & all beauty & all music belong to God— .... I would not lose a note of the lyre—& whatever He has included in His creation, I take to be holy subject enough for *me*" (*BC* 10:139). If such a creed sounds like William Blake's credo that "Everything that lives is holy," one should not be surprised, since EBB was shaped by Dissenting contexts as Blake was; discussed the poet with one of his friends and patrons, Charles Augustus Tulk, a family friend of the Barretts; copied out some of Blake's *Songs of Innocence and of Experience* in 1842; and drew on Blake's social critique in "The Cry of the Children" (1843).[1] Much like Blake, she declared, "To the 'Touch not, taste not, handle not' of the strict religionists, I feel inclined to cry 'Touch, taste handle—ALL THINGS ARE PURE'" (*BC* 10:105). Like Blake's, her beliefs were also much shaped by her reading of the heretical mystic, Emmanuel Swedenborg.[2] She succinctly summarized her belief: "I believe simply that the saved are saved by grace ... that the Lost are lost by their choice of free will," and that "the aspiration of christians sh^d simply be to *love more*" (*BC* 6:192, 171–72).

Like many other Victorians, EBB by no means invariably experienced a fixed and certain faith in a century when new scientific discoveries and textual analyses of the Bible challenged orthodox beliefs. Dorothy Mermin's comments that her "religious poems do not doubt, and rarely struggle," and that they do not "pay attention to the great religious questions of the time," have been increasingly called into question in recent criticism.[3] Nineteenth-century critics recognized the spiritual grounding of her poetry and its connec-

---

1 On EBB's knowledge of Blake and friendship with Tulk, see *BC* 5:308, 6:124, 127–28; *LTA*, 1:151, 176, 181; and the headnote to "The Cry of the Children."

2 Swedenborg (1688–1772), a Swedish philosopher, maintained that the universe comprises both a spirit world and a physical world. On the Swedenborgian elements in EBB's writings, see *Aurora Leigh* 5.116–25 and 7.840–50; Lewis 1998; and Lines 2004.

3 Mermin 1989, 69; on more recent responses to EBB's religious poetry, see Lewis 1998, Sadenwasser 1999, Straight 2000, Scheinberg 2002, Hoagwood 2004, Wörn 2004, Riede 2005, and Stone 2005.

tions to religious debates. The Victorian art and social critic John Ruskin deeply admired the Christian Gothic strains in her poetry, while the critic Peter Bayne found a "spirituality" burning with "the intensity of flame" in all her poems. In an 1846 lecture to the Working Men's Association in Holborn, William Johnson Fox, the prominent Unitarian and mentor to Robert Browning, noted how the religious impulse animating her poetry differed from sectarianism, and in 1896 Thomas Bradfield treated the "ethical impulse" of her poetry, as well as its political dimensions, as rooted in her "spiritual conviction."[1] Works by her such as "The Virgin Mary to the Child Jesus" entered into Victorian religious controversies, as the excerpt from the pamphlet *The True Mary* included here indicates (see Appendix B). As Cynthia Scheinberg has shown, EBB's poetry reflects the hegemony of Christian over Judaic perspectives in Victorian England, yet it also reveals how she drew upon her knowledge of Hebrew and Judaic traditions to create a "prophetic female identity" (2002, 66).

Woman's Voice, the Annuals, Ballads, and the Turn to Modernity in *Poems* (1844)

In 1842, describing her youthful enthusiasm for women's rights, EBB observed, "I read Mary Wolstonecraft [sic] when I was thirteen: no, twelve! .. and, through the whole course of my childhood, I had a steady indignation against Nature who made me a woman, & a determinate resolution to dress up in men's clothes as soon as ever I was free of the nursery, & go into the world 'to seek my fortune.' '*How*,' was not decided; but I rather leant towards being poor Lord Byron's PAGE" (*BC* 6:42). Family correspondence reveals that at fifteen she embraced Wollstonecraft's teachings so enthusiastically that her mother warned her against "visionary hopes" of founding happiness "upon yours & Mrs Wollstonecrafts [sic] system" (*BC* 1:132). Under Wollstonecraft's influence, probably by the time she was sixteen, she drafted the "Fragment of an 'Essay on Woman'" (a rejoinder to Pope's "Essay on Man"), condemning patriarchal practices that

---

1   Ruskin, Bayne, and Bradfield are cited in Stone 2005, 2; for Fox, see *BC* 12:388-404.

"pinion the wing" and "enslave the heart" of woman. Madame De Staël, author of the book EBB described as the "immortal" *Corinne*, was another one of her girlhood heroines (*BC* 3:25, 1:361). In the most ambitious poems of her twenties and thirties—"An Essay on Mind" and "The Seraphim"—EBB's youthful feminism largely disappears from view, muted by the repressive force of early nineteenth-century gender ideologies of the "proper lady," and the backlash against Wollstonecraft after her premature death in 1797.[1] The vital impact of Wollstonecraft and DeStaël on EBB's consciousness and identity resurfaces, however, in the ballads that EBB began to write for periodicals and annuals in the 1830s.

The increasingly woman-centered focus of EBB's poetry in the 1830s is accompanied by a more pronounced representation of her affiliations (and rivalries) with women writers among her contemporaries and precursors. While the principal protagonists in "The Seraphim" are male angels, in "The Virgin Mary to the Child Jesus," also in her 1838 collection, she gives voice to previously unrepresented aspects of the Virgin Mary's experience, writing in the vein of Hemans's *Records of Women* (1828). EBB's intertwined and mixed response to Hemans and Landon, "the two poetesses of our day" (*BC* 3:153), is most directly manifested in her elegy on Hemans's death, "Felicia Hemans: To L.E.L., Referring to Her Monody on the Poetess" prompted by Landon's "monody" or elegy on the death of Hemans, and in "L.E.L.'s Last Question," written on the occasion of Landon's own premature and mysterious death in 1839. Here, as in her correspondence, EBB represents a feminine tradition of "poetesses" ambivalently, subtly distancing herself from the models of poetic achievement embodied by Hemans and Landon much as she does in her often cited comment on her search for "grandmothers" within a national English poetic tradition (*BC* 10:4, 14).[2] As she became more aggressive in challenging

---

1   See Mary Poovey, *The Proper Lady and the Woman Writer: Ideology as Style in the Works of Mary Wollstonecraft, Mary Shelley, and Jane Austen* (Chicago: U of Chicago P, 1984); Margaret Kirkham details the backlash against Wollstonecraft in *Jane Austen, Feminism and Fiction* (Sussex: Harvester UP; New Jersey: Barnes & Noble, 1983), 39-50.

2   On constructions of the poetess and their relationship to emerging definitions of Englishness, see Chapman 2003a, and Susan Brown, "The Victorian Poetess," in *The Cambridge Companion to Victorian Poetry*, ed. Joseph Bristow (Cambridge: Cambridge UP, 2000), 180-202.

the poetic "grandfathers," her increasing focus on female perspectives and issues brought a more generous attitude toward women writers. Writing rather critically, shortly before her death in 1861, about recent poetry by Adelaide Procter, she commented to her friend Isa Blagden, "This is all between you and me—I admire her personally—and there's goodness and grace in what she writes.... It would, in fact, be <u>horrible</u> for me to be heard nibbling at another woman's poems. I would as soon that people said I dyed my hair."[1]

EBB's reputation as a poet of some genius was advanced in the 1835-40 period by her move to London and by the ballads she began to publish, both in leading periodicals and in the annuals—handsomely produced gift books in which poems and stories accompanied fashionable engravings. Like many of her contemporaries, she referred to these ballads using a variety of terms, including "romaunt" and "romance." With their exotic settings in time or place, archaic language, refrains, and kinship in plots to the traditional ballads returned to prominence by Thomas Percy's *Reliques of Ancient English Poetry* (1765), these poems capitalized on the widespread nineteenth-century enthusiasm for all things medieval. For EBB, however, it was not nostalgia or exoticism that made "the old burning ballads" (*BC* 6:268) appealing as much as their narrative thrust, elemental passions of love and revenge, frank physicality, and strong heroines. Like Wordsworth and Coleridge in *Lyrical Ballads* (1798), she often uses the ballad to portray socially marginalized speakers, exploring psychological complexities through dramatic events. Yet she differs from both these precursors in adapting the form for more polemical purposes, exploiting the ballad's power to elicit shared human sympathies: "All the passion of the heart will go into a ballad, & feel at home" (cited by Mermin 1989, 90). Most notably, the ballads she published increasingly carried a modern message and a feminist charge, concentrating as they do on female protagonists who both conform to and subvert nineteenth-century gender stereotypes. These dimensions are apparent even in one of her earliest ballads, "The Poet's Vow" (1836), which resembles Tennyson's "The Lady of Shalott" in its portrayal of Romantic isolationism, but more directly

---

1   Unpublished letter, the Berg Collection, New York Public Library, cited in Reynolds 1997, 61.

critiques Wordsworth's and Coleridge's portrayals of a solipsistic relationship with Nature.[1]

EBB's debut in the annuals and her developing sense of a community of women writers were facilitated by her friendship with the older, successful writer Mary Russell Mitford,[2] who supplemented her income by editing several issues of *Findens' Tableaux*, a fashionable gift-book. Mitford was introduced to EBB in May 1836 by EBB's wealthy distant cousin John Kenyon, himself an amateur poet. The day after this introduction, Kenyon invited his young literary cousin to dine in a group that included not only Mitford but also Wordsworth and the prominent poet Walter Savage Landor. Despite her skepticism of the literary value of the annuals (*BC* 3:273), which featured the engravings more prominently than the accompanying poems and stories, EBB saw that these volumes opened an opportunity for her to appear along-side famous writers—men as well as women. Between 1823 and the late 1830s, "demographic and economic alterations," new audiences, and new relations between authors and texts created by new markets made the annuals the period's principal medium for publishing verse, as Patricia Pulham and others have noted.[3] Responding to Mitford's invitations, EBB contributed three poems to the 1838, 1839, and 1840 issues of *Findens' Tableaux*:[4] "A Romance of the Ganges," "The Romaunt of the Page," and "The Legend of the Brown Rosarie," the first two praised by reviewers as the best poems of the collections in which they appeared. All three poems combine the use of exotic or medieval settings with a subtle interrogation of gender conventions that is clearly modern in implication. Not surprisingly, contemporary critics have been especially drawn to her ballads.[5]

Just as she was poised to enjoy growing literary recognition, EBB experienced a severe bronchial or pulmonary illness that led to her

---

1 For the text of this poem and its critique of Wordsworth, see the supplementary website: www.ebbarchive.org.

2 Mitford (1787-1855) was famous for her fiction and sketches, especially her memorialization of rural life in *Our Village* (1824-32). Her correspondence with EBB (*LTM*) provides an important window on literary culture in the early Victorian period.

3 Pulham, "'Jewels—delights—perfect loves': Victorian Women Poets and the Annuals," in Chapman 2003d, 9.

4 Some annual issues of *Findens'* appeared as *Finden's Tableaux*.

5 See Cooper 1988, Mermin 1989, Stephenson 1989, Stone 1995, and Bristow 2004.

removal from London to the clearer, warmer air of Torquay on England's south coast, initially accompanied by her sister Henrietta and two brothers, including her favorite, Bro. Between 1838 and 1841, she was bedridden, afflicted by chronically weak lungs, phlegm, racking cough, hemorrhaging, fever, loss of voice, and loss of appetite.[1] Treated with morphine and digitalis, she was forbidden to write poetry, a directive she ignored, writing her "wild and wicked ballad" about a cursing nun, "The Lay of the Brown Rosary," despite her physician's exclaiming "'In the very act, Miss Barrett!'" when he discovered her with "a pen guilty of ink" by her side (*BC* 4:169, 174). In February 1840, the death of her brother Sam in Jamaica further compromised her health. In July of the same year, she suffered a complete emotional and physical breakdown when Bro, her dearest brother, was lost at sea during a sailing party. This profound, unspeakable grief resonates in her poetry, in the posthumously published "De Profundis" and the sonnet "Grief," as well as in the *Sonnets from the Portuguese*. Returning to London in 1841, she led the life of a confirmed invalid, secluded in her room in the Barrett family's Wimpole Street home, cheered by her spaniel Flush (sent to her by Mitford after Bro's death), and surrounded by her books, busts of Chaucer and Homer, and engravings of contemporary writers—Wordsworth, Browning, Tennyson, Carlyle, and Harriet Martineau.

While both academic and popular versions of EBB's life story have credited Robert Browning, the dashing younger poet, with miraculously curing her and awakening her poetic creativity, in fact she experienced a return to moderately better health, as well as a flowering of her poetic powers, at least two years before first meeting him in May 1845. In 1842 she began an epistolary friendship with Benjamin Robert Haydon, the painter of large canvasses on historical subjects, leading to her celebrated sonnet on his portrait of Wordsworth. She also developed a correspondence and several literary projects with the

---

1 Having been treated by "four able physicians, two of them particularly experienced in diseases of the chest," EBB described her illness succinctly: "My case is very clear— not tubercular consumption—not what is called a 'decline',—but an affection of the lungs which leans towards it…. a blood vessel broke three years ago—& I never quite got over it" (*BC* 5:138-39). One of her physicians also attended Queen Victoria. For a fuller treatment of EBB's experience of illness see Taylor 1999, 81-82, 84, 86, 90.

poet and critic Richard Hengist Horne. They collaborated on *Psyche Apocalypté*, a poetic drama never completed; on his 1841 modernized edition of Chaucer; and on his 1844 collection of essays on contemporary writers, *A New Spirit of the Age*. For this project EBB provided substantial portions of various essays, including those on Carlyle and Tennyson, as well as many of the epigraphs (see *BC* 8:341-67). In 1843 Martineau, now famous as an invalid as well as a writer, joined her list of correspondents. In 1842, two substantial essays by EBB appeared in the *Athenaeum*: "Some Account of the Greek Christian Poets," demonstrating her command of the poets she had read and translated with H.S. Boyd, and "The Book of the Poets," a comprehensive "Survey of the English poets" from Chaucer up to the Romantic period, originating as a book review (*BC* 5:349). By 1843 she was also writing some of her best poetry yet, as she began to regain her strength and make periodic forays into the outside world.

This creative rebirth resulted in *Poems* (1844), widely reviewed in the major periodicals, establishing "Elizabeth Barrett Barrett" (the name on the title page) as a major poet of the age on both sides of the Atlantic. The ambitious treatment of sacred subjects that some reviewers had objected to in "The Seraphim" is even more evident in "A Drama of Exile," the lead work in this collection, and the title poem in its American edition, *A Drama of Exile: And Other Poems*. Taking up the subject of the fall of humanity at the point where John Milton's *Paradise Lost* leaves off, this verse drama in a form modeled on Greek tragedy dares to take Milton's epic in new directions, exploring the loss of Eden from Eve's point of view and celebrating human love and earth as home. The much cited "Preface" to *Poems* (1844) reveals the sense of transgression that she herself experienced in daring to invite comparison with *Paradise Lost* as her Romantic precursors had done—Blake, Wordsworth, and Byron among them. Though focusing on ostensibly "womanly" subjects such as grief and self-sacrifice, "A Drama of Exile" is self-consciously aggressive in venturing into a traditionally male subject and genre. As her "Preface" declares, she "took pleasure in driving in, like a pile, stroke upon stroke, the Idea of EXILE"—a subject that she as a woman writer knew firsthand: "*I* also an exile!"

Poems (1844) not only includes progressively more radical portrayals of women and female subjectivity than one finds in her poems of the 1830s, it also marks the shift to contemporary subjects, including political debates, that characterizes much of her poetry from the 1840s on. In dramatic lyrics such as "Caterina to Camoens" (which became a particular favorite of Browning's), she again treats a female figure silenced within literary tradition by giving a voice to the female muse addressed in love poems by the sixteenth-century Portuguese poet Luis de Camões. It is ballads such as "Rhyme of the Duchess May,"[1] with its star-crossed lovers on a stallion, and "The Romance of the Swan's Nest," however, that most strikingly anticipate the more outspoken critiques of gender stereotypes and conventions found in later works like *Aurora Leigh* (1856) and "Lord Walter's Wife" (1862). In "Lady Geraldine's Courtship," the last of the poems written for her 1844 collection, she abandoned the medieval setting of her earlier ballads, turning to overtly modern subject matter signaled by the subtitle to the poem, "A Romance of the Age." With its story of a love match involving an earl's daughter who courts a peasant poet as much as he courts her, this generically experimental work challenged Victorian assumptions about both class and gender hierarchies, while also constituting a riposte to Tennyson's "Locksley Hall" (1842), a poem read by many young Victorian men as an anthem of the age.

"Lady Geraldine's Courtship" is one among numerous works by EBB that enter into the mid-Victorian debate over the proper subject of poetry and whether it should focus on the past or the present. During the early Victorian period, critics increasingly questioned the relevance of poetry to a culture beset by problems of modernity, such as the human suffering resulting from the factory system, unregulated capitalism, and the rapid population shift to cities encouraged by these economic changes. The developing genre of the novel seemed more directly responsive to these problems than poetry, which to many seemed to be a vehicle for dreamy abstraction, escapism, and nostalgia. In the larger context of the Victorian debates between past and present, "Lady Geraldine's Courtship" thus marks a crucial shift in EBB's poetic vision and practice. Significantly, it forms the germ of *Aurora Leigh,* published more than ten years later, but first conceived in 1845, when EBB described to Browning her plans to one day

---

1   For this poem see the supplementary website: www.ebbarchive.org.

write "a poem as completely modern as 'Geraldine's Courtship,' ... meeting face to face & without mask, the Humanity of the age" (*BC* 10:102-03). In the middle of *Aurora Leigh*, a contemporary novel-epic that grapples with issues such as women's work, class conflict, and socialist experiments, the poet-protagonist utters a manifesto for poetic modernity, declaring, "if there's room for poets in this world / ... Their sole work is to represent the age, / Their age, not Charlemagne's,—this live, throbbing age..." (*AL* 5.200-3).

This "live, throbbing age" provides the subject matter of several political poems EBB wrote in the 1840s, as she returned to the direct political engagement that marked her youth. Like the historian and essayist Carlyle, who also bridged Romantic and Victorian periods and whose *On Heroes, Hero-Worship, and the Heroic in History* (1841) influenced her work, she increasingly adapted Romantic Promethean conceptions of the poet to Victorian demands for social usefulness. Also like Carlyle, who in *Past and Present* (1843) denounced the reduction of social relations in the nineteenth century to a "cash nexus," she criticized the excesses produced by unregulated Victorian industrialization. Most notably, she dramatized the need for reform and the regulation of child labor in "The Cry of the Children," first published in *Blackwood's* in 1843, a poem that directly responded to a series of parliamentary reports concerning the exploitation of women and children in factories and mines (see Appendix B). A companion poem, "The Cry of the Human," was inspired by EBB's desire to write something on the Corn Laws: "The rich preach 'rights' and 'future days,'" while "The poor die mute, with starving gaze / On corn-ships in the offing" (ll. 50, 52-53).[1] Including topical poems like "The Cry of the Children" along with "A Drama of Exile," medieval and contemporary ballads, lyrics, poems on nature, and many sonnets, EBB's 1844 volumes clearly marked her aspiration to enter the pantheon of immortal European "king-poets" depicted

---

1   Enacted in 1815 and repealed in 1846, these tariffs on imported grains protected English landlords and farmers from competition in trade but increased the price of bread. EBB long regretted that she did not write a more polemical poem protesting the Corn Laws in response to a request from a chapter of the Anti-Corn Law League in early 1845. She had "a regular quarrel" with her brothers over the issue and declared that she was "leagues before the rest of my house in essential radicalism," but she eventually yielded to their protests and those of her father (*BC* 10:65, 61; see also 34, 63-64).

in the Dantesque dream vision, "A Vision of Poets," the second longest work in the collection. Despite the fact that some thirty-five reviews appeared in 1844 and the early months of 1845, *Poems* (1844) had virtually disappeared from view by the middle of the next century, while Tennyson's *Poems* (1842) became pivotal works in the twentieth-century Victorian poetical canon.

Courtship, Marriage, and *Sonnets from the Portuguese*

> Enter the legend: sweet invalid, dear Miss Barrett.... Doll's face, those ringlets round her head. Dear Miss Barrett, lying there the day long, wasting away, waiting for—at last; it comes, the life-force incarnate, virile Robert Browning!... Miss Barrett runs away with Mr. Browning, into the warm sun, cured. Somewhere along the way she commits to paper the sum of what is on her mind.[1]

The romantic story of the Brownings' courtship, secret marriage, and subsequent flight from sooty London to sunny Italy has long had a powerful hold on the popular imagination. As Louise Bernikow's witty parody implies, however, it has had particularly distorting effects on perceptions of EBB, casting her as the pining, passive heroine of a sentimental romance, who is encapsulated in poet Francis Thompson's metaphor: "Browning stooped and picked up a fair-coined soul that lay rusting in a pool of tears."[2] The reality from which the story springs is considerably more complex, conflicted, and compelling—yet if anything, even more romantic, in a fuller sense of that word, than the "legend." Contrary to the gender stereotypes of the popular myth, it was EBB who made the first move in this relationship, opening a door in her life to her future husband by deftly weaving into "Lady Geraldine's Courtship" a sensuously flattering allusion to poetical works by Browning then appearing in a pamphlet series entitled *Bells and Pomegranates*: "Or

---

1   Louise Bernikow, ed., *The World Split Open: Four Centuries of Women Poets in England and America 1552-1950* (New York: Vintage Books, 1974), 29-30.

2   Viola Meynell, *Francis Thompson and Wilfrid Meynell: A Memoir* (London: Hollis & Carter, 1952), 87.

from Browning some 'Pomegranate,' which, if cut deep down the middle, / Shows a heart within blood-tinctured, of a veined humanity" (ll. 163-64). Browning responded warmly to this compliment, posting a letter to her on 10 January 1845, the first of 574 (all but one are extant) which they exchanged over the next twenty months. "I love your verses with all my heart, dear Miss Barrett," he declared, then amplified into praise of "the fresh strange music, the affluent language, the exquisite pathos and true new brave thought" of her "great living poetry." Reiterating, "I do, as I say, love these Books with all my heart—and I love you too," he added, "do you know I was once not very far from seeing .. really seeing you?," comparing the experience to being "close, so close, to some world's-wonder in chapel or crypt" (*BC* 10:17). It was a suggestive hint to the poet who had become one of the most celebrated recluses of the day. Browning addressed "Miss Barrett" as a celebrity, as a literary peer, and as a poet who had already attained the fame and critical acclaim that he himself so intensely desired in 1845.

Her immediate reply to his first letter, "I thank you, dear Mr Browning, from the bottom of my heart" (*BC* 10:18), echoed as his letter had done the imagery of the heart she had used to salute him in print, initiating a pattern of returning quotation for quotation pervading their correspondence. Their shared artistic aspirations, Dissenting backgrounds, family situations (both were still living at home, he at thirty-two, she at thirty-eight), passion for Greek literature, and mutual literary friends led to an immediate intellectual connection, then to a deepening spiritual and emotional intimacy. She did not immediately invite the meeting he hinted at, wryly responding to his suggestion that he venerated her like a saint in a chapel or crypt by commenting, "BUT, ... you know, .. if you had entered the 'crypt,' you might have caught cold, or been tired to death" (*BC* 10:19). As spring approached, he hinted more directly that he wished to meet her in person, expressing a desire to write something "in concert" with her (*BC* 10:201). She demurred at meeting him in person, even though she said her health was "*essentially better*" and had been "for several winters," then finally agreed, writing to caution him that her poetry was "the flower" of her: "the rest of me is nothing but a root, fit for the ground & the dark" (*BC* 10:111, 216).

They met in person on 20 May 1845, in EBB's bed-sitting room, an event rapidly followed by Browning's impulsive declaration of love (in a letter that he subsequently reclaimed and destroyed), precipitating her withdrawal in alarm, given her invalidism, age, and feelings of inadequacy. After this turbulent beginning, the two poets settled into a friendship, then into growing intimacy, as Browning called on EBB ninety-one times between 10 May 1845 and their marriage in September 1846 (*BC* 10:226n5). August and September 1845 brought a turning point, as EBB received medical advice urging her to travel to Italy to avoid another London winter but found her father firmly opposed to the idea, leaving her distraught and embittered. Browning condemned "the veriest slavery" her father subjected her to and declared on 25 September 1845, "I would marry you now," saying that he would be "no more than" a brother to her if her health required. His visit the next day led her to affirm in return, "I am yours for everything but to do you harm," promising that she would be to him what he chose, if God freed her from her "trailing chain" of ill health (*BC* 11:98, 100).

On 12 September 1846, they married quietly in St. Marylebone Church, attended only by EBB's maid Elizabeth Wilson and Browning's cousin James Silverthorne; a week later, they set out for Italy, accompanied by Wilson and Flush. EBB did not inform her two sisters or her brothers of the marriage in advance, in order to protect them from her father's wrath. Although Edward Moulton Barrett himself had married at twenty, apparently enjoyed a happy relationship with his wife, and sired twelve children, he unaccountably opposed the desires of any of his adult children to marry. EBB's worst fears were realized when he utterly repudiated her, refused to open any of the conciliatory letters she wrote over succeeding years, and similarly cast off two other adult children who dared to marry in his lifetime. When he died, in April 1857, without "a word, without a sign," she wrote bitterly to her sister Arabella, "Its [sic] like slamming a door on me as he went out" (*LTA* 2:298). Her marriage, nonetheless, brought great happiness and fulfillment, along with the birth of a son, Robert Wiedeman Barrett Browning or Penini (shortened to "Pen") on 9 March 1849. "*E un miraculo quello bambino e venuto da quel corpo,*" the Italian nurse declared ("It's a miracle that baby came from that body"; cited by Markus 1995, 130). This happy event was preceded by two miscarriages, and followed by two more life-threatening ones, the last in 1850 when EBB, forty-four years of age, almost died from hemorrhaging. In April 1847, the Brownings settled in Florence, eventually renting the second floor of a fifteenth-century palazzo, the Casa Guidi. This became their home base for the rest of their married life, though they would make extended visits to England, Paris, and Rome, as well as shorter ones to Vallombroso, Lucca, Siena, Milan, and Venice. Taking advantage of the cheapness of life on the Continent, they lived chiefly on income derived from the inheritances settled on EBB by her paternal grandmother and her Uncle Sam, with some additional small sums from their writing, until both poets received substantial bequests from EBB's benevolent cousin John Kenyon on his death in 1857 (see below, p. 38).

The two most important literary outcomes of the courtship period are the celebrated love letters exchanged by the Brownings and her *Sonnets from the Portuguese*. Although the syntax and erudition of the letters, as well as the many private references, can make them challenging reading, they nevertheless remain perennially fascinating, affording unique insight into the aesthetic principles, critical judgments, religious opinions, and cultural interests of two remarkable poets. As analyses of the letters by Karlin 1985, Sullivan 1987, Mermin 1989 (123-28), and Prins 1991 have shown, both poets initially refracted their growing desire through their discussion of each other's health and literary subject matter, each other's poems, and EBB's re-translation of *Prometheus Bound*. Robert requested her help in revising the poems he subsequently published in *Dramatic Romances and Lyrics* in November 1845; in response she provided pages of detailed commentary (*BC* 11:375-401). As the notes in this edition indicate, the courtship correspondence is especially important as an intertext for *Sonnets from the Portuguese*. Although the last of the sonnets was dated two days before the Brownings' marriage in September 1846, EBB kept them secret even from her husband until 1849: "I felt shy about them altogether .. even to him. I had heard him express himself strongly against 'personal' poetry & I shrank back," she explained to her sister Arabella after the Brownings decided to publish the *Sonnets* in the expanded collection of her poems published in 1850 (*LTA* 1:368). The sequence has remained EBB's most widely known and popular work, translated into many different languages, and now increasingly interpreted as a multi-faceted revision of the love sonnet tradition.

Poems (1850), Anti-Slavery Works, and Dramatic Monologues

Along with the *Sonnets from the Portuguese*, *Poems* (1850) included most of the titles previously published in the 1838 and 1844 collections—many of them in a heavily revised form—plus EBB's new and improved translation of *Prometheus Bound*, some other translations, and thirty-six poems that had earlier appeared in periodicals. Most notably, *Poems* (1850) brought to an English readership one of her most radical political poems, the anti-slavery work "The Runaway Slave at Pilgrim's Point," first published in December 1847 in the 1848 issue of the Boston abolitionist annual, *The Liberty Bell*. "The Runaway Slave at Pilgrim's Point" is the first of three anti-slavery poems written by EBB, after an invitation from the Boston Female Anti-Slavery Society pulled her into the currents of the trans-Atlantic abolitionist movement. A startling poem to come from the pen of a descendant of Jamaican slaveholders, "The Runaway Slave" invites comparison with both Frances Harper's later poem "The Slave Mother: A Tale of the Ohio" (1854) and Toni Morrison's novel *Beloved* (1987); it has also generated strikingly conflicted responses among critics today.[1] The impact of the trans-Atlantic abolitionist movement is also evident in a sonnet first published in *Poems* (1850), "Hiram Powers' 'Greek Slave,'" and in "A Curse for a Nation," first published in the 1856 issue of *The Liberty Bell*. The sonnet reflects the nexus between slavery and the oppression of women that EBB later articulated in an 1853 letter to the writer and women's activist Anna Jameson (1794-1860) apropos of Harriet Beecher Stowe's anti-slavery novel, *Uncle Tom's Cabin* (1852): "Oh, and is it possible that you think a woman has no business with questions like the question of slavery? Then she had better use a pen no more. She had better subside into slavery and concubinage herself, I think, as in the times of old, shut herself up

---

[1] On the parallels with Morrison's *Beloved*, see Battles 1991 and Stone 2002. For examples of divergent responses see Brown 1995, Brophy 1998, Leighton 1992, Stone 2003a, Slinn 2003, Lootens 2006, and Fish 2006.

with the Penelopes in the 'women's apartment,' and take no rank among thinkers and speakers" (*LEBB* 2:110-11). "A Curse for a Nation," most forcibly expresses the connection between the plight of slaves and the situation of women. In this poem EBB speaks in her own voice, publicly and politically, underscoring the fact with the ringing lines, "A curse from the depths of womanhood / Is very salt, and bitter, and good" (ll. 47-48).

While EBB continued to expand the range of poetic forms in which she worked in *Poems* (1850), "The Runaway Slave at Pilgrim's Point" together with several other works points to her accomplishment in a genre more often associated with her husband's name than with her own: the dramatic monologue. Her experimentation with this form, the most important of Victorian poetic genres, is frequently overlooked, in part because the term is so often narrowly defined in terms of a limited selection of Robert Browning's most familiar poems, and in part because women writers such as Hemans, EBB, Augusta Webster, and Amy Levy were generally excluded from literary histories of the form from the 1950s to the early 1990s—an approach now vigorously questioned by critics such as Isobel Armstrong, Cynthia Scheinberg, and Glennis Byron.[1] The majority of EBB's dramatic lyrics, monodramas, and monologues[2] bear out Glennis Byron's suggestion that women writers more often than men use the genre for "social critique," typically through giving voice to "marginalized and silenced figures" (96), and that they tend to "sympathise more with their

---

1   Armstrong 1993, 326; Scheinberg, "Recasting 'sympathy and judgment': Amy Levy and the Victorian Dramatic Monologue," *Victorian Poetry* 35 (1997): 173-91; and Byron 2003, 80.

2   EBB did not call these "dramatic monologues" because the term was not yet used in the early to mid-Victorian period. On Victorian terms for and concepts of dramatic monologues and the monodrama, see A. Dwight Culler, "Monodrama and the Dramatic Monologue," *PMLA* 90 (1975): 366-85; Ralph W. Rader, "The Dramatic Monologue and Related Lyric Forms," *Critical Inquiry* 3 (1976): 131-51; Alan Sinfield, *Dramatic Monologue* (London: Methuen, 1977); Herbert F. Tucker, "From Monomania to Monologue: 'St. Simeon Stylites' and the Rise of the Victorian Dramatic Monologue," *Victorian Poetry* 22 (1984): 121-37; Cornelia D.J. Pearsall, "The Dramatic Monologue," in *The Cambridge Companion to Victorian Poetry*, ed. Joseph Bristow (Cambridge: Cambridge UP, 2000), 67-88; Byron 2003; and Patricia Rigg, "Augusta Webster: The Social Politics of Monodrama," *Victorian Review* 26 (2001): 75-107.

speakers" (87). For example, in "Void in Law" (1862), EBB uses the dramatic monologue to portray the inner conflict of an abandoned single mother. Earlier experiments in which she moves towards the fully developed dramatic monologue form include "The Virgin Mary to the Child Jesus" (1838), "Catarina to Camoens" (1843), and the accomplished "Bertha in the Lane" (1844), much admired by Browning (e.g., *BC* 10:43; 11:16, 159). Even when her works do not exhibit all of the features some definitions associate with the dramatic monologue (a listener as well as a single speaker other than the poet and ironic character revelation), they reflect her interest in the fissured subjectivity critics have associated with the form.

Most of the dramatic speakers in EBB's monologues are female (just as the majority of Robert Browning's dramatic speakers in *Men and Women* are male, despite the collection's title). Nevertheless, she does on occasion experiment with male speakers, especially in the 1840s in works written before she met her future husband—for example, in "Lady Geraldine's Courtship" (1844), in the unpublished "Adam's Farewell to Eden—in his age" (see the headnote to *A Drama of Exile*), and in the original abandoned opening of "The Runaway Slave at Pilgrim's Point" (see Appendix CII). Her posthumously published experiment with what she termed a "monodram" (*BC* 10:102), portraying Aeschylus near the point of his bizarrely ironic death, raises provocative questions about the gender binaries that structure many definitions and histories of the dramatic monologue. First published under the title "Aeschylus' Soliloquy" in 1913, this poem was misattributed to Browning for seventy years, and highly praised in the process, until the rough draft manuscript confirmed EBB's authorship in 1982. These works aside, however, EBB resembles later female practitioners of the form such as Webster and Levy in achieving some of her most powerful effects through portraying women speakers. Influenced in part by her husband's example—much as he was influenced by hers in representing Pompilia in *The Ring and the Book* (1868-69)—she adopts a more realistic and colloquial technique in some of her later dramatic monologues. This technique bears fruit in the moving "Mother and Poet" in *Last Poems* (1862), exploring the anguish of an Italian mother and patriot who loses both her sons in the struggle for Italian nationhood that she taught them to revere. Overall, though, EBB's dramatic monologues, like Tennyson's, remain more rhetorical and lyrical than colloquial and realistic, as the pulsating lyric passion of "Bianca among the Nightingales" (1862) suggests.[1]

Continental Liberties: *Casa Guidi Windows* and *Risorgimento* Politics

The Brownings' move to the Continent, settlement in Florence, and extended stays in other major cities such as Paris and Rome brought EBB into dynamic circles of expatriate writers, artists, politicians, and activists. She also entered a world less trammeled by prudery and piety than mid-Victorian English society. In 1852 she fulfilled a long-held desire when she met the celebrated French writer George Sand, whom she had saluted in two sonnets published in *Poems* (1844) as "[t]rue genius, but true woman."[2] The Brownings' social circle between 1847 and 1861 included English writers such as Carlyle, Tennyson, Frederick Tennyson (Alfred's brother), and the poet Walter Savage Landor; Eliza Ogilvy, a successful Scottish poet living in Florence; the American sculptors Hiram Powers, Harriet Hosmer, and William Wetmore Story; Margaret Fuller Ossoli, the American transcendentalist writer and proponent of women's rights; the English actress Fanny Kemble, the estranged wife of a Georgia plantation owner and slave-holder, and her sister Adelaide Sartoris; the English painter Frederic Leighton; the writer Isa Blagden, one of their closest friends; and increasingly, in the later 1850s, Italian writers and politicians like Francesco Dall'Ongaro and Massimo d'Azeglio.[3] Visitors included William Makepeace Thackeray, Harriet Beecher Stowe, Nathaniel Hawthorne and his wife, and the English women's rights activist Frances Power Cobbe, among many others.

---

1   In *The Dramatic Monologue* (London: Methuen, 1977), Alan Sinfield notes of Tennyson's monologues that "dramatic speech may be rhetorical and lyrical as well as casual and colloquial" (20), a point more fully developed by Linda K. Hughes in *The Manyfacèd Glass: Tennyson's Dramatic Monologues* (Athens, OH: Ohio UP, 1987), Chapter 1.

2   See *LTA* 1:464 for the fullest account of this meeting; elsewhere EBB described Sand as sitting "like a priestess ... in a circle of eight or nine men" (*LEBB* 2:59) and noted that her "cigarette is really a feminine weapon if properly understood" (*LTM* 3:352).

3   On Francesco Dall'Ongaro (1808-73), poet, dramatist, journalist, professor, and patriot, and Massimo d'Azeglio (1798-1866), painter, writer, and patriot, see *LTA* 2:396, 426n9; also Petrioli 2001.

The move to the Continent and settlement in Florence also pulled EBB into the ferment of the revolutions, uprisings, and coups that swept through Europe in 1847-48 and the following years. Responding passionately and with partisan interest to these events, she avidly defended her "republicanism" and celebrated the fact that one of the first outcomes of the 1848 revolution in France was "the abolition of slavery" (*LTA* 1:156). She similarly underscored connections between the struggles for democracy and constitutional government in Europe and the growing mid-nineteenth-century campaign for women's rights. Responding to the 1848 revolution in France, she explicitly linked the political to the domestic sphere, commenting to her husband and to her sister Arabella that "*women* ought," like oppressed classes and nations, to "reorganize their position"—meaning, as she made clear, that "women in the mass," "the daughters & the wives, who must be obedient without regard to their own feelings or opinions," ought to study the example of the revolutionaries in France (*LTA* 1:160). Her views became more complicated as the French political situation changed. In Paris in December 1851, when Louis Napoleon, nephew of Napoleon Bonaparte, effected a coup to enable him to continue as president in defiance of the 1848 constitution, she described herself as living "the most vivid life possible." Unlike Robert, despite the deaths on the barricades, she did not see Louis Napoleon's action as contrary to her republican ideals because she believed that he had "the mass of the people clearly with him," according to a plebiscite he held on 20 December (*LTA* 1:434).[1] In Italy, she also approvingly noted the mingling of classes and genders: "England is not the place for the poor. They are treated like dogs there, and never enjoy anything like other human beings—The rich on one side, the poor on another ... Here we are all men & women & can reach to the same pleasures" (*LTA* 1:135).

Despite the insufficient reflection on the privileges of her own middle-class position in this statement, for the poet who in her youth had emulated Byron and called for Greek liberation,

---

1   Critics who have traditionally accused her of naïve hero-worship of Louis Napoleon tend to overlook the emphasis that EBB gave to the plebiscites indicating his popular support; as for his suppression of the press, she pointed out that the "republic in 1848" had also "gagged" "every adverse newspaper" (*LTA* 1:432).

immersion in the Italian *Risorgimento* proved to have profoundly transformative effects. From the Brownings' residence Casa Guidi, on 12 September 1847, the first anniversary of their marriage, they witnessed the jubilant popular processions that greeted progressive reforms in Tuscany, events soon followed by a chain of uprisings in other Italian states and the short-lived triumph of the "Roman Republic" in 1848. This burst of revolutionary enthusiasm was succeeded, however, by the crushing defeat of the Italian forces by the Austrians at the Battle of Novara in March 1849 and the restoration of reactionary governments throughout the Italian peninsula. Composed in two phases that reflect these transformations, the two-part *Casa Guidi Windows* (1851) was the most politically engaged work EBB had yet written. It is also the most generically complex and allusive work she produced up to 1851, mingling Italian and English traditions in a highly variable verse form, as it invokes Italy's rich cultural history (especially Dante and Michelangelo) as well as the chief political players in the 1847-48 wave of Italian nation-making. The poem reflects a civic spirit that Richard Cronin finds lacking in other "major Victorian poets" (2002, 180), an enthusiasm for nationalist movements, as well as an expanding internationalist vision, as EBB links these Italian revolutions to the struggle against slavery in America, and to other European democratic and nationalist uprisings in countries such as Poland and Hungary.

Though focused primarily on Italian current events, *Casa Guidi Windows* thus expressed EBB's increasing conviction that poetry should actively involve itself in the lives of the "people" and her resolute belief that a woman poet should speak out on political and social issues. Indeed, in its monitory apostrophes to leading figures of the *Risorgimento* such as Joseph Mazzini, its critiques of the policy of non-intervention in Italy promoted by the English "peace party," and its much cited satire of the global imperialism of the "Great Exhibition of the Works of Industry of All Nations" held triumphantly in London in 1851, the poem can be seen as a work of cultural diplomacy as well as a work of art. Throughout, EBB emphasizes the relations between the politics of gender and of nations: even "liberal nations" offer "no light" for the poor, sitting "in darkness when it is not night," and "[n]o help for women sobbing out of sight / Because men made the laws" (2.634-39).

Praised in Italy by some leaders of the *Risorgimento,* but actually read by relatively few Italians (Harris 2000, 123–27), *Casa Guidi Windows* inspired more mixed reviews in England. On the whole, however (see Appendix D), the mid-Victorian reception of this work was more positive than critics have traditionally assumed. Several noted its combination of "masculine" and "feminine" qualities, recalling EBB's own early praise of George Sand. The chief point of contention arose from EBB's pungent critique of the English peace movement and her call for English political intervention in Italy (*CGW* 2.373–424). While the *Eclectic Review* deplored her call for English military assistance in Italy's unification as "wrong, illogical, and halting in her otherwise manly and prominent progression," *The Spectator* praised her critique of the English peace movement as worthy of comparison with Milton and with Joan of Arc, and recommended the poem as a corrective to those who think women and politics "should be wide as the poles asunder."[1] After the successful achievement of Italian nationhood in 1870, *Casa Guidi Windows* fell into neglect, which persisted even after Julia Markus published her scholarly edition of the poem in 1977, as *Aurora Leigh* attracted the lion's share of feminist critical attention. This imbalance began to be addressed by studies in the 1990s exploring the poem's politics, poetics, epistemology, and innovative form.

Aurora Leigh in the Context of the Poems in This Edition[2]

Although scores of essays on *Aurora Leigh* (1856)[3] have appeared since Cora Kaplan recovered the text for twentieth-century readers in 1978, little attention has been paid to the ways in which it relates to the poems that preceded and followed it. For example, the tendency to read this work as a thinly veiled autobiography—despite the poet's own claim that it is a portrait of a representative

---

1 *Eclectic Review,* 5th series 2 (September 1851): 317; *Spectator* 24, no. 1200 (28 June 1851): 616–17. See Appendix D for excerpts from these reviews.

2 For excerpts from *Aurora Leigh* to accompany this edition, see the supplementary website: www.ebbarchive.org.

3 *Aurora Leigh,* which bore the date 1857 on its title page, was actually published in November 1856.

"artist woman" (*LEBB* 2:112)—has been promoted by inattention to the experimentation with dramatic speakers in EBB's earlier works that we note above.[1] Similarly, considerations of *Aurora Leigh* seldom take into account how it connects to *Casa Guidi Windows* (1851) and *Poems before Congress* (1860), the works on Italian and European politics that frame it in EBB's writing career. "A poet's heart / Can swell to a pair of nationalities, / However ill-lodged in a woman's breast" (6.50-51), Aurora observes in an often cited passage, as she reflects on her dual allegiance to Italy, the land of her Italian mother and her birth, and England, her father's homeland and the country that shapes her in adolescence. While Aurora, in her hybrid nationality, literally embodies a cosmopolitan aesthetic, it finds its first incarnation in *Casa Guidi Windows,* making EBB's 1851 intervention in the "Italian question" an essential precursor text to *Aurora Leigh,* as Matthew Reynolds points out (2001, 109). *Casa Guidi Windows* and *Aurora Leigh* are also linked by their woman-centered perspective on the broader political sphere, by their examination of the relation between poetics and politics, by their intertextual and topical allusiveness, and by their generic and stylistic hybridity. In the earlier work, the woman writer is positioned as an observer of larger political events (at a window, metaphorically). In the later work, the woman poet moves emphatically into the foreground, beginning with Aurora's opening assertion that she "will write ... Will write" her story, not for "others' uses" but for her "better self" (1.3-4).

As EBB explained, in *Aurora Leigh* she aimed to take her subject matter "from the times, 'hot and hot'" (as Byron had done in *Don Juan*), while also "showing how the practical & real (so called) is but the external evolution of the ideal & spiritual—that it is *from inner to outer,* .. whether in life, morals, or art" (cited *AL* 331). The poetry in this Broadview collection illustrates how she moved towards this fusion of the "practical & real" with the "ideal & spiritual" as the trajectory of her career manifested an increasing social engagement, particularly with the turn to the contemporary world in "Lady Geraldine's Courtship," the prototype of *Aurora*

---

1   For critiques of biographical readings of *AL*, see Margaret Reynolds, "Introduction," *AL* (Ohio), 7-12, and Stone 1995, 136-37.

Leigh. Much as the earlier poem alludes to railways and the telegraph, topical allusions jostle together in the pages of *Aurora Leigh*, especially in its multifaceted grappling with the "woman question." In 1845, EBB remarked that she was not "a very strong partizan on the Rights-of-woman-side of the argument—at least I have not been, since I was twelve years old" (*BC* 10:84), prompting some critics to judge her conservative on gender issues.[1] Her later poetry, correspondence, and artistic and political actions, however, clearly reflect her changing views and growing ties to the mid-Victorian women's rights movements. She numbered such notable advocates of women's issues as Anna Jameson, Harriet Martineau, Barbara Bodichon, and Bessie Rayner Parkes among her friends and correspondents, and in 1855 she signed a petition to Parliament, organized by Parkes, supporting property rights for married women—whose property, even personal effects, legally belonged to their husbands. In 1856, she also aligned herself with Parkes against the conservative ideas about women promoted by poet and essayist Coventry Patmore, saying "she & the rest of us militant, foam with rage" at his doctrines (cited *AL* 335). *Aurora Leigh* reflects this militance in multiple ways, continuing the concerns with woman's nature, rights, and voice evident in the unpublished juvenile "Fragment of an 'Essay on Woman,'" ballads such as "The Romaunt of the Page," and anti-slavery works such as "The Runaway Slave at Pilgrim's Point." While many of EBB's earlier poems subtly expose "a sort of masculine rampancy which w^d have a woman under the feet of a man that he might stroke her there like a hound" (*BC* 10:94), *Aurora Leigh* directly and polemically intertwines its treatment of the "condition of England" with the condition of women. Most notably, it brilliantly satirizes, as Wollstonecraft had done, the "score of books on womanhood" (1.427) teaching women subservience and idle accomplishments.[2] Through the representation of the working-class Marian, EBB also takes stock of women's limited employment opportunities; criticizes the exploitation of seamstresses; and confronts the issues of battered wives, systemic

---

1   See David 1987, and the response by Stott in Avery and Stott 2003, Chapter 8.

2   For a representative excerpt from Mrs. Sarah Ellis's conduct books, see the supplementary website: www.ebbarchive.org.

prostitution, and rape that are inextricable from the barriers to education and employment experienced by women. In its attention to the condition of women as well as the condition of England's poor, *Aurora Leigh* also opens the way to EBB's exploration of the sexual double standard in later poems such as "Bianca among the Nightingales," "Void in Law," and "Lord Walter's Wife."

Although EBB braced herself for harsh reviews of *Aurora Leigh,* the poem was more popular than she expected. While conservative reviewers objected to its independent heroine, its coarseness, and its stylistic hybridity, others called it a "modern epic," the work of a "master mind," saying, "It sings of our actual life, embodying the schemes and struggles, the opinions and social contrasts of our day."[1] *Aurora Leigh* was lauded by Walter Savage Landor, Leigh Hunt, Owen Meredith, D.G. Rossetti, George Eliot (who read it three times), and Swinburne, among many others; indeed, Ruskin called it "the greatest poem which the century has produced in any language."[2] EBB recorded her surprise at "quite decent women taking the part of the book in a sort of *effervescence*" (*LEBB* 2:252) and defended her representation of "unfeminine" topics such as rape and prostitution, observing, "If a woman ignores these wrongs, then may women as a sex continue to suffer them; there is no help for any of us—let us be dumb and die" (*LEBB* 2:254). The success of *Aurora Leigh* was quickly followed by two personal sorrows for EBB: the death of her benevolent cousin John Kenyon on 3 December 1856, and the death of her father on 17 April 1857. Whereas Kenyon in his will left £4,500 to EBB and £6,500 to Browning (*BC* 3:317), her father excluded EBB entirely from his (*BC* 1:287). After 1857, her health grew frailer, and she was drawn to the consolations that Swedenborgianism and spiritualism seemed to offer; she also, however, turned to renewed involvement in the Italian struggle for liberation, as unfolding events re-opened the promise of unification of the Italian states.

---

1   Cited by Stone 1995, 141, 143. On the reception of *Aurora Leigh* see also Mermin 1989, 223-24; Cooper 1988, 148-52; Reynolds, *AL* (Ohio), and Stott in Avery and Stott 2003, Chapter 8.

2   *The Elements of Drawing,* Appendix II, "Things to Be Studied," in *The Works of John Ruskin,* ed. E.T. Cook and Alexander Wedderburn, 39 vols. (London: George Allen, 1903-12), 15:227. See also his *Works* 36:247-48.

Poems before Congress, Death, and Last Poems

EBB's passionate engagement in Italian politics furnished the subject matter of *Poems before Congress* (1860), as well as the occasion for half of the poems in the posthumously published *Last Poems* (1862). In 1859, open conflict between the Italians and Austrians resumed, with Napoleon III of France intervening against the Austrians. The "Congress" in EBB's title was a scheduled meeting of the major powers involved in the conflict (although the meeting was ultimately indefinitely postponed). Through its title as well as its "Preface," *Poems before Congress* positions itself, more explicitly than *Casa Guidi Windows*, as an instrument of cultural diplomacy intervening in the politics of nations. Roundly stating in her "Preface" that "English readers" might find her poems "too pungently rendered to admit of a patriotic respect to the English sense of things," EBB emphasizes not only her "attachment to the Italian people," but also her belief in a transnationalist ethos replacing xenophobic patriotism. Like *Casa Guidi Windows*, *Poems before Congress* traces a trajectory of high hopes followed by disillusioned realism. Interspersed with poems presenting varying perspectives on Napoleon III and high-stakes diplomacy in the public sphere (see Montwieler 2005 and Woodworth 2006), EBB also presents other poems exploring women's roles in the conflicts, creating a counterpoint of genders. Published soon after the famous endeavors of Florence Nightingale in the Crimea, the collection strikingly emphasizes women's intellectual and artistic responsibility to intervene in war and nation-building rather than their nursing capacities. EBB declared, "I do not consider the best use to which we can put a gifted and accomplished woman is to *make her a hospital nurse*. If it is, why then woe to us all who are artists! The woman's question is at an end" (*LEBB* 2:189).

The indignation of English reviewers was particularly aroused by the closing poem, "A Curse for a Nation," here re-deployed by EBB in a new context that altered the work's meaning and rhetorical effect. English readers had largely ignored the poem when it had appeared in the 1856 issue of *The Liberty Bell* (see above, p. 29); however, they now interpreted it as a curse on England, not America, made more offensive by the fact that its author was England's most prominent woman poet. EBB protested in her letters that the poem had been misread; yet, as the annotation in this edition indicates, she revised "A Curse for a Nation" in republishing it in *Poems before Congress,* adding an entire stanza that underscores her oblique critique of England. The bold gender politics of "A Curse for a Nation" combined with the poem's direct intervention in the politics of nation-states explains the firestorm of protest that greeted it in England (the response was much less marked in America). Despite the insistent mid-Victorian refrain in conduct literature and periodicals counseling women to remain silent on politics, they had become increasingly vocal in the 1840s and 1850s in pressing for access to higher education, the professions, and the voting booth. By the 1860s, the successes of the women's movement in England, along with unsettled financial conditions and military embarrassments in the Crimea and in India, had created a conservative climate in which women were often figured symbolically as silently suffering, saintly mothers of the nation, rather than accepted as outspoken political critics. Instead of praising EBB's combination of womanly feeling and manly thought, as some reviewers of *Casa Guidi Windows* had done, many reviewers of this late volume aggressively critiqued her transgression into masculine subjects. *Blackwood's* declared "it is a good and wholesome rule that women should not interfere with politics ... the case is worse when women of real talent take part in political affray," and counseled that "to bless and not to curse is woman's function" (see Appendix D9). In our own time, critics have responded very differently, giving special attention to the rhetorical artistry and female agency of "A Curse for a Nation."[1]

EBB's intense preoccupation with events in Italy contributed to her physical decline, while a series of severe emotional blows in 1860 further eroded her health, among them the death of the Brownings' old friend, the art critic and essayist Anna Jameson, and of EBB's sister Henrietta. First elated in the spring of 1861 by thinking Italian independence was imminent, EBB was then devastated in June by the death of statesman Camillo di Cavour,[2] whom she viewed as the principal force for unifying Italy. In a low

---

1 See Arishtein 1969, Gladish 1969, Stone 1986, Slinn 2002, Montwieler 2005, and Woodworth 2006.

2 Camillo Benso di Cavour (1810–61), Prime Minister of Piedmont and a principal architect of modern Italy, died unexpectedly on 6 June 1861.

state of mind and having endured severe bronchial attacks every winter for the last six years, she fell ill on 20 June 1861. Suffering difficult breathing and pulmonary phlegm, she nevertheless insisted that this episode was not serious. But when abscesses broke in her lungs, despite her husband's tender care and the use of morphine to relieve her pain, she died on 29 June as dawn approached, cradled in his arms. With Pen, Robert left Florence within a month, and though in his last twelve years (1878-89) he traveled annually to northern Italy, he never returned to Florence. A tomb in the form of a raised sarcophagus, designed by the Brownings' artist friend Sir Frederic Leighton, was erected over EBB's grave in Florence's Protestant Cemetery. As Samantha Matthews notes, the monument became the subject of a number of tribute poems by "young male aspiring poets,"[1] as well as a site reflecting a fetishizing of the body of the dead "poetess," with some tourists chipping away bits of the tomb, as if to carry off a piece of the legendary author (2001, 37, 47). Less ostentatious, but ultimately more moving as a tribute to EBB's transnational fame, is the memorial tablet on the wall of Casa Guidi erected by a "Grateful Florence" for the poet and scholar "whose poems forged a golden ring / Between Italy and England" (see Appendix D10).

Early in 1862, Browning published *Last Poems*, a posthumous collection of twenty-eight poems by EBB, as well as some early translations from Greek and Latin. He said that he compiled the collection from a list EBB had drawn up in June 1861, the month of her death.[2] Many of the works included in the first half concern gender politics, while those in the second half concern Italian politics. The collection includes some of EBB's most anthologized works, suggesting ways in which she might have further developed as a poet had she lived as long as her husband or as Tennyson, instead of dying at fifty-five. Some of these poems treat acts of deception or betrayal by women, as *Aurora Leigh* does. A larger number explore male-female power imbalances, although in ways that complicate the simplistic gender binary of oppressor and victim, as EBB explores the power and possessiveness of female desire

---

1 See the tribute poems on the supplementary website: www.ebbarchive.org.
2 See the "Advertisement" to *Last Poems* written by RB and dated February 1862.

in "Void in Law" and "Bianca Among the Nightingales," and the hypocrisy of male inconstancy in "Lord Walter's Wife." The work in *Last Poems* that has won the widest praise—"A Musical Instrument"—is also the structural hinge that joins the collection's poems on women's experience to the poems on Italy grouped in the second half of the collection (see Chapman 2003b, 277). Among this latter group, "Mother and Poet" remains most powerfully resonant today through its fusion of the public and the private faces of war. A dramatic monologue, the poem was inspired by the experience of the Baroness Olimpia Rossi Savio, who led a Turin literary salon and wrote poetry urging patriotic self-sacrifice, before suffering the deaths of her two sons in battle. Here, as in *Aurora Leigh*, EBB uses female images of the body to convey, in Savio's words, how "the birth-pangs of nations will wring us at length / Into wail such as this" (ll. 93-4).

Obituaries, Reception History, and a Legacy of Innovation in Form and Technique

The clashing oppositions in the retrospective reviews and obituary essays prompted by EBB's death and *Last Poems* provide a fascinating glimpse into nineteenth-century gender wars, as the gathering strength of the multi-faceted Victorian women's rights movement led to a mounting backlash against its gains. On the one hand, reviewers sounded the chords of praise, claiming like Gerald Massey that EBB was "the greatest woman-poet of whom we have any record," Sappho included; the *English Woman's Journal* expressed a similar view. On the other hand, conservative reviewers acknowledged that EBB was England's greatest woman poet in order to use her as a rein to curb female aspirations: "Considering the great capabilities she possessed, her career may be accepted as some proof of the impossibility that women can ever attain to the first rank in imaginative composition," William Stigand concluded in the *Edinburgh Review,* after exclaiming at EBB's youthful "audacity" and denouncing her "grotesque" imagery, "eccentric" rhymes, and "coarsely masculine" tone. More bluntly, the *Saturday Review* harshly critiqued her poetry and asserted, "no woman can hope to achieve what Mrs. Browning failed to accomplish."[1] The misogynist agendas underlying such assertions are suggested by the private comments of Edward Fitzgerald, writer, translator, and friend of Tennyson: "Mrs. Browning's death is rather a relief to me," Fitzgerald confided to a friend on her death in 1861; "no more Aurora Leighs, thank God! A Woman of real Genius, I know: but what is the upshot of it all? She and her Sex had better mind the Kitchen and their Children; and perhaps the Poor: except in such things as little Novels, they only devote themselves to what Men do much better, leaving that which Men do worse or not at all."[2]

Despite the contradictory assessments of EBB's achievement in the reviews and obituaries of 1861-62, certain common features permeate this body of criticism. First, whether reviewers write to praise or condemn her, they assess EBB in distinctly gendered terms and repeatedly connect her achievement to the general advance of women writers, comparing her to Charlotte Brontë most often, but also to George Eliot and Mme De Staël.[3] Second, the obituary essays underscore how much EBB's fame was based on works published before and after *Aurora Leigh,* beginning with *Poems* (1844). The ballads from this collection in particular, along with "A Vision of Poets," and works from *Last Poems* are often cited and generally praised. Third, many reviewers incorporate details from EBB's life, laying the groundwork for the increasingly biographical readings that began to prevail in the ensuing decades. Finally, her supposed stylistic carelessness and/or eccentricities form a recurrent subject of discussion, even among critics who praise her achievement.

Claims about EBB's stylistic defects descended into unsupported critical platitudes by the twentieth century, although many of the objections can be traced back to stock objections to her

---

1 For Massey and Stigand, see Appendix A. "MRS. BROWNING," *The Saturday Review* (13 July 1861): 41-42; rpt. *Littel's Living Age,* 3rd series, 14 (July, August, September, 1861): 491-92.

2 *The Letters of Edward Fitzgerald,* ed. Alfred McKinley Terhune and Annabelle Burdick Terhune (Princeton: Princeton UP, 1980), 1:407.

3 On the importance of Mme De Staël's novel *Corinne* (1807) to nineteenth-century women writers, see Kaplan 1978, 17-18. For comparisons with Brontë, Eliot, and De Staël, see, for example, the Massey review cited above; Isaphene M. Luyster's "Mrs. Browning," *Christian Examiner,* 5th ser., 10 (January 1862): 87; "Elizabeth Barrett Browning," *Methodist Quarterly Review,* 44 (July 1862): 409-11.

poetic style, which were first articulated in mid-Victorian reviews of her poetry and in the obituaries. Standard criticisms include obscurity of expression, coining of words from Greek and Latin roots, violence or eccentricity of metaphors, and, above all, roughness in rhyme and meter. Most, if not all, of these objections were raised against Robert Browning's poetry as well, of course. In his case, however, modernist critics celebrated the formerly objectionable elements as technical innovations. There is copious evidence for seeing EBB's stylistic irregularities in a similar light. Much as she iconoclastically experimented with a wide range of genres, she pushed the boundaries of poetic convention through her experiments with diction, metaphor, rhyme, and meter.

In her handling of diction, EBB achieved imaginative precision by employing an expansive vocabulary enlivened by archaisms, neologisms, and fresh combinations of words, often derived from her largely self-taught command of French, Italian, Spanish, Latin, and Greek. In some cases, as in her use of "nympholeptic," the terms critics disparaged in her poetry had been used by earlier poets without arousing complaint.[1] She further energized her language by using ellipsis and compression, by employing adjectives as nouns (e.g., *God's possible*), and by creating or recovering from older English poetry compound words (*heart-fleshed, underweep*).[2] At times, as in the 1844 poem "Bertha in the Lane," where the dramatic speaker describes a swoon as being "flooded with a Dark" (l. 134), EBB's grammatical license anticipates Dickinson's, whom she clearly influenced in numerous ways (see Swyderski 2000). The same spirit of experimentation permeates her play with the figurative grounds of language through metaphors that can seem startling, violent, or "disconcertingly literal," as Mermin notes (1989, 6). Like Robert Browning's, her metaphors often require considerable unpacking, and, like his, they often have a disruptive physicality. To a greater degree than in his poetry, however, the transgressiveness of her figurative language for Victorian readers arose from its

---

1 See l. 32 and its note in "Lady Geraldine's Courtship," and *CGW* 1.140.

2 Hayter links these practices to Gerard Manley Hopkins's innovative methods of expressing "inscape," the essential or distinctive quality of a being, landscape, or thing (1962, 49).

grounding in explicitly female experience, as the allusion to "woman's figures" in *Aurora Leigh* suggests (8.1131)

EBB's innovative rhyming practices, involving a wide range of imperfect or slant rhymes, sight or "eye-rhymes," and double or feminine rhymes (two-syllable rhymes such as *bower / power*) aroused the greatest hostility among critics, followed closely by her experiments with meter. Poe's review of *Poems* (1844), alternating wildly between enthusiastic encomium and equally spirited denunciation, provides a veritable catalogue of the rhymes that Victorian critics objected to in her verse (see Appendix A2). Her wide-ranging survey of English poetical history, "The Book of the Poets" (*CW* 6:240-311), mapping five ages in English poetry, provides an important context for understanding her principled rejection of the "idol-worship of *rhyme*" (280) that she associated with the age of Dryden and Pope. Under the influence of the Romantic poets' questioning of traditional form and her wide reading in older English poetry, her skepticism developed into a deliberate poetic "license" that in her view manifested the spirit of the English language. "If I deal too much in licenses, it is not because I am idle, but because I am speculative for freedom's sake," she declared (*BC* 9:96). Less conventional readers among her contemporaries admired the outcome of these experiments, as Browning's praise of the "grand rhymes" in "The Dead Pan" indicates (*BC* 7:137).

EBB's innovations in meter and rhythm similarly reflect her belief that "a little varying of the accents, though at the obvious expence of injuring the smoothness of every line considered separately, gives variety of cadence & fuller harmony to the general effect" (*BC* 9:170). She acknowledged purposeful "roughness" in the rhythm of "The Cry of the Children" (*BC* 7:331) and noted that verse with "monotonous" rhythm was "defective" in "individuality," was "*melody*, without the intricacies, the varieties, the light & shade of *harmony*," and consequently "fatiguing to the ear" (*BC* 7:34-35). Sound is usually integrally related to sense in her poetry. For instance, when Bertram, the poet in "Lady Geraldine's Courtship," describes the difficulties young poets experience in reading their own works, she accentuates these difficulties through a jarring departure from the meter, emphasized by the placement of the caesura: "For the echo in you breaks upon the words which you are speaking, / And the chariot-wheels *jar* in the gate through which you drive them forth" (ll. 167-68, emphasis added). As in the case of her "licenses" with rhymes, she linked the rhythm of her own "jumping lines" to her "deeper study of the old master-poets, English poets, those of the Elizabeth & James ages, before the corruption of French rhythms" (*BC* 7:331-32), emphasizing that her apparent laxness in meter came "not of carelessness, but of *conviction*" (*BC* 9:66).

EBB's linguistic verve, her idiosyncratic diction, and her experi-ments in rhyme and rhythm produced what Browning in his first letter to her called her "fresh strange music" (*BC* 10:17)—a music that we recognize and value in the work of Dickinson, Hopkins, T.S. Eliot (who directly echoed her on occasion, as Cuda 2004 notes), Archibald MacLeish, W.H. Auden, and much of modernist verse. In 1939, Fred Manning Smith demonstrated through detailed analysis how EBB anticipated the innovations of many of these po-ets, while Alethea Hayter in 1962 offered a wide-ranging treatment of EBB's "Experiments with Poetic Technique" (37-57), noting that her "real innovation was the assonantal double rhyme—such a rhyme as 'benches/influences' or 'flowings/poems,'" which provides an antecedent for widespread practice in modern rhyme (46). Despite the studies by Smith (prominently placed in *PMLA*) and Hayter, however, and despite the earlier emphasis on EBB's deliberate experiments by Horne in 1877 (when he published her letters to him), as well as by Frederic Kenyon in his 1897 edition of her letters (*LEBB*), the complaint that EBB was simply careless or inept was reiterated throughout much of the twentieth century. As late as 1988 Bernard Richards's survey of Victorian poetry mentions EBB only in passing, in his chapter on "Victorian Versification," as a poet who was "technically inept."[1] More recently, however, her pioneering formal achievement and the intricate connections between sound, sense, and subject matter in her poetry have been investigated from a number of illuminating angles, including poli-tics, national traditions, and religion.[2]

A full appreciation of EBB's innovations in poetic form and

---

1 Richards, *English Poetry of the Victorian Period 1830-1890* (NY: Longman, 1988), 65.

2 See Morlier 1999, Reynolds 2001, and Sadenwasser 1999.

technique remains hampered by the fact that few scholars and students have discussed or even seen texts of the poems as they were first read in the nineteenth century or transcripts of the manuscripts charting changes that she made before and after initial publication. As the draft manuscripts and fair copies reveal, she actually crafted her verse with great care, often writing multiple drafts before publishing, and extensively reworking many published poems for subsequent printings. The printer's copy for her *Poems* (1850)—in many instances made up of revisions recorded on printed texts of works published in 1838 and 1844—shows that she made multiple substantive changes in many poems, adding whole stanzas and sections on occasion, as well as altering words and phrases. She also paid attention to the minute effects of punctuation, frequently altering this as well. While a comprehensive understanding of her stylistic practices must await completion of a full scholarly edition with detailed annotation on textual variants, we hope that the selective annotation in this edition will begin to suggest how much remains to be investigated in relation to her formal innovations. No other nineteenth-century poet of comparable range and historical impact has so long awaited the editorial practices that can help us to recognize the precise ways in which she was "speculative for freedom's sake," in matters of poetic form as well as in the treatment of subject matter that entered deeply into the principal social, political, and cultural movements of her time.

EBB's husband and fellow poet, Robert Browning, who knew her work intimately and often echoed it in his own (see Davies 2006), remains one of her most discerning readers. "I believed in your glorious genius and knew it for a true star from the moment I saw it,—long before I had the blessing of knowing it was MY star," he wrote in an 1845 letter to EBB (*BC* 11:159). In his subsequent brief, enigmatic poem "My Star" (1855), which held a special significance for him, he encapsulated this belief.[1] While the star he describes seems to stop "like a bird; like a flower, hangs furled" in the eyes of others, for him it is a "certain star" that "can

---

1 "My Star," *Robert Browning: The Poems*, ed. John Pettigrew and Thomas J. Collins (New Haven & London: Yale UP; Harmondsworth: Penguin, 1981), 1:580. RB frequently made signed copies of this poem and distributed it to friends and autograph seekers (see *R* E267–77).

throw ... / Now a dart of red, / Now a dart of blue"—iridescent, shape-changing, transformative in its power. The poems collected here are similarly multi-faceted in their darting allusiveness, innovative in their protean experiments with form, transgressive in their strength of conviction. Illuminating aesthetic, moral, ethical, and political issues that challenged EBB's era as they challenge our own, they manifest the "certain" energy and dynamism of the poet who called for subject matter that reflected the times she lived in, as well as new ways of artistically representing it. "[W]e want new *forms* . . as well as thoughts— ," she wrote to Browning. "The old gods are dethroned. Why should we go back to the antique molds.... Let us all aspire rather to *Life*—& let the dead bury their dead.... For there is poetry *everywhere*..." (*BC* 10:135).

1. Early Works

UNPUBLISHED JUVENILIA

On the Cruelty of Forcement to Man Alluding to the Press Gang

According to the notation "1812" in her mother's large commonplace book recording the early writings of EBB and her brother Edward,[1] EBB composed this, her earliest known poem, when she was only six years old. It refers to the English navy's practice of conscripting men from civilian life or from American ships, on the pretext that they were deserters, and pressing them into service. In 1812 this practice, debated in Parliament and protested in the press, provided a catalyst for war between Britain and the United States. Criticism: Avery and Stott 2003 and Taylor 2005a. Pub. 1914, *HUPS*. Text: Berg ms.

> Ah! the poor lad in yonder boat
> Forced from his Wife, his Friends, his home,
> Now gentle Maiden how can you
> Look at the misery of his doom?

Fragment of an "Essay on Woman"

"Yes—I know Mary Wolstonecraft. I was a great admirer at thirteen of the Rights of woman.[2] I know too certain letters[3] published under

---

1   Ms notebook in the Berg Collection, NY Public Library (*R* D666). The poem has been dated 1814 in *HUPS* and *R*, agreeing with the heading on a ms transcription by EBB's grandmother Elizabeth Moulton, "Poetry composed by my Grandaughter Elizabeth Barrett began at the age of eight years old August the 7th 1814" (see *R* D669). The prominence of discussions of impressments in the 1812 London *Times* argues for the earlier date. It also accords with EBB's recollection of her first poetic efforts: "At four I first mounted Pegasus but at six I thought myself priviledged [sic] to show off feats of horsemanship" (BC 1:349). Whether composed at age six or eight, the poem is remarkably precocious in anticipating her later work focused on social, political, and gender issues.

2   *A Vindication of the Rights of Woman: With Strictures on Political and Moral Subjects* (1792).

3   *Letters Written During a Short Residence in Sweden, Norway, and Denmark* (1796).

her name: but Godwin's Life[1] of her I never saw & sh^d like much to do so," EBB observed to her friend and fellow writer Mary Mitford in March 1842 (*BC* 5:282). A few months later, in July 1842, she repeated the same anecdote of reading Wollstonecraft at "thirteen: no, twelve!"—further commenting, "and, through the whole course of my childhood, I had a steady indignation against Nature who made me a woman" (*BC* 6:42).[2] Family correspondence confirms EBB's recollections of the dramatic impact of reading Wollstonecraft on her adolescent views of woman's position in society—although she may have been older than twelve or thirteen. In 1821, when she was fifteen, her mother warned her against "visionary hopes" of founding happiness "upon yours & Mrs Wolstonecrafts system" (*BC* 1:132). EBB's reading is especially interesting (and bold) in light of the backlash that followed William Godwin's injudicious revelations in 1798 about Wollstonecraft's private life and views.[3] Written in the manner of Alexander Pope's philosophical poem in heroic couplets *An Essay on Man* (pub. 1733-34), this "essay on woman" survives in a manuscript (*R* D308) carrying the watermark 1822 (when EBB turned sixteen). The date of composition may be earlier, however, since the manuscript is not a working draft but a signed fair copy. The poem was first published in 1984 by Eleanor Hoag.[4] The text here, based directly on the manuscript, differs from Hoag's transcription at several points. Criticism: Moser 1984.

Man's noble powers, the Poets pen sustains;
He stands superior in didactic strains.
For him, a Pope[5] awoke the living lays,

---

1 *Memoirs of the Author of a Vindication of the Rights of Woman*, published posthumously by Wollstonecraft's husband, the Romantic radical writer William Godwin (1756-1836).

2 In this same passage EBB describes her "determinate resolution," in her girlhood, "to seek my fortune" dressed "in men's clothes" as "Lord Byron's PAGE." (See "The Romaunt of the Page" 1839). For another reference to Wollstonecraft's impact on her, see *BC* 9:292.

3 The *Memoirs* led to attacks on Wollstonecraft as a "whore and an atheist." Consequently, other women writers such as Jane Austen were cautious about linking their names with hers, and Wollstonecraft's writings became increasingly difficult to obtain; see Margaret Kirkham, *Jane Austen, Feminism, and Fiction* (Sussex: Harvester P, New Jersey: Barnes and Noble, 1983), 48-49. Despite the scandal, Mitford defended Wollstonecraft as someone who "married or not married wrote like a modest woman—was a modest woman" (cited Kirkham, 167-68).

4 "Fragment of an 'Essay on Woman,'" *SBHC* 12 (1984), 11-12.

5 a Pope] Alexander Pope (1688-1744), alluding to his *An Essay on Man*.

And bade him triumph in immortal bays.[1]
Tis his, exalted midst the Universe,   5
The lord of Nature, & the pride of verse,
Unchecked, unvanquished, unsubdued to stand,
Pride in his post, and in his eye command.
But while we hail him potent, and devine,[2]
Shall gentle Woman claim no humble line?   10
Which may, perchance in simple couplet trace
The timid smile that lingers on her face;
And ah! that pledge of weakness, yet more dear,
The mild, reproachless, sympathetic tear—?
Paint the untutored blush—the fond caress   15
The trembling, melting voice of tenderness,
And all that Mother, Sister, Wife impart
To nurture, solace, and subdue the heart?

Yet not for this the breathing lyre rebounds,
It wakes to loftier, more exalted sounds.   20
Though sweet the hours of bliss domestic seem,
And bright the wings of Love's aerial dream,
Tho' gay the gentle voice that beguile,
And soft the April tear, and rainbow smile—
Yet be it mine to exert my humble care   25
To bend to nobler thoughts the British fair!
Found the proud path, where Glory's breezes fan,
She stands the equal of her Master Man.

Can Woman only triumph in the sigh,
The smile coquetish, or bewitching eye?   30
Are drawling words, & affectatious airs
The only claim on notice that are hers?
Are vases only prised[3] because they break?
Then why must Woman to be loved be weak?

Imperious Man! is this alone thy pride   35
T'enslave the heart that lingers at thy side?

---

1 bays] wreath of bay (laurel) leaves, traditionally the crown awarded to poets.

2 devine] divine.

3 prised] prized.

Smother each flash of intellectual fire,
And bid Ambition's noblest throb expire?
Pinion the wing, that yearns for glory's light,
Then boast the strength of thy superior flight? 40
Go! love the fabric of unmeaning clay,
The flattered creature of an idle day!
And as the trembling partner of thy lot
Hangs on thy steps unheeded, or forgot,
Thy cradle rocks, and weeps upon thy grave, 45
Tis thine to fetter, scorn, disdain, enslave!
And while she smiles, submissive, on thy breast,
Debase the faithful heart that loves thee best!
Teach her a lovely, abject thing, to be!
For such are *generous deeds*, and *worthy thee*! 50

Eternal Genius! thou mysterious tie,
That links the Mortal, and Divinity!
Say, hath thy sacred influence never stole,
With radiance unobscured, on Woman's soul;
Till, waking into greatness, it hath caught 55
The glow of fancy, and the life of thought,
Breathing Conception, eloquence that fires,
And all that learning gives, & Heav'n inspires?
Is Woman doomed obscure, & lone, to sigh?
Comnena,[1] Dacier,[2] More,[3] DeStael,[4] reply! 60

---

1 Comnena] Anna Comnena (1083-1148 or thereafter), eldest daughter of Alexius I
   Comnenus, Byzantine Emperor. She wrote the 15-volume *Alexiad* (written after 1137),
   a history of her father's life and of the First Crusades.

2 Dacier] Anne Lefevre Dacier (1654-1720), French translator of Homer, Sappho, Aris-
   tophanes, and other classical writers; her works included "Remarks upon Mr. Pope's
   Account of Homer" (1724).

3 More] Hannah More (1745-1833), dramatist, poet, novelist, abolitionist, and author
   of widely disseminated tracts and treatises on Christian morality, politics, universal
   education, and women's education.

4 DeStael] Madame De Staël (1766-1817), French-Swiss woman of letters, champion of
   women's rights, and author of the fictional works *Delphine* (1802) and *Corinne* (1807),
   as well as works on literature and on the passions. EBB described *Corinne* as an "im-
   mortal book," deserving to be read "three score & ten times" (*BC* 3:25). De Staël
   figures as a heroic model in EBB's untitled autobiographical essay on "Beth" (*BC*
   1:361) and forms the subject of the unpublished work of juvenile fiction, "Madame
   de Staëls Travels Thro Europe" (*R* L191), identified as the work of EBB's brother
   Edward, though possibly involving a collaboration with her.

FROM *AN ESSAY ON MIND, WITH OTHER POEMS* (1826)[1]

Stanzas on the Death of Lord Byron

Byron's death at Missolonghi in Greece on 19 April 1824, where he had gone to assist the Greek revolutionaries in their war against the Turks, inspired several elegiac tributes by EBB: these "Stanzas," first published 30 June 1824, in the London *Globe and Traveller* and reprinted, with revisions, in *An Essay on Mind, With Other Poems* (1826); the extended lament concluding the title poem in that collection, *An Essay on Mind* (ll. 1185-1262); and a poem in the 1826 volume entitled "Stanzas occasioned by a passage in Mr. Emerson's Journal." An unpublished ABL manuscript "Lines on the death of Lord Byron" records a more personal response to Byron's death and bears little resemblance to the poem below, written in the Spenserian stanzas used by Byron himself in *Childe Harold's Pilgrimage* (1812, 1816, 1818). P.B. Shelley had also used Spenserian stanzas in his elegy on the death of John Keats, "Adonais" (1821), providing EBB with a recent pattern for a poet's lament for a poet.

"——λέγε πᾶσιν ἀπώλετο." — *Bion.*[2]

"—I am not now
That which I have been." — *Childe Harold.*[3]

He *was*, and *is* not! Græcia's[4] trembling shore,
Sighing through all her palmy groves, shall tell
That Harold's pilgrimage at last is o'er—[5]

---

1 For a more extensive selection from this collection and from EBB's 1833 collection, *Prometheus Bound ... And Miscellaneous Poems*, see the supplementary website.

2 "λέγε πᾶσιν ἀπώλετο"] "Say to all he is dead," from the "Lament for Adonis," l. 5, by the Greek poet Bion (flourished c.100 BC). EBB's translation of "A Lament for Adonis" appeared in her *Poems* (1850).

3 *Childe Harold's Pilgrimage* 4.clxxxv, beginning "My task is done, my song hath ceased...."

4 Græcia's] Greece's.

5 Like the reading public, EBB conflates Byron with Childe Harold, his poem's pro-tagonist.

Mute the impassioned tongue, and tuneful shell,
That erst was wont¹ in noblest strains to swell,   5
Hush'd the proud shouts that rode Ægæa's² wave!
For lo! the great Deliv'rer breathes farewell!
Gives to the world his mem'ry and a grave—
Expiring in the land he only lived to save!

Mourn, Hellas,³ mourn! and o'er thy widow'd brow,   10
For aye, the cypress⁴ wreath of sorrow twine;
And in thy new-form'd beauty, desolate, throw
The fresh-cull'd flowers on *his* sepulchral shrine.
Yes! let that heart whose fervor was all thine,
In consecrated urn lamented be!   15
That generous heart where genius thrill'd divine,
Hath spent its last most glorious throb for thee—
Then sank amid the storm that made thy children free!

Britannia's Poet! Græcia's hero, sleeps!
And Freedom, bending o'er the breathless clay,   20
Lifts up her voice, and in her anguish weeps!
For *us*, a night hath clouded o'er our day,
And hush'd the lips that breath'd our fairest lay.
Alas! and must the British lyre resound
A requiem, while the spirit wings away   25
Of him who on its strings such music found,
And taught its startling chords to give so sweet a sound!

The theme grows sadder—but my soul shall find
A language in these tears! No more—no more!
Soon, 'midst the shriekings of the tossing wind,   30
The "dark blue depths"⁵ he sang of, shall have bore
Our *all* of Byron to his native shore!
His grave is thick with voices—to the ear

---

1   erst was wont] formerly was accustomed.
2   Ægæa's] the Aegean Sea's.
3   Hellas] ancient name of Greece.
4   Aye] always; cypress] traditionally associated with death.
5   "dark blue depths"] alluding to *Childe Harold* 4.clxxix.

Murm'ring an awful tale of greatness o'er;
But Memory strives with Death, and lingering near,   35
Shall consecrate the dust of Harold's lonely bier!

Figure 1: The picture for which EBB wrote "A Romance of the Ganges," from *Findens' Tableaux*, London, 1838.

2. *From* The Seraphim, and Other Poems *(1838)*

A Romance of the Ganges

Appearing in the 1838 *Findens' Tableaux: A Series of Picturesque Scenes of National Character, Beauty, and Costume* (published in October 1837 for Christmas sales), this ballad was EBB's first contribution to the gift books or annuals, which were sumptuously produced volumes that featured engravings and only secondarily the accompanying poems and tales, which were generally criticized for their mediocrity.[1] Although EBB wrote that she did not "hold any kind of annual, gild it as you please, in too much honour & awe" (*BC* 3:273), she supplied the poem on short notice (two to three weeks) partly out of friendship for the volume's editor Mary Russell Mitford (see the Introduction), and partly because it provided access to public recognition. Up to this time, EBB had published her poetry volumes anonymously, and she intended to print her name with this poem; her father objected, however, and was annoyed when the poem appeared signed with her initials (see *BC* 3:287, 289n3, 4:41n11). Mitford had requested "a poem in illustration of a very charming group of Hindoo girls floating their lamps upon the Ganges," referring to "that pretty superstition" (*BC* 3:252) that if her lover were faithful, the flame in a maiden's boat would continue to burn until the vessel passed from view (see *BC* 3:275).[2] EBB wrote that she did not need a copy of the engraving, for she had seen the original, an oil painting by William Daniell (1769-1837), in the Royal Academy exhibition (see Figure 1): "I remember that the subject is exactly the one you mention—moonlight & all" (*BC*

---

1 Whereas engravers or artists might receive as much as £150, EBB was to receive £5 for her poem (see *BC* 3:253). Notable writers, including the young Tennyson, published in the annuals even while disparaging them. With self-deprecating irony, EBB anticipated being "awestruck at having to stand" beside "some shining names" (*BC* 3:275).

2 Louis de Grandpré's *A Voyage in the Indian Ocean and to Bengal, Undertaken in the Year 1790*, first published in French and translated in several English editions, describes the practice but without relating it specifically to predictions regarding romantic fidelity (Boston, MA: W. Pelham and W.P. & L. Blake, 1803, 176), as does Thomas Moore's immensely popular "Lalla Rookh" (1817).

3:254). Unlike most pairings in the *Findens'* volume, EBB's poem develops the dramatic potential of the engraved image; it was praised by the *Literary Gazette* reviewer as "incomparably the best poem in the work" (*BC* 3:339). It included an epigraph, three lines from Alfred Tennyson's "Song: The Lintwhite and the Throstle-cock" (1830, ll. 13-15): "When thy light perisheth, / That from thee issueth, / Our life evanisheth." EBB made many revisions in the text in preparing *Poems* (1850); we note only a few below. Criticism: Leighton 1986, Mermin 1989, Stephenson 1989, Taylor 1993, Stone 1995, and Avery and Stott 2003.

I
Seven maidens 'neath the midnight
  Stand near the river-sea,
Whose water sweepeth white around
  The shadow of the tree.
The moon and earth are face to face,   5
  And earth is slumbering deep;
The wave-voice seems the voice of dreams
  That wander through her sleep.
       The river floweth on.

II
What bring they 'neath the midnight,   10
  Beside the river-sea?
They bring the human heart wherein
  No nightly calm can be,—
That droppeth never with the wind,
  Nor drieth with the dew.   15
Oh, calm it God! thy calm is broad
  To cover spirits, too.
       The river floweth on.

III
The maidens lean them over
  The waters, side by side,   20
And shun each other's deepening eyes,
  And gaze adown the tide;

For each within a little boat
  A little lamp hath put,
And heaped for freight some lily's weight   25
  Or scarlet rose half shut.
        The river floweth on.

IV[1]
Of shell of cocoa[2] carven,
  Each little boat is made.
Each carries a lamp, and carries a flower,   30
  And carries a hope unsaid;
And when the boat hath carried the lamp
  Unquenched, till out of sight,
The maiden is sure that love will endure,—
  But love will fail with light.   35
        The river floweth on.

V
Why, all the stars are ready
  To symbolize the soul,
The stars untroubled by the wind,
  Unwearied as they roll;   40
And yet the soul by instinct sad
  Reverts to symbols low—
To that small flame, whose very name
  Breathed o'er it, shakes it so!
        The river floweth on.   45

VI[3]
Six boats are on the river,
  Seven maidens on the shore,
While still above them stedfastly
  The stars shine evermore.
Go, little boats, go soft and safe,   50

---

1 Stanza IV was added in 1850.

2 cocoa] coconut.

3 In *Poems* (1850) the original version of stanza 6 was expanded to two stanzas by adding ll. 46-49 and 55-58.

And guard the symbol spark!—
The boats aright go safe and bright
  Across the waters dark.
            The river floweth on.

VII

The maiden Luti watcheth   55
  Where onwardly they float.
That look in her dilating eyes
  Might seem to drive her boat!
Her eyes still mark the constant fire,
  And kindling unawares   60
That hopeful while, she lets a smile
  Creep silent through her prayers.
            The river floweth on.

VIII

The smile—where hath it wandered?
  She riseth from her knee,   65
She holds her dark, wet locks away—
  There is no light to see!
She cries a quick and bitter cry—
  "Nuleeni, launch me thine!
We must have light abroad to-night,   70
  For all the wreck of mine."
            The river floweth on.

IX

"I do remember watching
  Beside this river-bed,
When on my childish knee was laid   75
  My dying father's head.[1]
I turned mine own, to keep the tears
  From falling on his face.
What doth it prove when Death and Love

---

1   In *Poems* (1850) and subsequent editions, EBB dropped a note she had included in the
    collections of 1837 and 1838: "The Hindoos carry their dying friends to the banks of
    the Ganges, believing in the after-blessedness of those who die there."

Choose out the self-same place?"   80
    The river floweth on.

X

"They say the dead are joyful
    The death-change here receiving.
Who say—ah, me!—who dare to say
    Where joy comes to the living?   85
Thy boat, Nuleeni! look not sad—
    Light up the waters rather!
I weep no faithless lover where
    I wept a loving father."
    The river floweth on.   90

XI

"My heart foretold his falsehood
    Ere my little boat grew dim:
And though I closed mine eyes to dream
    That one last dream of *him*,
They shall not now be wet to see   95
    The shining vision go.
From earth's cold love I look above
    To the holy house of snow."[1]
    The river floweth on.

XII

"Come thou—thou never knewest   100
    A grief, that thou shouldst fear one!
Thou wearest still the happy look
    That shines beneath a dear one.
Thy humming-bird is in the sun,[2]
    Thy cuckoo in the grove,   105
And all the three broad worlds, for thee
    Are full of wandering love."
    The river floweth on.

---

1 "The Hindoo heaven is localized on the summit of Mount Meru—one of the mountains of Himalaya or Himmeleh, which signifies, I believe, in Sanscrit, the abode of snow, winter, or coldness" [EBB's note]. Indra is the Hindu deity associated with this site.

2 "Hamadeva, the Indian god of love, is imagined to wander through the three worlds, accompanied by the humming-bird, cuckoo, and gentle breezes" [EBB's note]. Usually called Kamadeva, the god is also accompanied by his wife Rati.

XIII[1]

"Why, maiden, dost thou loiter?
  What secret wouldst thou cover?   110
That peepul[2] cannot hide thy boat,
  And I can guess thy lover.
I heard thee sob his name in sleep ...
  It was a name I knew.
Come, little maid, be not afraid,   115
  But let us prove him true!"
          The river floweth on.

XIV

The little maiden cometh,
  She cometh shy and slow.
I ween[3] she seeth through her lids,   120
  They drop adown so low.
Her tresses meet her small bare feet—
  She stands and speaketh nought,
Yet blusheth red, as if she said
  The name she only thought.   125
          The river floweth on.

XV

She knelt beside the water,
  She lighted up the flame,
And o'er her youthful forehead's calm
  The fitful radiance came:—   130
"Go, little boat, go, soft and safe,
  And guard the symbol spark!"
Soft, safe, doth float the little boat
  Across the waters dark.
          The river floweth on.   135

---

1 Stanza XIII was added in *Poems* (1850).

2 peepul] an Indian species of fig-tree, regarded as sacred; also known as the Bo-tree.

3 ween] surmise, suppose.

XVI

Glad tears her eyes have blinded,
  The light they cannot reach;
She turneth with that sudden smile
  She learnt before her speech—
"I do not hear his voice! the tears   140
  Have dimmed my light away!
But the symbol light will last to-night,
  The love will last for aye."[1]
          The river floweth on.

XVII

Then Luti spake behind her,   145
  Out-spake she bitterly.
"By the symbol light that lasts to-night,
  Wilt[2] vow a vow to me?"—
Nuleeni gazeth up her face,
  Soft answer maketh she.   150
"By loves that last when lights are past,
  I vow that vow to thee!"
          The river floweth on.

XVIII

An earthly look had Luti
  Though her voice was deep as prayer.   155
"The rice is gathered from the plains
  To cast upon thine hair.[3]
But when *he* comes, his marriage-band
  Around thy neck to throw,
Thy bride-smile raise to meet his gaze,   160
And whisper,—*There is one betrays,*
  While Luti suffers woe."[4]
          The river floweth on.

---

1 aye] ever, always.

2 Wilt] Will you.

3 "The casting of rice upon the head, and the fixing of the band or tali about the neck,
   are parts of the Hindoo marriage ceremonial" [EBB's note].

4 ll. 160-62] Toward his gaze thy bride-smile raise, / And ask of--Luti's woe!" *Poems*
   (1837, 1838).

XIX

"And when in seasons after,
  Thy little bright-faced son 165
Shall lean against thy knee and ask
  What deeds his sire hath done,
Press deeper down thy mother-smile
  His glossy curls among—
View deep his pretty childish eyes, 170
And whisper,—*There is none denies,*
  While Luti speaks of wrong."
        The river floweth on.

XX

Nuleeni looked in wonder,
  Yet softly answered she. 175
"By loves that last when lights are past,
  I vowed that vow to thee.
But why glads[1] it thee that a bride-day be
  By a word of *woe* defiled?
That a word of *wrong* take the cradle-song 180
  From the ear of a sinless child?"—
"Why?" Luti said, and her laugh was dread,[2]
  And her eyes dilated wild—
"That the fair new love may her bridegroom prove,
  And the father shame the child." 185
        The river floweth on.

XXI

"Thou flowest still, O river,
  Thou flowest 'neath the moon!
Thy lily hath not changed a leaf,[3]
  Thy charmèd lute a tune! 190
He mixed his voice with thine—and *his*
  Was all I heard around;
But now, beside his chosen bride,
  I hear the river's sound."
        The river floweth on. 195

---

1 glads] gladdens.

2 dread] awe-inspiring, frightful, inspiring dread.

3 "The Ganges is represented as a white woman, with a water lily in her right hand, and
   in her left a lute" [EBB's note].

XXII

"I gaze upon her beauty
  Through the tresses that enwreathe it.
The light above thy wave, is hers—
  My rest, alone beneath it.
Oh, give me back the dying look   200
  My father gave thy water!
Give back,—and let a little love
  O'erwatch his weary daughter!"
        The river floweth on.

XXIII

"Give back!" she hath departed—   205
  The word is wandering with her;
And the stricken maidens hear afar
  The step and cry together.
Frail symbols? None are frail enow[1]
  For mortal joys to borrow!—   210
While bright doth float Nuleeni's boat,
She weepeth, dark with sorrow.
        The river floweth on.

The Virgin Mary to the Child Jesus

First published in *The Seraphim, with Other Poems* (1838), this poem represents dimensions of female experience left unexplored by John Milton (1608-74). Whereas the later *A Drama of Exile* (1844) depicts the particular anguish of Eve after the loss of Paradise, EBB here gives voice to Mary's inner thoughts and feelings. She focuses not on the Nativity, the subject of Milton's ode "On the Morning of Christ's Nativity" (1629), but on the period following the holy birth, when the young mother meditates alone upon the sacred mystery of the child before her and the implications of her role in the Incarnation. This subject is untreated in either Milton's works or Scriptures; the closest analogue is the subject of the Virgin ador-

---

1 enow] enough.

ing the Christ child (the *Madonna Pia*) in medieval and Renaissance paintings, although in these depictions Mary is silent. In *Legends of the Madonna* (1852), the Victorian art critic Anna Jameson describes EBB's poem as an "interpretation worthy of the most beautiful of these representations," comparing it with the "high imaginings" conveyed by Michelangelo's "Silent Madonna."[1] The principal biblical source is the allusion to the marvelous sayings concerning Christ's birth in Luke 1-2, the most positive account of Mary in the Gospels, which may have indirectly provided EBB with an opening: "But Mary kept all these things, and pondered them in her heart." Formally, EBB adopts Milton's use of the irregular ode, while her use of a dramatic perspective to explore Mary's subjectivity may have been influenced by Felicia Hemans's *Records of Woman* (1828). The poem was separately published in a pamphlet *The True Mary* (1868; 2nd ed. 1870), with a preface and commentary defending it as a vindication of the Protestant interpretation of Mary as a flesh-and-blood woman in contrast to the Catholic interpretation of her as a Queen of Heaven.[2] EBB made many revisions to the 1838 text of the poem for her 1850 *Poems*, inserting new lines at some points. Criticism: Scheinberg 2002 and Stone 2005.

> But see the Virgin blest
> Hath laid her babe to rest.
> > Milton's *Hymn on the Nativity*.[3]

I

> Sleep, sleep, mine Holy One!
My flesh, my Lord!—what name? I do not know
A name that seemeth not too high or low,
> Too far from me or heaven.
My Jesus, *that* is best! that word being given   5
By the majestic angel whose command

---

1   Anna Brownell Jameson, *Legends of the Madonna: As Represented in the Arts* (London: Hutchinson, n.d.) 369. Jameson (1794-1860) was a prolific essayist, travel writer, and critic, and a close friend of the Brownings after their marriage.

2   See Appendix B for extracts from this pamphlet and the controversy it reflects.

3   *Nativity*] EBB cites ll. 237-38 from the final stanza of Milton's ode, immediately preceding his words, "Time is our tedious song should here have ending."

Was softly as a man's beseeching said,
When I and all the earth appeared to stand
        In the great overflow
Of light celestial from his wings and head.[1]   10
        Sleep, sleep, my saving One!

II
And art thou come for saving, baby-browed
And speechless Being—art thou come for saving?[2]
The palm that grows beside our door is bowed
By treadings of the low wind from the south,   15
A restless shadow through the chamber waving:
Upon its bough a bird sings in the sun;[3]
But Thou, with that close slumber on thy mouth,
Dost seem of wind and sun already weary.
Art come for saving, O my weary One?   20

III
Perchance this sleep that shutteth out the dreary
Earth-sounds and motions, opens on Thy soul
        High dreams on fire with God;
High songs that make the pathways where they roll
More bright than stars do theirs; and visions new   25
Of Thine eternal Nature's old abode.
        Suffer this mother's kiss,
        Best thing that earthly is,
To glide the music and the glory through,
Nor narrow in Thy dream the broad upliftings   30
        Of any seraph[4] wing.
Thus noiseless, thus. Sleep, sleep, my dreaming One!

---

1   At the time of the Annunciation, when he makes God's purpose known to Mary, the
    angel Gabriel declares, "thou shalt call his name JESUS" (Luke 1.31).

2   saving] alludes to Matthew 1.21: "and thou shalt call his name JESUS: for he shall save
    his people." The Greek word "Jesus" derives from the Hebrew "Joshua," meaning
    "Jehovah the Savior."

3   On the palm's associations with the life of Jesus, see John 12.13. Cf. the similar images
    of a palm and a bird in D.G. Rossetti's painting "The Girlhood of Mary Virgin"
    (1848-49) and the accompanying sonnet, "Mary's Girlhood."

4   seraph] singular form of "seraphim," the highest of the orders of angels.

IV

The slumber of His lips meseems[1] to run,
Through *my* lips to mine heart,—to all its shiftings
Of sensual life, bringing contrariousness   35
In a great calm. I feel, I could lie down
As Moses did, and die,[2]—and then live most.
I am 'ware of you, heavenly Presences,
That stand with your peculiar light unlost,
Each forehead with a high thought for a crown,   40
Unsunned i' the sunshine! I am 'ware. Ye throw
No shade against the wall! How motionless
Ye round me with your living statuary,
While through your whiteness, in and outwardly,
Continual thoughts of God appear to go,   45
Like light's soul in itself. I bear, I bear
To look upon the dropt lids of your eyes,
Though their external shining testifies
To that beatitude within, which were
Enough to blast an eagle at his sun.[3]   50
I fall not on my sad clay face before ye,—
          I look on His. I know
My spirit which dilateth with the woe
          Of His mortality,
          May well contain your glory.   55
          Yea, drop your lids more low.
Ye are but fellow-worshippers with me!
     Sleep, sleep, my worshipped One!

V

We sate[4] among the stalls at Bethlehem.
The dumb kine[5] from their fodder turning them,   60
     Softened their hornèd faces

---

1   meseems] seems to me.

2   die] "It is a Jewish tradition that Moses died of the kisses of God's lips." [EBB's note].

3   Traditionally eagles were said to have the keenest vision among birds and the ability
     to look directly at the sun.

4   sate] sat.

5   kine] archaic or poetic term for cattle. .

To almost human gazes
Toward the newly Born.
The simple shepherds from the star-lit brooks
Brought visionary looks,   65
As yet in their astonied[1] hearing rung
The strange, sweet angel-tongue.
The magi of the East,[2] in sandals worn,
Knelt reverent, sweeping round,
With long pale beards, their gifts upon the ground,   70
The incense, myrrh and gold
These baby hands were impotent to hold.
So, let all earthlies[3] and celestials wait
Upon thy royal state.
Sleep, sleep, my kingly One!   75

VI
I am not proud—meek angels, ye invest
New meeknesses to hear such utterance rest
On mortal lips,—"I am not proud"—*not proud!*
Albeit in my flesh God sent his Son,
Albeit over Him my head is bowed   80
As others bow before Him, still mine heart
Bows lower than their knees. O centuries
That roll, in vision, your futurities
My future grave athwart,—
Whose murmurs seem to reach me while I keep   85
Watch o'er this sleep,—
Say of me as the Heavenly said—"Thou art
The blessedest of women!"[4]—blessedest,
Not holiest, not noblest—no high name
Whose height misplaced may pierce me like a shame,   90
When I sit meek in heaven!
For me, for me,

---

1 astonied] astonished.

2 magi of the East] the "wise men" described in Matthew 2.1-12.

3 earthlies] earthly beings.

4 blessedest of women] alluding to the angel Gabriel's words to Mary, "blessed art thou
   among women" (Luke 1.28, 42, 48), echoed in Mary's song, the Magnificat, and in the
   Catholic prayer "Hail, Mary."

God knows that I am feeble like the rest!—[1]
I often wandered forth, more child than maiden,
Among the midnight hills of Galilee
      Whose summits looked heaven-laden, 95
Listening to silence as it seemed to be
God's voice, so soft yet strong—so fain to press
Upon my heart as Heaven did on the height,
And waken up its shadows by a light,
And show its vileness by a holiness. 100
Then I knelt down most silent like the night,
      Too self-renounced for fears,
Raising my small face to the boundless blue
Whose stars did mix and tremble in my tears.
God heard *them* falling after—with his dew. 105

VII

So, seeing my corruption, can I see
This Incorruptible now born of me,
This fair new Innocence no sun did chance
To shine on, (for even Adam was no child,)[2]
Created from my nature all defiled, 110
This mystery, from out mine ignorance,—
Nor feel the blindness, stain, corruption, more
Than others do, or *I* did heretofore?—
Can hands wherein such burden pure has been,
Not open with the cry "unclean, unclean," 115
More oft than any else beneath the skies?
      Ah King, ah Christ, ah son!
The kine, the shepherds, the abasèd wise,
      Must all less lowly wait
      Than I, upon thy state.— 120
      Sleep, sleep, my kingly One!

---

1 God knows ... rest!—] inserted in the 1850 copytext.

2 Adam was no child)] Adam was not born of woman, but fashioned by God in Genesis
   1.27.

VIII

Art Thou a King, then? Come, his universe,
    Come, crown me Him a King!
Pluck rays from all such stars as never fling
    Their light where fell a curse,   125
And make a crowning for this kingly brow!—
What is my word?—Each empyreal[1] star
          Sits in a sphere afar
          In shining ambuscade.[2]
          The child-brow, crowned by none,   130
          Keeps its unchildlike shade.
          Sleep, sleep, my crownless One!

IX

Unchildlike shade!—No other babe doth wear
An aspect very sorrowful, as thou.—
No small babe-smiles, my watching heart has seen,   135
To float like speech the speechless lips between.
No dovelike cooing in the golden air,
No quick short joys of leaping babyhood.
          Alas, our earthly good
In heaven thought evil, seems too good for Thee: 140
          Yet, sleep, my weary One!

X

And then the drear sharp tongue of prophecy,
With the dread sense of things which shall be done,
Doth smite me inly, like a sword! a sword?—
(*That* "smites the Shepherd.")[3] Then, I think aloud   145
The words "despised,"—"rejected,"[4]—every word
Recoiling into darkness as I view

---

1   empyreal] pertaining to the empyrean, the sphere of fire or highest heaven.

2   ambuscade] in ambush; in this context, in concealment.

3   "smites the Shepherd"] alludes to Zechariah 13.7, traditionally interpreted as a prophecy of the Crucifixion. EBB also alludes to this prophecy in "Stabat Mater," a poem that she wrote on the grieving Mary (see *LEBB* 2:80-81).

4   "despised,"—"rejected"] alludes to Isaiah 53.3, which is also traditionally interpreted as a prophecy of Christ's earthly suffering.

The DARLING on my knee.
Bright angels,—move not!—lest ye stir the cloud
Betwixt my soul and His futurity!   150
I must not die, with mother's work to do,
        And could not live—and see.

XI
        It is enough to bear
        This image still and fair—
        This holier in sleep,   155
        Than a saint at prayer:
        This aspect of a child
        Who never sinned or smiled;
        This Presence in an infant's face;
        This sadness most like love,   160
        This love than love more deep,
        This weakness like omnipotence
        It is so strong to move.
        Awful is this watching place
        Awful what I see from hence—   165
        A king, without regalia,
        A God, without the thunder,
        A child, without the heart for play;
        Ay, a Creator, rent asunder
        From His first glory and cast away   170
        On His own world, for me alone
To hold in hands created, crying—SON![1]

XII
        That tear fell not on thee
Beloved, yet thou stirrest in thy slumber!
THOU, stirring not for glad sounds out of number   175
Which through the vibratory palm trees run
        From summer wind and bird,
        So quickly hast thou heard
        A tear fall silently?—[2]
        Wak'st thou, O loving One?—   180

---

1 In the Berg ms of this poem, Stanza XI follows XII, forming the conclusion to the
   poem, and this line reads: "To hold with feeble hands, & say my Son."
2 Cf. the similar image in the conclusion of "A Drama of Exile."

Felicia Hemans: To L.E.L., Referring to her Monody on the Poetess[1]

EBB here acknowledges the two women poets with whom she was most often linked in the 1830s and 1840s. Felicia Dorothea Browne Hemans (1793-1835), a prolific poet and translator who published more than twenty volumes of verse, has been described as the woman poet in English most widely read by her contemporaries. Similarly prolific and popular, Letitia Elizabeth Landon (1802-38), known by her initials L.E.L., frequently contributed poetry and prose to periodicals, annuals, and gift books (some of which she edited) and published six poetry volumes and several novels. When Hemans died, L.E.L. printed "Stanzas on the Death of Mrs. Hemans" in the *New Monthly Magazine* (July 1835); the elegy celebrates Hemans's poetic accomplishment but laments the isolation imposed by artistic genius. EBB directly incorporated this work's title in the initial title of her own poem, first published in the September issue of the same periodical. Like the poem itself, the title evolved over time,[2] as did her views of both Hemans and Landon. Although she commended the work of both writers, calling them "the two poetesses of our day" (*BC* 3:153), she also frequently criticized their verse. Deeming that Hemans occupied a higher "pedestal" than Landon (*BC* 3:159), she nonetheless regarded Hemans as too "polished," "monotonous," and restrained: "she always does seem to me a lady rather than a woman, ... her refinement, like the prisoner's iron .. enters into her soul" (*BC* 6:165). EBB preferred Landon's work for its "*raw* bare powers" but judged it to be marred by conventional-

---

1   monody] a mournful song or dirge, i.e., an elegy.

2   A signed fair copy of the poem is entitled "Stanzas addressed to Miss Landon. Suggested by her 'Stanzas on the death of Mrs. Hemans'" (*R* D273), the title used (with *and* added before the subtitle) for the version in the *New Monthly Magazine*, n.s. 45 (September 1835): 82. In EBB's 1838 volume, the title is "Stanzas on the Death of Mrs. Hemans, written in reference to Miss Landon's poem on the same subject." The present title first appears in the printer's proofs for *Poems* (1850). The substitution of forms of reference for Hemans and Landon that do not convey their marital status occurred at a time when EBB was increasingly known as "Mrs. Browning."

ity and artificiality (see *BC* 5:75, 72).[1] In its early printings (1835, 1838), the poem's lines were halved, yielding eight-line stanzas, and EBB included an epigraph from William Habington (1605-54): "Nor grieve this christall streame so soone did fall / Into the ocean;--since she perfumed all / The banks she past—."[2] See also the related poem, "L.E.L.'s Last Question."[3] Criticism: Mermin 1989, Morlier 1993, and Furr 2002.

I
Thou bay-crowned[4] living One that o'er the bay-crowned Dead
   art bowing,
And o'er the shadeless moveless brow the vital shadow throwing,
And o'er the sighless songless lips the wail and music wedding,
And dropping o'er the tranquil eyes, the tears not of their shedding!—

II
Take music from the silent Dead, whose meaning is completer,[5] 5
Reserve thy tears for living brows, where all such tears are meeter,[6]
And leave the violets[7] in the grass to brighten where thou treadest!
No flowers for her! no need of flowers—albeit "bring flowers,"
   thou saidest.[8]

---

1 On occasion, however, she judged Hemans superior to L.E.L., whom she found "deficient in energy & condensation as well as in variety," though she also thought Landon's work was vivid, natural, and full of pathos (*BC* 3:159). For other comments by EBB on Hemans, see *BC* 7:214, 8:157-58, and on Landon, *BC* 3:193-94, 4:61.

2 "To Castara, upon the Death of a Lady" (ll. 7-9).

3 For the text of this poem, published in 1839, see the supplementary website.

4 bay-crowned] From classical antiquity, poets were traditionally crowned with wreaths made from the leaves of bay (laurel) trees.

5 In *Poems* (1850), EBB toned down the criticism of Landon in the 1838 version of the poem, which here read: "Go! take thy music from the dead, / Whose silentness is sweeter!"

6 meeter] more suitable, more fitting.

7 violets] associated with modesty in the Victorian language of flowers.

8 L.E.L.'s poem on Hemans's death begins: "Bring flowers to crown the cup and lute,— / Bring flowers,—the bride is near; / Bring flowers to soothe the captive's cell, / Bring flowers to strew the bier!" This opening stanza summarizes Hemans's poem "Bring Flowers"; obliquely refers to other poems by Hemans such as "The Broken Lute," "The Bridal Day," and "The Sicilian Captive"; and invokes classical elegies, which exhorted mourners to bring flowers to cover the grave of the lamented dead.

III

Yes, flowers, to crown the "cup and lute!" since both may come
  to breaking.
Or flowers, to greet the "bride!" the heart's own beating works
  its aching.   10
Or flowers, to soothe the "captive's" sight, from earth's free
  bosom gathered,
Reminding of his earthly hope, then withering as it withered.

IV

But bring not near the solemn corse,[1] a type of human seeming.
Lay only dust's stern verity upon the dust undreaming.
And while the calm perpetual stars shall look upon it solely,   15
Her spherèd[2] soul shall look on *them*, with eyes more bright and holy.

V

Nor mourn, O living One, because her part in life was mourning.[3]
Would she have lost the poet's fire for anguish of the burning?—
The minstrel harp, for the strained string? the tripod, for the afflated[4]
Woe? or the vision, for those tears in which it shone dilated?   20

VI

Perhaps she shuddered while the world's cold hand her brow was
  wreathing,
But never wronged that mystic breath which breathed in all her
  breathing,
Which drew from rocky earth and man, abstractions high and moving,
Beauty, if not the beautiful, and love, if not the loving.

---

1   corse] corpse.

2   spherèd] placed among the spheres, set in the heavens.

3   Hemans endured financial difficulties from childhood, regretted a failed marriage,
    and died at 41.

4   tripod] a three-legged ornamental vessel, often presented as a prize in classical liter-
    ary competitions; afflated] inspired (according to the *OED* an EBB coinage, derived
    from *afflatus*, meaning the miraculous communication of divine knowledge or poetic
    inspiration).

VII

Such visionings have paled in sight; the Saviour she descrieth,   25
And little recks[1] *who* wreathed the brow which on His bosom lieth.
The whiteness of His innocence o'er all her garments, flowing,
There, learneth she the sweet "new song," she will not mourn in
    knowing.

VIII

Be happy, crowned and living One! And, as thy dust decayeth,
May thine own England say for thee, what now for Her it sayeth—   30
"Albeit softly in our ears her silver song was ringing,
The foot-fall of her parting soul is softer than her singing!"

---

1   recks] knows, heeds, or cares.

3. *From* Poems *(1844)*

From The Preface

As the first poem of this collection, the "Drama of Exile," is the longest and most important work (to *me!*) which I ever trusted into the current of publication, I may be pardoned for entreating the reader's attention to the fact, that I decided on publishing it after considerable hesitation and doubt. The subject of the Drama rather fastened on me than was chosen; and the form, approaching the model of the Greek tragedy,[1] shaped itself under my hand, rather by force of pleasure than of design. But when the excitement of composition had subsided, I felt afraid of my position. My subject was the new and strange experience of the fallen humanity, as it went forth from Paradise into the wilderness; with a peculiar reference to Eve's allotted grief, which, considering that self-sacrifice belonged to her womanhood, and the consciousness of originating the Fall to her offence,—appeared to me imperfectly apprehended hitherto, and more expressible by a woman than a man. There was room, at least, for lyrical emotion in those first steps into the wilderness,— in that first sense of desolation after wrath,—in that first audible gathering of the recriminating "groan of the whole creation,"—in that first darkening of the hills from the recoiling feet of angels,—and in that first silence of the voice of God. And I took pleasure in driving in, like a pile,[2] stroke upon stroke, the Idea of EXILE,—admitting Lucifer[3] as an extreme Adam, to represent the ultimate tendencies of sin and loss,—that it might be strong to bear up the contrary idea of the Heavenly love and purity. But when all was done, I felt afraid, as I said before, of my position. I had promised my own prudence to shut close the gates of Eden

---

1 Early Greek tragedy generally had only two or three characters, plus a chorus which commented on the events.

2 pile] a heavy beam of timber driven into the earth to provide support for a structure.

3 Lucifer] As related in John Milton's epic poem *Paradise Lost* (1667), Lucifer, God's favorite angel (sometimes called Morning Star or Day Star), contested God's mastery and was cast out of Heaven with other angels who joined his rebellion. Renamed Satan, he set up a rival domain in Hell and sought revenge by seducing Adam and Eve from obedience to God, resulting in their expulsion from the Earthly Paradise.

between Milton and myself, so that none might say I dared to walk in his footsteps. He should be within, I thought, with his Adam and Eve unfallen or falling,—and I, without, with my EXILES,—*I* also an exile! It would not do. The subject, and his glory covering it, swept through the gates, and I stood full in it, against my will, and contrary to my vow,—till I shrank back fearing, almost desponding; hesitating to venture even a passing association with our great poet before the face of the public. Whether at last I took courage for the venture, by a sudden revival of that love of manuscript which should be classed by moral philosophers among the natural affections, or by the encouraging voice of a dear friend,[1] it is not interesting to the reader to inquire. Neither could the fact affect the question; since I bear, of course, my own responsibilities. For the rest, Milton is too high, and I am too low, to render it necessary for me to disavow any rash emulation of his divine faculty on his own ground; while enough individuality will be granted, I hope, to my poem, to rescue me from that imputation of plagiarism which should be too servile a thing for every sincere thinker. After all, and at the worst, I have only attempted, in respect to Milton, what the Greek dramatists achieved lawfully in respect to Homer.[2] They constructed dramas on Trojan ground; they raised on the buskin and even clasped with the sock,[3] the feet of Homeric heroes; yet they neither imitated their Homer nor emasculated him....

On a graver point I must take leave to touch, in further reference to my dramatic poem. The divine Saviour is represented in vision towards the close, speaking and transfigured; and it has been hinted to me that the introduction may give offence in quarters where I should be most reluctant to give any. A reproach of the same class, relating to the frequent recurrence of a Great Name in my pages,

---

1 After EBB's friend John Kenyon persuaded her not to destroy but to publish the manuscript, she wrote: "So my nerves are braced—& I grow a man again!" (*BC* 8:267-68, 269).

2 Homer's Greek epic the *Iliad* (probably eighth century BCE) recounts the siege and fall of Troy.

3 buskin] a thick-soled, laced boot worn by actors in Greek tragedies; sock] a light shoe worn by comic actors.

has already filled me with regret.[1] How shall I answer these things? .... There is a feeling abroad which appears to me (I say it with deference) nearer to superstition than to religion, that there should be no touching of holy vessels except by consecrated fingers, nor any naming of holy names except in consecrated places. As if life were not a continual sacrament to man, since Christ brake the daily bread of it in His hands! As if the name of God did not build a church, by the very naming of it! As if the word GOD were not, everywhere in His creation, and at every moment in His eternity, an appropriate word! ....

The next longest poem to the "Drama of Exile" in the collection, is the "Vision of Poets," in which I have endeavoured to indicate the necessary relations of genius to suffering and self-sacrifice.... I have attempted to express in this poem my view of the mission of the poet, of the self-abnegation implied in it, of the great work involved in it, of the duty and glory of what Balzac[2] has beautifully and truly called "la patience angélique du genie"; and of the obvious truth, above all, that if knowledge is power, suffering should be acceptable as a part of knowledge. It is enough to say of the other poems, that scarcely one of them is unambitious of an object and a significance.

.... In any case, while my poems are full of faults,—as I go forward to my critics and confess,—they have my heart and life in them,—they are not empty shells. If it must be said of me that I have contributed immemorable verses to the many rejected by the age, it cannot at least be said that I have done so in a light and irresponsible spirit. Poetry has been as serious a thing to me as life itself; and life has been a very serious thing: there has been no playing at skittles[3] for me in either. I never mistook pleasure for

---

1 Reviews of *The Seraphim* (*BC* 4:375-400, 408-09, 413-16) contributed to EBB's awareness of potential audience resistance to sacred subjects and "mystical tendencies" (*BC* 8:272).

2 Balzac] Honoré de Balzac (1799-1850), influential French novelist, author of interconnected works called the *Comédie humaine* (*Human Comedy*). EBB greatly admired his work (see, e.g., *BC* 8:316). The French quotation means "the angelic patience of genius."

3 skittles] a game of ninepins, in which a ball is thrown to knock down wooden pins. EBB here alludes to the comparison of writing poetry to playing at skittles by the French poet and critic Nicolas Boileau-Despréaux (1636-1711)—an analogy she refutes in the "Preface" to *An Essay on Mind* (1826). In England, the Utilitarian philosopher Jeremy Bentham (1748-1832) had similarly compared poetry to the child's game of push-pin to suggest poetry's unimportance.

the final cause of poetry; nor leisure, for the hour of the poet. I have done my work, so far, as work,—not as mere hand and head work, apart from the personal being,—but as the completest expression of that being, to which I could attain,—and as work I offer it to the public,—feeling its shortcomings more deeply than any of my readers, because measured from the height of my aspiration,—but feeling also that the reverence and sincerity with which the work was done, should give it some protection with the reverent and sincere.

From A Drama of Exile[1]

In 1841 when EBB first mentioned working on this poem, treating the events and experiences following the expulsion of Eve and Adam from the Earthly Paradise, she stressed the immediacy of their loss by calling it *"A day from Eden"* (*BC* 5:146).[2] At some point she treated the story from Adam's perspective, as evidenced by the manuscript poem "Adam's farewell to Eden—*in his age.*"[3] As she emphasized in her preface to the 1844 volume, however, "A Drama of Exile" differed from Milton's *Paradise Lost* in its new focus on the guilt and repentance of Eve: "The object is the development of the peculiar anguish of Eve—the fate of woman at its root." In her letters, she further explained that, while innumerable works in "the tradition" had written of Eve as "[*f*]irst in the transgression," nobody had written of Eve as *"first & deepest in the sorrow,"* and that the word "exile" applied not only to Adam and Eve but also "to Lucifer's exile, and to That other mystical exile of the Divine Being" [Christ] (*BC* 8:117, 267). Although EBB's drama includes choruses and lyrical speeches by entities such as "Eden Spirits," "Invisible Angels," "Morning Star," and "Earth Spirits," the sections excerpted here concentrate on the relationships among Eve, Adam, Lucifer, and Christ. Like EBB's previous treatment of

---

1 First published in the *United States Magazine and Democratic Review* (July and August 1844) and then in EBB's 1844 collection, *Poems*, which was published in America as *A Drama of Exile: And Other Poems.*

2 An 1843 notebook draft (*R* D214) is also titled "A Day from Eden."

3 See *R* D5, D6, published and discussed by Will and Mimosa Stephenson 1993.

Biblical narrative in "The Seraphim" (1838), "A Drama of Exile" resembles Romantic closet dramas such as P.B. Shelley's *Prometheus Unbound* (1820) and, in particular, Byron's *Cain* (1821), which she echoes and revises, much as she does in the case of Milton's *Paradise Lost*. Early reviews of the poem were mixed. While one reviewer dismissed numerous passages in it as "nothing but a mere conglomeration of glittering verbiage" (*BC* 9:331), others saw in it "mental energy and daring imagination," together with "*power* such as we do not remember in any lady's poetry" (*BC* 9:379, 369), and a combination of womanly heart and masculine intellect (see *BC* 9:319). Compared to Milton's Satan, EBB's Lucifer was deemed weak—more akin to Byron's portrait in *Cain* (*BC* 9:325). While some critics praised her representation of the tender love between Eve and Adam, the *Blackwood's* critic thought Eve's grief a subject too trivial "to sustain the weight of a dramatic poem"—at "the most, it might have furnished materials for a sonnet" (*BC* 9:357). In recent years, critics have been divided on the extent to which EBB succeeded in escaping the patriarchal frameworks of Milton and Byron in representing Eve and the story of the fall. Criticism: David 1987, Cooper 1988, Mermin 1989, Harrison 1990, Kimery 1993, Stone 1995, 2005, Lewis 1998, Riede 1999, 2005, Donaldson 2002, Melynk 2003, Hoagwood 2004, and Tucker 2006a.

[Outside the gate of Eden, now "shut fast with cloud, from the depth of which revolves a sword of fire self-moved," Lucifer boasts that he has prevailed against God by achieving the fall of Adam and Eve, and argues with the archangel Gabriel, who guards the gate of Eden, that mankind and earth belong to him. Spirits of Eden's trees, rivers, birds, and flowers bid farewell to Adam and Eve, who flee without looking back. At the edge of the glare cast by the sword, they pause.][1]

 Adam. What is this, Eve? thou droppest heavily   417
In a heap earthward, and thy body heaves
Under the golden floodings of thine hair!
 Eve. O Adam, Adam! by that name of Eve—   420

---

1 See the account of the loss of Eden in Genesis 2.15-3.24.

Thine Eve, thy life[1]—which suits me little now,
Seeing that I now confess myself thy death
And thine undoer, as the snake was mine,—
I do adjure thee, put me straight away,
Together with my name. Sweet, punish me!   425
O Love, be just! and, ere we pass beyond
The light cast outward by the fiery sword,
Into the dark which earth must be to us,
Bruise my head with thy foot,—as the curse said
My seed shall the first tempter's![2] strike with curse,   430
As God struck in the garden! and as HE,
Being satisfied with justice and with wrath,
Did roll His thunder gentler at the close,—
Thou, peradventure,[3] may'st at last recoil
To some soft need of mercy. Strike, my lord!   435
I, also, after tempting, writhe on the ground,
And I would feed on ashes from thine hand,
As suits me, O my tempted!
    Adam.   My beloved,
Mine Eve and life—I have no other name
For thee or for the sun than what ye are,   440
My utter life and light! If we have fallen,
It is that we have sinned,—we: God is just;
And, since His curse doth comprehend us both,
It must be that His balance holds the weights
Of first and last sin on a level. What!   445
Shall I who had not virtue to stand straight
Among the hills of Eden, here assume[4]
To mend the justice of the perfect God,
By piling up a curse upon His curse,
Against thee—thee—
    Eve.   For so, perchance, thy God   450
Might take thee into grace for scorning me;

---

1   *Eve* means *life* in Hebrew (see Genesis 3.20).
2   See Genesis 3.15.
3   peradventure] perhaps.
4   assume] presume.

Thy wrath against the sinner giving proof
Of inward abrogation of the sin.
And so, the blessed angels might come down
And walk with thee as erst,[1]—I think they would,—   455
Because I was not near to make them sad
Or soil the rustling of their innocence.

    Adam. They know me. I am deepest in the guilt,
If last in the transgression.
    Eve.   THOU!
    Adam.   If God,
Who gave the right and joyaunce[2] of the world   460
Both unto thee and me,—gave thee to me,
The best gift last, the last sin was the worst,
Which sinned against more complement[3] of gifts
And grace of giving. God! I render back
Strong benediction and perpetual praise   465
From mortal feeble lips (as incense-smoke,
Out of a little censer, may fill heaven),
That Thou, in striking my benumbèd hands
And forcing them to drop all other boons[4]
Of beauty and dominion and delight,—   470
Hast left this well-beloved Eve, this life
Within life, this best gift between their palms,
In gracious compensation!
    ....

    Eve.   Where is loss?   487
Am I in Eden?[5] can another speak
Mine own love's tongue?
    Adam.   Because with *her*, I stand
Upright, as far as can be in this fall,   490
And look away from heaven which doth accuse,
And look away from earth which doth convict,

---

1   erst] formerly, at first.
2   joyaunce] enjoyment.
3   more complement] a fuller quantity.
4   boons] blessings.
5   See *Paradise Lost*, Book 12, ll. 615-16.

Into her face, and crown my discrowned[1] brow
Out of her love, and put the thought of her
Around me, for an Eden full of birds,   495
And lift her body up—thus—to my heart,
And with my lips upon her lips,—thus, thus,—
Do quicken and sublimate my mortal breath
Which cannot climb against the grave's steep sides
But overtops this grief!
    Eve.   I am renewed.   500
My eyes grow with the light which is in thine;
The silence of my heart is full of sound.
Hold me up—so! Because I comprehend
This human love, I shall not be afraid
Of any human death; and yet because   505
I know this strength of love, I seem to know
Death's strength by that same sign. Kiss on my lips,
To shut the door close on my rising soul,—
Lest it pass outwards in astonishment
And leave thee lonely.
    Adam   Yet thou liest, Eve,   510
Bent heavily on thyself across mine arm,
Thy face flat to the sky.
    Eve.   Ay! and the tears
Running, as it might seem, my life from me,
They run so fast and warm. Let me lie so,
And weep so, as if in a dream or prayer,   515
Unfastening, clasp by clasp, the hard, tight thought
Which clipped my heart and showed me evermore
Loathed of thy justice as I loathe the snake,
And as the pure ones loathe our sin. To-day,
All day, beloved, as we fled across   520
This desolating radiance cast by swords
Not suns,—my lips prayed soundless to myself,
Striking against each other—"O Lord God!"
('Twas so I prayed) "I ask Thee by my sin,
And by thy curse, and by thy blameless heavens,   525

---

1 discrowned] uncrowned.

Make dreadful haste to hide me from thy face
And from the face of my beloved here
For whom I am no helpmeet, quick away
Into the new dark mystery of death!
I will lie still there, I will make no plaint,   530
I will not sigh, nor sob, nor speak a word,
Nor struggle to come back beneath the sun
Where peradventure I might sin anew
Against Thy mercy and his pleasure. Death,
Oh death, whate'er it be, is good enough   535
For such as I am.—While for Adam here
No voice shall say again, in heaven or earth,
It is not good for him to be alone."[1]
   Adam. And was it good for such a prayer to pass,
My unkind[2] Eve, betwixt our mutual lives?   540
If I am exiled, must I be bereaved?
   Eve. 'Twas an ill prayer: it shall be prayed no more;
And God did use it like a foolishness,
Giving no answer. Now my heart has grown
Too high and strong for such a foolish prayer;   545
Love makes it strong: and since I was the first
In the transgression, with a steady foot
I will be first to tread from this sword-glare
Into the outer darkness of the waste,—
And thus I do it....   550
   ....

[Lucifer appears]
   Luc. Now may all fruits be pleasant to thy lips,   642
Beautiful Eve! The times have somewhat changed
Since thou and I had talk beneath a tree,
Albeit ye are not gods yet.[3]
   Eve.   Adam! hold   645
My right hand strongly! It is Lucifer—
And we have love to lose.

---

1   An echo of Genesis 2.18.

2   unkind] besides the familiar definition, also means unnatural, contrary to the nature of one's kind.

3   albeit] although; yet] still.

Adam.   I' the name of God,
Go apart from us, O thou Lucifer!
And leave us to the desert thou hast made
Out of thy treason. Bring no serpent-slime   650
Athwart this path kept holy to our tears,
Or we may curse thee with their bitterness.
     Luc. Curse freely! curses thicken. Why, this Eve
Who thought me once part worthy of her ear
And somewhat wiser than the other beasts,—   655
Drawing together her large globes of eyes,
The light of which is throbbing in and out
Their steadfast continuity of gaze,—
Knots her fair eyebrows in so hard a knot,
And down from her white heights of womanhood   660
Looks on me so amazed,—I scarce should fear
To wager such an apple as she plucked
Against one riper from the tree of life,
That she could curse too—as a woman may—
Smooth in the vowels.[1]
     Eve.   So—speak wickedly!   665
I like it best so. Let thy words be wounds,—
For, so, I shall not fear thy power to hurt.
Trench on[2] the forms of good by open ill—
For, so, I shall wax strong and grand with scorn,
Scorning myself for ever trusting thee   670
As far as thinking, ere a snake ate dust,
He could speak wisdom.
     Luc.   Our new gods, it seems,
Deal more in thunders than in courtesies.
And, sooth, mine own Olympus, which anon[3]
I shall build up to loud-voiced imagery   675
From all the wandering visions of the world,
May show worse railing than our lady Eve

---

1 An echo of Lord Byron's 1821 closet drama *Cain*; see Stone 1995, 82–83.
2 trench on] encroach on.
3 Olympus] mountain dwelling of the classical gods; anon] soon.

Pours o'er the rounding of her argent[1] arm.
But why should this be? Adam pardoned Eve.
  Adam. Adam loved Eve. Jehovah pardon both.   680
  Eve. Adam forgave Eve—because loving Eve.
  Luc. So, well. Yet Adam was undone of Eve,
As both were by the snake. Therefore forgive,
In like wise, fellow-temptress, the poor snake—   .
Who stung there, not so poorly!   [*Aside.*
  Eve.   Hold thy wrath,   685
Beloved Adam! let me answer him;
For this time he speaks truth, which we should hear,
And asks for mercy, which I most should grant,
In like wise, as he tells us—in like wise!
And therefore I thee pardon, Lucifer,   690
As freely as the streams of Eden flowed
When we were happy by them. So, depart;
Leave us to walk the remnant of our time
Out mildly in the desert. Do not seek
To harm us any more or scoff at us   695
Or ere[2] the dust be laid upon our face
To find there the communion of the dust
And issue of the dust.—Go....

....

       LUCIFER *rises in the circle.*

 Luc.   .... Look around;—
Earth-spirits and phantasms hear you talk unmoved,   1325
As if ye were red clay again and talked!
What are your words to them? your grief to them?
Your deaths, indeed, to them? Did the hand pause
For *their* sake, in the plucking of the fruit,
That they should pause for *you*, in hating you?   1330
Or will your grief or death, as did your sin,
Bring change upon their final doom? Behold,

---

1 argent] silvery.
2 Or ere] before.

Your grief is but your sin in the rebound,
And cannot expiate for it.
    Adam.   That is true.
    Luc. Ay, that is true. The clay-king[1] testifies   1335
To the snake's counsel,—hear him!—very true....
....

    Luc. (*after a pause*). Dost thou remember, Adam, when the
        curse   1346
Took us in Eden? On a mountain-peak
Half-sheathed in primal woods and glittering
In spasms of awful sunshine at that hour,
A lion couched, part raised upon his paws,   1350
With his calm, massive face turned full on thine,
And his mane listening. When the ended curse
Left silence in the world,—right suddenly
He sprang up rampant and stood straight and stiff,
As if the new reality of death   1355
Were dashed against his eyes, and roared so fierce,
(Such thick carnivorous passion in his throat
Tearing a passage through the wrath and fear)
And roared so wild, and smote from all the hills
Such fast, keen echoes crumbling down the vales   1360
Precipitately,—that the forest beasts,
One after one, did mutter a response
Of savage and of sorrowful complaint
Which trailed along the gorges. Then, at once,
He fell back, and rolled crashing from the height   1365
Into the dusk of pines.[2]
....

    That lion is the type of what I am.   1368
And as he fixed thee with his full-faced hate,
And roared, O Adam, comprehending doom,
So, gazing on the face of the Unseen,
I cry out here between the Heavens and Earth

---

1   clay-king] From dust or clay God made Adam, who is "like the clay in the potter's
    hand" of God (Genesis 2.7; Jeremiah 18.6). The Hebrew words for *man* and *ground* are
    '*adham* and '*adhamah*.

2   Ll. 1347-66 were praised by Edgar Allan Poe for their "Homeric force" (*BC* 10:351).

My conscience of this sin, this woe, this wrath,
Which damn me to this depth.
....

Pass along   1415
Your wilderness, vain mortals! Puny griefs
In transitory shapes, be henceforth dwarfed
To your own conscience, by the dread extremes
Of what I am and have been. If ye have fallen,
It is but a step's fall,—the whole ground beneath   1420
Strewn woolly soft with promise! if ye have sinned,
Your prayers tread high as angels! if ye have grieved,
Ye are too mortal to be pitiable,
The power to die disproves the right to grieve.
Go to! ye call this ruin? I half-scorn   1425
The ill I did you! Were ye wronged by me,
Hated and tempted and undone of me,—
Still, what's your hurt to mine of doing hurt,
Of hating, tempting, and so ruining?
This sword's *hilt* is the sharpest, and cuts through   1430
The hand that wields it.
Go—I curse you all.
Hate one another—feebly—as ye can;....
....

[Lucifer vanishes, and the spirits of earth and beasts condemn him,
allaying Adam and Eve's fears of the creatures in their new environ-
ment. A vision of Christ appears, admonishing the Earth Spirits to
submit to Adam and Eve, who in their transgression demonstrated
the free will that elevates them above Nature and its creatures.]

   Eve. Speak on still, Christ! Albeit thou bless me not   1821
In set words, I am blessed in harkening[1] thee—
Speak, Christ.
   CHRIST.   Speak, Adam. Bless the woman, man—
It is thine office.
   Adam.   Mother of the world,

---

1   harkening] listening to.

Take heart before this Presence. Lo, my voice,   1825
Which, naming erst[1] the creatures, did express
(God breathing through my breath) the attributes
And instincts of each creature in its name,
Floats to the same afflatus,[2]—floats and heaves
Like a water-weed that opens to a wave,   1830
A full-leaved prophecy affecting thee,
Out fairly and wide. Henceforward, rise, aspire
To all the calms and magnanimities,
The lofty uses and the noble ends,
The sanctified devotion and full work,   1835
To which thou art elect for evermore,
First woman, wife, and mother.
    Eve.   And first in sin.
    Adam. And also the sole bearer of the Seed
Whereby sin dieth! raise the majesties
Of thy disconsolate brows, O well-beloved,   1840
And front with level eyelids the To come,[3]
And all the dark o' the world. Rise, woman, rise
To thy peculiar and best altitudes
Of doing good and of enduring ill,
Of comforting for ill, and teaching good,   1845
And reconciling all that ill and good
Unto the patience of a constant hope,—
Rise with thy daughters! If sin came by thee,
And by sin, death,—the ransom-righteousness,
The heavenly life and compensative rest   1850
Shall come by means of thee. If woe by thee
Had issue to the world, thou shalt go forth
An angel of the woe thou didst achieve,
Found acceptable to the world instead
Of others of that name, of whose bright steps   1855
Thy deed stripped bare the hills. Be satisfied;
Something thou hast to bear through womanhood,

---

1   erst] previously.

2   afflatus] creative impulse.

3   the To come] the future; that which is to come.

Peculiar suffering answering to the sin,—
Some pang paid down for each new human life,[1]
Some weariness in guarding such a life,   1860
Some coldness from the guarded, some mistrust
From those thou hast too well served, from those beloved
Too loyally some treason; feebleness
Within thy heart, and cruelty without,
And pressures of an alien tyranny   1865
With its dynastic reasons of larger bones
And stronger sinews. But, go to! thy love
Shall chant itself its own beatitudes[2]
After its own life-working. A child's kiss
Set on thy sighing lips, shall make thee glad;   1870
A poor man served by thee, shall make thee rich;
A sick man helped by thee, shall make thee strong;
Thou shalt be served thyself by every sense
Of service which thou renderest. Such a crown
I set upon thy head,—Christ witnessing   1875
With looks of prompting love—to keep thee clear
Of all reproach against the sin forgone,
From all the generations which succeed.
Thy hand which plucked the apple, I clasp close,
Thy lips which spake wrong counsel, I kiss close,   1880
I bless thee in the name of Paradise
And by the memory of Edenic joys
Forfeit and lost,—by that last cypress tree
Green at the gate, which thrilled as we came out,
And by the blessed nightingale which threw   1885
Its melancholy music after us,—
And by the flowers, whose spirits full of smells
Did follow softly, plucking us behind
Back to the gradual banks and vernal bowers
And fourfold river-courses.—By all these,   1890

---

1 See God's pronouncement concerning Eve's punishment in Genesis 3:16

2 beatitudes] supreme blessedness, exalted joy or happiness. In a passage known as the
   Beatitudes (Matthew 5.3-11; Luke 6.20-23), Christ in the Sermon on the Mount an-
   nounces that those who have suffered or given to others on earth will be blessed in
   heaven.

I bless thee to the contraries of these,
I bless thee to the desert and the thorns,
To the elemental change and turbulence,
And to the roar of the estranged beasts,
And to the solemn dignities of grief,—   1895
To each one of these ends,—and to their END
Of Death and the hereafter!
    Eve.   I accept
For me and for my daughters this high part
Which lowly shall be counted. Noble work
Shall hold me in the place of garden-rest,   1900
And in the place of Eden's lost delight
Worthy endurance of permitted pain;
While on my longest patience there shall wait
Death's speechless angel, smiling in the east
Whence cometh the cold wind. I bow myself   1905
Humbly henceforward on the ill I did,
That humbleness may keep it in the shade.
Shall it be so? shall I smile, saying so?
O seed! O King! O God, who *shalt* be seed,—
What shall I say? As Eden's fountains swelled   1910
Brightly betwixt their banks, so swells my soul
Betwixt thy love and power!
                        And, sweetest thoughts
Of foregone Eden! now, for the first time
Since God said "Adam," walking through the trees,
I dare to pluck you as I plucked erewhile   1915
The lily or pink, the rose or heliotrope.
So pluck I you—so largely—with both hands,
And throw you forward on the outer earth
Wherein we are cast out, to sweeten it.
....

    CHRIST. In the set noon of time, shall one from Heaven,   1959
An angel fresh from looking upon God,
Descend before a woman,[1] blessing her

---

1   Christ forecasts the Annunciation, when the angel Gabriel will tell the Virgin Mary
    that she is to bear God's son (Luke 1.26-35).

With perfect benediction of pure love,
For all the world in all its elements,
For all the creatures of earth, air, and sea,
For all men in the body and in the soul,   1965
Unto all ends of glory and sanctity.
    Eve. O pale, pathetic Christ—I worship thee!
I thank thee for that woman!
    CHRIST.   Then, at last,
I, wrapping round me your humanity,
Which being sustained, shall neither break nor burn   1970
Beneath the fire of Godhead, will tread earth,
And ransom you and it, and set strong peace
Betwixt you and its creatures. With my pangs
I will confront your sins; and since those sins
Have sunken to all Nature's heart from yours,   1975
The tears of my clean soul shall follow them
And set a holy passion to work clear
Absolute consecration. In my brow
Of kingly whiteness, shall be crowned anew
Your discrowned human nature. Look on me!   1980
As I shall be uplifted on a cross
In darkness of eclipse and anguish dread,
So shall I lift up in my piercèd hands,
Not into dark, but light—not unto death,
But life,—beyond the reach of guilt and grief,   1985
The whole creation.[1] Henceforth in my name
Take courage, O thou woman,—man, take hope!
Your grave shall be as smooth as Eden's sward,
Beneath the steps of your prospective thoughts,
And, one step past it, a new Eden-gate   1990
Shall open on a hinge of harmony
    And let you through to mercy....

[As the "vision of CHRIST vanishes," "ADAM and EVE stand in an
ecstasy" and the drama concludes with a "chant from the two
Earth Spirits"]

---

1   For EBB's earlier narrative of the Crucifixion, see "The Seraphim" (1838).

Chorus.

> Future joy and far light   2255
> Working such relations,
> Hear us singing gently
> *Exiled is not lost.*
> God, above the starlight,
> God, above the patience,   2260
> Shall at last present ye
> Guerdons¹ worth the cost.
> Patiently enduring,
> Painfully surrounded,
> Listen how we love you,   2265
> Hope the uttermost.
> Waiting for that curing
> Which exalts the wounded,
> Hear us sing above you—
> EXILED, BUT NOT LOST!   2270

[The drama concludes with the following stage directions: "*The stars shine on brightly while* ADAM *and* EVE *pursue their way into the far wilderness. There is a sound through the silence, as of the falling tears of an angel.*"²]

Sonnets

Having published several sonnets in her volume of 1838, in the early 1840s EBB experimented more extensively with the genre. Employing the Petrarchan form compatible with the rich rhyming possibilities in the Italian language, but more challenging for English writers, she described it as "imperious," but "very fine," and declared, "I never *would* believe that our language is unqualified for the very strictest Italian form" (*BC* 6:111). Her pocket notebooks from 1842-44 include unpublished translations of several love sonnets by Petrarch alongside versions of original sonnets on

---

1   guerdons] rewards.

2   Some reviewers (especially Poe) criticized this concluding image (*BC* 10: 351); cf. Keats's 1817 sonnet "To one who has been long in city pent": "E'en like the passage of an angel's tear / That falls through clear ether silently" (ll. 13-14).

varied topics published or collected in *Poems* (1844). Like Italian sonnets, those in England had traditionally focused primarily on amatory themes, the ephemerality of life, and the permanence of poetry, until John Milton (1608-74) expanded the form's subject matter to explore personal, religious, and political topics. This range was further enlarged by William Wordsworth (1770-1850), who in the Romantic period's explosion of sonnet writing composed well over five hundred sonnets. During her 1845-46 courtship EBB would recast and challenge many of the formulaic patterns of Italian and English amatory sequences in *Sonnets from the Portuguese* (1850), but she also often employed the form for individual philosophical, religious, and commemorative poems. Although contemporary reviewers praised her miscellaneous sonnets, finding them "rich in poetic beauty," "worthy to be classed with the best of the best writers," her stylistically "most finished" works, marked by "depth and purity of sentiment" (*BC* 9:320, 341, 351), the extreme popularity of *Sonnets from the Portuguese* has long dwarfed her achievement in other well crafted works such as those presented here. Criticism: Billone 2001 and Morlier 2003.

The Soul's Expression

In arranging her works for publication in 1844 and thereafter, EBB consistently introduced her sonnets with this poem.[1] In subject matter, it is associated with an unfinished poetic drama on which she collaborated with her correspondent and fellow poet, Richard Hengist Horne (1802?-84) in 1841. Entitled "Psyche Apocalypté," the drama explores "the terror attending spiritual consciousness." As she explained to Horne, "The awe of this self consciousness, breaking ... through the chasms of our conventionalities has struck me, in my own self observation as a mystery of nature ... & is quite a distinct mystery from *conscience*. Conscience has to do with action ... & not with abstract existence. There are moments when we are startled at the footsteps of our own Being, more than at the thunders of God" (*BC* 5:7). Criticism: Chapman 2002.

---

1   First published in *Graham's Magazine* (July 1843).

With stammering lips and insufficient sound
I strive and struggle to deliver right
That music of my nature, day and night
With dream and thought and feeling interwound,   4
And inly[1] answering all the senses round
With octaves of a mystic depth and height
Which step out grandly to the infinite
From the dark edges of the sensual ground!   8
This song of soul I struggle to outbear
Through portals of the sense, sublime and whole,
And utter all myself into the air.
But if I did it,—as the thunder-roll   12
Breaks its own cloud, my flesh would perish there,
Before that dread apocalypse of soul.

On a Portrait of Wordsworth by B.R. Haydon[2]

Beginning their epistolary friendship in 1842, the noted painter of history scenes Benjamin Robert Haydon (1786-1846) sent EBB the unfinished portrait he was then making of poet William Wordsworth for her to enjoy until he wished to complete it. She responded with delight to the portrait, with its "magnificent head, its white hair glittering like a crown," and immediately planned "to send a sonnet back with it" to Haydon as "witness" to her feeling (*BC* 6:106), a poem which Haydon subsequently sent to Wordsworth himself. Despite her acute shyness, EBB had met Wordsworth at a London dinner hosted by her friend John Kenyon in May 1836 and had traveled with "him & Miss Mitford to Chiswick" (*BC* 3:205). She later recalled as a highlight of their conversation his reciting a sonnet translated from Dante (*BC* 3:217). Revering Wordsworth as "the king-poet of our times" (*BC* 6:28)—but also expressing a subtle sense of rivalry with him—she commented extensively on his works in her correspondence, especially in 1842-43, comparing

---

1 inly] inwardly.

2 Entitled "Sonnet on Mr. Haydon's Portrait of Mr. Wordsworth" when first printed in the *Athenaeum* (29 October 1842), the poem bore various titles in mss (e.g., "Mr. Haydon's portrait of Mr. Wordsworth," *R* D617).

him to other poets such as Byron and Coleridge (see especially *BC* 6:171).[1] Wordsworth's poetry and poetic manifestos consistently celebrate Nature for its beauty and sublimity and for its embodiment of transcendent spiritual values. In one fair copy manuscript (*R* D617) EBB wrote beneath this sonnet, "Evangelist of Nature!" Criticism: Woolford 1993, 1995; and Billone 2001.

Wordsworth upon Helvellyn![2] Let the cloud
Ebb[3] audibly along the mountain-wind
Then break against the rock, and show behind
The lowland valleys floating up to crowd   4
The sense with beauty. He with forehead bowed
And humble-lidded eyes, as one inclined
Before the sovran[4] thought of his own mind,
And very meek with inspirations proud,   8
Takes here his rightful place as poet-priest
By the high altar, singing prayer and prayer
To the higher Heavens. A noble vision free
Our Haydon's hand has flung out from the mist!   12
No portrait this, with Academic air![5]
This is the poet and his poetry.

Past and Future

This sonnet (first published in the 1844 *Poems*) is integrally connected to Sonnet XLII of *Sonnets from the Portuguese,* which begins by quoting its opening line. When EBB first published her sonnet sequence in *Poems* (1850), she printed it without Sonnet XLII,

---

1 Her review essay "The Book of the Poets" (*CW* 6: 240-311) also includes extended comments on Wordsworth and his place in literary history.

2 Helvellyn] a ridge (elevation 3,313 feet) near Wordsworth's home in England's Lake District.

3 When Haydon sent a copy of EBB's sonnet to Wordsworth, the elder poet counseled her that the word *ebb* would be "obscure to nine readers out of ten" (*BC* 6:121). Undeterred, she retained the pun on the initials by which she normally signed her letters and poems (see Woolford 1993, 57-58).

4 sovran] sovereign.

5 An allusion to the stiff, formal portraits associated with the Royal Academy of painters.

with its identifiable allusion to this poem, to preserve the illusion that the sequence might be translations rather than essentially autobiographical works (see the headnote to the sequence, p. 205. Criticism: Stone 1994).

My future will not copy fair my past
On any leaf but Heaven's. Be fully done,
Supernal Will! I would not fain[1] be one
Who, satisfying thirst and breaking fast   4
Upon the fulness of the heart, at last
Says no grace after meat. My wine has run
Indeed out of my cup, and there is none
To gather up the bread of my repast   8
Scattered and trampled,—yet I find some good
In earth's green herbs, and streams that bubble up
Clear from the darkling ground,—content until
I sit with angels before better food.   12
Dear Christ! when thy new vintage fills my cup,[2]
This hand shall shake no more, nor that wine spill.

Grief[3]

By the time EBB wrote this sonnet, she had suffered the deaths of her beloved mother, her maternal grandmother, her favorite uncle, Samuel Moulton Barrett (1787-1837), and her brother Samuel Barrett Moulton-Barrett (1812-40). Her most intense grief, however, arose from the 1840 death of her best loved companion, the eldest of her brothers and closest to her in age, Edward or "Bro." Blaming herself for his death because she had persuaded her father to allow him to stay as a companion in her illness at Torquay, where he drowned during a sudden storm while sailing, she suffered a total breakdown and long period of misery rarely relieved by tears (see the Introduction). Criticism: Leighton 1986 and Mermin 1989.

---

1   Supernal] heavenly, exalted; fain] gladly, willingly.
2   The imagery recalls the story of Christ's turning water into wine (John 2.1-10).
3   Untitled when first published in *Graham's Magazine* (December 1842).

I tell you, hopeless grief is passionless;
That only men incredulous of despair,
Half-taught in anguish, through the midnight air
Beat upward to God's throne in loud access   4
Of shrieking and reproach. Full desertness
In souls as countries, lieth silent-bare
Under the blanching,[1] vertical eye-glare
Of the absolute Heavens. Deep-hearted man, express   8
Grief for thy Dead in silence like to death:—
Most like a monumental statue set
In everlasting watch and moveless woe,[2]
Till itself crumble to the dust beneath.   12
Touch it: the marble eyelids are not wet.
If it could weep, it could arise and go.

To George Sand: A Desire

Though her unconventional private life and the frank sexuality of
her novels stigmatized French novelist George Sand (pen name of
Aurore Dudevant,[3] 1804-76), EBB declared her "the first female
genius of any country or age" and "the greatest female poet the
world ever saw" (*BC* 10:15, 8:240; see also 6:163). Yet even as she
delighted in Sand's romances, EBB judged her work sometimes
marred by "soul-slime" and "vileness" (*BC* 6:233). Meeting Sand
in Paris in 1852 reaffirmed EBB's sense of her genius, despite
RB's disapproval of the novelist's bohemian manner (see the
Introduction). When her two sonnets on Sand first appeared in
1844, one reviewer commended EBB's courage in praising her:
amid the general fashion of deploring French novels, these poems
reveal "that the pulses of one strong and warm woman's heart
are unchecked by the fear of opinion" (*BC* 9:376). As Morlier
shows, some of the more bizarre metaphors used in the sonnets

---

1   blanching] causing to turn pale, whitening.

2   An evocation of the Egyptian Sphinx as well as P.B. Shelley's poem "Ozymandias"
    (1818).

3   EBB's admiration for Sand may have influenced the name of her heroine in *Aurora*
    Leigh (1856).

reveal EBB's engagement with the debate in English periodicals over Sand's morality.[1] Criticism: Donaldson 1977, Cooper 1988, Mermin 1989, Morlier 2003, Lewis 2003, and Saunders 2006.

Thou large-brained woman and large-hearted man,[2]
Self-called George Sand! whose soul, amid the lions
Of thy tumultuous senses, moans defiance,
And answers roar for roar, as spirits can!   4
I would some mild miraculous thunder ran
Above the applauded circus, in appliance[3]
Of thine own nobler nature's strength and science,
Drawing two pinions, white as wings of swan,   8
From thy strong shoulders, to amaze the place
With holier light! that thou to woman's claim,
And man's, might'st join beside the angel's grace
Of a pure genius sanctified from blame,—   12
Till child and maiden pressed to thine embrace,
To kiss upon thy lips a stainless fame.

To George Sand: A Recognition

True genius, but true woman! dost deny
Thy woman's nature with a manly scorn,
And break away the gauds[4] and armlets worn
By weaker women in captivity?   4
Ah, vain denial! that revolted cry
Is sobbed in by a woman's voice forlorn!—

---

1 See the "Tribute Poems" on the supplementary website for the related poem "To George Sand on her Interview with Elizabeth Barrett Browning" (1873) by EBB's close friend Isa Blagden.

2 Morlier 2003 (321) cites an essay on Sand by the Italian exile Joseph Mazzini (see the headnote to *Casa Guidi Windows*) reflecting Victorian gender stereotypes: "'man lives more by the brain, and woman by the heart.'" On reviewers' impressions of EBB as combining feminine feeling with masculine intellect, see, e.g., *BC* 9:319.

3 appliance] application.

4 gauds] jewelry or finery. Besides her love affairs with notable men (e.g., writer Alfred de Musset, composer Frederic Chopin), Sand's scandalous behavior included some-times wearing men's clothing.

Thy woman's hair, my sister, all unshorn,
Floats back dishevelled strength in agony,   8
Disproving thy man's name! and while before
The world thou burnest in a poet-fire,
We see thy woman-heart beat evermore
Through the large flame. Beat, purer, heart, and higher   12
Till God unsex thee on the heavenly shore,
Where unincarnate spirits purely aspire.[1]

---

[1] In 1844, the last two lines read, "Till God unsex thee on the spirit-shore; / To which
alone unsexing, purely aspire." EBB revised them in 1850, making her redefinition
of the normally pejorative term *unsex* clearer (see Morlier 1990, 322). Despite the
revision, a reviewer who affirmed that the "moral difference" between the sexes is
"necessary, radical, and most unchangeable" lamented the lines as a "beautiful insan-
ity.... Did she dream that God, who made such a beautiful creation, would deny his
wisdom and work to 'unsex' it?"; C.B. Conant, *North American Review*, 94 (1862): 342,
345.

Figure 2: The picture for which EBB wrote "The Romaunt of the Page," from *Finden's Tableaux*, London, 1839.

The Romaunt of the Page[1]

One of EBB's most popular ballads in the nineteenth century, this first appeared as the lead poem in the annual, *Finden's Tableaux of The Affections; A Series of Picturesque Illustrations of The Womanly Virtues. From Paintings by W. Perring* (1839), edited by her friend Mary Mitford.[2] EBB observed of the engraved painting it illustrated (see Figure 2), "the pictured one pretty as she is, has a good deal exaggerated the ballad-receipt[3] for making a ladye page—Do you remember?———

> 'And you must cut your gowne of green
>   An INCH above the knee'!——

She comes within the fi fa fum of the prudes, in consequence—" (*BC* 4:38). The quotation from "Child Waters," a traditional ballad in *Reliques of Ancient English Poetry* (1765), compiled by Thomas Percy (1729-1811), points to one of the works at play—often ironically—in the poem's intertextual echoes. Although EBB said the subject was "not of [her] choosing" in her "very long barbarous ballad" (*BC* 4:33), it clearly chimed with her girlhood "indignation" at being a woman (inspired by reading Mary Wollstonecraft[4]) and her consequent longing to be "Lord Byron's PAGE," recollected in her letters in 1842 and playfully described in her semi-autobiographical essay about a girl named Beth (*BC* 6:42, 1:360-62). Byron's *Lara* (1814) is one of the many influences on the poem. With its archaic diction and chivalric setting, the poem reflects the medievalism associated with the ballad revival inspired by Percy's *Reliques*, Sir Walter Scott's *Minstrelsy of the Scottish Border* (1802-03), and the *Lyrical Ballads* (1798) of William Wordsworth and Samuel Taylor Coleridge. Mitford told EBB that

---

1   A "romaunt" (archaic) is a romantic tale or poem; a "page" is a boy or youth employed as a personal attendant, a male servant, or an apprentice to knighthood. All three senses of *page* are relevant here.

2   *Finden's Tableaux*: Other issues are titled *Findens' Tableaux*, but the title page of this issue uses the singular possessive. On Mitford and EBB's contributions to these gift books, see the headnote to "A Romance of the Ganges."

3   ballad-receipt] ballad recipe, i.e., ballad convention.

4   Wollstonecraft] see the Introduction and the headnote to "Fragment of an 'Essay on Woman,'" pp. 49–50.

"The Romaunt of the Page" was "the finest thing" she had written and entreated her to write more such poems "of human feelings and human actions" (*BC* 5:135). Victorian reviewers of the 1839 *Finden's* also singled it out as "full of fancy and originality," "distinguished by poetical qualities of the highest order," and marked by "true and original genius," finding it filled "with the spirit of the elder and better day of poetry in every line" and "dipped in the hues of ballad minstrelsy" (*BC* 4:405-06). In reviews of *Poems* (1844), it was praised for its "subjective" handling of the ballad form and described as "foremost among 'Records of Woman'" (*BC* 9:342, 320; see also *BC* 9:339, 347, 365, 370)—an allusion connecting it to one of the most popular collections by Felicia Hemans (1793-1835).[1] EBB heavily revised the ballad for *Poems* (1844), adding entire stanzas and substantially rewriting many passages. Most notably, the *Finden's* text lacks Stanza V and narrates the story told in Stanzas XV to XIX below in only two stanzas, without many of the details added in 1844 (see l. 147n).[2] In 1839 and 1844, the poem was preceded by an epigraph from Beaumont and Fletcher deleted from the later collections.[3] Criticism: Hickock 1984, Leighton 1986, Mermin 1989, Stephenson 1989, Stone 1993, and Shires 2001.

I

A knight of gallant deeds
   And a young page at his side,
From the holy war in Palestine[4]
   Did slow and thoughtful ride,
As each were a palmer and told for beads[5]   5
   The dews of the eventide.

---

1 *Records of Woman: With Other Poems* (1828). On Hemans, see "Felicia Hemans: To L.E.L.," pp. 73–76.

2 Stone (1993, 1995) discusses the major revisions.

3 "The trustiest, loving'st, and the gentlest boy, / That ever master had.—Beaumont and Fletcher"] Francis Beaumont (1584-1616) and John Fletcher (1579-1625), dramatists and collaborators; the quotation comes from Philaster (produced 1611; printed 1620), Act 1, scene 2, ll. 159-60.

4 holy war in Palestine] alluding to the Crusades.

5 As] as if; palmer ... beads] a pilgrim or itinerant monk, counting beads on a rosary.

II

"O young page," said the knight,
　　"A noble page art thou!
Thou fearest not to steep in blood
　　The curls upon thy brow;
And once in the tent, and twice in the fight,
　　Didst ward[1] me a mortal blow."　　　　　　　　10

III

"O brave knight," said the page,
　　"Or ere[2] we hither came,
We talked in tent, we talked in field,　　　　　　15
　　Of the bloody battle-game;
But here, below this greenwood bough,
　　I cannot speak the same.

IV

"Our troop is far behind,
　　The woodland calm is new;　　　　　　　　　　20
Our steeds, with slow grass-muffled hoofs,
　　Tread deep the shadows through;
And in my mind, some blessing kind
　　Is dropping with the dew.

V

"The woodland calm is pure—　　　　　　　　　25
　　I cannot choose but have
A thought from these, o' the beechen-trees
　　Which in our England wave,
And of the little finches fine
Which sang there, while in Palestine　　　　　　30
　　The warrior-hilt we drave.[3]

1　ward] fend off.
2　Or ere] before.
3　warrior-hilt we drave] we drove the warrior sword into the enemy.

VI

"Methinks, a moment gone,
    I heard my mother pray!
I heard, sir knight, the prayer for *me*
    Wherein she passed away;   35
And I know the Heavens are leaning down
    To hear what I shall say."

VII

The page spake calm and high,
    As of no mean degree.
Perhaps he felt in nature's broad   40
    Full heart, his own was free.
And the knight looked up to his lifted eye,
    Then answered smilingly:—

VIII

'Sir page, I pray your grace!
    Certes,[1] I meant not so   45
To cross your pastoral mood, sir page,
    With the crook of the battle-bow;
But a knight may speak of a lady's face,
I ween, in any mood or place,
    If the grasses die or grow.   50

IX

"And this I meant to say,—
    My lady's face shall shine
As ladies' faces use, to greet
    My page from Palestine;
Or, speak she fair or prank[2] she gay,   55
    She is no lady of mine.

---

1   certes] certainly.
2   prank] deck oneself out; adorn or display oneself.

X

"And this I meant to fear,—
  Her bower may suit thee ill!
For, sooth,[1] in that same field and tent,
  Thy *talk* was somewhat still;   60
And fitter thy hand for my knightly spear,
  Than thy tongue for my lady's will."

XI

Slowly and thankfully
  The young page bowed his head:
His large eyes seemed to muse a smile,   65
  Until he blushed instead,
And no lady in her bower pardiè,[2]
  Could blush more sudden red.
"Sir Knight,—thy lady's bower to me
  Is suited well," he said.   70

XII

Beati, beati, mortui![3]
From the convent on the sea,
One mile off, or scarce as nigh,
Swells the dirge[4] as clear and high
As if that, over brake and lea,[5]   75
Bodily the wind did carry
The great altar of St. Mary,
And the fifty tapers burning o'er it,
And the lady Abbess dead before it,
And the chanting nuns whom yesterweek   80

---

1 sooth] in truth.

2 pardiè] by God (from French *pardieu*).

3 *Beati, beati, mortui!*] Blessed be the dead! A parallel use of convent music to create
   narrative counterpoint appears in Scott's *Marmion* (1808).

4 dirge] generally, a funeral song; here referring to the first part of the antiphonal song
   or chant sung in the Service of the Dead. EBB commented that convent music is heard
   "when the page is happiest, & so absorbed in happy thought that he is unconscious
   even of the sound" (*BC* 4:43).

5 brake and lea] bush and grass land.

Her voice did charge and bless,—
Chanting steady, chanting meek,
Chanting with a solemn breath
Because that they are thinking less
Upon the Dead than upon death! 85
Beati, beati, mortui!
Now the vision in the sound
Wheeleth on the wind around.
Now it sweepeth back, away—
The uplands will not let it stay 90
To dark[1] the western sun.
Mortui!—away at last,—
Or ere the page's blush is past!
And the knight heard all, and the page heard none.

XIII

"A boon, thou noble knight, 95
    If ever I servèd thee!
Though thou art a knight and I am a page,
    Now grant a boon to me;
And tell me sooth, if dark or bright,
If little loved or loved aright 100
    Be the face of thy ladye."[2]

XIV

Gloomily looked the knight;—
    "As a son thou hast servèd me,
And would to none I had granted boon
    Except to only thee! 105
For haply then I should love aright,
For then I should know if dark or bright
    Were the face of my ladye.

---

1 dark] darken, cloud, dim, or obscure.
2 ladye] archaic spelling of *lady*.

XV

"Yet ill it suits my knightly tongue
   To grudge that granted boon!   110
That heavy price from heart and life
   I paid in silence down.
The hand that claimed it, cleared in fine[1]
My father's fame: I swear by mine,
   That price was nobly won.   115

XVI

"Earl Walter was a brave old earl,—
   He was my father's friend;
And while I rode the lists[2] at court
   And little guessed the end,
My noble father in his shroud,   120
Against a slanderer lying loud,
   He rose up to defend.

XVII

"Oh, calm, below the marble grey
   My father's dust was strown!
Oh, meek, above the marble grey   125
   His image prayed alone!
The slanderer lied—the wretch was brave,—
For, looking up the minster-nave,[3]
He saw my father's knightly glaive[4]
   Was changed from steel to stone.   130

XVIII

"Earl Walter's glaive was steel,
   With a brave old hand to wear it,
And dashed the lie back in the mouth
Which lied against the godly truth

---

1 in fine] conclusively, with connotations here of its original sense of *fine*, medieval
   Latin for the sum paid on concluding a lawsuit.

2 lists] an enclosed space or arena for tournaments.

3 minster-nave] the central space of a cathedral leading up to the altar.

4 glaive] a lance or spear; more loosely, a sword.

And against the knightly merit! 135
The slanderer, 'neath the avenger's heel,
Struck up the dagger in appeal
From stealthy lie to brutal force—
And out upon the traitor's corse[1]
    Was yielded the true spirit. 140

XIX
"I would mine hand had fought that fight
    And justified my father!
I would mine heart had caught that wound
    And slept beside him rather!
I think it were a better thing 145
Than murthered friend and marriage-ring
    Forced on my life together.[2]

XX
"Wail shook Earl Walter's house;
    His true wife shed no tear;
She lay upon her bed as mute 150
    As the earl did on his bier:
Till—'Ride, ride fast,' she said at last,
    'And bring the avengèd's son anear!
Ride fast—ride free, as a dart can flee,
For white of blee[3] with waiting for me 155
    Is the corse in the next chambère.'

XXI
"I came—I knelt beside her bed—
    Her calm was worse than strife;
'My husband, for thy father dear,
Gave freely when thou wert not here 160

---

1   corse] corpse.

2   Stanzas XV-XIX] In place of these five stanzas detailing the story of the enemy knight and Earl Walter, 1839 presents a much shorter account featuring a nameless Baron (rather than Earl Walter) who championed the dead father of the knight here speaking to his page.

3   blee] complexion.

His own and eke[1] my life.
A boon! Of that sweet child we make
An orphan for thy father's sake,
   Make thou, for ours, a wife.'

XXII

"I said, 'My steed neighs in the court,   165
   My bark rocks on the brine,
And the warrior's vow I am under now
   To free the pilgrim's shrine;
But fetch the ring and fetch the priest
   And call that daughter of thine,   170
And rule she wide from my castle on Nyde[2]
   While I am in Palestine.'

XXIII

"In the dark chambère, if the bride was fair,
   Ye wis,[3] I could not see,
But the steed thrice neighed, and the priest fast prayed, 175
   And wedded fast were we.
Her mother smiled upon her bed
As at its side we knelt to wed,
   And the bride rose from her knee
And kissed the smile of her mother dead,   180
   Or ever she kissed me.

XXIV

"My page, my page, what grieves thee so,
   That the tears run down thy face?"—
"Alas, alas! mine own sistèr[4]
   Was in thy lady's case!   185
But *she* laid down the silks she wore

---

1   eke] also.

2   Nyde] the Nidd River in Yorkshire, also spelled Nyde and Nyd in Walter Kaye's
   Parish Records of Harrogate 1560-1812 (1923).

3   Ye wis] you know.

4   "Alas, alas! mine own sister] the 1839 text presents only a hypothetical parallel with
   the page's sister here] "Alas! What if my own sister."

And followed him she wed before,[1]
Disguised as his true servitor,
   To the very battle-place."

XXV

And wept the page, but laughed the knight,—   190
   A careless laugh laughed he:
"Well done it were for thy sistèr,
   But not for my ladye!
My love, so please you, shall requite
No woman, whether dark or bright,   195
   Unwomaned if she be."

XXVI

The page stopped weeping and smiled cold—
   "Your wisdom may declare
That womanhood is proved the best
By golden brooch and glossy vest   200
   The mincing ladies wear;
Yet is it proved, and was of old,
Anear as well, I dare to hold,
   By truth, or by despair."

XXVII

He smiled no more, he wept no more,   205
   But passionate he spake,—
"Oh, womanly she prayed in tent,
   When none beside did wake!
Oh, womanly she paled in fight,
   For one belovèd's sake!—   210
And her little hand defiled with blood,
Her tender tears of womanhood
   Most woman-pure did make!"

---

1   she wed before] the Berg ms (R D795)—"beloved more"—makes no mention of marriage here.

XXVIII

—"Well done it were for thy sistèr,
   Thou tellest well her tale!   215
But for my lady, she shall pray
   I' the kirk of Nydesdale.
Not dread for me but love for me
   Shall make my lady pale;
No casque shall hide her woman's tear—   220
It shall have room to trickle clear
   Behind her woman's veil."

XXIX

—"But what if she mistook thy mind
   And followed thee to strife,
Then kneeling, did entreat thy love,   225
   As Paynims[1] ask for life?"
—"I would forgive, and evermore
Would love her as my servitor,
   But little as my wife.[2]

XXX

"Look up—there is a small bright cloud   230
   Alone amid the skies!
So high, so pure, and so apart,
   A woman's honor lies."
The page looked up—the cloud was sheen[3]—
A sadder cloud did rush, I ween,   235
   Betwixt it and his eyes:

---

1 Paynims] pagans or heathens; in the Christian, medieval context here, especially Moslems or Arabs.

2 as my servitor/ But little as my wife] Cf. Marmion's treatment of his unwed lover Constance as a horse boy in Scott's *Marmion* and the treatment of Ellen, the unmarried companion of Child Waters, who runs pregnant and bare-foot by his horse's side as his footpage in "Child Waters" (Stone 1995, 126-27).

3 sheen] shining, bright, or resplendent.

XXXI

Then dimly dropped his eyes away
　From welkin[1] unto hill—
Ha! who rides there?—the page is 'ware,
　Though the cry at his heart is still! 240
And the page seeth all and the knight seeth none,
Though banner and spear do fleck the sun,
　And the Saracens[2] ride at will.

XXXII

He speaketh calm, he speaketh low,—
　"Ride fast, my master, ride, 245
Or ere within the broadening dark
　The narrow shadows hide."
"Yea, fast, my page, I will do so,
　And keep thou at my side."

XXXIII

"Now nay, now nay, ride on thy way, 250
　Thy faithful page precede.
For I must loose on saddle-bow
My battle-casque that galls, I trow,[3]
　The shoulder of my steed;
And I must pray, as I did vow, 255
　For one in bitter need.

XXXIV

"Ere night I shall be near to thee,—
　Now ride, my master, ride!
Ere night, as parted spirits cleave[4]
To mortals too beloved to leave, 260
　I shall be at thy side."
The knight smiled free at the fantasy,[5]
　And adown the dell did ride.

1　welkin] sky or firmament.

2　Saracens] Arabs or Moslems, especially in the context of the Crusades.

3　galls] chafes, opens a wound or sore by rubbing; trow] believe.

4　cleave] cling fast to.

5　fantasy] here, fanciful or whimsical idea.

XXXV

Had the knight looked up to the page's face,
    No smile the word had won: 265
Had the knight looked up to the page's face,
    I ween he had never gone:
Had the knight looked back to the page's geste,[1]
    I ween he had turned anon![2]
For dread was the woe in the face so young,   270
And wild was the silent geste that flung
Casque, sword to earth—as the boy down-sprung,
    And stood—alone, alone.

XXXVI

He clenched his hands as if to hold
    His soul's great agony—   275
"Have I renounced my womanhood,
    For wifehood unto *thee*,
And is this the last, last look of thine
    That ever I shall see?

XXXVII

"Yet God thee save, and mayst thou have   280
    A lady to thy mind,
More woman-proud and half as true
    As one thou leav'st behind!
And God me take with HIM to dwell—
For HIM I cannot love too well,   285
    As I have loved my kind."

---

1   geste] gesture.
2   anon] at once.

XXXVIII

SHE looketh up, in earth's despair,
   The hopeful Heavens to seek.
That little cloud still floateth there,
   Whereof her Loved did speak.   290
How bright the little cloud appears!
Her eyelids fall upon the tears,
   And the tears down either cheek.

XXXIX

The tramp of hoof, the flash of steel—
   The Paynims round her coming!   295
The sound and sight have made her calm,—
   False page, but truthful woman!
She stands amid them all unmoved.
A heart once broken by the loved
   Is strong to meet the foeman.   300

XL

"Ho, Christian page! art[1] keeping sheep,
   From pouring wine-cups resting?"—
"I keep my master's noble name,
   For warring, not for feasting;
And if that here Sir Hubert were,   305
My master brave, my master dear,
   Ye would not stay to question."

XLI

"Where is thy master, scornful page,
   That we may slay or bind him?"—
"Now search the lea and search the wood,   310
   And see if ye can find him!
Nathless,[2] as hath been often tried,
Your Paynim heroes faster ride
   Before him than behind him."

---

1 art] are you.
2 Nathless] nevertheless.

XLII

"Give smoother answers, lying page,   315
   Or perish in the lying."—
"I trow that if the warrior brand[1]
Beside my foot, were in my hand,
   'Twere better at replying."
They cursed her deep, they smote her low,   320
They cleft her golden ringlets through;
   The Loving is the Dying.

XLIII

She felt the scimitar gleam down,
   And met it from beneath
With smile more bright in victory   325
   Than any sword from sheath,—
Which flashed across her lip serene,
Most like the spirit-light between
   The darks of life and death.

XLIV

   Ingemisco, ingemisco![2]   330
From the convent on the sea,
Now it sweepeth solemnly!
As over wood and over lea
Bodily the wind did carry
The great altar of St. Mary,   335
And the fifty tapers paling o'er it,
And the Lady Abbess stark before it,
And the weary nuns with hearts that faintly
Beat along their voices saintly—
   Ingemisco, ingemisco!   340
Dirge for abbess laid in shroud,
Sweepeth o'er the shroudless Dead,
Page or lady, as we said,

---

1 brand] here, the blade of a sword.

2 *Ingemisco, ingemisco!*] I lament (i.e., my sins), Latin; from the Requiem or the Mass for
   the Dead.

With the dews upon her head,[1]
All as sad if not as loud.   345
   Ingemisco, ingemisco!
Is ever a lament begun
By any mourner under sun,
Which, ere it endeth, suits but *one?*

Lady Geraldine's Courtship
A Romance of the Age

EBB completed the last one hundred and forty lines of this "long modern ballad," as she first referred to it, in a single day in July 1844, to balance the length of the two volumes of her *Poems* (1844) (*BC* 9: 65, 73). Critical legend held that the entire poem had been composed in a day or twelve hours.[2] EBB described the poem as "treating of railroads, routes, & all manner of 'temporalities'" in a deliberately "radical" temper, with the aim of throwing "conventionalities (turned asbestos for the nonce) into the fire of poetry, to make them glow & glitter" (*BC* 9:65, 165). The poem reflected the urging of her friend and correspondent Mary Mitford that she write poems of "Humanity," not "Mysticism"—though EBB maintained it had "more mysticism ... hid in the story .. than all the other ballad-poems" in her 1844 collection (*BC* 6:219-20; 9:293, 304). Integrating the traditional with the modern, EBB combines courtly love conventions with allusions to railroads and the telegraph. The contemporary cast of characters and narrative led one reviewer to call the poem a "capital magazine story" (*BC* 10:387). Generically, the work is a hybrid, as a ballad or "romaunt" incorporated in an epistolary dramatic monologue framed with a "Conclusion." One *Blackwood's* writer, who read it "at least six times aloud," called the work a "beautiful *sui generis* drama" (*BC* 9:171). The "apparent roughness" of the meter and rhyme—to a degree deliberate, given that EBB was "playing at ball" with the placement of the caesura or "the *pause*" (*BC* 9:177)—was smoothed

---

1 Dirge ... head] in the Berg ms, ll. 341-44 differ substantially, and include an echo of "Woman on the Field of Battle" by Hemans (Stone 1995, 120).

2 See obituary in *The Edinburgh Review* 114 (1861): 518; Mary Mitford may have contributed to the myth (*BC* 10:330).

out by the many revisions she made in the poem in subsequent collections of her poetry, some addressing the "rhymes left unrhymed" (*LEBB* 2:111). The poem is filled with echoes (including the meter) of "Locksley Hall," a work in Tennyson's *Poems* (1842) that became a kind of anthem for the age, and that EBB much admired but also here challenges (*BC* 6:219-20). Critics repeatedly connected the two works, as Edgar Allan Poe (1809-49) did (see Appendix A.2 and *BC* 10:352). Victorians found the poem's class politics relatively radical. EBB's own brother George Barrett (1816-95) considered it "very immoral" for a man to accept "a fortune from a wife" (*BC* 6:86), while the *Blackwood's* reviewer asked "how the match between the peasant's son and the peer's daughter was found to answer" (*BC* 9:362). "Lady Geraldine's Courtship" rapidly became a "popular favorite," which EBB attributed to "the fact of there being a *story*" in the poem; it was praised by Thomas Carlyle (1795-1881) and Harriet Martineau (1802-76), among many others (*BC* 9:213, 219, 165).[1] RB's echoes of it suggest that it was a favorite of his as well (*BC* 11:21, 29)—understandably, given its sensuous compliment to his own poetry (see l. 163). "Lady Geraldine's Courtship" is especially important in EBB's poetic development as the prototype for her novel-poem *Aurora Leigh* (1856). The earlier poem's success stimulated her aspiration to write "some day a longer poem of a like class," a work treating "this real everyday life of our age"—a "sort of novel-poem ... running into the midst of our conventions, & rushing into drawingrooms ... & so, meeting face to face & without mask, the Humanity of the age" (*BC* 9:177, 304; 10:102-03). Criticism: Mermin 1989, Homans 1998, Stephenson 1989, and Avery and Stott 2003.

A poet writes to his friend. PLACE—*A room in Wycombe Hall.*
    TIME—*Late in the evening.*

Dear my friend and fellow-student, I would lean my spirit o'er you!
Down the purple of this chamber, tears should scarcely run at will.
I am humbled who was humble. Friend,—I bow my head before you.
You should lead me to my peasants,—but their faces are too still.

---

1   James Thomson (1834-82) complimented the work by writing a "prequel," "Bertram to the Most Noble and Beautiful Lady Geraldine" (1857); see *The Poetical Works of James Thomson* (London: Reeves & Turner, 1895), 2: 337-50.

There's a lady—an earl's daughter,—she is proud and she is noble,   5
And she treads the crimson carpet, and she breathes the perfumed air,
And a kingly blood sends glances up her princely eye to trouble,
And the shadow of a monarch's crown is softened in her hair.

She has halls among the woodlands, she has castles by the breakers,
She has farms and she has manors, she can threaten and command,   10
And the palpitating engines snort in steam across her acres,[1]
As they mark upon the blasted heaven the measure of the land.

There are none of England's daughters who can show a prouder
   presence.
Upon princely suitors praying, she has looked in her disdain.
She was sprung of English nobles, I was born of English peasants;   15
What was *I* that I should love her—save for competence to pain?[2]

I was only a poor poet, made for singing at her casement,[3]
As the finches or the thrushes, while she thought of other things.
Oh, she walked so high above me, she appeared to my abasement,
In her lovely silken murmur, like an angel clad in wings!   20

Many vassals[4] bow before her as her carriage sweeps their door-ways;
She has blest their little children,—as a priest or queen were she.
Far too tender, or too cruel far, her smile upon the poor was,
For I thought it was the same smile which she used to smile on *me*.

She has voters in the commons,[5] she has lovers in the palace;   25
And of all the fair court-ladies, few have jewels half as fine.

---

1   palpitating engines ... acres] among the first mentions of steam trains in English
    poetry; the 1844 text alluded, more indirectly, to "resonant steam-eagles," an image
    disparaged by one reviewer (*BC* 9:339-40).

2   competence to pain] here, the capacity to experience pain.

3   singing ... casement] serenading her at the window, following the courtly love tradi-
    tion. Cf. Sonnet 3 in *Sonnets from the Portuguese* (1850), in which the female speaker
    sings at the casement.

4   vassals] servants or subordinates (a term associated with the feudal system).

5   voters in the commons] members of Parliament representing the ridings controlled by
    her aristocratic family, as was the practice prior to the democratizing Second Reform
    Bill (1867).

Oft the prince has named her beauty 'Twixt the red wine and the
    chalice.
Oh, and what was *I* to love her? my beloved, my Geraldine!

Yet I could not choose but love her. I was born to poet-uses,
To love all things set above me, all of good and all of fair.   30
Nymphs of mountain, not of valley, we are wont to call the Muses;[1]
And in nympholeptic[2] climbing, poets pass from mount to star.

And because I was a poet, and because the public praised me,
With a critical deduction for the modern writer's fault,
I could sit at rich men's tables,—though the courtesies that raised me,   35
Still suggested clear between us the pale spectrum of the salt.[3]

And they praised me in her presence;—"Will your book appear
    this summer?"
Then returning to each other—"Yes, our plans are for the moors."
Then with whisper dropped behind me—"There he is! the latest
    comer!
Oh, she only likes his verses! what is over, she endures.   40

"Quite low-born! self-educated! somewhat gifted though by nature,—
And we make a point of asking him,—of being very kind.
You may speak, he does not hear you! and besides, he writes no
    satire,—
All these serpents kept by charmers,[4] leave the natural sting behind."

I grew scornfuller, grew colder, as I stood up there among them,   45
Till as frost intense will burn you, the cold scorning scorched my
    brow,—

---

1   Muses] in Greek mythology, the nine goddesses who personify and inspire artistic
    creativity.

2   nympholeptic] characterized by enthusiasm or passion, especially for unattainable
    deals; from "nympholepsy" (Greek for "caught by nymphs"); 1844 reads "silver-
    footed." See *Casa Guidi Windows* 1:190n, for EBB's explanation of "nympholepsy."

3   spectrum of the salt] guests of distinction were seated near the head of the table "above
    the salt" (the silver salt cellar placed in the table's center); dependents and inferior
    guests were seated below it.

4   serpents ... charmers] *i.e.*, artists patronized by wealthy ladies.

When a sudden silver speaking, gravely cadenced, over-rung them,
And a sudden silken stirring touched my inner nature through.

I looked upward and beheld her. With a calm and regnant[1] spirit,
Slowly round she swept her eyelids, and said clear before them all—   50
"Have you such superfluous honor, sir, that able to confer it
You will come down, Mister Bertram, as my guest to Wycombe Hall?"

Here she paused,—she had been paler at the first word of her speaking,
But because a silence followed it, blushed somewhat, as for shame,
Then, as scorning her own feeling, resumed calmly—"I am
      seeking   55
More distinction than these gentlemen think worthy of my claim.

"Ne'ertheless, you see, I seek it—not because I am a woman,"
(Here her smile sprang like a fountain, and, so, overflowed her
      mouth)
"But because my woods in Sussex have some purple shades at gloaming[2]
Which are worthy of a king in state, or poet in his youth.   60

"I invite you, Mister Bertram, to no scene for worldly speeches—
Sir, I scarce should dare—but only where God asked the
      thrushes first—
And if *you* will sing beside them, in the covert of my beeches,
I will thank you for the woodlands,... for the human world, at worst."

Then she smiled around right childly,[3] then she gazed around
      right queenly,   65
And I bowed—I could not answer; alternated light and gloom—
While as one who quells the lions,[4] with a steady eye serenely,
She, with level fronting eyelids, passed out stately from the room.

---

1   regnant] ruling, exercising sway or influence.

2   gloaming] twilight.

3   childly] here, in a manner like a youth of gentle or high lineage (the adverbial form of
    "child" or "childe," an honorific title, as in RB's 1855 poem, "Childe Roland to the
    Dark Tower Came").

4   lions] lions in an arena, but here also suggesting artists "lionized" or sought after as
    persons of note.

Oh, the blessèd woods of Sussex, I can hear them still around me,
With their leafy tide of greenery still rippling up the wind.[1]   70
Oh, the cursèd woods of Sussex! where the hunter's arrow[2] found me,
When a fair face and a tender voice had made me mad and blind!

In that ancient hall of Wycombe, thronged the numerous guests
     invited,
And the lovely London ladies trod the floors with gliding feet;
And their voices low with fashion, not with feeling, softly
     freighted   75
All the air about the windows, with elastic laughters sweet.

For at eve, the open windows flung their light out on the terrace,
Which the floating orbs of curtains did with gradual shadow
     sweep,
While the swans upon the river, fed at morning by the heiress,
Trembled downward through their snowy wings at music in their
     sleep.   80

And there evermore was music, both of instrument and singing,
Till the finches of the shrubberies grew restless in the dark;
But the cedars stood up motionless, each in a moonlight ringing,
And the deer, half in the glimmer, strewed the hollows of the park.

And though sometimes she would bind me with her silver-corded
     speeches   85
To commix[3] my words and laughter with the converse and the jest,
Oft I sate[4] apart, and gazing on the river through the beeches,
Heard, as pure the swans swam down it, her pure voice o'erfloat
     the rest.

---

1   In 1844, l. 70 is followed by two additional lines deleted in the 1850 Printer's Copy:
    "Oh, the cursed woods of Sussex! Oh, the cruel love that bound me / Up against
    the boles of cedars, to be shamed where I pined!" Cf. the volley of four lines (ll.
    59-62) beginning with "Cursèd" and the four quick iterations of "O" (ll. 39-40) in
    Tennyson's "Locksley Hall" (see headnote).

2   hunter's arrow] i.e., Cupid's arrow.

3   commix] to mix or mingle together, to intermix.

4   sate] sat.

In the morning, horn of huntsman, hoof of steed, and laugh of rider,
Spread out cheery from the court-yard till we lost them in the hills, 90
While herself and other ladies, and her suitors left beside her,
Went a-wandering up the gardens through the laurels and abeles.[1]

Thus, her foot upon the new-mown grass, bareheaded, with the
    flowing
Of the virginal white vesture gathered closely to her throat,—
And the golden ringlets in her neck just quickened by her going, 95
And appearing to breathe sun for air, and doubting if to float,—

With a branch of dewy maple, which her right hand held above her,
And which trembled a green shadow in betwixt her and the skies,
As she turned her face in going, thus, she drew me on to love her,
And to worship the divineness of the smile hid in her eyes.   100

For her eyes alone smile constantly: her lips have serious sweetness,
And her front[2] is calm—the dimple rarely ripples on the cheek;
But her deep blue eyes smile constantly, as if they in discreetness
Kept the secret of a happy dream she did not care to speak.

Thus she drew me the first morning, out across into the garden, 105
And I walked among her noble friends and could not keep behind.
Spake she unto all and unto me—"Behold, I am the warden
Of the song-birds in these lindens, which are cages to their mind.

"But within this swarded[3] circle, into which the lime-walk brings us,
Whence the beeches, rounded greenly, stand away in reverent fear, 110
I will let no music enter, saving what the fountain sings us,
Which the lilies round the basin may seem pure enough to hear.

"The live air that waves the lilies waves the slender jet of water
Like a holy thought sent feebly up from soul of fasting saint.

---

1   abeles] while poplars.
2   front] face as expressive of emotion or character; expression of countenance; de-
    meanor.
3   swarded] covered with grass.

Whereby lies a marble Silence, sleeping! (Lough the sculptor[1]
   wrought her)   115
So asleep she is forgetting to say Hush!—a fancy quaint.

"Mark how heavy white her eyelids! not a dream between them lingers.
And the left hand's index droppeth from the lips upon the cheek;
While the right hand,—with the symbol rose[2] held slack within
   the fingers,—
Has fallen backward in the basin—yet this Silence will not speak!   120

"That the essential meaning growing may exceed the special symbol,
Is the thought as I conceive it: it applies more high and low.
Our true noblemen will often through right nobleness grow humble,
And assert an inward honour by denying outward show."

"Nay, your Silence," said I, "truly, holds her symbol rose but slackly,   125
Yet *she holds it*—or would scarcely be a Silence to our ken.[3]
And your nobles wear their ermine[4] on the outside, or walk blackly
In the presence of the social law as mere ignoble men.

"Let the poets dream such dreaming! madam, in these British islands,
'Tis the substance that wanes ever, 'Tis the symbol that exceeds.   130
Soon we shall have nought but symbol! and, for statues like this
   Silence,
Shall accept the rose's image—in another case, the weed's."

"Not so quickly," she retorted,—"I confess, where'er you go, you
Find for things, names—shows for actions, and pure gold for
   honour clear.

---

1   marble Silence ... Lough the sculptor] a statue of Silence, here personified as a woman,
   by John Graham Lough (1806-76), the English neoclassical sculptor, a friend of the
   Barretts (*BC* 8:93, 95; 9:288-89).

2   the symbol rose] in Roman myth, the rose given to Harpocrates, the god of silence,
   by Cupid to persuade him not to betray the amorous escapades of Venus (Cupid's
   mother); Harpocrates is traditionally depicted as male, with his finger to his lips hold-
   ing this "symbol rose." For EBB's association of Harpocrates's rose with secrecy, see
   BC 4:147, 5:320.

3   ken] knowledge or sight.

4   ermine] white fur emblematic of purity, worn by judges and nobles.

But when all is run to symbol in the Social, I will throw you   135
The world's book which now reads drily, and sit down with
   Silence here."

Half in playfulness she spoke, I thought, and half in indignation;
Friends who listened, laughed her words off, while her lovers
   deemed her fair.
A fair woman, flushed with feeling, in her noble-lighted station
Near the statue's white reposing—and both bathed in sunny air!—   140

With the trees round, not so distant but you heard their vernal
   murmur,
And beheld in light and shadow the leaves in and outward move,
And the little fountain leaping toward the sun-heart to be warmer,
Then recoiling in a tremble from the too much light above.

'Tis a picture for remembrance. And thus, morning after morning,   145
Did I follow as she drew me by the spirit to her feet.
Why, her greyhound followed also! dogs—we both were dogs for
   scorning—
To be sent back when she pleased it and her path lay through the wheat.

And thus, morning after morning, spite of vows and spite of sorrow,
Did I follow at her drawing, while the week-days passed along,   150
Just to feed the swans this noontide, or to see the fawns to-morrow,
Or to teach the hill-side echo some sweet Tuscan[1] in a song.

Ay, for sometimes on the hill-side, while we sate down in the gowans,[2]
With the forest green behind us, and its shadow cast before,
And the river running under, and across it from the rowans[3]   155
A brown partridge whirring near us, till we felt the air it bore,—

There, obedient to her praying, did I read aloud the poems
Made to Tuscan flutes, or instruments more various of our own;

---

1   Tuscan] an inhabitant of Tuscany (a region in Italy), such as Petrarch (see l. 160n,
    below).

2   gowans] white or yellow flowers, especially daisies.

3   rowans] a small tree with white flowers and red berries.

Read the pastoral parts of Spenser[1]—or the subtle interflowings
Found in Petrarch's sonnets[2]—here's the book—the leaf is folded
    down!—   160

Or at times a modern volume,—Wordsworth's solemn-thoughted idyl,[3]
Howitt's ballad-verse,[4] or Tennyson's enchanted reverie,—[5]
Or from Browning some "Pomegranate,"[6] which, if cut deep
    down the middle,
Shows a heart within blood-tinctured, of a veined humanity.

Or at times I read there, hoarsely, some new poem of my making.   165
Poets ever fail in reading their own verses to their worth,—
For the echo in you breaks upon the words which you are speaking,
And the chariot-wheels jar in the gate through which you drive
    them forth.

After, when we were grown tired of books, the silence round us
    flinging
A slow arm of sweet compression, felt with beatings at the breast,   170
She would break out, on a sudden, in a gush of woodland singing,
Like a child's emotion in a god—a naiad[7] tired of rest.

---

1   the pastoral parts of Spenser] poems about idealized rural life by Edmund Spenser (1552-99).

2   Petrarch's sonnets] the love poems of Italian poet Petrarch (1304-74) to his lady Laura. For
    Petrarch's influence on EBB, see the headnote to *Sonnets from the Portuguese* (1850), p. 206.

3   Wordsworth's solemn-thoughted idyl] poetry about rural life by the Romantic poet
    William Wordsworth (1770-1850); the reference to Wordsworth replaced "such as
    Mitford's dewy idyl" in the Printer's Copy for the American edition of EBB's 1844
    collection (*R* D721).

4   Howitt's ballad-verse] ballads by English poet Mary Howitt (1799-1888), often praised
    in EBB's letters (*BC* 6:204, 7:164, 8:176).

5   Tennyson's enchanted reverie] works published in Tennyson's *Poems* (1832) and *Poems*
    (1842); EBB spoke of their dream-like beauty and the "spells" Tennyson "cast upon
    the ear" (*BC* 6:219, 8:362).

6   from Browning some "Pomegranate"] EBB's famous salute to RB alludes to the
    title—*Bells and Pomegranates*—of a pamphlet series he published and accords with her
    praise of his "graphic & passionate" manner; she called him a "master in clenched
    passion," defended his poetry against charges of obscurity, and linked his name with
    Tennyson's as a true poet (*BC* 6:226, 325, 142, 77). RB returned her public compliment
    in his praise of her poems expressed in his first letter to her in January 1845 (see the
    Introduction, pp. 25–26).

7   naiad] a water nymph in classical mythology.

Oh, to see or hear her singing! scarce I know which is divinest—
For her looks sing too—she modulates her gestures on the tune;
And her mouth stirs with the song, like song; and when the notes
    are finest,   175
'Tis the eyes that shoot out vocal light and seem to swell them on.

Then we talked—oh, how we talked! her voice, so cadenced in
    the talking,
Made another singing—of the soul! a music without bars.
While the leafy sounds of woodlands, humming round where we
    were walking,
Brought interposition[1] worthy-sweet,—as skies about the stars.   180

And she spake such good thoughts natural, as if she always thought them;
She had sympathies so rapid, open, free as bird on branch,
Just as ready to fly east as west, whichever way besought them
In the birchen-wood a chirrup, or a cock-crow in the grange.[2]

In her utmost lightness there is truth—and often she speaks lightly, 185
Has a grace in being gay, which even mournful souls approve,
For the root of some grave earnest thought is understruck[3] so rightly
As to justify the foliage and the waving flowers above.

And she talked on—*we* talked, rather! upon all things, substance,
    shadow,
Of the sheep that browsed the grasses, of the reapers in the corn,   190
Of the little children from the schools, seen winding through the
    meadow—
Of the poor rich world beyond them, still kept poorer by its scorn.

So, of men, and so, of letters—books are men of higher stature,
And the only men that speak aloud for future times to hear;

---

1   interposition] here, a digression from the music of her voice, sounding in its
    intervals.
2   grange] here, a granary or barn.
3   understruck] struck from below.

So, of mankind in the abstract, which grows slowly into nature,[1]   195
Yet will lift the cry of "progress," as it trod from sphere to sphere.

And her custom was to praise me when I said,—"The Age culls simples,[2]
With a broad clown's[3] back turned broadly to the glory of the stars.
We are gods by our own reck'ning, and may well shut up the temples,
And wield on, amid the incense-steam, the thunder of our cars.   200

"For we throw out acclamations of self-thanking, self-admiring,
With, at every mile run faster,—'O the wondrous wondrous age,'[4]
Little thinking if we work our SOULS as nobly as our iron,
Or if angels will commend us at the goal of pilgrimage.

"Why, what *is* this patient entrance into nature's deep resources,   205
But the child's most gradual learning to walk upright without bane?[5]
When we drive out, from the cloud of steam, majestical white horses,
Are we greater than the first men who led black ones by the mane?

"If we trod the deeps of ocean, if we struck the stars in rising,
If we wrapped the globe intensely with one hot electric breath,[6]   210
'Twere but power within our tether,[7] no new spirit-power comprising,
And in life we were not greater men, nor bolder men in death,

She was patient with my talking; and I loved her, loved her certes,[8]
As I loved all heavenly objects, with uplifted eyes and hands!

---

1   grows slowly into nature] unfolds slowly into its true nature, possibly suggesting
     as well that this potential is realized through gaining knowledge of Nature (see ll.
     205-06).

2   'The Age culls simples'] gathers or picks plants or herbs.

3   clown's] refers here to an uncouth or ignorant peasant or rustic.

4   wondrous, wondrous age] cf. the "wondrous Mother-Age" celebrated by the speaker
     in Tennyson's "Locksley Hall" (l. 108) for its technological marvels and progress.

5   bane] harm or woe.

6   hot electric breath] alluding to the electromagnetic telegraph, invented by Samuel
     Morse in the 1830s. The first telegraph line (between Baltimore and Washington) was
     opened in May 1844, although the first trans-Atlantic cable would not be successfully
     laid until 1866.

7   tether] the length of rope tying an animal such as a horse.

8   certes] certainly.

As I loved pure inspirations, loved the graces, loved the virtues,   215
In a Love content with writing his own name on desert sands.

Or at least I thought so, purely!—thought no idiot Hope was raising
Any crown to crown Love's silence—silent Love that sate alone.
Out, alas! the stag is like me—he, that tries to go on grazing
With the great deep gun-wound in his neck, then reels with
    sudden moan.   220

It was thus I reeled. I told you that her hand had many suitors;
But she smiles them down imperially, as Venus did the waves,[1]
And with such a gracious coldness, that they cannot press their futures
On the present of her courtesy, which yieldingly enslaves.

And this morning, as I sat alone within the inner chamber,   225
With the great saloon beyond it, lost in pleasant thought serene,
For I had been reading Camoëns—that poem you remember,
Which his lady's eyes are praised in, as the sweetest ever seen.[2]

And the book lay open, and my thought flew from it, taking from it
A vibration and impulsion to an end beyond its own,   230
As the branch of a green osier,[3] when a child would overcome it,
Springs up freely from his clasping and goes swinging in the sun.

As I mused I heard a murmur,—it grew deep as it grew longer—
Speakers using earnest language—"Lady Geraldine, you *would!*"
And I heard a voice that pleaded ever on, in accents stronger   235
As a sense of reason gave it power to make its rhetoric good.

Well I knew that voice—it was an earl's, of soul that matched his station,
Soul completed into lordship—might and right read on his brow;
Very finely courteous—far too proud to doubt his domination
Of the common people, he atones for grandeur by a bow.   240

---

1   as Venus did the waves] alluding to the birth of Venus from the foam of the sea.
2   Camoëns] the Portuguese poet Luis de Camoëns (1524-79); Bertram is inspired by the
    same work that inspired EBB's poem "Caterina to Camoens" (1844; see that poem's
    headnote, p. 166).
3   osier] a species of willow.

High straight forehead, nose of eagle, cold blue eyes, of less expression
Than resistance, coldly casting off the looks of other men,
As steel, arrows,—unelastic lips, which seem to taste possession,
And be cautious lest the common air should injure or distrain.[1]

For the rest, accomplished, upright,—ay, and standing by his order   245
With a bearing not ungraceful; fond of art and letters too;
Just a good man made a proud man,—as the sandy rocks that border
A wild coast, by circumstances, in a regnant ebb and flow.

Thus, I knew that voice—I heard it, and I could not help the
    harkening.[2]
In the room I stood up blindly, and my burning heart within   250
Seemed to seethe and fuse my senses, till they ran on all sides
    darkening,
And scorched, weighed, like melted metal round my feet that
    stood therein.

And that voice, I heard it pleading, for love's sake, for wealth, position,
For the sake of liberal uses,[3] and great actions to be done—
And she interrupted gently, "Nay, my lord, the old tradition   255
Of your Normans,[4] by some worthier hand than mine is, should
    be won."

"Ah, that white hand!" he said quickly,—and in his he either drew it
Or attempted—for with gravity and instance she replied,
"Nay, indeed, my lord, this talk is vain, and we had best eschew it,
And pass on, like friends, to other points less easy to decide."   260

What he said again, I know not. It is likely that his trouble
Worked his pride up to the surface, for she answered in slow scorn,
"And your lordship judges rightly. Whom I marry, shall be noble,
Ay, and wealthy. I shall never blush to think how he was born."

---

1   distrain] to distress or afflict.
2   harkening] listening or hearing with attention.
3   liberal uses] customs pertaining to or suitable for persons of superior social station.
4   Normans] French precursors (from Normandy) of many English noble families, dat-
    ing back to the Norman Conquest of England in 1066.

There, I maddened! her words stung me. Life swept through me
    into fever,   265
And my soul sprang up astonished, sprang, full-statured in an hour.
Know you what it is when anguish, with apocalyptic NEVER,
To a Pythian[1] height dilates you,—and despair sublimes[2] to power?

From my brain, the soul-wings budded,—waved a flame about
    my body,
Whence conventions coiled to ashes. I felt self-drawn out, as man,   270
From amalgamate[3] false natures, and I saw the skies grow ruddy
With the deepening feet of angels, and I knew what spirits can.

I was mad—inspired—say either! (anguish worketh inspiration)
Was a man, or beast—perhaps so, for the tiger roars, when speared;
And I walked on, step by step, along the level of my passion—   275
Oh my soul! and passed the doorway to her face, and never feared.

He had left her, peradventure,[4] when my footstep proved my coming—
But for *her*—she half arose, then sate—grew scarlet and grew pale.
Oh, she trembled!—'tis so always with a worldly man or woman
In the presence of true spirits—what else *can* they do but quail?   280

Oh, she fluttered like a tame bird, in among its forest-brothers
Far too strong for it; then drooping, bowed her face upon her hands—
And I spake out wildly, fiercely, brutal truths of her and others.
I, she planted in the desert, swathed her, windlike, with my sands.

I plucked up her social fictions, bloody-rooted though leaf-
    verdant,—   285
Trod them down with words of shaming,—all the purple and the gold,
All the "landed stakes"[5] and lordships, all, that spirits pure and
    ardent
Are cast out of love and honor because chancing not to hold.

---

1   Pythian] of or resembling Pythia, priestess of the Greek god of poetry Apollo, who at
    Delphi delivered oracles in an inspired state.
2   sublimes] raises to an elevated or exalted state; sublimates (as in a chemical conversion).
3   amalgamate] mixed or alloyed (as in a chemical mixed compound).
4   peradventure] perhaps.
5   "landed stakes"] landed properties providing a stake in the country, or the class hav-
    ing such stakes.

"For myself I do not argue," said I, "though I love you, madam,
But for better souls that nearer to the height of yours have trod.   290
And this age shows, to my thinking, still more infidels to Adam,[1]
Than directly, by profession, simple infidels to God.

"Yet, O God," I said, "O grave," I said, "O mother's heart and bosom,
With whom first and last are equal, saint and corpse and little child!
We are fools to your deductions, in these figments of heart-
     closing.[2]   295
We are traitors to your causes, in these sympathies defiled.

"Learn more reverence, madam, not for rank or wealth—*that*
     needs no learning,
That comes quickly—quick as sin does, ay, and culminates to sin;
But for Adam's seed, MAN! Trust me, 'Tis a clay above your scorning,
With God's image stamped upon it, and God's kindling breath
     within.   300

"What right have you, madam, gazing in your palace mirror daily,
Getting so by heart your beauty which all others must adore,
While you draw the golden ringlets down your fingers, to vow gaily
You will wed no man that's only good to God, and nothing more?

"Why, what right have you, made fair by that same God—the
     sweetest woman   305
Of all women He has fashioned—with your lovely spirit-face,
Which would seem too near to vanish if its smile were not so human,
And your voice of holy sweetness, turning common words to grace,

"What right *can* you have, God's other works to scorn, despise,
     revile them
In the gross, as mere men, broadly—not as *noble* men, forsooth,—   310
As mere Parias[3] of the outer world, forbidden to assoil them[4]
In the hope of living, dying, near that sweetness of your mouth?

---

1   infidels to Adam] people unfaithful to their own humanity.

2   figments of heart-closing] fictitious notions of heart-to-heart union; *heart-closing* may
     be a term coined by EBB, or possibly one adopted from her "study of our old English
     writers" (*BC* 9:165).

3   Parias] pariahs, members of a low Hindu caste shunned as unclean by higher castes; outcasts.

4   assoil them] absolve themselves of sin, pardon themselves.

"Have you any answer, madam? If my spirit were less earthly,
If its instrument were gifted with a better silver string,
I would kneel down where I stand, and say—Behold me! I am
    worthy   315
Of thy loving, for I love thee! I am worthy as a king.

"As it is—your ermined pride, I swear, shall feel this stain upon her,
That *I*, poor, weak, tost with passion, scorned by me and you again,
Love you, madam—dare to love you—to my grief and your dishonor,
To my endless desolation, and your impotent disdain!"   320

More mad words like these—mere madness! friend, I need not
    write them fuller,
For I hear my hot soul dropping on the lines in showers of tears.
Oh, a woman! friend, a woman! why, a beast had scarce been duller
Than roar bestial loud complaints against the shining of the spheres.

But at last there came a pause. I stood all vibrating with thunder   325
Which my soul had used. The silence drew her face up like a call.
Could you guess what word she uttered? She looked up, as if in
    wonder,
With tears beaded on her lashes, and said "Bertram!" it was all.

If she had cursed me, and she might have—or if even, with queenly
    bearing
Which at need is used by women, she had risen up and said,   330
"Sir, you are my guest, and therefore I have given you a full hearing,
Now, beseech you, choose a name exacting somewhat less, instead,"

I had borne it!—but that "Bertram"—why it lies there on the paper
A mere word, without her accent,—and you cannot judge the weight
Of the calm which crushed my passion. I seemed drowning in a
    vapour,—   335
And her gentleness destroyed me whom her scorn made desolate.

So, struck backward and exhausted by that inward flow of passion
Which had rushed on, sparing nothing, into forms of abstract truth,
By a logic agonising through unseemly demonstration,
And by youth's own anguish turning grimly grey the hairs of
    youth,—   340

By the sense accursed and instant, that if even I spake[1] wisely
I spake basely—using truth, if what I spake, indeed was true,
To avenge wrong on a woman—*her*, who sate there weighing nicely
A poor manhood's worth, found guilty of such deeds as I could do!—

By such wrong and woe exhausted—what I suffered and
    occasioned,—   345
As a wild horse through a city runs with lightning in his eyes,
And then dashing at a church's cold and passive wall, impassioned,
Strikes the death into his burning brain, and blindly drops and dies—

So I fell, struck down before her! do you blame me, friend, for
    weakness?
'Twas my strength of passion slew me!—fell before her like a
    stone.   350
Fast the dreadful world rolled from me, on its roaring wheels of
    blackness—
When the light came, I was lying in this chamber, and alone.

Oh, of course, she charged her lacqueys[2] to bear out the sickly burden,
And to cast it from her scornful sight—but not *beyond* the gate;
She is too kind to be cruel, and too haughty not to pardon   355
Such a man as I—'twere something to be level to her hate.

But for me—you now are conscious why, my friend, I write this letter,
How my life is read all backward, and the charm of life undone.
I shall leave her house at dawn; I would to-night, if I were better—
And I charge my soul to hold my body strengthened for the sun. 360

When the sun has dyed the oriel,[3] I depart, with no last gazes,
No weak moanings, (one word only, left in writing for her hands,)
Out of reach of all derision, and some unavailing praises,
To make front against this anguish in the far and foreign lands.

---

1   spake] spoke.
2   lacqueys] lackeys, here signifying her footmen.
3   oriel] a stained glass window in an oriel (a recess with a window projecting from a
    building's upper storey).

Blame me not. I would not squander life in grief—I am abstemious. 365
I but nurse my spirit's falcon that its wing may soar again.
There's no room for tears of weakness in the blind eyes of a Phemius![1]
Into work the poet kneads them,—and he does not die *till then*.

CONCLUSION

Bertram finished the last pages, while along the silence ever
Still in hot and heavy splashes, fell the tears on every leaf.   370
Having ended he leans backward in his chair, with lips that quiver
From the deep unspoken, ay, and deep unwritten thoughts of grief.

Soh![2] how still the lady standeth! 'tis a dream—a dream of mercies!
'Twixt the purple lattice-curtains, how she standeth still and pale!
'Tis a vision, sure, of mercies, sent to soften his self-curses—   375
Sent to sweep a patient quiet o'er the tossing of his wail.

"Eyes," he said, "now throbbing through me! are ye eyes that did
     undo me?
Shining eyes, like antique jewels set in Parian statue-stone![3]
Underneath that calm white forehead, are ye ever burning torrid[4]
O'er the desolate sand-desert of my heart and life undone?"   380

With a murmurous stir uncertain, in the air, the purple curtain
Swelleth in and swelleth out around her motionless pale brows,
While the gliding of the river sends a rippling noise for ever
Through the open casement whitened by the moonlight's slant repose.

Said he—"Vision of a lady! stand there silent, stand there steady!   385
Now I see it plainly, plainly; now I cannot hope or doubt—
There, the brows of mild repression—there, the lips of silent passion,
Curvéd like an archer's bow to send the bitter arrows out."

---

1   Phemius] in Homer's *Odyssey*, the minstrel who stays with Ulysses' wife Penelope
    during her husband's absence.

2   Soh!] here, an exclamation expressing surprise.

3   Parian statue-stone] marble renowned for its whiteness, from the Greek island of Paros.

4   torrid] intensely hot, burning, scorching; also burning with passion.

Ever, evermore the while in a slow silence she kept smiling,
And approached him slowly, slowly, in a gliding measured pace;   390
With her two white hands extended, as if praying one offended,
And a look of supplication, gazing earnest in his face.

Said he—"Wake me by no gesture,—sound of breath, or stir of vesture!
Let the blessèd apparition melt not yet to its divine!
No approaching—hush, no breathing! or my heart must swoon to
    death in   395
The too utter[1] life thou bringest—O thou dream of Geraldine!"

Ever, evermore the while in a slow silence she kept smiling—
But the tears ran over lightly from her eyes, and tenderly.
"Dost thou, Bertram, truly love me? Is no woman far above me
Found more worthy of thy poet-heart than such a one as *I*?"   400

Said he—"I would dream so ever, like the flowing of that river,
Flowing ever in a shadow greenly onward to the sea!
So, thou vision of all sweetness—princely to a full completeness,—
Would my heart and life flow onward—deathward—through this
    dream of THEE!"

Ever, evermore the while in a slow silence she kept smiling,   405
While the silver tears ran faster down the blushing of her cheeks;
Then with both her hands enfolding both of his, she softly told him,
"Bertram, if I say I love thee, ... 'Tis the vision only speaks."[2]

Softened, quickened to adore her, on his knee he fell before her—
And she whispered low in triumph, "It shall be as I have sworn!   410
Very rich he is in virtues,—very noble—noble, certes;
And I shall not blush in knowing that men call him lowly born."

---

1   utter] complete or absolute.

2   Victorian conduct literature emphasized that a lady must never avow her love before the
    man proposed marriage. Rank could trump gender, however; there was wide discussion
    of the appropriate protocol for the proposal in the case of the courtship of Queen Victoria
    (1819-1901) and her cousin, Albert of Saxe-Coburg-Gotha (1819-61), whom she married on
    10 February 1840, an occasion prompting EBB's "Crowned and Wedded" (1840, 1844).

From **A Vision of Poets**

First published as the lead poem in Volume II of *Poems* (1844), this was the second longest and most ambitious poem in the collection, after "A Drama of Exile." Drafted in three sections in three different notebooks between 1838-39 and 1843-44,[1] it explores, as EBB explains in her "Preface" (see above), the poet's "mission" and the "relations of genius to self-sacrifice." The poem employs the dream vision and allegorical quest integral both to Dante's work and to much medieval and Romantic English poetry, as well as a simplified form of the *terza rima* used by Dante (1265-1321) in the *Divine Comedy*. EBB portrays an unnamed male "pilgrim poet" (l. 679) who, guided by a muse-like lady, travels across a barren heath and experiences a vision after drinking from a pool representing "*World's Cruelty*" (l. 183). In this vision, which is also his initiation into poetic identity, he sees the assembled immortal "king-poets" (l. 728) of the past, described in a bravura passage excerpted here that displays EBB's command of the English and Western European poetic traditions. The split between the male "pilgrim-poet" protagonist in "A Vision of Poets" and a shadowy narrator of indeterminate gender who enters the poem in a concluding section may manifest the anxiety of authorship EBB experienced as a woman poet aspiring to enter a European tradition of "king-poets" and their "worthy son[s]" (ll. 728-29). "A Vision of Poets" was widely cited up to the end of the nineteenth century, by Emily Dickinson (1830-86) among others (see ll. 289-91n), and was praised by RB and reviewers, who were especially struck by EBB's catalogue of "king-poets." RB exclaimed, "how perfect, absolutely perfect, are those three or four pages in the 'Vision' which present the Poets—a line, a few words, and the man there,—one twang of the bow—and the arrowhead in the white—Shelley's 'white ideal all statue-blind' is—perfect,—how can I coin words?"(*BC* 11:15). While not all readers agreed, many were similarly impressed: "you feel, as you proceed, that you are in the company of one to whom all the masters of the Greek, Latin, and Italian schools are familiar in the originals," one reviewer observed (*BC* 10:370). Victorian critics particularly remarked on the parallels with Dante and Keats (see *BC*

---

1   See R D1090, 1091, 1092, and *BC* 7:265, 270, 332; 11:295.

10:340; 11:342). The appetite for poetic power evident in the poem
was not lost on some conservative reviewers, who found it inappro-
priate in a woman.[1] Criticism: Mermin 1989, Stone 1995, Scheinberg
2002, Riede 2005, and Johnson 2006.

The poet knew them. Faint and dim   286
His spirits seemed to sink in him,
Then, like a dolphin, change and swim

The current. These were poets true,
Who died for Beauty, as martyrs do   290
For Truth—the ends being scarcely two.[2]

God's prophets of the Beautiful
These poets were; of iron rule,
The rugged cilix, serge of wool.[3]

Here, Homer,[4] with the broad suspense   295
Of thunderous brows, and lips intense
Of garrulous god-innocence.

There, Shakespeare,[5] on whose forehead climb
The crowns o' the world. O eyes sublime,
With tears and laughters for all time!   300

---

1 In *Blackwood's*, James Ferrier urged "Miss Barrett" to "wash her hands completely" of
   the "poets, either great, or whom she takes for such," and to "come before the public
   in the graces of her own feminine sensibilities" (*BC* 9:363).

2 Beauty ... two] The most direct of several echoes of Keats in the poem. EBB here invokes
   the conclusion to Keats's "Ode on a Grecian Urn" (1820): "'Beauty is truth, truth beauty,'—
   that is all / Ye know on earth, and all ye need to know." Emily Dickinson alludes to these
   lines by EBB in her Poem 544, on the "Martyr Poets" (see Swyderski 2000).

3 rugged cilix, serge of wool] a garment made from the hair of goats found in Cicilia, in
   Asia Minor; here, invoking the "iron" discipline and haircloth habit worn by monks
   who mortify the flesh.

4 Homer] On EBB's love of Greek epic poet Homer, see the Introduction, and l. 329n below.
   She possessed a bust of Homer, possibly influencing the portrait here (*BC* 4:41n12; 7:149).

5 Shakespeare] here coupled with Homer because the two topped EBB's hierarchy of
   poets in "antique and modern literatures" respectively (see "The Book of the Poets,"
   CW 6:272, also *CW* 6:261, 272-75).

Here, Æschylus,[1] the women swooned
To see so awful, when he frowned
As the gods did![2]—he standeth crowned.

Euripides,[3] with close and mild
Scholastic lips,—that could be wild,   305
And laugh or sob out like a child

Even in the classes. Sophocles,[4]
With that king's look which, down the trees,
Followed the dark effigies

Of the lost Theban.[5] Hesiod[6] old,   310
Who, somewhat blind and deaf and cold,
Cared most for gods and bulls. And bold

Electric Pindar,[7] quick as fear,
With race-dust on his cheeks, and clear

---

1   Æschylus] c.525-456 BCE, the first great Greek writer of tragedy and in EBB's view
the "sublimest of the sublime Greeks"; she also called him "the obscurest poet in the
world, .. with the exception of ... we will say .. Mr. Browning!" (BC 6:148). She had
read all of Aeschylus's plays by the end of January 1832 (Diary 207), and subsequently
published two different translations of Prometheus Bound in her 1833 and 1850 collec-
tions. See also ["Aeschylus's Monodrama"] in this edition.

2   the women swooned ... did!] James Ferrier observed of this passage in Blackwood's: "It
is well known that no pregnant woman could look Æschylus in the face when the fit of
inspiration was on him, without having cause to regret her indiscretion"—i.e., suffer a
miscarriage; "delicacy" dictated the matter be "only barely hinted at," Ferrier added,
punningly complaining of what he saw as "miscarried" grammar in the passage (BC
9:360). Porter and Clark (CW 2:388) suggest that EBB was alluding to the effect on
Athenian women of the Furies during the performance of the Eumenides (458 BCE).

3   Euripides] Greek tragic poet (c. 484-c. 406 BCE).

4   Sophocles] Greek tragic poet (c. 495-c. 405 BCE), known for his trilogy of plays about
Oedipus, King of Thebes, to which ll.308-10 allude. EBB had read all the plays of both
Sophocles and Euripides by the end of March 1832 (Diary 229).

5   lost Theban] Oedipus, King of Thebes, who, after blinding himself, is led by the gods
from an olive grove into the underworld.

6   Hesiod] Greek poet (c. eighth c. BCE) credited with writing the Theogony (chiefly
about gods) and Works and Days (about bulls and farm creatures). EBB translated
extracts from Hesiod in the 1840s (see R D1221-25).

7   Pindar] Greek lyric poet (c. 522-c. 446 BCE), whose poetry commemorated Olympic
games victories.

Slant startled eyes that seem to hear 315

The chariot rounding the last goal,
To hurtle past it in his soul.
And Sappho,[1] with that gloriole[2]

Of ebon[3] hair on calméd brows.
O poet-woman! none forgoes 320
The leap, attaining the repose!

Theocritus,[4] with glittering locks
Dropt sideway, as betwixt the rocks
He watched the visionary flocks.

And Aristophanes,[5] who took 325
The world with mirth, and laughter-struck
The hollow caves of Thought and woke

The infinite echoes hid in each.
And Virgil:[6] shade of Mantuan beech[7]
Did help the shade of bay to reach 330

---

1   Sappho] On Sappho, and EBB's private comparison of herself to the celebrated Greek
    poet, see the Introduction; the "leap" in l. 321 is an allusion to Sappho's legendary sui-
    cide. EBB also compared George Sand (see her two 1844 sonnets "To George Sand")
    to Sappho, "who broke off a fragment of her soul to be guessed by—as creation did by
    its fossils" (*BC* 8:211).

2   gloriole] aureole or halo; derived from "glory," and literally meaning, a bit of glory.

3   ebon] black or ebony in color.

4   Theocritus] Greek poet (c. 308-c. 240 BCE) from Syracuse, famed for his pastoral
    idylls—poems on rustic subjects. Cf. EBB's allusion to Theocritus in the opening of
    Sonnets from the Portuguese (1850).

5   Aristophanes] Greek poet-dramatist (c. 447-c. 386 BCE), renowned for his com-
    edies.

6   Virgil] Roman poet Publius Vergilius Maro (c. 70-c. 19 BCE), author of the epic *The
    Aeneid*.

7   Mantuan beech] alluding to Virgil's birth in Mantua and his mother's prophetic dream
    that she gave birth to a laurel or bay tree that took root and sprang up full grown. EBB's
    scant praise reflects her view that Homer and the Greeks were generally superior to
    Virgil and the Roman poets. She "tried hard to like olives & the Æneid upon principle,"
    but was much more drawn to "Homer's fire," declaring that one might as well "compare
    the mouse with the mountain!" as Virgil with Homer (*BC* 2:107).

And knit around his forehead high.
For his gods wore less majesty
Than his brown bees hummed deathlessly.[1]

Lucretius[2]—nobler than his mood;
Who dropped his plummet[3] down the broad   335
Deep universe, and said "No God,"

Finding no bottom: he denied
Divinely the divine, and died
Chief poet on the Tiber-side[4]

By grace of God! his face is stern,   340
As one compelled, in spite of scorn,
To teach a truth he would not learn.

And Ossian,[5] dimly seen or guessed:
Once counted greater than the rest,
When mountain-winds blew out his vest.   345

---

1 His brown bees ... deathlessly] Virgil's fourth *Georgic* describes the lives and habits of bees.

2 Lucretius] Titus Lucretius Carus (c. 99-c. 55 BCE), Roman poet and philosopher, whose philosophical epic *De Rerum Natura* (*On the Nature of the Universe*) claimed the world could be explained without recourse to divine intervention. EBB saw him as a "Heathen" writer whose works paradoxically testified to "the reflection of divinely revealed lights" (*BC* 2:213). Cf. Tennyson's dramatic monologue "Lucretius" (1868).

3 plummet] a leaden weight used to determine vertical distance or depth.

4 Tiber-side] the Tiber River runs through the city of Rome.

5 Ossian] a reference to *The Poems of Ossian, Translated by James Macpherson* (1762), presented as the works of a third-century Gaelic bard. The veiled skepticism of ll. 342-45 reflects EBB's agreement with the view of Samuel Johnson (1709-84), Sir Walter Scott (1771-1832), and others that Macpherson was an "impostor." She considered Ossian "as the poetical lay figure upon which Mr. Macpherson dared to cast his personality" (*BC* 6:268) and carried on an extended debate with Hugh Stuart Boyd (see the Introduction) in 1842-43 concerning the authenticity and quality of "Ossian's" poems, a subject much discussed in the earlier decades of the nineteenth century (see *BC* 6: 267-68, 281-83, 297-98, 306-07, 318, 328, 335, 345-46; *BC* 7:35, 73-74, 80).

And Spenser[1] drooped his dreaming head
(With languid sleep-smile you had said
From his own verse engenderèd)[2]

On Ariosto's,[3] till they ran
Their curls in one.—The Italian   350
Shot nimbler heat of bolder man

From his fine lids. And Dante stern
And sweet,[4] whose spirit was an urn
For wine and milk poured out in turn.

Hard-souled Alfieri;[5] and fancy-willed   355
Boiardo,[6]—who with laughter filled
The pauses of the jostled shield.

And Berni,[7] with a hand stretched out
To sleek that storm. And, not without
The wreath he died in, and the doubt   360

1   Spenser] Edmund Spenser, author of the *Faerie Queene* (1590, 1596), echoed in EBB's
    representation of the lady on the white palfrey in an earlier passage of "A Vision of
    Poets."

2   engenderèd] begotten.

3   Ariosto's] Ludovico Ariosto (1474-1533), Italian poet who wrote the epic *Orlando
    Furioso*. Spenser's indebtedness to Ariosto is made clear in Spenser's letters to friend
    and critic, Gabriel Harvey (1550-1631).

4   Dante] "Dante's poetry seems to come down in hail, rather than in rain—but count
    me the drops congealed in one hail stone!," EBB said, defending his poetic "crown"
    to RB (*BC* 10:189).

5   Alfieri] Vittorio Alfieri (1749-1803), Italian dramatist important in the rise of Italian
    nationalism.

6   Boiardo] Matteo Maria Boiardo (c.1441-94), Italian poet; his greatest work, the
    unfinished *Orlando Inamorato*, inspired Ariosto's *Orlando Furioso*.

7   Berni] Francesco Berni (c.1497-1536), Italian poet who stylistically reworked Boiardo's
    Orlando Inamorato.

He died by, Tasso![1] bard and lover,
Whose visions were too thin to cover
The face of a false woman over.

And soft Racine,[2]—and grave Corneille,[3]
The orator of rhymes, whose wail   365
Scarce shook his purple.[4] And Petrarch[5] pale,

From whose brainlighted heart were thrown
A thousand thoughts beneath the sun,
Each lucid with the name of One.

And Camoens,[6] with that look he had,   370
Compelling India's Genius sad
From the wave through the Lusiad,—

The murmurs of the storm-cape ocean
Indrawn in vibrative emotion
Along the verse. And while devotion   375

In his wild eyes fantastic shone
Under the tonsure[7] blown upon
By airs celestial,—Calderon.[8]

---

1 Tasso] The author of *Gerusalemme Liberata* (*Jerusalem Delivered*, published 1581), Torquato Tasso (1544-95) was an Italian poet and courtier in the court of Duke Alfonso II of Ferrara (1533-97), the model for the Duke in RB's "My Last Duchess" (1842). Tasso's doomed love for Leonara or Eleonore d'Este of Ferrara made him a tragic hero of interest to RB and others. Psychological instability led to his intermittent confinement; he died in Rome shortly before he was to be crowned as Italy's poet laureate (an event alluded to in the "wreath"—i.e., wreath of laurels—of l. 360).

2 Racine] Jean Racine (1639-99), French dramatist and poet of the neoclassical style.

3 Corneille] Pierre Corneille (1606-84), French dramatist.

4 his purple] a reference to the purple or declamatory style that EBB associated with Corneille. In "An Essay on Mind" (1826), ll. 1061-68, she commends English poets for not imitating the style of Corneille and Racine.

5 Petrarch] the famous Italian poet who wrote sonnets to his lady Laura, the "One" alluded to in l. 369. On EBB's response to these, see the headnote to *Sonnets from the Portuguese*, p. 206.

6 Camoens] Luis Vaz de Camoëns (1524-80), Portuguese author of the epic *The Lusiads*, on the discovery of the passage to the East Indies or India by his kinsman, the explorer Vasco de Gama (c. 1469-1524). See also EBB's "Catarina to Camoens" in this edition.

7 tonsure] the part of a priest's or monk's head left bare by shaving it.

8 Calderon] Pedro Calderon de la Barca (1600-81), Spanish dramatist; he became a devoted priest in 1651.

And bold De Vega,[1]—who breathed quick
Verse after verse, till death's old trick   380 .
Put pause to life and rhetorick.

And Goethe[2]—with that reaching eye
His soul reached out from, far and high,
And fell from inner entity.[3]

And Schiller,[4] with heroic front,[5]   385
Worthy of Plutarch's[6] kiss upon't,
Too large for wreath of modern wont.[7]

And Chaucer, with his infantine
Familiar clasp of things divine.[8]
That mark upon his lip is wine.[9]   390

---

1 De Vega] Felix de Lope de Vega Carpio (1562-1635), Spanish dramatist and poet;
   despite joining the priesthood in c. 1614, de Vega continued his many love affairs and
   fathered many children.

2 Goethe] Johann Wolfgang von Goethe (1749-1832), German poet, playwright, novelist,
   and natural philosopher, perhaps best known for his two-part drama *Faust* (1808, 1832).

3 fell from inner entity] i.e., from inner essence or being.

4 Schiller] Johann Christoph Friedrich von Schiller (1759-1805), German poet, drama-
   tist, essayist, and historian. EBB's "The Death of Pan" (1844) is a poetic response to
   Schiller's "The Gods of Greece" (1788).

5 front] forehead.

6 Plutarch's] Mestrius Plutarchus (c. 45-c. 125 CE), Greek essayist best known for his
   biographies of Greek and Roman heroes in *Parallel Lives*.

7 wont] custom or habit; EBB implies that Schiller is a heroic figure (like Plutarch's
   heroes), too large to be measured by a modern "wreath," or conventional modes of
   tribute.

8 Chaucer ... divine] Although Chaucer is best known for *The Canterbury Tales*, the work
   most directly echoed in "A Vision of Poets" is his *House of Fame*. EBB spoke of Chaucer's
   "familiarity" in referring to God as frequently "as a child has its father's name" on its lips
   in an 1843 letter to her cousin John Kenyon (*BC* 7:21) and contributed to *The Poems of
   Geoffrey Chaucer, Modernized* (1841), edited by Richard Hengist Horne (see the Introduc-
   tion). She also owned a bust of Chaucer that presided over her collection of English poetry
   in her bedroom-study in Wimpole Street (*BC* 7:149), described the first era of English
   poetry as "the Chaucerian," and included extensive comments on his contributions to
   English poetry in "The Book of the Poets" (see *CW* 6:243-62, 278-79).

9 That mark ... is wine] alluding to the royal grant providing Chaucer with a daily
   pitcher of wine (*CW* 2:393).

Here, Milton's[1] eyes strike piercing-dim.
The shapes of suns and stars did swim
Like clouds from them, and granted him

God for sole vision. Cowley,[2] there;
Whose active fancy debonaire[3]   395
Drew straws like amber—foul to fair.

Drayton[4] and Browne,[5] —with smiles they drew
From outward nature, still kept new
From their own inward nature true.

And Marlowe,[6] Webster,[7] Fletcher,[8] Ben—[9]   400
Whose fire-hearts sowed our furrows when
The world was worthy of such men.

And Burns,[10] with pungent passionings
Set in his eyes. Deep lyric springs
Are of the fire-mount's issuings.   405

---

1   Milton's] John Milton (1608-74), the author of *Paradise Lost*, became blind in 1651. For
    EBB's poetic responses to Milton, see "The Virgin Mary to the Child Jesus" (1838),
    her "Preface" to Poems (1844), and "A Drama of Exile"; for her comments on him as
    a lesser genius than Homer, see *CW* 6:287-89.

2   Cowley] Abraham Cowley (1618-67), English metaphysical poet; for EBB's view of
    him see *CW* 6:283-85.

3   debonaire] of a gentle or gracious disposition.

4   Drayton] Michael Drayton (1563-1631), English poet; see CW 6:264.

5   Browne] William Browne, author of the poem's epigraph.

6   Marlowe] Christopher Marlowe (1564-93), English dramatist and poet; Shakespeare's
    short-lived rival and greatest predecessor.

7   Webster] John Webster (c. 1580-c. 1625), English dramatist, known for his Jacobean
    masterpieces such as *The Duchess of Malfi* (c. 1614).

8   Fletcher] John Fletcher (1576-1625), English dramatist who collaborated with Francis
    Beaumont (1584-1616), Shakespeare, and others; see *CW* 6:264, 276-77.

9   Ben] Ben Jonson (1574-1637), English dramatist and poet laureate, known for his
    comedies of humors such as *Every Man in His Humour* (c. 1598); see *CW* 6:275-76.

10 Burns] Robert Burns (1759-96), Scottish poet, author of over four hundred songs and
    ballads (including "Auld Lang Syne"); EBB saw him as contributing to the "move-
    ment towards Nature" in English poetry (*CW* 6:299-300).

And Shelley,[1] in his white ideal,
All statue-blind! And Keats the real
Adonis,[2] with the hymeneal[3]

Fresh vernal buds half sunk between
His youthful curls, kissed straight and sheen[4]   410
In his Rome-grave, by Venus queen.

And poor, proud Byron,—sad as grave,
And salt as life: forlornly brave,[5]
And quivering with the dart he drave.[6]

And visionary Coleridge,[7] who   415
Did sweep his thoughts as angels do
Their wings, with cadence[8] up the Blue.

---

1   Shelley] Percy Bysshe Shelley (1792-1822), English Romantic poet. EBB describes her
    early response to his poetry in her 1831-32 *Diary* (102,138). In her letters she is more
    critical, describing him as "that high & yet too low, elemental poet, who froze in cold
    glory between Heaven & earth" (*BC* 5:60), although she still considered him a "great
    poet" (*BC* 6:144; see also 243; 8:76).

2   Keats ... the real Adonis] alluding to Shelley's representation of Keats as Adonis (in Greek
    mythology, a beautiful youth who became a consort of Venus, goddess of love) in his elegy
    for Keats, *Adonais* (1821), which EBB describes as "perfectly exquisite" in her 1831-32 *Diary*
    (138). EBB had read many of Keats's other poems by 1831-32, including *Hyperion* (1820),
    which she praised as "poetry of wonderful grandeur" (*Diary* 93-94). In December 1842
    she also received two pages of Keats's poetry in ms and a sketch of Keats's profile from the
    painter Benjamin Robert Haydon (1786-1846), and she drew her own sketch of Keats in
    response. For her high praise of Keats's "fine genius" and her correspondence concerning
    him, see *BC* 6:113, 126, 243, 246, 251, 254; 8:92; 9:81; 11: 67-68.

3   hymeneal] pertaining to marriage (from Hymen, the classical god of marriage).

4   sheen] beautiful, bright, resplendent.

5   Byron] on Byron, a major influence on EBB's poetic formation, see the Introduction and
    "Stanzas on the Death of Lord Byron" (1824, 1826). The characterization of Byron here reflects
    EBB's repeated critique of the mid-Victorian reaction against him—"the present fashion of
    decrying Byron as a poet" (*BC* 6:171). See also *BC* 6:192; 8:176, 216; 13:280; and *CW* 6:301-02).

6   drave] past tense of drive.

7   Coleridge] Samuel Taylor Coleridge (1772-1824), who collaborated with William
    Wordsworth on *Lyrical Ballads* (1798). On EBB's defense of Coleridge's obscurity and
    her view in 1842-43 that he had an "intenser" or "grander genius" than Wordsworth,
    see *BC* 6:75; 7:123; also *BC* 6:142, 148, 171.

8   cadence] rhythm; here a reference to the meter of Coleridge's poetry.

These poets faced, and many more,
The lighted altar looming o'er
The clouds of incense dim and hoar:[1]   420

And all their faces, in the lull
Of natural things, looked wonderful
With life and death and deathless rule.

All, still as stone, and yet intense;
As if by spirit's vehemence   425
That stone were carved, and not by sense.

But where the heart of each should beat,
There seemed a wound instead of it,
From whence the blood dropped to their feet,

Drop after drop—dropped heavily,   430
As century follows century
Into the deep eternity.

The Cry of the Children

"The first stanza came into my head in a hurricane, & I was obliged
to make the other stanzas like it," EBB said of this widely influen-
tial poem (*BC* 7:331), first published in August 1843 in *Blackwood's*
and collected in EBB's 1844 *Poems*. Her poetic articulation of
the "cry" of England's children owed "its utterance," she testi-
fied, to the work of her friend, correspondent, and collaborator
R.H. Horne[2] with the Royal Commission for the Employment of
Children in Mines and Factories and to the Commission reports
(*BC* 7:274). Established in 1840, the Commission generated har-
rowing accounts of the working conditions and lack of educational
opportunities among child laborers, some of them as young as

---

1   hoar] here, grayish-white in color, with connotations of another common sense of the
    word—old or venerable.
2   Horne] Richard Hengist Horne (1802-84), author of dramas, critical essays, and
    poetry. On EBB's correspondence and collaborations with him, see the Introduction
    and *BC* 4:317-20.

four and working up to sixteen hours a day (see Appendix B.II). Horne's report on the small metal industries of Wolverhampton in South Staffordshire detailed many instances of stunted, illiterate, deformed, and mutilated children, and was subsequently cited by Friedrich Engels[1] in *The Condition of the Working Class in England in 1844* (1845). EBB's poem draws on Romantic representations of the child's vision by William Wordsworth and by William Blake, in particular Wordsworth's lyrical ballad "We Are Seven" (1798) and Blake's *Songs of Innocence and of Experience* (1794), which EBB read in 1842.[2] The poem's pointed address to factory owners and legislators as "my brothers" gains added resonance from an unpublished fragment EBB addressed to "My sisters!," and from the "regular quarrel" she subsequently had with her own brothers when they strongly opposed and ridiculed her interest in writing an invited poem for the Anti-Corn Law League.[3] Surviving drafts support EBB's description of the compositional process as a "hurricane," yet also underscore the revising that followed. She continued to make minor revisions in the poem up to 1856.[4] In her 1850 *Poems* and subsequent editions, she "arranged" that this poem should immediately follow "The Runaway Slave at Pilgrim's Point" in order "to appear impartial as to national grievances" (*LTM* 3:310); in these collections, it is followed by the contrasting representation of protected childhood innocence in "A Child Asleep."

"The Cry of the Children" was credited with helping to increase the public pressure that led to the limited regulations to improve working conditions imposed by the 1844 Labour in Factories Act and the 1847 Factory Act known as the "Ten Hours Act." Although one reviewer criticized "Miss Barrett" for joining in the "mistaken clamour" against the "factory system," observing that she had never

---

1 Engels] Friedrich Engels (1820-95), German socialist and intellectual; collaborator with Karl Marx (1819-83) on the *Communist Manifesto* (1848).

2 EBB was lent a copy of Blake's work as well as a biography of him; like many other Victorians, she assumed Blake had a "shattered intellect," yet found "wild glances of the poetical faculty" in his work (*BC* 5:308). She transcribed several poems from *Songs of Innocence and of Experience* (see R D1415, D1427).

3 On the fragment beginning "My sisters!" see Stone and Taylor 2006; on EBB's quarrel with her brothers, see the Introduction, p. 24, note 1.

4 For the 1843 *Blackwood's* text of the poem, see the supplementary website.

visited "one of those 'hives of industry,'" most reviewers praised the poem's power (*BC* 9:379; 8:290, 375; 9:344, 372, 375). The poem figured prominently in a lecture given by William Johnson Fox[1] in 1846 in the National Hall of the Workingmen's Association in Holborn (*BC* 12:388, 401-03), and its impact spanned the Atlantic: "It is known throughout America," Cornelius Mathews[2] observed in 1844 (*BC* 9:344). The poem was later translated into Italian and Russian,[3] and inspired both the title and the scenario of the 1912 film *The Cry of the Children*.[4] The poet herself acknowledged the "roughness" of the poem's "versification," criticized by both Victorian and twentieth-century readers (see *BC* 7:331 and Leighton 1992, 96)—but she also pointed out, in the same letter, the purposeful nature of her licenses with meter (see the Introduction and *BC* 7:331-32). "The cadence, lingering, broken, and full of wail, is one of the mos[t] perfect adaptations of sound to sense in literature," one Victorian reviewer noted (*BC* 9:365). The title echoes the words of God to Moses in Exodus 3.9, concerning "the cry of the children of Israel" under the "oppression" of the Egyptians, where the term "children" applies metaphorically to the Israelites generally. Criticism: Cooper 1988, Mermin 1989, Leighton 1992, Dillon 2001, Shires 2001, Avery and Stott 2003, Levine 2006, and Tucker 2006b.

"Φεῦ, φεῦ, τί προσδέρκεσθέ μ' ὄμμασιν, τέκνα"—Medea.[5]

---

1 William Johnson Fox] (1786-1864), Unitarian preacher and author, a founder of *The Westminster Review*, co-editor of *The Monthly Repository*, and a mentor to RB; see BC 3:313-14.

2 Cornelius Mathews] (1817-89), American author and editor who helped arrange for the publication of EBB's periodical poems and 1844 collection in the United States. See *BC* 6:363-64.

3 On the Italian translations, see Bisignano 1964, 207-08, 214-15; on the Russian, see Waddington 1997.

4 The most famous film produced by the Thanhouser Company, established in 1909 by the American film producer Edwin Thanhouser (1865-1956).

5 MEDEA] "Woe, Woe, why do you look upon me with your eyes, my children?"—or, more freely translated, "Alas, alas, my children, why do you look at me?" From the tragedy *Medea* (431 BCE) by the Greek playwright Euripides (c. 480-406 BCE). The betrayed and anguished Medea utters the words of the epigraph as she contemplates her children just before murdering them.

I

Do ye hear the children weeping, O my brothers,
       Ere the sorrow comes with years?
They are leaning their young heads against their mothers,
       And *that* cannot stop their tears.
The young lambs are bleating in the meadows,   5
   The young birds are chirping in the nest,
The young fawns are playing with the shadows,
   The young flowers are blowing¹ toward the west—
But the young, young children, O my brothers,
       They are weeping bitterly!   10
They are weeping in the playtime of the others,
       In the country of the free.

II

Do you question the young children in the sorrow,
       Why their tears are falling so?
The old man may weep for his to-morrow   15
       Which is lost in Long Ago.
The old tree is leafless in the forest,
   The old year is ending in the frost,
The old wound, if stricken, is the sorest,
   The old hope is hardest to be lost.   20
But the young, young children, O my brothers,
       Do you ask them why they stand
Weeping sore before the bosoms of their mothers,
       In our happy Fatherland?

III

They look up with their pale and sunken faces,   25
       And their looks are sad to see,
For the man's hoary anguish draws and presses
       Down the cheeks of infancy.
"Your old earth," they say, "is very dreary;
   Our young feet," they say, "are very weak!   30
Few paces have we taken, yet are weary—

---

1 blowing] blooming.

Our grave-rest is very far to seek.
Ask the aged why they weep, and not the children;
     For the outside earth is cold;
And we young ones stand without, in our bewildering,   35
     And the graves are for the old."

IV
"True," say the children, "it may happen
     That we die before our time.
Little Alice died last year—her grave is shapen
     Like a snowball, in the rime.[1]   40
We looked into the pit prepared to take her.
    Was no room for any work in the close clay!
From the sleep wherein she lieth none will wake her,
    Crying, 'Get up, little Alice! it is day.'
If you listen by that grave, in sun and shower,   45
    With your ear down, little Alice never cries.
Could we see her face, be sure we should not know her,
    For the smile has time for growing in her eyes.
And merry go her moments, lulled and stilled in
     The shroud by the kirk-chime![2]   50
It is good when it happens," say the children,
     "That we die before our time."

V
Alas, alas, the children! they are seeking
     Death in life, as best to have.
They are binding up their hearts away from breaking,   55
     With a cerement[3] from the grave.
Go out, children, from the mine and from the city,
    Sing out, children, as the little thrushes do.
Pluck you handfuls of the meadow-cowslips pretty,
    Laugh aloud, to feel your fingers let them through!   60
But they answer, "Are your cowslips of the meadows

---

1 rime] hoar frost or frozen mist. Cf. the child in the graveyard in Wordsworth's "We
   Are Seven," ll. 57-60.

2 kirk-chime] chime of the church bells.

3 cerement] shroud.

Like our weeds anear[1] the mine?
Leave us quiet in the dark of the coal-shadows,
      From your pleasures fair and fine!

VI

"For oh;" say the children, "we are weary,   65
      And we cannot run or leap.
If we cared for any meadows, it were merely
      To drop down in them and sleep.
Our knees tremble sorely in the stooping,
   We fall upon our faces, trying to go;   70
And, underneath our heavy eyelids drooping,
   The reddest flower would look as pale as snow.
For, all day, we drag our burden tiring
      Through the coal-dark, underground—
Or, all day, we drive the wheels of iron   75
      In the factories, round and round.

VII

"For, all day, the wheels are droning, turning,—
      Their wind comes in our faces,—
Till our hearts turn,—our heads, with pulses burning,
      And the walls turn in their places.   80
Turns the sky in the high window blank and reeling,
   Turns the long light that drops adown[2] the wall,
Turn the black flies that crawl along the ceiling,
   All are turning, all the day, and we with all.
And all day, the iron wheels are droning,   85
      And sometimes we could pray,
'O ye wheels,' (breaking out in a mad moaning)
      'Stop! be silent for to-day!'"

VIII

Ay! be silent! Let them hear each other breathing
      For a moment, mouth to mouth!   90

---

1 anear] near to.
2 adown] archaic for downward or down.

Let them touch each other's hands, in a fresh wreathing[1]
    Of their tender human youth!
Let them feel that this cold metallic motion
    Is not all the life God fashions or reveals.
Let them prove their living souls against the notion   95
    That they live in you, or under you, O wheels!—
Still, all day, the iron wheels go onward,
    Grinding life down from its mark;
And the children's souls, which God is calling sunward,
    Spin on blindly in the dark.   100

IX

Now tell the poor young children, O my brothers,
    To look up to Him and pray;
So the blessèd One who blesseth all the others,
    Will bless them another day.
They answer, "Who is God that He should hear us,   105
    While the rushing of the iron wheels is stirred?
When we sob aloud, the human creatures near us
    Pass by, hearing not, or answer not a word.
And *we* hear not (for the wheels in their resounding)
    Strangers speaking at the door.   110
Is it likely God, with angels singing round him,
    Hears our weeping any more?

X

"Two words, indeed, of praying we remember,
    And at midnight's hour of harm,
'Our Father,' looking upward in the chamber,   115
    We say softly for a charm.[2]
We know no other words, except 'Our Father,'

---

1 wreathing] intertwining.

2 charm] "A fact rendered pathetically historical by Mr. Horne's report of his commission. The name of the poet of 'Orion' and 'Cosmo de' Medici' has, however, a change of associations, and comes in time to remind me that we have some noble poetic heat of literature still,—however open to the reproach of being somewhat gelid in our humanity.—1844" [EBB's note]; *gelid*, i.e., ice-cold. See the report on Eliza Field, in Appendix B.II.2. For the very different response of another poet, Eliza Cook (1817-89), to Horne's account of this case, see Leighton 1992, 95.

And we think that, in some pause of angels' song,
God may pluck them with the silence sweet to gather,
    And hold both within His right hand which is strong.   120
'Our Father!' If He heard us, He would surely
        (For they call Him good and mild)
Answer, smiling down the steep world very purely,
        'Come and rest with me, my child.'

XI
"But, no!" say the children, weeping faster,   125
        "He is speechless as a stone.
And they tell us, of His image is the master
        Who commands us to work on.
Go to!" say the children,—"up in Heaven,
    Dark, wheel-like, turning clouds are all we find.   130
Do not mock us; grief has made us unbelieving—
    We look up for God, but tears have made us blind."
Do you hear the children weeping and disproving,
        O my brothers, what ye preach?
For God's possible is taught by His world's loving,   135
        And the children doubt of each.

XII
And well may the children weep before you!
        They are weary ere they run.
They have never seen the sunshine, nor the glory,
        Which is brighter than the sun.   140
They know the grief of man, without his wisdom.
    They sink in man's despair, without its calm;
Are slaves, without the liberty in Christdom,
    Are martyrs, by the pang without the palm,— [1]
Are worn, as if with age, yet unretrievingly   145
        The harvest of its memories cannot reap,—
Are orphans of the earthly love and heavenly.
        Let them weep! let them weep!

---

1   palm] branches of the palm tree, carried by martyrs and associated with Christ and
    holiness; see John 12.12-19.

XIII

They look up, with their pale and sunken faces,
    And their look is dread to see,   150
For they mind[1] you of their angels in high places,
    With eyes turned on Deity!—
"How long" they say, "how long, O cruel nation,
  Will you stand, to move the world,[2] on a child's heart,—
Stifle down with a mailed[3] heel its palpitation,   155
    And tread onward to your throne amid the mart?[4]
Our blood splashes upward, O gold-heaper,
    And your purple shows your path!
But the child's sob in the silence curses deeper
    Than the strong man in his wrath."   160

Bertha in the Lane

Singled out by RB along with his favorite "Catarina to Camoens" (*BC* 10:43, 11:16, 159), "Bertha in the Lane" (published 1844) also frequently won praise from mid-Victorian reviewers, who generally interpreted it as a sentimental portrayal of feminine self-sacrifice, like the *Blackwood's* reviewer who judged it "the purest picture of a broken heart that ever drew tears from the eyes of woman or of man" (*BC* 9:354). Another reviewer termed it "the truest to the human heart of any [poem] in the language" (*BC* 9:374), while the poet herself reported a "tradition" that the poem provoked a "gush of tears" down "the Plutonian cheeks of a lawyer" (*BC* 10:140; see also *BC* 9:330, 347; 10:347, 370; *BC* 11:355). Reviewers (including Edgar Allan Poe) categorized it generically as a "ballad" (*BC* 10:352, 370)—the term "dramatic monologue" was not yet in use. One reviewer pointed to its affinities with the English idyls of Tennyson, terming it "a

---

1   mind] remind.

2   stand, to move the world] alluding to a declaration attributed to the Greek mathematician Archimedes (c. 278-212 BCE), echoed in EBB's letters (*BC* 2:75; 9:66): "Give me a firm place to stand and I will move the earth."

3   mailed] armored with metal.

4   mart] marketplace.

village tragedy" and pairing it with Tennyson's "New Year's Eve," a portion of the 1832 poem "The May Queen" (*BC* 9:322), which intimates a similar rivalry between sisters. Stephenson notes the poem's parallels with the traditional ballad "The Twa Sisters" (1989, 44). EBB also knew Tennyson's variant on this ballad, "The Sisters" (1842), in which the narrative unfolds somewhat differently (*BC* 6:212). Recent critical response has been divided on whether the poem is a lyric portrait of a virtuously self-sacrificing woman or a dramatic monologue in which ironic character revelation betrays the speaker. Criticism: Cooper 1988, Mermin 1989, Lewis 1998, Stephenson 1989, Stone 1994, and Simonsen 1997.[1]

I

Put the broidery-frame[2] away,
   For my sewing is all done.
The last thread is used to-day,
   And I need not join it on.
   Though the clock stands at the noon   5
   I am weary. I have sewn,
   Sweet, for thee, a wedding-gown.

II

 Sister, help me to the bed,
   And stand near me, Dearest-sweet.
Do not shrink nor be afraid,   10
   Blushing with a sudden heat!
   No one standeth in the street?—
   By God's love I go to meet,
   Love I thee with love complete.

III

Lean thy face down! drop it in   15
   These two hands, that I may hold

---

1 See also W. David Shaw, *Origins of the Monologue: The Hidden God* (Toronto: U of Toronto P, 1999).

2 broidery] embroidery.

'Twixt their palms thy cheek and chin,
   Stroking back the curls of gold.
   'Tis a fair, fair face, in sooth[1]—
   Larger eyes and redder mouth   20
   Than mine were in my first youth.

IV

Thou art younger by seven years—
   Ah!—so bashful at my gaze,
That the lashes, hung with tears,
   Grow too heavy to upraise?   25
   I would wound thee by no touch
   Which thy shyness feels as such.
   Dost thou mind me, Dear, so much?

V

Have I not been nigh a mother
   To thy sweetness—tell me, Dear?   30
Have we not loved one another
   Tenderly, from year to year,
   Since our dying mother mild
   Said with accents undefiled,
   "Child, be mother to this child!"   35

VI

Mother, mother, up in heaven,
   Stand up on the jasper sea,[2]
And be witness I have given
   All the gifts required of me,—
   Hope that blessed me, bliss that crowned,   40
   Love, that left me with a wound,
   Life itself, that turneth round!

VII

Mother, mother, thou art kind,

---

1   sooth] truth.

2   jasper] see Revelation 21.11: "Even like a jasper stone, clear as crystal."

Thou art standing in the room,
In a molten glory shrined,   45
  That rays off into the gloom!
  But thy smile is bright and bleak
  Like cold waves—I cannot speak,
  I sob in it, and grow weak.

VIII
Ghostly mother, keep aloof   50
  One hour longer from my soul—
For I still am thinking of
  Earth's warm-beating joy and dole[1]!
  On my finger is a ring
  Which I still see glittering,   55
  When the night hides everything.

IX
Little sister, thou art pale!
  Ah, I have a wandering brain—
But I lose that fever-bale,[2]
  And my thoughts grow calm again.   60
  Lean down closer—closer still!
  I have words thine ear to fill,—[3]
  And would kiss thee at my will.

X
Dear, I heard thee in the spring,
  Thee and Robert—through the trees,—   65
When we all went gathering
  Boughs of May-bloom for the bees.
  Do not start so! think instead
  How the sunshine over head
  Seemed to trickle through the shade.   70

---

1   dole] grief or sorrow.
2   fever-bale] fever torment (with connotations of death).
3   Lean ... ear to fill,—] cf. Eve's dream of a tempting voice (Satan's) "Close at mine ear" in Milton's *Paradise Lost* (5:36).

XI

What a day it was, that day!
   Hills and vales did openly
Seem to heave and throb away
   At the sight of the great sky.
   And the Silence, as it stood   75
   In the Glory's golden flood,
   Audibly did bud—and bud.

XII

Through the winding hedgerows green,
   How we wandered, I and you,—
With the bowery tops shut in,   80
   And the gates that showed the view!
   How we talked there! thrushes soft
   Sang our praises out—or oft
   Bleatings took them, from the croft[1]

XIII

Till the pleasure grown too strong   85
   Left me muter evermore,
And, the winding road being long,
   I walked out of sight, before,
   And so, wrapt in musings fond,
   Issued (past the wayside pond)   90
   On the meadow-lands beyond.

XIV

I sate[2] down beneath the beech
   Which leans over to the lane,
And the far sound of your speech
   Did not promise any pain;
   And I blessed you full and free,   95
   With a smile stooped tenderly
   O'er the May-flowers on my knee.

---

1   croft] small enclosed field or pasture.

2   sate] sat.

XV

But the sound grew into word
    As the speakers drew more near—   100
Sweet, forgive me that I heard
    What you wished me not to hear.
    Do not weep so—do not shake—
    Oh,—I heard thee, Bertha,* make
    Good true answers for my sake.   105

XVI

Yes, and HE too! let him stand
    In thy thoughts, untouched by blame.
Could he help it, if my hand
    He had claimed with hasty claim?
    That was wrong perhaps—but then   110
    Such things be—and will, again.
    Women cannot judge for men.

XVII

Had he seen thee, when he swore
    He would love but me alone?
Thou wert absent—sent before   115
    To our kin in Sidmouth town.[1]
    When he saw thee who art best
    Past compare, and loveliest,
    He but judged thee as the rest.

XVIII

Could we blame him with grave words,   120
    Thou and I, Dear, if we might?
Thy brown eyes have looks like birds,
    Flying straightway to the light:
    Mine are older.—Hush!—look out—
    Up the street! Is none without?   125
    How the poplar swings about.

---

1 Sidmouth] a town on the southern coast of Devonshire where EBB's family lived from
    August 1832 to 1835.

XIX

And that hour—beneath the beech,
  When I listened in a dream,
And he said in his deep speech,
    That he owed me all *esteem*,—   130
    Each word swam in on my brain
    With a dim, dilating pain,
    Till it burst with that last strain.[1]

XX

I fell flooded with a Dark,
  In the silence of a swoon.   135
When I rose, still cold and stark,
    There was night,—I saw the moon.
    And the stars, each in its place,
    And the May-blooms on the grass,
    Seemed to wonder what I was.   140

XXI

And I walked as if apart
  From myself, when I could stand—
And I pitied my own heart,
    As if I held it in my hand,
    Somewhat coldly,—with a sense   145
    Of fulfilled benevolence,
    And a "Poor thing" negligence.

XXII

And I answered coldly too,
  When you met me at the door;
And I only *heard* the dew   150
    Dripping from me to the floor.
    And the flowers I bade you see,
    Were too withered for the bee,—
    As my life, henceforth, for me.

---

1   strain] a sequence of sounds, a tune; also a pressure that taxes one's endurance.

XXIII

Do not weep so—Dear—heart-warm!   155
 All was best as it befell.
If I say he did me harm,
 I speak wild,—I am not well.
 All his words were kind and good—
 He esteemed me! Only, blood   160
 Runs so faint in womanhood.

XXIV

Then I always was too grave,—
 Like the saddest ballad sung,—
With that look, besides, we have
 In our faces, who die young.   165
 I had died, Dear, all the same;
 Life's long, joyous, jostling game
 Is too loud for my meek shame.

XXV

We are so unlike each other,
 Thou and I, that none could guess   170
We were children of one mother,
 But for mutual tenderness.
 Thou art rose-lined from the cold,
 And meant, verily, to hold
 Life's pure pleasures manifold.   175

XXVI

I am pale as crocus grows
 Close beside a rose-tree's root;
Whosoe'er would reach the rose,
 Treads the crocus underfoot.
 I, like May-bloom on thorn-tree—   180
 Thou, like merry summer-bee!
 Fit that I be plucked for thee.

XXVII

Yet who plucks me?—no one mourns,
   I have lived my season out,
And now die of my own thorns   185
   Which I could not live without.
   Sweet, be merry! How the light
   Comes and goes! If it be night,
   Keep the candles in my sight.

XXVIII

Are there footsteps at the door?   190
   Look out quickly. Yea, or nay?
Some one might be waiting for
   Some last word that I might say.
   Nay? So best!—so angels would
   Stand off clear from deathly road,   195
   Not to cross the sight of God.

XXIX

Colder grow my hands and feet.
   When I wear the shroud I made,
Let the folds lie straight and neat,
   And the rosemary be spread,[1]   200
   That if any friend should come,
   (To see *thee*, sweet!) all the room
   May be lifted out of gloom.

XXX

And, dear Bertha, let me keep
   On my hand this little ring,
Which at nights, when others sleep,   205
   I can still see glittering.
   Let me wear it out of sight,
   In the grave,—where it will light
   All the Dark up, day and night.   210

---

1   rosemary] traditionally signifies remembrance; see *Hamlet* act 4, scene 5, l. 174.

XXXI

On that grave, drop not a tear!
   Else, though fathom-deep[1] the place,
Through the woollen shroud I wear
    I shall feel it on my face.
    Rather smile there, blessëd one,   215
    Thinking of me in the sun,
    Or forget me[2]—smiling on!

XXXII

Art thou near me? nearer? so!
   Kiss me close upon the eyes,
That the earthly light may go   220
    Sweetly, as it used to rise,
    When I watched the morning-gray
    Strike, betwixt the hills, the way
    He was sure to come that day.

XXXIII

So,—no more vain words be said!—   225
   The hosannas[3] nearer roll.
Mother, smile now on thy Dead,
   I am death-strong in my soul.
    Mystic Dove alit on cross,[4]
    Guide the poor bird of the snows   230
    Through the snow-wind above loss!

XXIV

Jesus, Victim, comprehending
   Love's divine self-abnegation,
Cleanse my love in its self-spending,
   And absorb the poor libation!   235

---

1 fathom-deep] six feet deep (normally a nautical measurement), the usual depth of a grave.

2 forget me] cf. ll. 7-8 in "Song" ("When I am dead my dearest") by Christina Rossetti (1830-94): "And if thou wilt, remember/ And if thou wilt, forget."

3 hosannas] expressions of adoration or praise addressed to God.

4 Mystic Dove alit on cross] alludes to God's incarnations as both Holy Ghost and Christ.

Wind my thread of life[1] up higher,
Up, through angels' hands of fire!—
I aspire while I expire.

Catarina to Camoens;
Dying in his Absence Abroad, and Referring to the Poem in which He Recorded the Sweetness of Her Eyes

First published in the American periodical *Graham's Magazine* in October 1843,[2] this was one of EBB's most loved and often cited poems in the nineteenth century. In it she represents the perspective of Catarina de Ataide, the storied, silent muse of love lyrics by the Portuguese poet Luis de Camöens (1524-80).[3] The poem focuses on the period just before Catarina dies during the long exile from the Portuguese court of her suitor, who had lauded her beautiful eyes in his poetry. EBB's principal source for details of Camöens' life, as George Monteiro has shown, was *Poems, from the Portuguese of Luis de Camoen* (1803), by Lord Viscount Strangford (1780-1855). The romantic story of Camöens's life had attracted the interest of Lord Byron and Felicia Hemans (1793-1835), among others.[4] Strangford's comment about Catarina—"There can scarcely be conceived a more interesting theme for the visions of romance, than the death of this young and amiable being" (cited Monteiro 1980, 14)—may have provided an opening for EBB's dramatization of a female voice. As her 1831-32 *Diary* shows (181), a draft of the poem was first composed

---

1 thread of life] In classical myth, the three Fates (Atropos, Clotho, and Lachesis) measure the duration of a human life in the length of thread spun from Clotho's spindle, which is then cut by Atropos with great shears.

2 Published under the title "Caterina to Camoens." A parenthetical note appears in place of the subtitle used in 1844 and later editions: "[The lady died during the absence of her poet, and is supposed to muse thus while dying; referring to the verse in which he had recorded the sweetness of her eyes.]"

3 Camöens (the various spellings include Camoëns and Camões) is best known for his love sonnets and his epic poem on the Portuguese discovery of India, *The Lusiads* (1572), to which EBB alludes in "A Vision of Poets" (ll. 370-75).

4 See Byron's "Stanzas to a Lady, With the Poems of Camoens" (1807) and Hemans's *Translations from Camoens, and Other Poets* (1818); also Byron's satirical description of Camoens's "plaintive strain" admired by "each love-sick miss" in *English Bards and Scotch Reviewers* (1809), ll. 297-308.

17 November 1831. EBB engaged in another round of revisions of the *Graham's Magazine* version in republishing "Catarina to Camoens" in *Poems* (1844), reordering and altering stanzas, deleting an entire stanza, and adding two new stanzas (stanzas 7-8).[1] In the courtship period, RB could recite "Catarina to Camoens" by heart "'in a voice & manner as good as singing'" (*BC* 12:321), and his letters abound with playful and amorous echoes of the poem (see *BC* 11:131; 12:8, 11, 64, 261, 295, 319, 338). It also suggested the title of the *Sonnets from the Portuguese* (*LTA* 1:368-69), and directions in the printer's copy for EBB's *Poems* (1850) indicate that she deliberately positioned it immediately before that sonnet sequence.[2] During the nineteenth century, the poem was generally read as a lyric of saintly female "self-renouncement" (*BC* 10:377). "Who can read without emotion a picture of womanly devotion, and self-abnegation like this?," one reviewer exclaimed (*BC* 9:368). The Victorian art critic John Ruskin (1819-1900) called it his "favourite" work in a volume that left his eyes "wet" more often than they had been in "five years"(cited Monteiro 1980, 8). The poem is echoed and subtly critiqued by Christina Rossetti (1830-94) in a poem she left unpublished, "Three Nuns" (Stone 1994, 347-49), while its concluding image of a maiden looking down from heaven on her lover below has parallels with "The Blessed Damozel" (1850, 1870) by D.G. Rossetti (1828-82).[3] In America, as Monteiro notes (1980, 8), "Catarina to Camoens" was well known to Emily Dickinson (1830-86) and Herman Melville (1819-91), among others. Additional criticism: Mermin 1989, Stephenson 1989 and Neri 2000.[4]

---

1 For early ms drafts and the *Graham's Magazine* texts of the poem, see the supplementary website: www.ebbarchive.org.

2 In *Poems* (1856), EBB inserted a cluster of six autobiographical love lyrics between "Catarina" and *Sonnets from the Portuguese* (see the headnote to the sonnet sequence, p. 205).

3 See Appendix A.1 for D.G. Rossetti's youthful response to EBB's poetry.

4 See also Bill Goldman, "The Archæology of a Letter: RB to EBB, 9 July 1846," *Browning Society Notes* 28 (2003): 29-32.

I

On the door you will not enter,
　I have gazed too long—adieu!
Hope withdraws her peradventure—[1]
　Death is near me,—and not *you.*
　　　Come, O lover,　　　　　　　　　　　　　　5
　　　Close and cover
These poor eyes, you called, I ween,[2]
"Sweetest eyes, were ever seen."

II

When I heard you sing that burden[3]
　In my vernal days and bowers,　　　　　　　　　10
Other praises disregarding,
　I but harkened that of yours—
　　　Only saying
　　　In heart-playing,
"Blessed eyes mine eyes have been,　　　　　　　15
If the sweetest, HIS have seen!"

III

But all changes. At this vesper,[4]
　Cold the sun shines down the door.
If you stood there, would you whisper
　"Love, I love you," as before,—　　　　　　　　20
　　　Death pervading
　　　Now, and shading
Eyes you sang of, that yestreen,[5]
As the sweetest ever seen?

IV

Yes, I think, were you beside them,　　　　　　　25
　Near the bed I die upon,—

1　peradventure] the possibility of a thing being so or not.

2　ween] think or believe.

3　burden] refrain or chorus of a song.

4　vesper] evening; also evening prayers or devotion.

5　yestreen] yesterday evening (poetic).

Though their beauty you denied them,
  As you stood there, looking down,
    You would truly
    Call them duly,   30
For the love's sake found therein,—
"Sweetest eyes, were ever seen."

V
And if *you* looked down upon them,
  And if *they* looked up to *you*,
All the light which has foregone them   35
  Would be gathered back anew.
    They would truly
    Be as duly
Love-transformed to beauty's sheen,—[1]
"Sweetest eyes, were ever seen."   40

VI
But, ah me! you only see me,
  In your thoughts of loving man,
Smiling soft perhaps and dreamy
  Through the wavings of my fan,—
    And unweeting[2]   45
    Go repeating,
In your reverie serene,
"Sweetest eyes, were ever seen."

VII
While my spirit leans and reaches
  From my body still and pale,   50
Fain[3] to hear what tender speech is
  In your love to help my bale—[4]
    O my poet,

---

1 sheen] brightness, luster, or radiance.
2 unweeting] unwitting or unaware.
3 fain] glad.
4 bale] here, the evil of physical and/or mental suffering; woe.

Come and show it!
Come, of latest love, to glean   55
"Sweetest eyes were ever seen."

VIII

O my poet, O my prophet,
   When you praised their sweetness so,
Did you think, in singing of it,
   That it might be near to go?   60
      Had you fancies
      From their glances,
That the grave would quickly screen
"Sweetest eyes, were ever seen?"

IX

No reply! the fountain's warble   65
   In the court-yard sounds alone.
As the water to the marble
   So my heart falls with a moan
      From love-sighing
      To this dying.   70
Death forerunneth Love to win
"Sweetest eyes, were ever seen."

X

Will you come? When I'm departed
   Where all sweetnesses are hid;
Where thy voice, my tender-hearted,   75
   Will not lift up either lid.
      Cry, O lover,
      Love is over!
Cry, beneath the cypress green—
"Sweetest eyes, were ever seen."   80

XI

When the angelus[1] is ringing,
  Near the convent will you walk,
And recall the choral singing
  Which brought angels down our talk?
    Spirit-shriven[2]   85
    I viewed Heaven,
Till you smiled—"Is earth unclean,
Sweetest eyes, were ever seen?"

XII

When beneath the palace-lattice,
  You ride slow as you have done,   90
And you see a face there—that is
  Not the old familiar one,—
    Will you oftly[3]
    Murmur softly,
"Here, ye watched me morn and e'en,   95
Sweetest eyes, were ever seen!"

XIII

When the palace-ladies, sitting
  Round your gittern,[4] shall have said,
"Poet, sing those verses written
  For the lady who is dead,"   100
    Will you tremble,
    Yet dissemble,—
Or sing hoarse, with tears between,
"Sweetest eyes, were ever seen?"

---

1 angelus] the angelus bell, marking the devotional exercise commemorating the mystery of Christ's incarnation, repeated by Roman Catholics in the morning, at noon, and at sunset.

2 Spirit-shriven] with a spirit or soul absolved and purified through confession.

3 oftly] often.

4 gittern] an old instrument of the guitar family.

XIV

"Sweetest eyes!" how sweet in flowings,   105
  The repeated cadence is!
Though you sang a hundred poems,
  Still the best one would be this.
    I can hear it
     'Twixt my spirit   110
And the earth-noise intervene—
"Sweetest eyes, were ever seen!"

XV

But the priest waits for the praying,
  And the choir are on their knees,
And the soul must pass away in   115
  Strains more solemn high than these.
    Miserere[1]
    For the weary!
Oh, no longer for Catrine,
"Sweetest eyes, were ever seen!"   120

XVI

Keep my riband,[2] take and keep it,
  (I have loosed it from my hair)[3]
Feeling, while you overweep it,
  Not alone in your despair,
    Since with saintly   125
    Watch unfaintly
Out of heaven shall o'er you lean
"Sweetest eyes, were ever seen."

---

1 *Miserere*] the first word of the penitential psalm, *Miserere mei Deus* ("Have mercy upon me, oh God").

2 riband] ribbon.

3 "She left him the riband from her hair." [EBB's note]. In the earliest ms draft, the note reads, "Which she gave to him at their parting."

XVII

But—but *now*—yet unremovèd
  Up to Heaven, they glisten fast.   130
You may cast away, Belovèd,
  In your future all my past.
    Such old phrases
    May be praises
For some fairer bosom-queen—   135
"Sweetest eyes, were ever seen!"

XVIII

Eyes of mine, what are ye doing?
  Faithless, faithless,—praised amiss
If a tear be of your showing,
  Dropt for any hope of HIS!   140
    Death has boldness
    Besides coldness,
If unworthy tears demean
"Sweetest eyes, were ever seen."

XIX

I will look out to his future;   145
  I will bless it till it shine.
Should he ever be a suitor
  Unto sweeter eyes than mine,
    Sunshine gild them,
    Angels shield them,   150
Whatsoever eyes terrene[1]
Be the sweetest HIS have seen!

The Romance of the Swan's Nest

One of EBB's ballads popular with Victorian readers, this
poem, written in July 1844 (*BC* 9:58) and published in her im-
portant collection of that year, evokes the patterns of love and

---

1 terrene] belonging to the earth or this world; terrestrial.

courtship established by medieval romances. In them knights won fair damsels through daring feats, devoted service, and courtly manners expressed in lofty language evoking religious devotion. EBB's use of these patterns invites comparison with Aurora Leigh's "distrust" of ballad writers' focus on the "chivalric bones" of medieval rather than modern life (see *AL* 5:189-98; for more on EBB's ballads and Victorian medievalism, see the headnote to "Romaunt of the Page," p. 103). Although EBB referred to this poem as being "of a lighter & brighter colouring than the predominant tone of my poetry" (*BC* 9:58) and Victorian reviewers read it as a delineation of childhood's playfulness and poignancy (see, e.g., *BC* 9:353; 10:359), recent critics have discussed its challenges to gendered power relations and the sexual double standard, its eroticism, and its relationship to the ballad tradition. Criticism: Leighton 1986, Cooper 1988, Mermin 1989, Stephenson 1989, and Stone 1995.

So the dreams depart,
So the fading phantoms flee,
And the sharp reality
Now must act its part.
—Westwood's *Beads from a Rosary*[1]

I
  Little Ellie sits alone
'Mid the beeches of a meadow,
  By a stream-side on the grass,
  And the trees are showering down
Doubles of their leaves in shadow,   5
  On her shining hair and face.

II
  She has thrown her bonnet by,
And her feet she has been dipping

---

1 Minor poet Thomas Westwood (1814-88) corresponded with EBB in the 1840s, mostly 1842-46. The preface of his 1843 collection *Beads from a Rosary*, a copy of which he sent to EBB, warmly praises her poetry (see *BC* 8:159-60). He described "The Romance of the Swan's Nest" as "a sweet little poem" (*BC* 9:108).

In the shallow water's flow.
　Now she holds them nakedly　　　　　　　　　10
In her hands, all sleek and dripping,
　　While she rocketh to and fro.

III

　Little Ellie sits alone,
And the smile she softly uses,
　Fills the silence like a speech,　　　　　　　15
　　While she thinks what shall be done,—
And the sweetest pleasure chooses
　For her future within reach.

IV

　Little Ellie in her smile
Chooses ... "I will have a lover,　　　　　　　20
　Riding on a steed of steeds!
　He shall love me without guile,
And to *him* I will discover
　The swan's nest among the reeds.

V

　"And the steed shall be red-roan,¹　　　　　　25
And the lover shall be noble,
　With an eye that takes the breath.
　And the lute he plays upon,
Shall strike ladies into trouble,
　As his sword strikes men to death.　　　　　　30

VI

　"And the steed it shall be shod
All in silver, housed² in azure,
　And the mane shall swim the wind;
　And the hoofs along the sod
Shall flash onward and keep measure,　　　　　　35

1　roan] a horse with a coat whose dominant color is mingled with another (usually
　　white or gray).

2　housed] covered (housings are the cloth coverings put on horses).

Till the shepherds look behind.

VII

"But my lover will not prize
All the glory that he rides in,
  When he gazes in my face.
  He will say, 'O Love, thine eyes   40
Build the shrine my soul abides in,
  And I kneel here for thy grace.'

VIII

  "Then, ay, then—he shall kneel low,
With the red-roan steed anear him
  Which shall seem to understand—   45
  Till I answer, 'Rise and go!
For the world must love and fear him
  Whom I gift with heart and hand.'

IX

  "Then he will arise so pale,
I shall feel my own lips tremble   50
  With a *yes* I must not say,
  Nathless¹ maiden-brave, 'Farewell,'
I will utter, and dissemble—
  'Light to-morrow with to-day.'

X

  "Then he'll ride among the hills   55
To the wide world past the river,
  There to put away all wrong;
  To make straight distorted wills,
And to empty the broad quiver
  Which the wicked bear along.   60

XI

  "Three times shall a young foot-page
Swim the stream and climb the mountain

---

1   nathless] nonetheless.

And kneel down beside my feet—
　'Lo, my master sends this gage,[1]
Lady, for thy pity's counting!　　　　　　　　　　　65
　What wilt thou exchange for it?'

XII
　"And the first time, I will send
A white rosebud for a guerdon,—[2]
　And the second time, a glove;
　But the third time—I may bend　　　　　　　　70
From my pride, and answer—'Pardon,
　If he comes to take my love.'

XIII
　"Then the young foot-page will run—
Then my lover will ride faster,
　Till he kneeleth at my knee:　　　　　　　　　75
　'I am a duke's eldest son!
Thousand serfs do call me master,—
　But, O Love, I love but *thee!'*

XIV
　"He will kiss me on the mouth
Then, and lead me as a lover　　　　　　　　　　80
　Through the crowds that praise his deeds:
　And, when soul-tied by one troth,[3]
Unto *him* I will discover
　That swan's nest among the reeds."

1　gage] something, such as a glove, given as token of a pledge.

2　guerdon] reward, recompense.

3　troth] vow of fidelity, betrothal.

XV

    Little Ellie, with her smile   85
Not yet ended, rose up gaily,
    Tied the bonnet, donned the shoe,
    And went homeward, round a mile,
Just to see, as she did daily,
    What more eggs were with the two.   90

XVI

    Pushing through the elm-tree copse,[1]
Winding up the stream, light-hearted,
    Where the osier[2] pathway leads—
    Past the boughs she stoops—and stops.
Lo, the wild swan had deserted—   95
    And a rat had gnawed the reeds.

XVII

    Ellie went home sad and slow.
If she found the lover ever,
    With his red-roan steed of steeds,
    Sooth I know not! but I know   100
She could never show him—never,
    That swan's nest among the reeds!

---

1   copse] thicket.
2   osier] willow.

4. [Aeschylus's Monodrama] (Unpublished, 1845)

This dramatic monologue, mistakenly attributed to Robert Browning on the basis of a manuscript in his hand now in the British Library (R D1160), here appears for the first time in a collection of EBB's poetry. After the poem's initial publication by Frederic Kenyon in 1913, the misattribution persisted for almost seventy years. In 1935, in *A Browning Handbook,* W.C. DeVane described the poem as "thoroughly mature," "steadily excellent," and "one of the best of the poems which [Robert] Browning left unpublished."[1] In 1981 it was included in a scholarly edition of RB's poetry by John Pettigrew and Thomas H. Collins, despite Martha Hale Shackford's earlier reasoned arguments for EBB's authorship in the *Times Literary Supplement* in 1942.[2] Shackford's hypothesis was confirmed in 1982 by the discovery of EBB's rough draft in a small notebook in the Huntington Library (R D1159), yet the poem was still incorrectly identified as her verse translation of lines from Aeschylus.[3] It was clearly presented as EBB's own original poem to a wide community of scholars only in 1997, when Margaret Reynolds and Barbara Rosenbaum published "'Aeschylus' Soliloquy' by Elizabeth Barrett Browning."[4] Whereas others have followed the untitled poem's first editor, Frederic Kenyon, in identifying it as "Aeschylus' Soliloquy," the title given to it here derives from EBB's own description of the monologue.

EBB first mentioned this poem in a letter to RB on 27 February 1845, when she had completed her second translation of Aeschylus's

---

1   William Clyde DeVane. *A Browning Handbook* (New York: Appleton Crofts, 1935): 514-15.

2   See John Woolford and Daniel Karlin, "'Aeschylus' Soliloquy': Transcript and Notes," *Browning Society Notes* 8.2 (August 1978): 14-18; Robert Browning, *The Poems,* ed. John Pettigrew and Thomas J. Collins (New Haven & London: Yale UP; Harmondsworth: Penguin, 1981), 2:948-51; and Martha Hale Shackford, "The Authorship of 'Æschylus' Soliloquy,'" *Times Literary Supplement* (21 March 1942): 144 (hereafter *TLS*). G.D. Hobson's 16-line rebuttal of Shackford in "'Aeschylus' Soliloquy,'" *TLS* (11 April 1942): 189, did not clearly address most of her evidence.

3   See Barbara Rosenbaum, *Index of English Literary Manuscripts,* vol. 4, ed. Barbara Rosenbaum and Pamela White, Part I (London: Mansell, 1982), xxxi, 107, 109, and item BrEB 1104.

4   See Reynolds and Rosenbaum 1997; hereafter referred to as R&R.

Prometheus Bound: "I have in my head to associate with the version, .. a monodram of my own—not a long poem, .. but a monologue of Æschylus as he sate a blind exile on the flats of Sicily and re-counted the past to his own soul, just before the eagle cracked his great massy skull with a stone." Three months later she reported that "The Prometheus is done—but the monodram is where it was" (*BC* 10:102, 233). In calling this poem a "monodram" or drama of one (more usually termed a "monodrama"), EBB used a term employed by Victorian poets—along with "lyrical drama," "dramatic lyric," "dramatic romance," "dramatic idyll," "dramatic study," and even "ballad"—for what we now describe as a dramatic monologue (a label not widely used until late in the nineteenth century).[1] The poem is today known only from her draft and RB's copy, probably made shortly after her death (along with the transcriptions of other ms fragments by her which were later misattributed to him), when he was working on a collection of her complete works.

The monodrama and its dramatic situation reflect EBB's long-standing enthusiasm for the Greek tragedian Aeschylus (525-456 BCE), evident not only from her two translations of his *Prometheus Bound* (1833, 1850), but also from her diary's 1832 declarations that she had read all of his plays and from many references in her cor-respondence, where, for example, she judges him "the divinest of all the divine Greek souls" (*BC* 10:111). Legendary accounts of his death in several classical sources held that Aeschylus, having offended Athenian audiences with his play *The Eumenides* and/or having been defeated in the dramatic competition, had gone into self-imposed exile in Sicily. Fearing a prophecy that a falling house (or in some versions, a blow from heaven) would kill him, the aged poet sought open spaces—but in vain, since he died when a flying eagle, trying to open the shell of a tortoise, mistook his bald head

---

1   By the 1840s, the term *monodrama* commonly referred to a dramatic performance by a single actor or to a dramatic poem spoken by a single character; it was applied by EBB's friend and collaborator R.H. Horne to Tennyson's monologue "St. Simeon Stylites," and in 1875 Tennyson subtitled Maud (1855) "A Monodrama" following the lead of crit-ics in the 1850s. See A. Dwight Culler, "Monodrama and the Dramatic Monologue," *PMLA* 90 (1975): 366-85; and Christopher Ricks, *Tennyson: A Selected Edition* (London: Longman, 1989), 512. On the various terms for dramatic monologues and nineteenth-century developments in the genre, see the Introduction, p. 30, note 2..

for a rock. EBB briefly relates the story in *Aurora Leigh* (5:292-99) to illustrate the fate of dramatists undervalued by audiences.

The ms, in ink over a faded pencil draft beneath, is typical of her rough drafts, with many deletions, additions, substitutions, and on occasion, alterations in line sequencing. Although her intentions are usually clear, in some instances she entered an alternative word or line choice without canceling the first, especially towards the end of the ms, much as Emily Dickinson tends to do in her mss. The text printed here is based on our own examination of the Huntington ms, in light of both RB's copy and R&R's transcriptions.[1]

I am an old and solitary man
And now at set of sun in Sicily
I sit down in the middle of this plain
Which drives between the mountains and the sea
Its blank of nature.[2] If a traveller came   5
Seeing my bare bald skull and my still brows
And massive features coloured to a stone
The tragic mask of a humanity
Whose part is played to an end,—he might mistake [me]
For some god Terminus[3] set on these flats   10
Or broken marble Faunus.[4] Let it be
Life has ebbed from me—I am on dry ground
All sounds of life I held so thunderous sweet[5]
Shade off to silence—all the perfect shapes
Born of perception and men's images   15
Which thronged against the outer rim of earth

---

1 For a text with detailed notes explaining less finished aspects of the ms, textual vari-
   ants, and the differences between our version of the poem and those of RB and R&R,
   see the supplemental website: www.ebbarchive.org.

2 On the facing page EBB wrote a version of the five opening lines in the third person,
   experimenting with a narrative rather than dramatic utterance. The alternative ver-
   sion begins, "An old man sate* upon a rugged stone, …"; *sate] i.e., sat.

3 Terminus] classical god of boundaries whose image, often a bust, was used to mark
   property lines.

4 Faunus] a mythological figure usually represented as having a man's body and a goat's
   ears, legs, and feet.

5 EBB termed Aeschylus "the thunderous" in "Wine of Cyprus" (1844) and elsewhere
   describes his "thundering" lines (*BC* 8:259).

And hung with floating faces over it
Grow dim and dimmer—all the motions drawn
From Beauty in action which spun audibly
My brain round in a rapture, have grown still   20
There's a gap twixt me and the life once mine,
Now others' and not mine, which now roars off
In gradual declination[1]—till at last
I hear it in the distance droning small
Like a bee at sunset. Ay, and that bee's hum   25
The buzzing fly and mouthing of the grass
Cropped slowly near me by some straying sheep
Are strange to me with life—and separate from me
The outside of my being—I myself
Grow to the silence, fasten to the calm   30
Of an organic nature .. sky and rocks—
I pass onto their general unity
As if in preparation for my death
When dying down into impersonal dust
                  Ah ha—these flats are wide.   35
The prophecy which said the house would fall
And thereby crush me, must bring down the sky
The only roof above me where I sit
Or ere[2] it prove its oracle today.
Stand fast ye pillars of the constant Heavens   40
As Life does in me. I who did not die
That day in Athens when the people's scorn
Hissed toward the sun as if to darken it
Over my head, because I spoke my Greek
Too deep down in my soul to suit their ears   45
Who did not die to see the solemn vests
Of my white chorus round the thymele[3]
Flutter like doves, and sweep back like a cloud

---

1   Declination] decline. Plutarch suggests that in 458 BCE Aeschylus's reputation began
    to decline when Sophocles defeated him in Athens' annual dramatic competition
    (Plutarch, *Life of Kimon*).

2   Or ere] i.e., before.

3   chorus round the thymele] choral speakers around the altar to the god Dionysus, god
    of wine and revelry, in the center of the ancient Greek theater.

Before the shrill lipped people .. but stood calm
And cold, and felt the theatre wax hot   50
With mouthing whispers——the man Æschylus
Is gray I fancy and his wrinkles ridge—
The smoothest of his phrases—or the times
Have grown too polished for this old rough work—
We have no sphinxes in the Parthenon[1]   55
Nor, any flints at Delphos—[2]or forsooth
I think the sphinxes wrote this Attic Greek[3]
Our Sophocles[4] hath something more than this
Cast out on a thin smile—.—I would not die
At this time by the crushing of a house   60
Who lived that day out .. I would go to death
With voluntary and majestic steps
Jove[5] thundering on the right hand. Let it be.

I am an old and solitary man—
Mine eyes feel dimly out the setting sun   65
Which drops its great red fruit of bitterness
Today as other days, as every day
Within the patient waters. What do I say
I whistle out my scorn against the sun
Who knelt his trilogy, morn, noon and night   70
And set this tragic world against the sun—
Forgive me great Apollo—Bitter fruit
I think we never found that holy sun
Or ere with conjurations of our hands
Drove up the saltness of our hearts to it   75

A blessed fruit a full Hesperian fruit[1]
Which the fair sisters with their starry eyes
Did warm to scarlet bloom. O holy sun
My eyes are weak and cannot hold thee round.
But in my large soul there is room for thee—   80
All human wrongs and shames cast out from it,—
And I invite thee, Sun, to sphere thyself
In my large soul, and let my thoughts in white
Keep chorus round thy glory—Oh the days
In which I sate upon Hymettus hill[2]   85
A little tuniced[3] child, and felt my thoughts
Rise past the golden bees against thy face
Great sun upon the sea. The city lay
Beneath me like an eaglet in an egg
The beak and claws shut whitely up in calm—   90
And calm were the great waters—and the hills
Ilissus[4] seeming louder—and the groves
Of blessed olive thinking of their use
Holding at arms length their unmolten snows
Plunged in the light of Heaven which trickled back   95
On all sides .. [a] libation[5] to the world ..
          There I sate, a child,
Half hidden in purple thyme with knees drawn up
By clasping of my little arms, and cheek
Laid slant across them with obtruded nose—   100
And full eyes gazing—Ay, my eyes climbed up
Against the heated metal of thy shield
Till their persistent look clove through the fires
And struck it into manyfolded fires
And opened out the secret of the night   105
Hid in the day-source—Darkness mixed with light

---

1   Hesperian fruit] golden apples growing in the Garden of the Hesperides (called "the
    fair sisters" in the next line), the daughters or granddaughters of Hesperus, the eve-
    ning star. Cf. Tennyson's poem "The Hesperides" (1832).

2   Hymettus hill] a mountain near Athens, famed for its prized honey.

3   Tuniced] wearing a tunic, the typical Greek garment for men and women.

4   Ilissus] river near Athens.

5   Libation] a drink poured on the ground as an offering to the gods.

Then shot innumerous arrows in my eyes
From all sides of the Heavens,—so blinding me—
As countless as the Norland[1] snowflakes fall
Before the northwind—rapid, wonderful,   110
Some shafts as bright as sunrays nine times drawn
Thro the heart of the sun, .. some black as night in Hell—
All mixed, sharp, driven against me! And as I gazed
(For I gazed still) I saw the sea and earth
Leap up as wounded by the innumerous shafts   115
And hurry round, and whirl into a blot
Across which evermore fell thick the shafts
As Norland snow fall[s] thick before the wind
Until the northmen at the cavern's mouth
Can see no pinetree through. I could see nought   120
No earth, no sea, no sky, no sun itself
Only that arrowy rush of black and white
Across a surge of rainbows infinite
Drove piercing and blinding and astonishing
And then it was revealed, it was revealed   125
That I should be a priest of the Unseen
And build a bridge of sounds across the straights
From Heaven to earth whence all the Gods might walk
Nor bend it with their soles—
And through it all Homerus the blind man[2]   130
Did chant his vowelled music in my brain
And then I saw the Gods tread past me slow
From out the portals of the hungry dark ..
And each one as he past breathed in my face
And made me greater: First old Saturn[3] came   135
Blind with eternal watches .. calm and blind ..

---

1 Norland] North land; on EBB's use of this term see R&R 327.

2 Homerus the blind man] On EBB's love of the Greek epic poet, Homer, whom tradi-
tion held to be blind, see "A Vision of Poets," l. 295n. Her classical mentor Hugh
Stuart Boyd (see the Introduction) was also blind. Writing to RB in March 1845, EBB
observed that her own life of seclusion had made her like "a blind poet," with "much
of the inner life," but lacking "experience of life & man" (BC 10:133).

3 Saturn] also called Cronos (Time), once the chief god, overthrown and replaced by
his son Zeus/Jove.

Then Zeus, his eagle blinking on his wrist[1]
To the lightning fires he moved on—in a roll
Of thunder sounding hollows of the worlds
He glode[2] on grandly—while the troop of Prayers   140
Buzzed dimly in the shadow of his light.
With murmurous sounds, and poor beseeching brows.
And Neptune[3] with beard and locks drawn straight
As seaweed .. ay and Pluto[4] with his Dark
Cutting the dark as lightening cuts the sun   145
Made individual by intensity—
And then Apollo trenching[5] on the dark
With a white glory white the lute he bore
Struck on the air

---

1   eagle blinking on his wrist] the bird sacred to Zeus/Jove.
2   Glode] glided. EBB used *glode* in this sense in her second translation of *Prometheus Bound* (l. 336), the work with which she associated this monologue (see R&R, 348).
3   Neptune] god of the sea.
4   Pluto] god of the underworld.
5   trenching] entrenching, encroaching.

5. *From* Poems *(1850)*

Flush or Faunus

EBB's spaniel Flush, her constant companion, was a gift from the writer Mary Russell Mitford, who sent the puppy in January 1841 to console her younger friend in the emotional and physical collapse following the drowning of her favorite brother Edward ("Bro") the previous July. Before writing this poem, EBB had praised Flush for his devotion in "some very light cobwebby verses" (*BC* 7:253) called "To Flush, My Dog" (1843). In that poem and her correspondence, EBB feminizes the dog as unheroic and ladylike: "never born for a hero," he whines until he is "covered ... up all but the nose like a Turkish lady"; "so fine-ladyly delicate, ... he expects ... to be nourished upon macaroons" (*BC* 5:105, 236). In contrast, this poem (pub. 1850) associates Flush with the masculine sexual energy of the classical deity Faunus or Pan, the part man, part beast god of fields and forests, crops, flocks, wildlife, and fertility. The sonnet was probably written during EBB's courtship with RB—whom Flush regarded as a rival[1]— when she was also responding to her suitor in Petrarchan sonnets that became the sequence *Sonnets from the Portuguese*.[2] Earlier, in "The Dead Pan" (1844) EBB had employed Pan to represent the pagan values supplanted by Christianity; later, in "A Musical Instrument" (1860) she would associate Pan with a fearful sexual power that brutalizes but also creates. Flush was immortalized as the protagonist of Virginia Woolf's comic novel *Flush* (1933), which sold nearly 19,000 copies in the first six months.[3] Criticism: Merivale 1965.

---

1   Flush bit RB twice (see *BC* 13:138, 177–78), eventually making peace with him and accompanying the Brownings to Italy, where he died in 1854.

2   Manuscript evidence associates the poem with a cluster of sonnets written in 1845–46 when EBB was also at work on the *Sonnets from the Portuguese* (see R D294, D540, D726, D752).

3   See Anna Snaith, "Of Fanciers, Footnotes, and Fascism: Virginia Woolf's *Flush*," *Modern Fiction Studies*, 48 (2002): 617.

You see this dog. It was but yesterday
I mused forgetful of his presence here
Till thought on thought drew downward tear on tear,
When from the pillow, where wet-cheeked I lay,
A head as hairy as Faunus, thrust its way   5
Right sudden against my face,—two golden-clear
Great eyes astonished mine,—a drooping ear
Did flap me on either cheek to dry the spray!
I started first, as some Arcadian,[1]
Amazed by goatly god in twilight grove;   10
But, as the bearded vision closelier ran
My tears off, I knew Flush, and rose above
Surprise and sadness,—thanking the true PAN,
Who, by low creatures, leads to heights of love.

Hiram Powers' Greek Slave

This sonnet (pub. 1850) reflects EBB's intervention in the aesthetic
and political debates surrounding "The Greek Slave" (1844), a
statue of a nude white slave by the American sculptor Hiram
Powers (1805-73) that became one of the most popular, frequently
replicated, and widely exhibited works of art in America and
Europe by the mid-nineteenth century (see Figure 3).[2] EBB notes
in her correspondence that the statue was exhibited in London in
1846; in May 1847 the Brownings met Powers in Florence and saw
in his studio "The Greek Slave" together with a statue of Eve "yet
unworked in the marble" which EBB much admired (LTA 1:83,
85n26, 89-90). When Powers's "Greek Slave" was exhibited in the
Crystal Palace in the 1851 Great Exhibition, it inspired a parodic
cartoon by John Tenniel in Punch magazine of a black slave in the
same pose entitled "The Virginian Slave." A catalogue accompa-
nying exhibits of "The Greek Slave" observed, "The ostensible

1 Arcadian] an inhabitant of a region in Greece symbolizing the ideal life.
2 See Jean Fagin Yellin, Women and Sisters: The Anti-slavery Feminists in America (New
   Haven, CT: Yale UP, 1989), 99-125; Joy S. Kasson, Marble Queens and Captives:
   Women in Nineteenth-Century American Sculpture (New Haven, CT: Yale UP, 1990); and
   Stone 2002.

subject is merely a Grecian maiden, made captive by the Turks and exposed at Constantinople, for sale." The catalogue also drew attention to "the cross and locket visible amid the drapery" near the slave's chained hands and described her as a "type of resignation, uncompromising virtue, or sublime patience." Nevertheless, some viewers objected to the statue as an immoral exhibition. Like Powers's statue, EBB's sonnet has itself generated considerable disagreement. While some have read it as a critique of the passivity of Powers's figure, others have interpreted it as endorsing an implicit race politics in its association of an idealized whiteness with beauty and the sublime. Criticism: Mermin 1989, Stone 2002, Gaja 2003.[1]

Figure 3: Hiram Powers' Sculpture "The Greek Slave."

---

1   See also Jennifer DeVere Brody, *Impossible Purities: Blackness, Femininity, and Victorian Culture* (Durham, NC: Duke UP, 1998), 67-69.

They say Ideal beauty cannot enter
The house of anguish. On the threshold stands
An alien Image with enshackled hands,
Called the Greek Slave! as if the artist meant her
(That passionless perfection which he lent her,   5
Shadowed, not darkened where the sill expands)
To, so, confront man's crimes in different lands
With man's ideal sense. Pierce to the centre,
Art's fiery finger!—and break up ere long
The serfdom of this world! appeal, fair stone,   10
From God's pure heights of beauty against man's wrong!
Catch up in thy divine face, not alone
East griefs but west,[1]—and strike and shame the strong,
By thunders of white silence, overthrown.

The Runaway Slave at Pilgrim's Point

First mentioned by EBB on 1 December 1845, this poem responded
to an invitation "to write for the anti-slavery people at Boston" (*BC*
11:213), abolitionists associated with the American Anti-Slavery Soci-
ety, and, more immediately, with its very active auxiliary organization,
the Boston Female Anti-Slavery Society. Unlike the American and
Foreign Anti-Slavery Society, the American Anti-Slavery Society,
headed by William Lloyd Garrison (1805-79), supported the move-
ment for women's rights within the anti-slavery movement and thus
protested the exclusion of women delegates from the first World Anti-
Slavery Convention in London in 1840. Beginning in 1839, the Boston
Female Anti-Slavery Society began producing an anti-slavery annual,
The Liberty Bell, for sale at its Christmas bazaar, an important fund-
raiser for the cause. "The Runaway Slave at Pilgrim's Point" was first
published in the 1848 issue, available for purchase at the 1847 bazaar. *The
Liberty Bell* was a miscellany featuring poems, fiction, and other works
by writers of both sexes and of different races and nationalities, among
them the great African American orator, author, and activist Frederick

---

1   not alone / East griefs but west] the grief of slavery in the "west" (i.e., America) as
    well as in the east, i.e., in the Turkish Empire, where there was a trade in white slave
    women.

Douglass (c. 1818-95) and the English writer Harriet Martineau (1802-76), who began corresponding with EBB in 1843 (*BC* 4:326). The invitation to contribute may have come from the annual's principal editor, Maria Weston Chapman (1806-85) or from the American poet James Russell Lowell (1819-91), EBB's correspondent since 1842 (*BC* 5:373).[1] She mailed the completed poem to Lowell on 23 December 1846, three and a half months after her marriage on 12 September (*BC* 14:86), commenting to her scholarly friend Hugh Stuart Boyd that it was "too ferocious, perhaps, for the Americans to publish" and to her friend Mary Mitford that "nobody will print it, I am certain, because I could not help making it bitter" (*BC* 14:86, 117). EBB descended on her father's side from generations of Jamaican slave-holders and received legacies derived from colonial trade (see Marks 1938; Barrett 2000; and *R*, xv). Nevertheless, she supported the Emancipation Act of 1833, which brought gradual emancipation in British colonies, saying that she was "glad" that the slaves were "virtually—free!" (*BC* 3:86). RB, who also had West Indian connections through his father, shared her anti-slavery views; in June 1846 she ironically described to him the "infinite traditions" of her "great great grandfather, who flogged his slaves like a divinity" (*BC* 13:24). Critics approaching the poem biographically have interpreted it as an act of rebellion against the poet's father Edward Moulton Barrett or, more extremely, have linked it to unfounded speculations about the poet's own ancestry.[2] Several critics have also assumed that it was derived from an account of a Jamaican runaway slave given to the poet by her cousin Richard Barrett (1789-1839), a speaker in Jamaica's House of Assembly (*BC* 5:212). However, that account, published as "A Jamaican Story" in an appendix to *Richard Barrett's Journal*, bears very little resemblance to the published poem.[3]

The draft manuscript of "The Runaway Slave at Pilgrim's Point" (*R* D799) reveals an unusually convoluted compositional

---

1   EBB received presentation copies of the 1844 and 1845 issues, the first from Chapman and the second from Eliza L. Follen (1787-1860), a friend of Martineau's and like her a contributor to *The Liberty Bell*; see *R* A619, A620; *BC* 10:161, 163n2; and Stone 2003a 39.

2   Markus 1995 argued on the basis of evidence refuted by Kennedy and critiqued by Phelan 2003 that EBB "believed she had African blood through her grandfather Charles Moulton" (106).

3   Edited by Thomas Brott and Philip Kelley (Winfield, KS: Wedgestone P, 1983). Richard Barrett's story did leave its mark, however, on a 688-line unpublished work of juvenilia by EBB entitled "The African."

process and includes an abandoned opening section in which the speaker is a male, not a female slave (see Appendix C.II). The decision to situate the fugitive at Pilgrim's Point came relatively late in the poem's composition. The first fair copy of the poem, with the cancelled title "Black and Mad at Pilgrim's Point," now exists in three portions (R D800, 801, 802) and includes RB's pencilled suggestions for revision. This ms is signed, as was her practice, with the initials "EBB," a designation that remained unchanged after her marriage (see the Introduction). In a fond gesture, the newlywed RB added "<u>my</u>" before the signature initials in this ms and enclosed "<u>my</u> EBB" in the enfolding arms of heavy brackets.[1] The annotation below cites some of his marginalia. EBB made numerous minor textual revisions in the poem after its initial publication, especially for *Poems* (1850).[2] Stanza XV was inserted in this first fair copy. In her 1850 *Poems,* EBB "arranged" that "The Runaway Slave at Pilgrim's Point" should "come next" to "The Cry of the Children" in order "to appear impartial as to national grievances" (*LTM* 3:310). The pamphlet edition of the poem dated 1849 is a forgery produced in 1888 by the notorious Thomas Wise.[3] Critical response to the poem has been diverse. Praised as a "noble" poem in the nineteenth century by black and white readers alike (see the extract from Charlotte Forten's journal in Appendix C.III.2), it fell into obscurity with many of EBB's other poems for the first half of the twentieth century. In the 1950s it was criticized as "too blunt and shocking to have any enduring artistic worth"(Taplin 1957, 194); in the 1980s and 1990s it was criticized by some for being idealized, melodramatic, or complicit in patriarchal structures, but it was defended by others as a radical treatment of racial and sexual politics. While EBB herself identified this poem as a "ballad" (*LTM* 3:310), it has been generally interpreted as a dramatic monologue. Criticism: Leighton 1986, 1992; Parry 1988; Cooper 1988; Forster 1988; Mermin 1989; Battles 1991; Markus 1995; Brown 1995; Brophy 1998; Stauffer 1997; Slinn 2003; Stone 1986, 2002, 2003a, 2003b, 2005; Davies and Stone 2006; Lootens 2006; and Fish 2006.

---

1 Davies and Stone 2006 debate the significance of this gesture.

2 On these textual revisions, see Stauffer 1997; for *The Liberty Bell* version of the poem, see the supplementary website.

3 Wise] See the headnote to *Sonnets from the Portuguese,* p. 204.

I

I stand on the mark beside the shore
  Of the first white pilgrim's bended knee,
Where exile turned to ancestor,
  And God was thanked for liberty.[1]
I have run through the night, my skin is as dark,   5
I bend my knee down on this mark[2] ..
  I look on the sky and the sea.

II

O pilgrim-souls, I speak to you!
  I see you come out proud and slow
From the land of the spirits pale as dew,   10
  And round me and round me ye go!
O pilgrims, I have gasped and run
All night long from the whips of one
  Who in your names works sin and woe.

III

And thus I thought that I would come   15
  And kneel here where ye knelt before,
And feel your souls around me hum
  In undertone to the ocean's roar;
And lift my black face, my black hand,[3]
Here, in your names, to curse this land   20
  Ye blessed in freedom's evermore.

---

1 God was thanked for Liberty] alludes to the landing of the Pilgrim Fathers at Plymouth, Massachusetts, in December 1620, mythologized as the founding moment in the development of the United States of America and frequently invoked in *The Liberty Bell*. In Felicia Hemans's "The Landing of the Pilgrim Fathers in New England" (1825), the "band of exiles" is depicted singing an "anthem of the free" on the "soil where first they trod."

2 bend my knee down on this mark] Images of an enchained and beseeching kneeling slave were widely disseminated in anti-slavery publications and artifacts, following the pattern first made popular in a clay cameo emblem created by the pottery manufacturer Josiah Wedgwood (1730-95) in 1787, inscribed with the words, "Am I Not a Man and a Brother?" Female versions followed, inscribed "Am I Not a Woman and a Sister?"

3 black hand] "black" was RB's suggestion; EBB initially wrote "& my hand."

IV

I am black, I am black!
    And yet God made me, they say.
But if He did so, smiling back
    He must have cast his work away   25
Under the feet of his white creatures,
With a look of scorn,—that the dusky features
    Might be trodden again to clay.[1]

V

And yet He has made dark things
    To be glad and merry as light.   30
There's a little dark bird, sits and sings;
    There's a dark stream ripples out of sight;
And the dark frogs chant in the safe morass,[2]
And the sweetest stars are made to pass
    O'er the face of the darkest night.   35

VI

But *we* who are dark, we are dark!
    Ah God, we have no stars!
About our souls in care and cark[3]
    Our blackness shuts like prison-bars.
The poor souls crouch so far behind,   40
That never a comfort can they find
    By reaching through the prison-bars.

VII[4]

Indeed we live beneath the sky,
    That great smooth Hand of God[5] stretched out
On all His children fatherly,   45

---

1   He must have ... clay.] See the representation of God as a potter in Jeremiah 18.1–6; cf.
    the similar allusion in l. 97 of RB's "Caliban Upon Setebos" (1864).

2   morass] marsh or bog.

3   cark] a burden of anxiety, labor, or toil (archaic, usually linked with "care," as here).

4   Stanza VII] not in *The Liberty Bell* text (hereafter, *LB*) or the first (eventually dismem-
    bered) fair copy (*R* D800, D801, D802) with RB's marginalia.

5   Hand of God] cf. the similar image in "The Cry of the Children," l. 120.

To save them from the dread and doubt
Which would be, if, from this low place,
All opened straight up to His face
    Into the grand eternity.

VIII

And still God's sunshine and His frost,   50
    They make us hot, they make us cold,
As if we were not black and lost;
    And the beasts and birds, in wood and fold,
Do fear and take us for very men!
Could the weep-poor-will[1] or the cat of the glen[2]   55
    Look into my eyes and be bold?

IX

I am black, I am black!—
    But, once, I laughed in girlish glee,
For one of my color stood in the track
    Where the drivers[3] drove, and looked at me,   60
And tender and full was the look he gave—
Could a slave look *so* at another slave?—
    I look at the sky and the sea.

X

And from that hour our spirits grew
    As free as if unsold, unbought.   65
Oh, strong enough, since we were two,
    To conquer the world, we thought!
The drivers drove us day by day;
We did not mind, we went one way,
    And no better a freedom sought.   70

---

1   weep-poor-will] i.e., a whippoorwill, as it is referred to in *LB*; a species of bird.

2   cat of the glen] a wildcat living in a glen or mountain valley. EBB initially wrote "stag of the glen," and RB questioned it, asking, "could not some more characteristic creature be found—and smaller, to pair with the whippoorwill? martin, raccoon opossum, wild cat & c."

3   drivers] the immediate overseers of slave gangs, compelling them to work by driving them on with whips.

XI

In the sunny ground between the canes,
    He said "I love you" as he passed:
When the shingle-roof rang sharp with the rains,
    I heard how he vowed[1] it fast.
While others shook he smiled in the hut,   75
As he carved me a bowl of the cocoa-nut
    Through the roar of the hurricanes.

XII

I sang his name instead of a song.
    Over and over I sang his name—
Upward and downward I drew it along   80
    My various notes,—the same, the same!
I sang it low, that the slave-girls near
Might never guess from aught they could hear,
    It was only a name—a name.

XIII

I look on the sky and the sea.   85
    We were two to love, and two to pray,—
Yes, two, O God, who cried to Thee,
    Though nothing didst Thou say.
Coldly Thou sat'st behind the sun!
And now I cry who am but one,   90
    Thou wilt not speak to-day.—[2]

XIV

We were black, we were black.
    We had no claim to love and bliss,
What marvel, if each went to wrack?[3]
    They wrung my cold hands out of his,—   95
They dragged him ... where? .. I crawled to touch

---

1   vowed] EBB initially wrote "swore," but RB questioned this: "Does one swear fast or more than once? One breathes fast, & c."

2   Cf. the children's comment about God in "The Cry of the Children" (l. 126).

3   wrack] ruin, waste, destruction.

His blood's mark in the dust! .. not much,
 Ye pilgrim-souls, .. though plain as *this!*[1]

XV

Wrong, followed by a deeper wrong!
 Mere grief's too good for such as I. 100
So the white men brought the shame ere long
 To strangle the sob of my agony.[2]
They would not leave me for my dull
Wet eyes!—it was too merciful
 To let me weep pure tears and die. 105

XVI

I am black, I am black!
 I wore a child upon my breast ...
An amulet[3] that hung too slack,
 And, in my unrest, could not rest.
Thus we went moaning, child and mother, 110
One to another, one to another,
 Until all ended for the best.

XVII

For hark! I will tell you low .. low ..
 I am black, you see,—
And the babe who lay on my bosom so, 115
 Was far too white .. too white for me;
As white as the ladies who scorned to pray
Beside me at church but yesterday,
 Though my tears had washed a place for my knee.

XVIII

My own, own child! I could not bear 120
 To look in his face, it was so white.
I covered him up with a kerchief there;

---

1 as this!] i.e., as the mark of the pilgrim's knee on the shore mentioned in Stanza 1.

2 To strangle the sob of my agony.] EBB revised to stress the slave's suffering in the rape;
 LB here reads "To stifle the sob in my throat thereby."

3 amulet] charm worn to protect against evil.

I covered his face in close and tight:
And he moaned and struggled, as well might be,
For the white child wanted his liberty—   125
 Ha, ha! he wanted the master-right.

XIX

He moaned and beat with his head and feet,
 His little feet that never grew—
He struck them out, as it was meet,
 Against my heart to break it through.   130
I might have sung and made him mild—
But I dared not sing to the white-faced child
 The only song I knew.

XX

I pulled the kerchief very close:
 He could not see the sun, I swear,   135
More, then, alive, than now he does
 From between the roots of the mango[1] ... where?
.. I know where. Close! a child and mother
Do wrong to look at one another,
 When one is black and one is fair.   140

XXI

Why, in that single glance I had
 Of my child's face, .. I tell you all,
I saw a look that made me mad!
 The *master's* look, that used to fall
On my soul like his lash .. or worse!—   145
And so, to save it from my curse,
 I twisted it round in my shawl.[2]

---

1 mango] "mangles" in *LB*, a Spanish form of "mangrove." Cf. the burial of the infant
 in William Wordsworth's ballad "The Thorn" (1798).

2 shawl] underlined twice in pencil in first fair copy (portion two, D801) by RB, with
 accompanying comment, also in pencil, in right margin: "Does that sound like a
 slave's article of clothing?"

XXII

And he moaned and trembled from foot to head,
   He shivered from head to foot;
Till, after a time, he lay instead   150
   Too suddenly still and mute.
I felt, beside, a stiffening cold
I dared to lift up just a fold, ..
   As in lifting a leaf of the mango-fruit.

XXIII

But *my* fruit ... ha, ha!—there, had been   155
   (I laugh to think on't at this hour!)
Your fine white angels (who have seen
   Nearest the secret of God's power)
And plucked my fruit to make them wine,
And sucked the soul of that child of mine,   160
   As the humming-bird sucks the soul of the flower.

XXIV

Ha, ha, the trick of the angels white!
   They freed the white child's spirit so.
I said not a word, but, day and night,
   I carried the body to and fro,   165
And it lay on my heart like a stone .. as chill.
—The sun may shine out as much as he will:
   I am cold, though it happened a month ago.

XXV

From the white man's house, and the black man's hut,
   I carried the little body on.   170
The forest's arms did round us shut,
   And silence through the trees did run.[1]
They asked no question as I went,—
They stood too high for astonishment,—
   They could see God sit on his throne.   175

---

1 ll. 169-72] Cf. the father's journey through the forest with his dead child in "The Indian With His Dead Child" (1830) by Felicia Hemans (1793-1835).

XXVI

My little body, kerchiefed fast,
    I bore it on through the forest .. on;
And when I felt it was tired at last,
    I scooped a hole beneath the moon.
Through the forest-tops the angels far,   180
With a white sharp finger from every star,
    Did point and mock at what was done.

XXVII

Yet when it was all done aright, ..
    Earth, 'twixt me and my baby, strewed, ..
All, changed to black earth, .. nothing white, ..   185
    A dark child in the dark!—ensued
Some comfort, and my heart grew young.
I sate down smiling there and sung
    The song I learnt in my maidenhood.

XXVIII

And thus we two were reconciled,   190
    The white child and black mother, thus;
For, as I sang it soft and wild,
    The same song, more melodious,
Rose from the grave whereon I sate.
It was the dead child singing that,   195
    To join the souls of both of us.

XXIX

I look on the sea and the sky!
    Where the pilgrims' ships first anchored lay
The free sun rideth gloriously,
    But the pilgrim-ghosts have slid away   200
Through the earliest streaks of the morn.
My face is black, but it glares with a scorn[1]
    Which they dare not meet by day.

---

1   but it glares with a scorn] RB's suggested phrasing, reinscribed in ink in EBB's hand
    above her cancelled phrase "my soul forlorn."

XXX

Ah!—in their 'stead, their hunter sons![1]
    Ah, ah! they are on me—they hunt in a ring—   205
Keep off! I brave you all at once—
    I throw off your eyes like snakes that sting!
You have killed the black eagle at nest, I think.
Did you never stand still in your triumph, and shrink
    From the stroke of her wounded wing?   210

XXXI

(Man, drop that stone you dared to lift!—)
    I wish you who stand there five a-breast,
Each, for his own wife's joy and gift,
    A little corpse as safely at rest
As mine in the mangos!—Yes, but *she*   215
May keep live babies on her knee,
    And sing the song she likes the best.

XXXII

I am not mad: I am black.
    I see you staring in my face—
I know you staring, shrinking back,   220
    Ye are born of the Washington-race.[2]
And this land is the free America,
And this mark on my wrist .. (I prove what I say)
    Ropes tied me up here to the flogging-place.

XXXIII

You think I shrieked then? Not a sound!   225
    I hung, as a gourd hangs in the sun.
I only cursed them all around
    As softly as I might have done
My very own child.—From these sands
Up to the mountains, lift your hands,   230
    O slaves, and end what I begun!

---

1   hunter sons!] i.e., the slave hunters whom she regards as descendents of the Pilgrim fathers.

2   Washington-race] the descendents of George Washington (1732-99), first President of the United States.

XXXIV

Whips, curses; these must answer those!
    For in this UNION,[1] you have set
Two kinds of men in adverse rows,
    Each loathing each; and all forget   235
The seven wounds in Christ's body fair,[2]
While HE sees gaping everywhere
    Our countless wounds that pay no debt.

XXXV

Our wounds are different. Your white men
    Are, after all, not gods indeed,   240
Nor able to make Christs again
    Do good with bleeding. *We* who bleed
(Stand off!) we help not in our loss!
We are too heavy for our cross,
    And fall and crush you and your seed.   245

XXXVI

I fall, I swoon! I look at the sky.
    The clouds are breaking on my brain.
I am floated along, as if I should die
    Of liberty's exquisite[3] pain.
In the name of the white child waiting for me   250
In the death-dark where we may kiss and agree,
White men, I leave you all curse-free
    In my broken heart's disdain!

---

1   UNION] Frequently figuring in works in *The Liberty Bell*, "UNION" is capitalized thus in "The American Union" by William Lloyd Garrison in the 1845 issue (see Appendix C.I.4).

2   seven wounds in Christ's body fair] the wounds caused by the scourging of Christ, his crowning with thorns, and the five that were inflicted on him when he was stretched on the Cross.

3   exquisite] RB's penciled suggestion, as D802 shows. EBB first wrote "glorious," then deleted it, tried another word (illegible because deleted), then inserted "wonderful."

A Reed

The multiple signed copies of "A Reed," combined with its first-person declarations, suggest that it can be read as a kind of signature poem for EBB, testifying obliquely to her values, modes of self-representation, and sense of identity.[1] She returns to the metaphor of the reed in "A Musical Instrument" (1860), which makes its associations with the myth of Pan and Syrinx more evident. "A Reed" seems to have been especially significant to RB. A transcript by him of stanzas one and two appears on a leaf with a signed quotation from his brief lyric "My Star," published in *Men and Women* (1855) and usually interpreted as an autobiographical tribute to EBB.[2]

I

I am no trumpet, but a reed:
No flattering breath shall from me lead
  A silver sound, a hollow sound.
I will not ring, for priest or king,
One blast that in re-echoing   5
  Would leave a bondsman faster bound.

II

I am no trumpet, but a reed,—
A broken reed, the wind indeed
  Left flat upon a dismal shore;
Yet if a little maid, or child,   10
Should sigh within it, earnest-mild,
  This reed will answer evermore.

III

I am no trumpet, but a reed.
Go, tell the fishers, as they spread

---

1   A preliminary draft of this poem (*R* D761) appears in a notebook dated 1842; a second draft (D762) closer in phrasing to the poem as published in *Blackwood's Edinburgh Magazine* in October 1846 (and in *Poems*, 1850) exists in a notebook dating from the 1844–46 period. Another signed copy is dated April 1845 (D763), while still another (D764) appears on a leaf with lines of RB's *Paracelsus* (1835; Part V, 186–92).

2   On "My Star," see the conclusion to the Introduction.

Their nets along the river's edge,   15
I will not tear their nets at all,
Nor pierce their hands, if they should fall;
    Then let them leave me in the sedge.

Sonnets from the Portuguese

First published in *Poems* (1850), this sonnet sequence remains EBB's
most widely known and popular work. In less than a century be-
tween 1886, when the first separate edition appeared, and 1962, at
least 170 editions and reprints were published (see Barnes 1967).
The sequence has been translated into German (many times, most
notably by the German lyric poet Rainer Maria Rilke), French (by
André Maurois, among others), Italian, Spanish (in separate editions
published in Spain, Mexico, and Argentina), Portuguese, Dutch,
Russian, Hungarian, and Polish. The pamphlet edition published
at "Reading" in "1847" is the most famous among many forgeries
by the notorious Thomas Wise,[1] who sought to capitalize on the
sequence's popularity. The perennial and international appeal of
the *Sonnets from the Portuguese* in the decades following the turn of
the twentieth century helps to explain the immediate popularity of
the play and film representing the courtship of EBB and RB, *The
Barretts of Wimpole Street* (see the Introduction). EBB composed the
poems during her nineteen-month courtship with RB in 1845-46
but kept them secret from him until after their marriage and the
birth of their son, giving him the manuscript in 1849 when RB was
deeply depressed by his mother's recent death. Because of his reluc-
tance to exhibit their personal lives to the public (see his 1876 poem
"House"), he described the poems as "a strange, heavy crown, that
wreath of Sonnets, put on me one morning unawares, three years

---

1   Thomas J. Wise (1859-1937), collector, bibliophile, and producer of multiple forged
     pamphlet editions of nineteenth-century works, including the ostensible 1849 edition
     of "The Runaway Slave at Pilgrim's Point." See John Carter and Graham Pollard, *An
     Enquiry into the Nature of Certain Nineteenth Century Pamphlets* (London: Constable;
     New York: Charles Scribner's Sons, 1934); Richard D. Altick, *The Scholar Adventurers*
     (NY: Macmillan, 1950), ch. 2; and Barker 2003.

after it had been twined."[1] Although EBB did not originally intend to publish them, he nevertheless "could not consent ... that they should be lost" (*LTA* 1:368). The Brownings devised the enigmatic title to shield the personal elements of the sonnets by implying that they are translations—a ruse EBB playfully sustained, briefly, with her "impertinent" skeptical sister Arabella: "How can you possibly know that I have not been studying Portuguese, a language rich in sonnets, all these four years!" (*LTA* 1:361). The title's masquerade simultaneously conceals and reveals the poems' intimacy, however, for it refers indirectly to one of RB's favorites among EBB's works, "Catarina to Camoens"[2] (1843), in which the dying Catarina addresses her absent poet-lover, the sixteenth-century Portuguese poet Luiz de Camões, himself a writer of love sonnets.[3] EBB wrote that "[i]n a loving fancy," Robert "had always associated me with Catarina" (*LTA* 1:368). The sequence was positioned immediately after "Catarina to Camöens," following directions to the printer in RB's hand, when it was initially published in *Poems* (1850). EBB further shielded the personal matter of the sonnets by removing one from the sequence in 1850 and printing it separately—number XLII, which quotes her previously published sonnet "Past and Future" (1844). In 1850 she also separated the sequence from a group of six personal lyrics directly associated with its subject matter. In *Poems* of 1856, however, the full sequence of 44 sonnets appeared, prefaced by this cluster of six lyrics,[4] which followed "Catarina to Camoens."

Although reading the Brownings' courtship correspondence vividly underscores the autobiographical dimensions of *Sonnets from the Portuguese*, their literary achievement can be appreciated only

1 *Robert Browning and Julia Wedgwood: A Broken Friendship as Revealed by Their Letters*, ed. Richard Curle (NY: Frederick A. Stokes, 1937), 99.

2 In their courtship correspondence, RB quoted or referred to "Catarina to Camoens" at least fourteen times. Edmund Gosse, in a patently inventive account, reported that EBB initially intended to call the sequence "Sonnets translated from the Bosnian" (see Appendix A.8), but RB argued for the personal associations of Portuguese (see *RB and Julia Wedgwood*, 100).

3 Camöens's sonnets fit the traditional courtly love pattern, celebrating an unattainable earthly love which ultimately leads to the divine; see the allusion to Camöens (c. 1524-80) in "A Vision of Poets," ll. 370-75; and the headnote to "Catarina to Camoens."

4 These six lyrics—"Life and Love," "A Denial," "Proof and Disproof," "Question and Answer," "Inclusions," and "Insufficiency"—are also associated with *Sonnets from the Portuguese* through manuscript evidence; see R D875.

by viewing them in the tradition of the sonnet sequence tracing back to the Italian poet Petrarch (1304-74) and the 317 sonnets in his *Rime sparse* or *Canzoniere* ("scattered rhymes" or "songs"), many of which express his adoration of Laura, an idealized woman who remained unattainable but spiritually inspiring.[1] While *Sonnets from the Portuguese* echoes the conventions and thematic patterns of Renaissance sonnet sequences, EBB dramatically varies their formulaic relationships by reversing conventional gender roles and asserting female passion and desire, in part through the sensuous images of the sequence. She also counters the typical representation of love as frustrated desire which imprisons the lover and makes him ill, instead portraying love as a force that liberates, restores health, and renews life. Unlike most English poets who wrote love sonnet sequences, including Sir Philip Sidney (1554-86), Edmund Spenser (1552-99), and Shakespeare (1564-1616), EBB employed the demanding Italian (Petrarchan) sonnet form. She treated its organization into an octave and a sestet rather freely, often achieving complex effects by abbreviating and expanding these structural units, and making innovative use of slant rhymes, off rhymes, and near rhymes.

Biographical approaches to the *Sonnets from the Portuguese* as the unmediated revelation of a woman's heart chiefly prevailed from the late Victorian period until the 1970s, but since then a growing body of scholarship has emphasized the negotiation and revision of sonnet conventions in the sequence, its gender politics, its artistry, its complex rhetorical strategies, and its intertextual connections with the courtship correspondence or with poems by RB and other Victorian poets such as Christina Rossetti (1830-94). On the gender politics of the sequence and EBB's engagement with the love sonnet tradition and other Victorian sonnet sequences, see Mermin 1981; Agajanian 1985; Leighton 1986, 1988; Cooper 1988; Stephenson 1989; Paul 1989; Mazzaro 1991; Lootens 1996; Riede 2005; Reynolds 1997; Stone 1999; Neri 2000, 2003, 2005; Houston 2002; Moore 2000; Gray 2002; Avery and Stott 2003; and Marshall 2006. Morlier 1999 analyzes EBB's adaptation of

---

1   EBB translated several of Petrarch's sonnets in 1842-44 (see *R* D1245-1255), when she was also drafting a substantial number of original sonnets on subjects other than love published in *Poems* (1844).

the political sonnet and the rhyming strategies of social reform poetry. On the connections between the sonnets, the courtship correspondence, and RB's poems see Karlin 1985, 1997, Sullivan 1987, Mermin 1989, Chapman 1998, Pollock 2003, and Davies and Stone 2006. A variorum edition by Miroslava Wein Dow (1980) incorporates detailed annotation on the surviving manuscripts and textual variants.

I

I thought once how Theocritus[1] had sung
Of the sweet years, the dear and wished for years,
Who each one in a gracious hand appears
To bear a gift for mortals, old or young:
And, as I mused it in his antique tongue,   5
I saw, in gradual vision through my tears,
The sweet, sad years, the melancholy years,
Those of my own life, who by turns had flung
A shadow across me. Straightway I was 'ware,
So weeping, how a mystic Shape did move   10
Behind me, and drew me backward by the hair,[2]
And a voice said in mastery while I strove, ..
"Guess now who holds thee?"—"Death," I said. But, there,
The silver[3] answer rang .. "Not Death, but Love."

II

But only three in all God's universe
Have heard this word thou hast said,—Himself, beside
Thee speaking, and me listening! and replied
One of us .. *that* was God, .. and laid the curse[4]

---

1 Theocritus] Greek poet (c. 308-c. 240 BCE), in whose bucolic Idyl 15, Adonis, welcoming the advent of Spring and the reawakening of Love, describes the Hours bringing gifts to mortals.

2 Echoes the *Iliad* 1.204, where an invisible Athena pulls Achilles backward by his hair.

3 Alludes to Shakespeare's "silver sound" of music in *Romeo and Juliet*, act 4, scene 5, ll. 125-38. In her letters EBB refers to the "silver sound" in RB's words or voice: e.g., "those words of the letter which were of a better silver in the sound than even your praise could be" (*BC* 11:165).

4 Responding to RB's renewed declarations of love, EBB wrote, "But something worse than even a sense of unworthiness, GOD has put between us!" (*BC* 11:78; see also *BC* 11:100).

So darkly on my eyelids, as to amerce[1]   5
My sight from seeing thee,—that if I had died,
The deathweights,[2] placed there, would have signified
Less absolute exclusion. "Nay" is worse
From God than from all others, O my friend!
Men could not part us with their worldly jars,   10
Nor the seas change us, nor the tempests bend;
Our hands would touch for all the mountain-bars,—
And, heaven being rolled between us at the end,
We should but vow the faster for the stars.

III
Unlike are we, unlike, O princely Heart!
Unlike our uses and our destinies.
Our ministering two angels[3] look surprise
On one another, as they strike athwart
Their wings in passing. Thou, bethink thee, art   5
A guest for queens to social pageantries,
With gages[4] from a hundred brighter eyes
Than tears even can make mine, to ply thy part
Of chief musician. What hast *thou* to do
With looking from the lattice-lights at me,   10
A poor, tired, wandering singer, .. singing through
The dark, and leaning up a cypress[5] tree?
The chrism[6] is on thine head,—on mine, the dew,—
And Death must dig the level where these agree.

IV
Thou hast thy calling to some palace-floor,
Most gracious singer of high poems! where

---

1   amerce] deprive; also to penalize, especially financially, as in levying a fine.
2   deathweights] weights customarily placed on the eyelids of the dead to keep them closed.
3   ministering two angels] evokes medieval and Renaissance notions that human beings
    are influenced by their personal good and evil spirits; see Shakespeare's sonnet 144.
4   gages] pledges.
5   cypress] tree traditionally associated with death.
6   chrism] the oil used to anoint a king at his coronation.

The dancers will break footing,[1] from the care
Of watching up thy pregnant lips for more.
And dost thou lift this house's latch too poor   5
For hand of thine? and canst thou think and bear
To let thy music drop here unaware
In folds of golden fulness at my door?
Look up and see the casement broken in,
The bats and owlets builders in the roof!   10
My cricket chirps against thy mandolin.
Hush, call no echo up in further proof
Of desolation! there's a voice within
That weeps .. as thou must sing .. alone, aloof.

V
I lift my heavy heart up solemnly,
As once Electra her sepulchral urn,[2]
And, looking in thine eyes, I overturn
The ashes at thy feet. Behold and see
What a great heap of grief lay hid in me,   5
And how the red wild sparkles dimly burn
Through the ashen greyness. If thy foot in scorn
Could tread them out to darkness utterly,
It might be well perhaps. But if instead
Thou wait beside me for the wind to blow   10
The grey dust up, ... those laurels[3] on thine head,
O my belovèd, will not shield thee so,
That none of all the fires shall scorch and shred
The hair beneath. Stand further off then! go.

VI
Go from me. Yet I feel that I shall stand
Henceforward in thy shadow. Nevermore

---

1   break footing] make a mistake in their steps or choreography.

2   In Sophocles's drama *Electra*, Electra receives a funeral urn ostensibly containing the ashes
    of her brother Orestes (she eventually discovers he is still alive); EBB uses the allusion to
    refer to her intense grief over her brother Edward's 1840 death (see her sonnet "Grief").

3   laurels] triumphant poets were traditionally crowned with wreaths made of laurel
    (bay) leaves.

Alone upon the threshold of my door
Of individual life,[1] I shall command
The uses of my soul, nor lift my hand   5
Serenely in the sunshine as before,
Without the sense of that which I forbore,[2] ..
Thy touch upon the palm. The widest land
Doom takes to part us, leaves thy heart in mine
With pulses that beat double. What I do   10
And what I dream include thee, as the wine
Must taste of its own grapes. And when I sue[3]
God for myself, He hears that name of thine,
And sees within my eyes, the tears of two.

VII

The face of all the world is changed, I think,
Since first I heard the footsteps of thy soul
Move still, oh, still, beside me, as they stole
Betwixt me and the dreadful outer brink
Of obvious death, where I, who thought to sink,   5
Was caught up into love, and taught the whole
Of life in a new rhythm. The cup of dole[4]
God gave for baptism, I am fain[5] to drink,
And praise its sweetness, Sweet, with thee anear.
The names of country, heaven, are changed away   10
For where thou art or shalt be, there or here;
And this .. this lute and song .. loved yesterday,
(The singing angels know) are only dear,
Because thy name moves right in what they say.

---

1   EBB wrote to RB, "you do not know what my life meant before you touched it…. My
    wonder is greater than your wonders, .. I who sate [i.e., sat] here alone but yesterday,
    so weary of my own being" (*BC* 11:147).

2   forebore] endured the loss of.

3   sue] petition, beseech.

4   dole] grief or sorrow.

5   fain] glad, eager.

VIII

What can I give thee back, O liberal
And princely giver, who has brought the gold
And purple of thine heart, unstained, untold,[1]
And laid them on the outside of the wall
For such as I to take or leave withal,[2]   5
In unexpected largesse? am I cold,
Ungrateful, that for these most manifold
High gifts, I render nothing back at all?
Not so; not cold,—but very poor instead.
Ask God who knows. For frequent tears have run   10
The colours from my life,[3] and left so dead
And pale a stuff, it were not fitly done
To give the same as pillow to thy head.
Go farther! let it serve to trample on.

IX

Can it be right to give what I can give?[4]
To let thee sit beneath the fall of tears
As salt as mine, and hear the sighing years
Re-sighing on my lips renunciative
Through those infrequent smiles which fail to live   5
For all thy adjurations? O my fears,
That this can scarce be right! We are not peers,
So to be lovers; and I own, and grieve,
That givers of such gifts as mine are, must
Be counted with the ungenerous. Out, alas!   10
I will not soil thy purple with my dust,

---

1   untold] uncounted, beyond enumeration. Gold and purple are traditionally associated
with wealth and royalty. EBB wrote to RB, "What could I give you, which it would
not be ungenerous to give?" (*BC* 11:54).

2   withal] along with the rest.

3   EBB wrote RB, "Have I not been ground down to browns & blacks? & is it my fault
if I am not green?"; "my poetry … is the flower of me-- I have lived most & been
most happy in it, & so it has all my colours,--the rest of me is nothing but a root, fit
for the ground & the dark" (*BC* 10:254, 216).

4   EBB wrote to RB, "if you gave [your life] to me & I put my whole heart into it,
what should I put but anxiety, & more sadness than you were born to? What could
I give you, which it would not be ungenerous to give?" (*BC* 11:54).

Nor breathe my poison on thy Venice-glass,[1]
Nor give thee any love ... which were unjust.
Beloved, I only love thee! let it pass.

X

Yet, love, mere love, is beautiful indeed
And worthy of acceptation.[2] Fire is bright,
Let temple burn, or flax. An equal light
Leaps in the flame from cedar-plank or weed.
And love is fire; and when I say at need   5
I love thee .. mark! .. I love thee! .. in thy sight
I stand transfigured,[3] glorified aright,
With conscience[4] of the new rays that proceed
Out of my face toward thine. There's nothing low
In love, when love the lowest: meanest creatures   10
Who love God, God accepts while loving so.
And what I *feel*, across the inferior features
Of what I *am*, doth flash itself, and show
How that great work of Love enhances Nature's.

XI

And therefore if to love can be desert,[5]
I am not all unworthy. Cheeks as pale
As these you see, and trembling knees that fail
To bear the burden of a heavy heart,—
This weary minstrel-life that once was girt[6]   5
To climb Aornus,[7] and can scarce avail

---

1   Venice-glass] Venetian glass was reputed to be so fine that poison would shatter it.

2   acceptation] favourable reception or approval, implying assent, acquiescence, or belief.

3   transfigured] transformed, with connotations of the Transfiguration, the sudden radiance emitted by Christ after his contact with God (Matthew 17.2; Mark 9.2).

4   conscience] consciousness.

5   desert] deserved; something deserved.

6   girt] encircled, especially referring to clothing, recalling the Biblical admonition "gird up thy loins" to prepare for a challenging encounter (e.g., 2 Kings 4.29, Job 38.3).

7   Aornus] a high rock plateau in the Himalayan foothills thought to be impregnable (mythic Hercules failed to conquer it), but captured by Alexander the Great (326 BCE).

To pipe now 'gainst the valley nightingale
A melancholy music,—why advert[1]
To these things? O Beloved, it is plain
I am not of thy worth nor for thy place!   10
And yet, because I love thee, I obtain
From that same love this vindicating grace,
To live on still in love, and yet in vain, ..
To bless thee, yet renounce thee to thy face.

XII

Indeed this very love which is my boast,
And which, when rising up from breast to brow,
Doth crown me with a ruby large enow[2]
To draw men's eyes and prove the inner cost, ..
This love even, all my worth, to the uttermost,   5
I should not love withal, unless that thou
Hadst set me an example, shown me how,
When first thine earnest eyes with mine were crossed,
And love called love. And thus, I cannot speak
Of love even, as a good thing of my own.   10
Thy soul hath snatched up mine all faint and weak,
And placed it by thee on a golden throne,—
And that I love (O soul, we must be meek!)
Is by thee only, whom I love alone.

XIII

And wilt thou have me fashion into speech
The love I bear thee, finding words enough,
And hold the torch out, while the winds are rough,
Between our faces, to cast light on each?—
I drop it at thy feet. I cannot teach   5
My hand to hold my spirit so far off
From myself .. me .. that I should bring thee proof
In words, of love hid in me out of reach.
Nay, let the silence of my womanhood

---

1 advert] refer.
2 enow] enough.

Commend my woman-love to thy belief,— 10
Seeing that I stand unwon, however wooed,
And rend the garment of my life, in brief,
By a most dauntless, voiceless fortitude,
Lest one touch of this heart convey its grief.

XIV

If thou must love me, let it be for nought
Except for love's sake only.[1] Do not say
"I love her for her smile .. her look .. her way
Of speaking gently, .. for a trick of thought
That falls in well with mine, and certes[2] brought 5
A sense of pleasant ease on such a day"—
For these things in themselves, Belovèd, may
Be changed, or change for thee,—and love, so wrought,
May be unwrought so. Neither love me for
Thine own dear pity's wiping my cheeks dry,—[3] 10
A creature might forget to weep, who bore
Thy comfort long, and lose thy love thereby!
But love me for love's sake, that evermore
Thou may'st love on, through love's eternity.

XV

Accuse me not, beseech thee, that I wear
Too calm and sad a face in front of thine;
For we two look two ways,[4] and cannot shine
With the same sunlight on our brow and hair.
On me thou lookest, with no doubting care, 5
As on a bee shut in a crystalline,—

---

1   EBB wrote to RB, "The first moment in which I seemed to admit to myself … the
possibility of your affection for me … was that when you intimated … that you cared
for me not for a reason, but because you cared for me" (*BC* 11:165). RB had previously
declared, "I love you because I love you" (*BC* 11:135).

2   certes] certainly.

3   EBB wrote to RB, "I have sometimes felt jealous of myself .. of my own infirmities,
.. & thought that you cared for me only because your chivalry touched them with a
silver sound" (*BC* 11:137).

4   EBB wrote to RB, "while you see from above & I from below, we cannot see the same
thing in the same light" (*BC* 11:91).

Since sorrow hath shut me safe in love's divine,
And to spread wing and fly in the outer air
Were most impossible failure, if I strove
To fail so. But I look on thee .. on thee ..   10
Beholding, besides love, the end of love,[1]
Hearing oblivion beyond memory!
As one who sits and gazes from above,
Over the rivers to the bitter sea.

XVI

And yet, because thou overcomest so,[2]
Because thou art more noble and like a king,
Thou canst prevail against my fears and fling
Thy purple round me,[3] till my heart shall grow
Too close against thine heart, henceforth to know   5
How it shook when alone. Why, conquering
May prove as lordly and complete a thing
In lifting upward,[4] as in crushing low!
And as a vanquished soldier yields his sword
To one who lifts him from the bloody earth,[5]—   10
Even so, Belovèd, I at last record,
Here ends my strife. If *thou* invite me forth,
I rise above abasement at the word.
Make thy love larger to enlarge my worth.

---

1   EBB feared that RB's interest in her would fade: "I tremble! When you come to know
    me as well as I know myself, what can save me, do you think, from disappointing &
    displeasing you?" (*BC* 11:244).

2   EBB referred to RB's allaying her fears and doubts concerning their relationship:
    "How you overcome me as always you do" (*BC* 11:176).

3   RB used similar imagery in a letter: "you take me in your mantle, and we shine
    together" (*BC* 11:292).

4   Hoping that she could love him without neglecting her poetry, RB wrote to EBB:
    "if you can lift me with one hand, while the other suffices to crown you—there is
    queenliness in that, too!" (*BC* 11:159).

5   And as a vanquished soldier...earth] one of the more notable revisions between *Poems*
    (1850) and *Poems* (1856): in the former, this passage read, "And, as a soldier struck down
    by a sword / May cry, 'My strife ends here,' and sink to earth."

XVII

My poet, thou canst touch on all the notes
God set between His After and Before,
And strike up and strike off the general roar
Of the rushing worlds, a melody that floats
In a serene air purely. Antidotes   5
Of medicated music,[1] answering for
Mankind's forlornest uses, thou canst pour
From thence into their ears. God's will devotes
Thine to such ends, and mine to wait on thine.
How, Dearest, wilt thou have me for most use?[2]   10
A hope, to sing by gladly? .. or a fine
Sad memory, with thy songs to interfuse?
A shade, in which to sing ... of palm or pine?[3]
A grave, on which to rest from singing? .. Choose.

XVIII

I never gave a lock of hair away
To a man, Dearest, except this to thee,[4]
Which now upon my fingers thoughtfully
I ring out to the full brown length and say
"Take it." My day of youth went yesterday;   5
My hair no longer bounds to my foot's glee,
Nor plant I it from rose or myrtle-tree,[5]
As girls do, any more. It only may

---

1 Antidotes of medicated music] cf. the use of music by the biblical David to soothe
   King Saul in I Samuel 16.14-23, the subject of RB's poem "Saul" (1845, expanded
   version 1855), discussed by the two poets (*BC* 11: 388-90).

2 Before he began to visit her, RB wrote EBB, "are you not my dear friend already, and
   shall I not use you?" (*BC* 10:107).

3 palm or pine] The palm tree is traditionally associated with life, the pine with death.

4 Responding to RB's request for a lock of her hair, EBB wrote, "I never gave away
   what you ask me to give you, to a human being, except my nearest relatives & once
   or twice or thrice to female friends" (*BC* 11:197); she had earlier refused Richard
   Hengist Horne's request for a lock of hair as a "'memento'" (*BC* 11:149), despite her
   extended correspondence and collaborations with him (see the Introduction, p. 22).
   The exchange of hair between lovers traditionally bore an erotic charge. Cf. the
   association of "loose long hair" with "flame" and desire in *Aurora Leigh* 5:1126-32.

5 She no longer adorns her hair with sprigs of rose or myrtle (both associated with
   love).

Now shade on two pale cheeks, the mark of tears,
Taught drooping from the head that hangs aside   10
Through sorrow's trick.[1] I thought the funeral-shears[2]
Would take this first, but Love is justified,—
Take it thou, .. finding pure, from all those years,
The kiss my mother left here when she died.[3]

XIX

The soul's Rialto[4] hath its merchandise;
I barter curl for curl upon that mart,
And from my poet's forehead to my heart,
Receive this lock[5] which outweighs argosies,—
As purply black, as erst,[6] to Pindar's eyes,   5
The dim purpureal tresses gloomed athwart
The nine white Muse-brows.[7] For this counterpart, ..
The bay-crown's shade, Belovèd, I surmise,
Still lingers on thy curl, it is so black!
Thus, with a fillet[8] of smooth-kissing breath,   10
I tie the shadow safe from gliding back,
And lay the gift where nothing hindereth,
Here on my heart,[9] as on thy brow, to lack

---

1 Portraits and photographs of EBB record this characteristic tilt of her head.

2 Alludes to the classical custom of cutting the hair of the dead and also to the Victorian
   practice of cutting locks from the dead for memorial jewelry, especially rings and
   pins. On the many locks of hair from both of the Brownings that still survive as relics
   in various collections, see R H474-498.

3 EBB's mother died in 1828.

4 Rialto] the Rialto Bridge in Venice, lined with shops.

5 In exchange for the lock of hair EBB gave to RB (see sonnet XVIII), she required one
   of his, insisting (in language echoing Shakespeare's *The Merchant of Venice*) on an equal
   exchange of "pure merchandise" (*BC* 11:198).

6 erst] formerly.

7 The first Pythian ode of the Greek poet Pindar (c. 518-c. 483 BCE) describes the
   Muses' locks as a black of purplish hue (here "purpureal"). In Greek mythology, the
   Muses were the nine daughters of Zeus and Mnemosyne who each presided over an
   art or science. See also EBB's allusion to the legendary lock of purple that grew in the
   gray hair of Nisus, King of Megara, insuring the safety of his kingdom and his life (*BC*
   11:207).

8 fillet] headband or ribbon used to tie back the hair, fashionable in ancient Greece.

9 EBB wore the lock of RB's hair in a treasured locket; she sent hers to him in a ring.

No natural heat till mine grows cold in death.

XX

Beloved, my Beloved, when I think
That thou wast in the world a year ago,[1]
What time I sate[2] alone here in the snow
And saw no footprint, heard the silence sink
No moment at thy voice, .. but, link by link,   5
Went counting all my chains,[3] as if that so
They never could fall off at any blow
Struck by thy possible hand ... . why, thus I drink
Of life's great cup of wonder! Wonderful,
Never to feel thee thrill the day or night   10
With personal act or speech,—nor ever cull
Some prescience of thee with the blossoms white
Thou sawest growing![4] Atheists are as dull,
Who cannot guess God's presence out of sight.

XXI

Say over again, and yet once over again,
That thou dost love me. Though the word repeated
Should seem "a cuckoo-song,"[5] as thou dost treat it,
Remember never to the hill or plain,
Valley and wood, without her cuckoo-strain,   5
Comes the fresh Spring in all her green completed.
Beloved, I, amid the darkness greeted

---

1   EBB wrote to RB on 19 May 1846: "how I had different thoughts of you & of myself & of the world & of life, last year at this hour!" (*BC* 12:339).

2   sate] sat.

3   EBB wrote to RB, "no man was ever before to any woman what you are to me—the fulness must be in proportion, you know, to the vacancy .. & only I know what was behind .. the long wilderness without the 'footstep', .. without the blossoming rose .. & the capacity for happiness, like a black gaping hole, before this silver flooding" (*BC* 11:305).

4   Early in their correspondence RB anticipated the advent of Spring, when EBB had suggested she might allow him to visit her, by noting early blossoms (e.g., *BC* 10:202).

5   RB wrote to EBB: "what is in my mind," a "cuckoo-song," is "that I love & love & love again my own, dearest love" (*BC* 11:248). The cuckoo is the first English bird to return in the spring.

By a doubtful spirit-voice, in that doubt's pain
Cry .. "Speak once more .. thou lovest!" Who can fear
Too many stars, though each in heaven shall roll— 10
Too many flowers, though each shall crown the year?
Say thou dost love me, love me, love me—toll
The silver iterance!—only minding, Dear,
To love me also in silence, with thy soul.

XXII

When our two souls stand up erect and strong,
Face to face, silent, drawing nigh and nigher,
Until the lengthening wings break into fire
At either curvéd point,—what bitter wrong
Can the earth do to us, that we should not long 5
Be here contented? Think. In mounting higher,
The angels would press on us, and aspire
To drop some golden orb of perfect song
Into our deep, dear silence. Let us stay
Rather on earth, Belovèd,—where the unfit 10
Contrarious moods of men recoil away
And isolate pure spirits, and permit
A place to stand and love in for a day,[1]
With darkness and the death-hour rounding it.

XXIII

Is it indeed so? If I lay here dead,
Would'st thou miss any life in losing mine?
And would the sun for thee more coldly shine,
Because of grave-damps[2] falling round my head?
I marvelled, my Belovèd, when I read 5

---

1 Alludes to a declaration attributed to the Greek mathematician Archimedes (c. 278-212 BCE): "Give me a firm place to stand and I will move the earth." Six months before meeting RB, EBB had written that poetry "is my pou stoo [Greek "place to stand"]... not to move the world, .. but to live on in" (*BC* 9:66).

2 grave-damps] grave moisture forming into drops; possibly a nonce compound, like EBB's "grave-deep," in l. 132 of "Crowned and Buried" (1844).

Thy thought so in the letter.[1] I am thine—
But .. *so* much to thee? Can I pour thy wine
While my hands tremble? Then my soul, instead
Of dreams of death, resumes life's lower range.
Then, love me, Love! look on me .. breathe on me!   10
As brighter ladies do not count it strange,
For love, to give up acres and degree,
I yield the grave for thy sake, and exchange
My near sweet view of Heaven, for earth with thee!

XXIV

Let the world's sharpness like a clasping knife[2]
Shut in upon itself and do no harm
In this close hand of Love, now soft and warm,
And let us hear no sound of human strife
After the click of the shutting. Life to life—   5
I lean upon thee, Dear, without alarm,
And feel as safe as guarded by a charm
Against the stab of worldlings, who if rife[3]
Are weak to injure. Very whitely still
The lilies of our lives may reassure   10
Their blossoms from their roots, accessible
Alone to heavenly dews that drop not fewer;
Growing straight, out of man's reach, on the hill.
God only, who made us rich, can make us poor.

XXV

A heavy heart, Belovèd, have I borne
From year to year until I saw thy face,
And sorrow after sorrow took the place
Of all those natural joys as lightly worn

---

1 On 18 December 1845 EBB wrote, "I have thought sometimes that, if I considered
myself wholly, I should choose to die this winter .. now .. before I had disappointed
you in anything." RB protested passionately in his next two letters, written on 20 and
21 December (*BC* 11:244, 250, 254).

2 clasping knife] a knife (like a modern pocket knife) on which the blade folds into the
handle.

3 rife] quick; also numerous.

As the stringed pearls .. each lifted in its turn   5
By a beating heart at dance-time. Hopes apace[1]
Were changed to long despairs, till God's own grace
Could scarcely lift above the world forlorn
My heavy heart. Then *thou* didst bid me bring
And let it drop adown thy calmly great   10
Deep being! Fast it sinketh, as a thing
Which its own nature doth precipitate,
While thine doth close above it, mediating
Betwixt the stars and the unaccomplished fate.

XXVI

I lived with visions for my company,[2]
Instead of men and women,[3] years ago,
And found them gentle mates, nor thought to know
A sweeter music than they played to me.
But soon their trailing purple[4] was not free   5
Of this world's dust,—their lutes did silent grow,
And I myself grew faint and blind below
Their vanishing eyes. Then THOU didst come .. to be,
Belovèd, what they seemed. Their shining fronts,[5]
Their songs, their splendours, (better, yet the same,   10
As river-water hallowed into fonts)
Met in thee, and from out thee overcame
My soul with satisfaction of all wants—
Because God's gifts put man's best dreams to shame.

---

1   apace] rapidly.

2   EBB described her sheltered life to RB: "I have lived only inwardly.... had my heart
    in books & poetry, .. & my experience, in reveries.... Books & dreams were what I
    lived in.... and afterwards, when my illness came ... I turned to thinking with some
    bitterness ... that I had seen no Human nature" (*BC* 10:133). For one example of her
    "reveries," see "A Vision of Poets" (1844).

3   RB used the phrase "men and women" as the title of his 1855 collection of poetry, and
    its dedicatory poem addressed to EBB, "One Word More," begins: "There they are,
    my fifty men and women...."

4   purple] here, associated both with royalty and the cloth used to drape caskets and graves.

5   fronts] foreheads; here more generally suggesting faces.

XXVII

My own belovèd, who hast lifted me
From this drear flat of earth where I was thrown,
And, in betwixt the languid ringlets, blown
A life-breath, till the forehead hopefully
Shines out again, as all the angels see,   5
Before thy saving kiss! My own, my own,
Who camest to me when the world was gone,
And I who looked for only God, found *thee!*
I find thee; I am safe, and strong, and glad.
As one who stands in dewless asphodel,[1]   10
Looks backward on the tedious time he had
In the upper life,—so I, with bosom-swell,
Make witness, here, between the good and bad,
That Love, as strong as Death, retrieves as well.

XXVIII

My letters![2] all dead paper, .. mute and white!—
And yet they seem alive and quivering
Against my tremulous hands which loose the string
And let them drop down on my knee to-night.
This said, .. he wished to have me in his sight   5
Once, as a friend:[3] this fixed a day in spring
To come and touch my hand[4] ... a simple thing,

---

1   asphodel] the flower of immortality that in Greek mythology grows in the Elysian
    Fields of the blessed.

2   Refers to the 287 letters RB sent to EBB during their courtship minus the one letter
    that she returned and he destroyed (see *BC* 10:238, 11:151, and note to l. 9 below).
    They exchanged a total of 573 letters, each treasuring the other's in a special box.
    Cf. the allusions to love letters in Sonnets XLIII and XLVIII of the *Amoretti* (1595) by
    Edmund Spenser (1552?-99).

3   RB's first letter to EBB explained that he once had nearly met her, accompany-
    ing their mutual friend John Kenyon, but she had been too unwell to receive
    him: "I feel ... as if I had been close, so close, to some world's-wonder in chapel
    or crypt, .. only a screen to push and I might have entered—but there was some
    slight ... and just-sufficient bar to admission, and the half-opened door shut,
    and I went home my thousands of miles, and the sight was never to be!" (*BC*
    10:17-18).

4   On 16 May 1845 RB wrote, "I will call at 2: on Tuesday" (*BC* 10:224); he first visited
    her on 20 May.

Yet I wept for it![1]—this, .. the paper's light ..
Said, *Dear, I love thee;*[2] and I sank and quailed
As if God's future thundered on my past.   10
This said, *I am thine*[3]—and so its ink has paled
With lying at my heart that beat too fast.
And this ... O Love, thy words have ill availed,
If, what this said, I dared repeat at last!

XXIX

I think of thee!—my thoughts do twine and bud
About thee, as wild vines, about a tree,
Put out broad leaves, and soon there's nought to see
Except the straggling green which hides the wood.
Yet, O my palm-tree,[4] be it understood   5
I will not have my thoughts instead of thee
Who art dearer, better! rather instantly
Renew thy presence. As a strong tree should,
Rustle thy boughs and set thy trunk all bare,
And let these bands of greenery which insphere[5] thee,   10
Drop heavily down, .. burst, shattered, everywhere!
Because, in this deep joy to see and hear thee
And breathe within thy shadow a new air,
I do not think of thee—I am too near thee.

---

1   EBB later admitted, "When I wrote that letter to let you come the first time, do you
    know, the tears ran down my cheeks .. I could not tell why: partly it might be mere
    nervousness" (*BC* 11:148).

2   Two letters seem pertinent here. Either EBB is metaphorically alluding to the
    impulsive letter RB wrote to her directly after their first meeting on 20 May
    1845, "wildly" declaring his feelings for her, which she returned to him and he
    destroyed (*BC* 10:232, 236); she later recalled how the "deeps" of her heart were
    "shaken" by this letter (*BC* 12:340). Or she may be referring to a letter of 30
    August 1845 in which, despite her having forbidden him to speak of love, he
    reiterated his feelings (*BC* 11:52), leading to a crescendo in her conflict of loyalties
    to her father and her suitor as each debated her plan to winter in Pisa (see *BC*
    11:42–45, 52, 55, 57–58).

3   RB declared his wish to marry her in a letter of 25 September 1845 (*BC* 11:98); the
    next day she replied, "Henceforward I am yours for everything but to do you harm"
    (*BC* 11:100).

4   palm-tree] EBB linked the palm to RB and his life-renewing love: "I was in the
    desert & ... I am among the palm-trees" (*BC* 11:242).

5   insphere] encircle.

XXX

I see thine image[1] through my tears to-night,
And yet to-day I saw thee smiling. How
Refer the cause?—Belovèd, is it thou
Or I? who makes me sad? The acolyte
Amid the chanted joy and thankful rite,   5
May so fall flat, with pale insensate brow,
On the altar-stair. I hear thy voice and vow
Perplexed, uncertain, since thou art out of sight,
As he, in his swooning ears, the choir's amen.
Belovèd, dost thou love? or did I see all   10
The glory as I dreamed, and fainted when
Too vehement light dilated my ideal,
For my soul's eyes? Will that light come again,
As now these tears come ... falling hot and real?

XXXI

Thou comest! all is said without a word.
I sit beneath thy looks, as children do
In the noon-sun,[2] with souls that tremble through
Their happy eyelids from an unaverred[3]
Yet prodigal inward joy. Behold, I erred   5
In that last doubt! and yet I cannot rue
The sin most, but the occasion ... that we two
Should for a moment stand unministered
By a mutual presence. Ah, keep near and close,
Thou dovelike help! and, when my fears would rise,   10
With thy broad heart serenely interpose.
Brood down with thy divine sufficiencies

---

1 Before she met him, EBB had hung a framed picture of RB in her room, along
   with those of Thomas Carlyle, Alfred Tennyson, William Wordsworth, and Harriet
   Martineau that had been published in *The New Spirit of the Age* (1844), a series of essays
   on contemporary writers in which EBB had collaborated with R.H. Horne. On the
   day RB first visited her, she had removed his portrait before he arrived; she eventually
   pasted it in a copy of his poem *Paracelsus* (*BC* II:221).

2 Agjanian 1985 notes the parallels here with Petrarch's comparisons of Laura to the sun
   and with Sonnet LXXVI of *Astrophel and Stella* (1591) by Sir Philip Sidney (1554-86),
   opening with "She comes."

3 unaverred] unconfessed, unaffirmed.

These thoughts which tremble when bereft of those,
Like callow[1] birds left desert[2] to the skies.

XXXII

The first time that the sun rose on thine oath
To love me, I looked forward to the moon
To slacken all those bonds which seemed too soon
And quickly tied to make a lasting troth.[3]
Quick-loving hearts, I thought, may quickly loathe;   5
And, looking on myself, I seemed not one
For such man's love!—more like an out of tune
Worn viol, a good singer would be wroth
To spoil his song with, and which, snatched in haste,
Is laid down at the first ill-sounding note.   10
I did not wrong myself so, but I placed
A wrong on *thee.* For perfect strains may float
'Neath master-hands, from instruments defaced,—
And great souls, at one stroke, may do and doat.[4]

XXXIII

Yes, call me by my pet-name![5] let me hear
The name I used to run at, when a child,
From innocent play, and leave the cowslips piled,
To glance up in some face that proved me dear
With the look of its eyes. I miss the clear   5
Fond voices, which, being drawn and reconciled
Into the music of Heaven's undefiled,
Call me no longer. Silence on the bier,
While I call God .. call God!—So let thy mouth

---

1 callow] downy, without feathers.

2 desert] deserted, abandoned.

3 troth] pledge, particularly a betrothal or promise to marry.

4 doat] dote, love excessively.

5 EBB explained her nickname from early childhood, "Ba" (rhymes with "ah"), to RB
   in a letter of 9 September 1845, but he did not venture to use it until 19 December (*BC*
   11:66, 248). See her 1838 poem "The Pet-Name."

Be heir to those who are now exanimate.[1]   10
Gather the north flowers to complete the south,
And catch the early love up in the late.
Yes, call me by that name,—and I, in truth,
With the same heart, will answer, and not wait.

XXXIV

With the same heart, I said, I'll answer thee
As those, when thou shalt call me by my name—
Lo, the vain promise! is the same, the same,
Perplexed and ruffled by life's strategy?
When called before, I told how hastily   5
I dropped my flowers or brake[2] off from a game,
To run and answer with the smile that came
At play last moment, and went on with me
Through my obedience. When I answer now,
I drop a grave thought,—break from solitude;—   10
Yet still my heart goes to thee ... ponder how ..
Not as to a single good, but all my good!
Lay thy hand on it, best one, and allow
That no child's foot could run fast as this blood.

XXXV

If I leave all for thee, wilt thou exchange
And be all to me? Shall I never miss
Home-talk and blessing and the common kiss
That comes to each in turn,[3] nor count it strange,

---

1   exanimate] dead; formerly, but no longer, animate. EBB's mother died in 1828 and her
    closest brother, Edward, in 1840; other close relatives dead by this time included her
    grandmother Elizabeth Moulton, her uncle Samuel Moulton Barrett, and her brother
    Sam.

2   brake] broke.

3   EBB dreaded the rupture with her father that she expected to follow her marriage.
    Edward Moulton Barrett had made it clear that he would break off relations with any
    of his children who married without his permission—and he refused permission to
    all who sought it. EBB at one point explained this bitter truth in a jest: "If a prince
    of Eldorado should come, with a pedigree of lineal descent from some signory in
    the moon in one hand, & a ticket of good-behaviour from the nearest Independent
    chapel, in the other," her father would still judge the suitor unacceptable (*BC* 11:238;
    see also 78).

When I look up, to drop on a new range 5
Of walls and floors .. another home than this?
Nay, wilt thou fill that place by me which is
Filled by dead eyes too tender to know change?
That's hardest. If to conquer love, has tried,
To conquer grief, tries more ... as all things prove; 10
For grief indeed is love and grief beside.
Alas, I have grieved so I am hard to love.
Yet love me—wilt thou? Open thine heart wide,
And fold within, the wet wings of thy dove.[1]

XXXVI

When we met first and loved, I did not build
Upon the event with marble. Could it mean
To last, a love set pendulous between
Sorrow and sorrow? Nay, I rather thrilled,
Distrusting every light that seemed to gild 5
The onward path, and feared to overlean
A finger even. And, though I have grown serene
And strong since then, I think that God has willed
A still renewable fear .. O love, O troth ..
Lest these enclaspèd hands should never hold, 10
This mutual kiss drop down between us both
As an unowned thing, once the lips being cold.
And Love, be false! if *he*, to keep one oath,
Must lose one joy, by his life's star foretold.

XXXVII

Pardon, oh, pardon, that my soul should make
Of all that strong divineness which I know
For thine and thee, an image only so
Formed of the sand, and fit to shift and break.
It is that distant years which did not take 5
Thy sovranty, recoiling with a blow,
Have forced my swimming brain to undergo
Their doubt and dread, and blindly to forsake

1   See the biblical story of Noah releasing a dove from the ark (Genesis 8.8-9).

Thy purity of likeness, and distort
Thy worthiest love to a worthless counterfeit.   10
As if a shipwrecked Pagan, safe in port,
His guardian sea-god to commemorate,
Should set a sculptured porpoise, gills a-snort,
And vibrant tail, within the temple-gate.[1]

XXXVIII

First time he kissed me, he but only kissed
The fingers of this hand wherewith I write;[2]
And, ever since, it grew more clean and white, ..
Slow to world-greetings .. quick with its "Oh, list,"[3]
When the angels speak. A ring of amethyst   5
I could not wear here, plainer to my sight,
Than that first kiss. The second passed in height
The first, and sought the forehead, and half missed
Half falling on the hair. O beyond meed![4]
That was the chrism[5] of love, which love's own crown,   10
With sanctifying sweetness, did precede.
The third upon my lips was folded down
In perfect, purple state; since when, indeed,
I have been proud and said, "My love, my own."

XXXIX

Because thou hast the power and own'st the grace
To look through and behind this mask of me,
(Against which years have beat thus blanchingly
With their rains,) and behold my soul's true face,
The dim and weary witness of life's race!—   5

---

1   Refers to the ancient practice of giving thanks to a sea god for one's safe arrival after
    a voyage by erecting a statue in a temple.

2   RB wrote EBB that he "would not have dared to take the blessing of kissing your
    hand, much less your lip," had he not feared that she "might fancy I only felt a dreamy,
    abstract passion for a phantom of my own creating out of your books and letters, and
    which only took your name" (*BC* 13:18-19).

3   list] listen.

4   meed] a merited gift or reward.

5   chrism] oil consecrated for use in sacraments such as baptism.

Because thou hast the faith and love to see,
Through that same soul's distracting lethargy,
The patient angel waiting for a place
In the new Heavens!—because nor sin nor woe,
Nor God's infliction, nor death's neighbourhood,   10
Nor all which others viewing, turn to go, ..
Nor all which makes me tired of all, self-viewed, ..
Nothing repels thee, .. Dearest, teach me so
To pour out gratitude, as thou dost, good.

XL

Oh, yes! they love through all this world of ours![1]
I will not gainsay love, called love forsooth.[2]
I have heard love talked in my early youth,
And since, not so long back but that the flowers
Then gathered, smell still. Mussulmans and Giaours[3]   5
Throw kerchiefs at a smile, and have no ruth[4]
For any weeping. Polypheme's white tooth
Slips on the nut,[5] if, after frequent showers,
The shell is over-smooth,—and not so much
Will turn the thing called love, aside to hate,   10
Or else to oblivion. But thou art not such
A lover, my Belovèd! thou canst wait
Through sorrow and sickness, to bring souls to touch,
And think it soon when others cry "Too late."

---

1 EBB wrote to RB about the world's misuse of the word "love": "I have not a high
   appreciation of what passes in the world … under the name of love…. To see the
   marriages which are made everyday! worse than solitudes & more desolate!" (*BC*
   11:259).

2 forsooth] in truth.

3 Mussulmans] Muslims; Giaours] what Turks scornfully called non-Muslims, espe-
   cially Christians. The terms here identify as "infidels" those who do not follow the
   "true faith" in love.

4 ruth] pity, compassion.

5 Alludes to the unrequited love, in classical myth, of Polyphemus the one-eyed
   Cyclops, a giant son of Neptune, for the sea nymph Galatea, who eluded him, much
   as the desired nut slips from his mouth.

XLI

I thank all who have loved me in their hearts,
With thanks and love from mine. Deep thanks to all
Who paused a little near the prison-wall,
To hear my music in its louder parts,
Ere they went onward, each one to the mart's   5
Or temple's occupation, beyond call.
But thou, who, in my voice's sink and fall,
When the sob took it, thy divinest Art's
Own instrument didst drop down at thy foot,
To harken what I said between my tears, ..   10
Instruct me how to thank thee!—Oh, to shoot
My soul's full meaning into future years,
That *they* should lend it utterance, and salute
Love that endures, from Life that disappears!

XLII

"My future will not copy fair my past"—[1]
I wrote that once; and thinking at my side
My ministering life-angel justified
The word by his appealing look upcast
To the white throne of God, I turned at last,   5
And there, instead, saw thee, not unallied
To angels in thy soul![2] Then I, long tried
By natural ills, received the comfort fast,
While budding, at thy sight, my pilgrim's staff[3]
Gave out green leaves with morning dews impearled.[4]   10
I seek no copy now of life's first half:
Leave here the pages with long musing curled,

---

1   Quotes the opening line of EBB's sonnet "Past and Future" (1844), which RB had
     written "affects me more than any poem I ever read," "as a true utterance of yours" (*BC*
     11:174). See the headnote on the omission of this sonnet from the sequence in 1850.

2   EBB frequently characterized RB as a rescuing angel, as in her letter of 31 October
     1845 (alluding to Acts 5.19): "o my angel at the gate of the prison!" (*BC* 11:147).

3   In medieval writings, the pilgrim's walking staff miraculously sprouted green leaves
     to symbolize his spiritual renewal; cf. Petrarch's Rime 16, comparing the lover to an
     unsuccessful pilgrim.

4   Possibly an allusion to RB's poem *Pippa Passes* (1841), which describes a "dew-pearled"
     hillside at morning when "God's in his heaven— / All's right with the world!" (I.221-28).

And write me new my future's epigraph,
New angel mine, unhoped for in the world!

XLIII

How do I love thee? Let me count the ways.
I love thee to the depth and breadth and height[1]
My soul can reach, when feeling out of sight
For the ends of Being and ideal Grace.
I love thee to the level of everyday's   5
Most quiet need, by sun and candlelight.
I love thee freely, as men strive for Right;
I love thee purely, as they turn from Praise.
I love thee with the passion put to use
In my old griefs, and with my childhood's faith.   10
I love thee with a love I seemed to lose
With my lost saints,—I love thee with the breath,
Smiles, tears, of all my life!—and, if God choose,
I shall but love thee better after death.

XLIV

Belovèd, thou hast brought me many flowers[2]
Plucked in the garden, all the summer through
And winter, and it seemed as if they grew
In this close room, nor missed the sun and showers.
So, in the like name of that love of ours,   5
Take back these thoughts which here unfolded too,
And which on warm and cold days I withdrew
From my heart's ground. Indeed, those beds and bowers
Be overgrown with bitter weeds and rue,[3]

---

1 Alludes to the description of Christ's love in Ephesians 3.17-19.

2 Beginning with his sixth visit (28 June 1845), RB often brought EBB flowers from his mother's garden; she considered it "among the miracles" that the flowers survived in her close room (*BC* 11:268).

3 rue] associated with regret, also repentance, grace, and purification. (See Ophelia's mad song in Shakespeare's *Hamlet*, act 4, scene 5, l. 180.) EBB used similar imagery of weeds entwined with flowers to explain that if her father had been more openly loving, she would never have been able to defy his wishes and develop a love relationship with RB: "So the nightshade & the eglantine are twisted, twined, one in the other, .. & the little pink roses lean up against the pale poison of the berries .. we cannot tear this from that, let us think of it ever so much!" (*BC* 13:168).

And wait thy weeding; yet here's eglantine,[1]
Here's ivy![2]—take them, as I used to do
Thy flowers, and keep them where they shall not pine.
Instruct thine eyes to keep their colours true,
And tell thy soul, their roots are left in mine.

---

1   eglantine] sweetbrier rose, associated with poetry.
2   ivy] associated with friendship, especially with fidelity in friendship.

6. *From* Casa Guidi Windows *(1851)*

EBB's marriage in September 1846 and subsequent move to Italy swept her into the upheaval of the *Risorgimento,* the nineteenth-century struggle for Italian liberation and nationhood. In *Casa Guidi Windows* (hereafter *CGW*) she bears witness to historically resonant events in one critical phase of this struggle between 1846 and 1850. In 1846, Italy was a collection of city states oppressed by absolutist governments. After the defeat of Napoleon Bonaparte at the Battle of Waterloo (1815), the representatives of the European powers at the Congress of Vienna sought to root out the ideas of liberty and republicanism sown in the Italian states by the French Revolution. They eliminated parliaments and freedom of the press, suppressed the concept of "Italy" as a national entity, and in some states censored the very word "liberty." The northern states of Lombardy and Venetia were incorporated into the Austrian Empire (whose influence extended throughout Italy). Piedmont, Sardinia, and Savoy in the northwest and west were under French control; in the south, the Kingdom of the Two Sicilies (Sicily and Naples) was ruled by the Spanish monarchy; the Papal States in central Italy were governed by the Pope as a temporal sovereign; other states north of these in central Italy, including Tuscany, were ruled by Dukes or Grand Dukes under Austrian control.

As the "Advertisement" to the first edition (1851) indicates, *CGW* was written in two successive parts, reflecting two phases in the *Risorgimento*: the agitation for democratic governance and Italian unification culminating in the revolutions of 1848 (coinciding with revolutions in several other European countries) and the disillusionment and political repression following the defeat of Italian liberal and patriotic forces in 1849. The poem's title is taken from the palazzo in Florence, Casa Guidi,[1] in which the Brownings first rented an apartment in 1847; from May 1848 they made it their principal residence in Italy until EBB's death in 1861.

Part I reflects the high hopes raised by progressive reforms

---

1   Casa Guidi] Casa (Italian for *house*) Guidi is a fifteenth-century building near the Pitti Palace in Florence. Today restored to approximate its appearance during the Brownings' occupancy, it is open to the public at specified times.

within the Papal States by Pope Pius IX (1792-1878), or "Pio Nono," after his election as Pope in June 1846. In Tuscany, Grand Duke Leopold II (1797-1870) followed with democratic concessions, most notably, granting permission for the Florentine people to form a civic guard. From the front windows of Casa Guidi, on 12 September 1847—auspiciously for her, the first anniversary of her marriage—EBB witnessed the jubilant celebrations and political procession that greeted the Duke's concessions. She vividly described these events in a letter to her sisters written 13 September 1847 (*LTA* 1:130-38) that were echoed in the poem itself (Part I, ll. 446-576). "My poem ... was begun in this very palazzo Guidi last autumn, and finished in the winter," EBB told her sister Henrietta on 17 July 1848, referring to the work as a "Meditation in Tuscany" (*LTH* 89).[1] In Part I of *CGW,* she uses "the name of greatness unforgot, / To meditate what greatness may be done" (ll. 647-48), as she first muses on Italy's (and especially Tuscany's) rich artistic heritage and contemporary struggles, then calls for a "civic spirit" (l. 746) and for "civic heroes" (l. 795) to advance the cause of Italy's liberty and unification, with help from "lands of Europe" (l. 1104). Publication of "A Meditation in Tuscany" did not proceed as quickly as EBB hoped after she sent it to *Blackwood's* magazine in late winter or spring 1848; in fact, *Blackwood's* did not publish the poem even after she supplied notes, as the editor requested, explaining some of the Italian references (*LTA* 1:199, 203n25). By 23 January 1850, she was planning to "write a second part" and to publish the two parts "separately" from the new expanded edition of her *Poems* published in 1850 (*LTA* 1: 294).

The interval between the composition of Parts I and II of *CGW* brought the birth of the Brownings' only child, Robert Wiedeman Barrett Browning, or "Pen," on 9 March 1849.[2] It also brought, on 23 March 1849, the crushing defeat of the Italian forces by Austria at the Battle of Novara, resulting in the restoration of reactionary governments throughout Italy, a new clampdown on civil rights,

---

1   The poem's relationship, if any, to an unrealized joint publishing venture contemplated by the Brownings in the spring of 1847—"a new book on Italy which is to move the world" (*LTA* 1:43)—is unclear.

2   Two miscarriages preceded Pen's birth (March 1847 and March 1848), and two more followed (November or December 1849 and July 1850), the last one life threatening.

and the Austrian occupation of Tuscany. Part II records the bitter feelings of betrayal EBB experienced, together with liberal Italians, when potential leaders of the unification movement such as Pope Pius IX and Grand Duke Leopold II became mere pawns in the hands of the Austrians. "The blood boils in my veins sometimes— but poor Tuscany is now 'a province of Austria' indeed," she wrote on 23 June 1849, commenting on the censorship forced on the Florentine people and the possibility of her letters being opened by the authorities (*LTA* 1:255). In Part II she relates the fate of the Italian revolutionaries to that of other European revolutionaries in 1846-49—in Poland and Hungary, for example (ll. 415-17)—as well as to the oppression of American slaves (ll. 393-96).

Generically and thematically, *CGW* draws simultaneously on English and Italian poetic forms, as well as cultural traditions, but emphasizes the Italian to a greater degree. Combining lyric meditation, artistic and political history and prophecy, letters from the front, religious satire, and cultural diplomacy, the poem is hybrid not only in its genre but also in its verse form. The meter varies in differing parts of the poem, form mirroring content. In Part II, ll. 286-318, for example, the heavy jackboot beat of the "regular tramp of horse and tread of men" (l. 288) conveys the oppressive effect of the occupying "Austria's thousands" (l. 301) entering a subjugated, silenced Florence. The poem teems with references to Italy's rich cultural heritage, although EBB critiques those who aestheticize Italy's past glory while ignoring its modern political struggles for liberty and nationhood. The great Florentine poet Dante Alighieri (1265-1321) and the sculptor, painter, architect, and poet Michelangelo Buonarroti (1475-1564) are especially key artistic and political figures. Among contemporary political figures, Giuseppe Mazzini (1805-72), the chief theorist of the *Risorgimento,* looms large. This is not surprising given the prominence Mazzini attained living in London as an exiled patriot in the 1840s (especially given the public scandal in 1844-45 occasioned by the discovery that the British government had been opening his private mail), as well as his correspondence with RB at this time (*BC* 11:169-71, 181n3) and his friendship with other English writers such as Thomas Carlyle (1795-1881). In a reference to recent events, EBB also portrays, near the close of her poem (Part II, ll. 678-94), the death of Anita Garibaldi (1821-49), the heroic Brazilian wife and companion in arms of the master of guerrilla warfare and general of Italian volunteer armies, Giuseppe Maria Garibaldi (1807-82). English preoccupations of the mid–Victorian period also animate *CGW,* including the debate between past and present; controversies over faith and religion; Carlylean hero worship (see Part I, l. 772n); a critique of the age's industrial materialism, especially evident in the often cited satire of the 1851 Great Exhibition (Part II, ll. 577-657); and a related critique of the English peace movement (Part II, ll. 373-424), reversing EBB's call for peaceful democratic change in Italy in Part I. As critics have noted, the poet's English and Protestant biases are sometimes evident.

Given its foreign subject matter, sales of *CGW* were "very slow" (*LTA* 2:91), even though, among EBB's English contemporaries, it generated positive as well as negative reviews (see Appendix D and *LTA* 1:384n11, 390n6, 397n9, 399-400, 401-02n14). In Italy reception was more uniformly positive, at least among liberal Italians. Piedmont's prime minister from May 1849 to October 1852, the writer and patriot Massimo d'Azeglio (1798-1866), quoted from Part II (ll. 694-723) in an 1852 address to the Piedmont Chamber of Deputies (*LTA* 2:397n14). Later response to the poem was shaped by the British outrage over EBB's next volume of poems on the Italian question, *Poems before Congress* (1860), in particular the poem "A Curse for a Nation." After the Victorian period, *CGW* had fewer readers, as the *Risorgimento* receded in history. Julia Markus's scholarly edition (1977) rescued the poem from more than a century of neglect and misinterpretation. In the 1980s interpretations of *CGW* focused on the poem's gender politics. Since that time, scholars have explored its political, cultural, technological, and historical contexts; its central "windows" metaphor; the relation between its poetics and its politics; its themes of nation-building and citizenship; and its innovative meter and verse form. Criticism: Alaya 1978, Rosenblum 1985, Cooper 1988, Mermin 1989, Phelan 1993, Dillon and Frank 1997, Schor 1998, Harris 2000, Groth 2000, Reynolds 2001, Chapman 2001a, 2003c, Cronin 2002, Armstrong 2003, and Avery and Stott 2003. EBB's correspondence, especially Scott Lewis's *LTA,* is an indispensable background resource. On the revisions and corrections in the 1851 edition that EBB made in republishing *CGW* in her fourth edition of *Poems* (1856), see the Markus edition (1977, 115-30).

Advertisement to the First Edition

This poem contains the impressions of the writer upon events in Tuscany of which she was a witness. "From a window," the critic may demur. She bows to the objection in the very title of her work. No continuous narrative nor exposition of political philosophy is attempted by her. It is a simple story of personal impressions, whose only value is in the intensity with which they were received, as proving her warm affection for a beautiful and unfortunate country, and the sincerity with which they are related, as indicating her own good faith and freedom from partisanship.

Of the two parts of this poem, the first was written nearly three years ago, while the second resumes the actual situation of 1851. The discrepancy between the two parts is a sufficient guarantee to the public of the truthfulness of the writer, who, though she certainly escaped the epidemic "falling sickness" of enthusiasm for Pio Nono,[1] takes shame upon herself that she believed, like a woman, some royal oaths, and lost sight of the probable consequences of some obvious popular defects. If the discrepancy should be painful to the reader, let him understand that to the writer it has been more so. But such discrepancies we are called upon to accept at every hour by the conditions of our nature, implying the interval, between aspiration and performance, between faith and dis-illusion, between hope and fact.

"O trusted broken prophecy,
O richest fortune sourly crost,
Born for the future, to the future lost!"[2]
nay, not lost to the future in this case. The future of Italy shall not be disinherited.
        FLORENCE, 1851.

---

1   Pio Nono] Pope Pius IX; see headnote.
2   From "Threnody," ll. 173-75, by American poet and essayist Ralph Waldo Emerson (1802-82).

Part I

I heard last night a little child go singing[1]
    'Neath Casa Guidi windows, by the church,[2]
O bella libertà,[3] *O bella!* stringing
    The same words still on notes he went in search
So high for, you[4] concluded the upspringing   5
    Of such a nimble bird to sky from perch
Must leave the whole bush in a tremble green,
    And that the heart of Italy must beat,
While such a voice had leave to rise serene
    'Twixt church and palace[5] of a Florence street!   10
A little child, too, who not long had been
    By mother's finger steadied on his feet,
And still *O bella libertà* he sang.

Then I thought, musing, of the innumerous
    Sweet songs which still for Italy outrang   15
From older singers' lips,[6] who sang not thus
    Exultingly and purely, yet, with pang
Fast sheathed in music, touched the heart of us
    So finely, that the pity scarcely pained.
I thought how Filicaja[7] led on others,   20
    Bewailers for their Italy enchained,
And how they called her childless among mothers,

---

1   child go singing] children's liberty songs were noted in the *Tuscan Athenaeum* (Markus, *CGW*, 72), and EBB said that even children of two lisped "'Vivas'" ("long live …") (*LTA* 1:131).

2   church] San Felice, the church directly across from the Brownings' apartment balcony in Casa Guidi.

3   O bella libertà] O beautiful liberty!

4   you] here, a representative observer or perhaps RB, whom EBB addresses directly in ll. 1129 ff.

5   palace] Casa Guidi, also called "Palazzo Guidi."

6   older singers' lips] the lips of earlier poets described below, beginning at l. 20.

7   Filicaja] Vincenzo da Filicaja (1642–1707), Florentine poet, patriot, and administrator, whose lyric laments for Italy were echoed by later Italian and European poets such as Byron (see ll. 25–26n below).

Widow of empires,[1] ay, and scarce refrained
Cursing her beauty to her face, as brothers
   Might a shamed sister's,—"Had she been less fair   25
She were less wretched,"[2]— how, evoking so
   From congregated wrong and heaped despair
Of men and women writhing under blow,
   Harrowed and hideous in a filthy lair,
Some personating Image, wherein woe   30
   Was wrapt in beauty from offending much,
They called it Cybele,[3] or Niobe,[4]
   Or laid it corpse-like on a bier for such,
Where all the world might drop for Italy
   Those cadenced tears which burn not where they touch,— 35
"Juliet of nations, canst thou die as we?
   And was the violet crown that crowned thy head
So over-large, though new buds made it rough,
   It slipped down and across thine eyelids dead,
O sweet, fair Juliet?"[5] Of such songs enough,   40
   Too many of such complaints! behold, instead,
Void at Verona, Juliet's marble trough.[6]
   As void as that is, are all images
Men set between themselves and actual wrong,
   To catch the weight of pity, meet the stress   45

---

1 Widow of empires] Cf. Byron's "Lone mother of dead empires!" in *Childe Harold's Pilgrimage* (1818) 4.78.

2 "Had she ... wretched,"] adapted from Filicaja's sonnet, "Italia, Italia, O tu cui diè la sorte / Dono infelice di bellezza." The lines were freely translated by Byron as "Italia! oh Italia! thou who hast / The fatal gift of beauty" in *Childe Harold's Pilgrimage* 4.42, and by Felicia Hemans (1793-1835) as "ITALIA! thou, by lavish Nature graced / With ill-starr'd beauty," in *Translations from Camoens, And Other Poets, With Original Poetry* (1818).

3 Cybele] Phrygian mother goddess identified by the Greeks with Ceres or Demeter, goddess of earth.

4 Niobe] Queen of Thebes, punished by the gods for her excessive pride in her children by their deaths; cf. Byron's calling Rome "The Niobe of nations" in *Childe Harold's Pilgrimage* 4.79.

5 Juliet] alluding to Shakespeare's *Romeo and Juliet* (1599). Violets are traditionally associated with faithfulness, modesty, and love.

6 marble trough] "They show at Verona, as the tomb of Juliet, an empty trough of stone" [EBB's note].

Of conscience,—since 'tis easier to gaze long
  On mournful masks, and sad effigies,
Than on real, live, weak creatures crushed by strong.

  For me who stand in Italy to-day
Where worthier poets stood and sang before,   50
  I kiss their footsteps, yet their words gainsay.
I can but muse in hope upon this shore
  Of golden Arno[1] as it shoots away
Through Florence' heart beneath her bridges four!
  Bent bridges, seeming to strain off like bows,   55
And tremble while the arrowy undertide
  Shoots on and cleaves the marble as it goes,
And strikes up palace-walls on either side,
  And froths the cornice out in glittering rows,
With doors and windows quaintly multiplied,   60
  And terrace-sweeps, and gazers upon all,
By whom if flower or kerchief were thrown out
  From any lattice there, the same would fall
Into the river underneath no doubt,
  It runs so close and fast 'twixt wall and wall.   65
How beautiful! the mountains from without
  In silence listen for the word said next.
What word will men say,—here where Giotto[2] planted
  His campanile,[3] like an unperplexed
Fine question Heaven-ward, touching the things granted   70
  A noble people who, being greatly vexed
In act, in aspiration keep undaunted?
  What word will God say? Michel's[4] Night and Day

---

1 Arno] the river that flows through Florence.
2 Giotto] Giotto di Bondone (c.1266-1337), the celebrated Florentine painter and
   architect.
3 campanile] the bell tower of the Cathedral of Santa Maria del Fiore, designed by
   Giotto but left unfinished at his death and not completed until the end of the four-
   teenth century.
4 Michel] i.e., Michelangelo; see headnote.

And Dawn and Twilight wait in marble scorn,[1]
    Like dogs upon a dunghill, couched on clay   75
From whence the Medicean stamp's[2] outworn,
    The final putting off of all such sway
By all such hands, and freeing of the unborn
    In Florence and the great world outside Florence.
Three hundred years his patient statues wait   80
    In that small chapel of the dim St. Lawrence.
Day's eyes are breaking bold and passionate
    Over his shoulder, and will flash abhorrence
On darkness and with level looks meet fate,
    When once loose from that marble film of theirs;   85
The Night has wild dreams in her sleep, the Dawn
    Is haggard as the sleepless, Twilight wears
A sort of horror; as the veil withdrawn
    'Twixt the artist's soul and works had left them heirs
Of speechless thoughts which would not quail nor fawn,   90
    Of angers and contempts, of hope and love;
For not without a meaning did he place
    The princely Urbino[3] on the seat above
With everlasting shadow[4] on his face,
    While the slow dawns and twilights disapprove   95
The ashes of his long-extinguished race,
    Which never more shall clog the feet of men.
I do believe, divinest Angelo,
    That winter-hour, in Via Larga,[5] when

---

1   Night and Day / And Dawn and Twilight wait in marble scorn] "These famous
statues recline in Sagrestia Nuova, on the tombs of Giuliano de' Medici, third son of
Lorenzo the Magnificent, and Lorenzo of Urbino, his grandson. Strozzi's epigram on
the Night, with Michel Angelo's rejoinder, is well known" [EBB's note]. She alludes
to Michelangelo's haunting statues in the New Sacristy of the Church of San Lorenzo
and Vasari's account of the artist's poem in which Night says, "Happy am I to sleep,
and still more blest / To be of stone, while grief and shame endure; / To see, nor feel,
is now my utmost hope, / Wherefore speak softly, and awake me not."

2   Medicean stamp's] the coat-of-arms of the Medici, the powerful Florentine banking
family that also figures in RB's "Fra Lippo Lippi" (1855); metaphorically, an allusion
to their influence.

3   Urbino] Lorenzo de Medici (1492-1519), who was Duke of Urbino from 1516-19.

4   everlasting shadow] a symbol of the eclipse of Florentine liberty described in the
following lines.

5   Via Larga] now Via Cavour, in front of the Palazzo Medici (now the Palazzo Riccardi).

They bade thee build a statue up in snow,[1]   100
    And straight that marvel of thine art again
Dissolved beneath the sun's Italian glow,
    Thine eyes, dilated with the plastic[2] passion,
Thawing too, in drops of wounded manhood, since,
    To mock alike thine art and indignation,   105
Laughed at the palace-window the new prince,—
    ("Aha! this genius needs for exaltation,
When all's said, and howe'er the proud may wince,
    A little marble from our princely mines!")
I do believe that hour thou laughedst too,   110
    For the whole sad world and for thy Florentines,
After those few tears—which were only few!
    That as, beneath the sun, the grand white lines
Of thy snow-statue trembled and withdrew,—
    The head, erect as Jove's, being palsied first,   115
The eyelids flattened, the full brow turned blank,—
    The right hand, raised but now as if it cursed,
Dropt, a mere snowball, (till the people sank
    Their voices, though a louder laughter burst
From the royal window) thou couldst proudly thank   120
    God and the prince for promise and presage,
And laugh the laugh back, I think verily,
    Thine eyes being purged by tears of righteous rage
To read a wrong into a prophecy,
    And measure a true great man's heritage   125
Against a mere great duke's posterity.
    I think thy soul said then, "I do not need
A princedom and its quarries, after all;
    For if I write, paint, carve a word, indeed,
On book or board or dust, on floor or wall,   130
    The same is kept of God, who taketh heed
That not a letter of the meaning fall
    Or ere[3] it touch and teach His world's deep heart,

---

1   in snow] "This mocking task was set by Pietro, the unworthy successor of Lorenzo
    the Magnificent" [EBB's note]. Her account is based on an anecdote in Vasari about
    Piero de Medici (1471-1503), the untalented oldest son of Lorenzo the Magnificent
    (1449-92), ruler of Florence and patron of the arts.

2   plastic] shaping or moulding.

3   Or ere] before.

Outlasting, therefore, all your lordships, sir!
    So keep your stone, beseech you, for your part,   135
To cover up your grave-place and refer
    The proper titles; *I* live by my art.
The thought I threw into this snow shall stir
    This gazing people when their gaze is done;
And the tradition of your act and mine,   140
    When all the snow is melted in the sun,
Shall gather up, for unborn men, a sign
    Of what is the true princedom,—ay, and none
Shall laugh that day, except the drunk with wine."

    Amen, great Angelo! the day's at hand.[1]   145
If many laugh not on it, shall we weep?
    Much more we must not, let us understand.
Through rhymers sonneteering in their sleep,
    And archaists mumbling dry bones up the land,
And sketchers lauding ruined towns a-heap,—   150
    Through all that drowsy hum of voices smooth,
The hopeful bird mounts carolling from brake,[2]
    The hopeful child, with leaps to catch his growth,
Sings open-eyed for liberty's sweet sake!
    And I, a singer also, from my youth,   155
Prefer to sing with these who are awake,
    With birds, with babes, with men who will not fear
The baptism of the holy morning dew,
    (And many of such wakers now are here,
Complete in their anointed manhood, who   160
    Will greatly dare and greatlier persevere,)
Than join those old thin voices with my new,
    And sigh for Italy with some safe sigh
Cooped up in music 'twixt an oh and ah,—
    Nay, hand in hand with that young child, will I   165
Go singing rather, "*Bella libertà*,"

---

1   the day's at hand] the day of Italian liberty when Michelangelo's statue Night would
    be happy to wake.
2   brake] a thicket of bushes or briers.

Than, with those poets, croon the dead or cry
"*Se tu men bella fossi, Italia!* "[1]

"Less wretched if less fair." Perhaps a truth
Is so far plain in this—that Italy,   170
Long trammelled[2] with the purple of her youth
Against her age's ripe activity,
Sits still upon her tombs, without death's ruth,[3]
But also without life's brave energy.
"Now tell us what is Italy?" men ask: 175
And others answer, "Virgil, Cicero,
Catullus, Cæsar." What beside? to task
The memory closer—"Why, Boccaccio,
Dante, Petrarca,"— and if still the flask
Appears to yield its wine by drops too slow,—   180
"Angelo, Raffael, Pergolese,"[4]— all
Whose strong hearts beat through stone, or charged again
The paints with fire of souls electrical,
Or broke up heaven for music. What more then?
Why, then, no more. The chaplet's[5] last beads fall   185
In naming the last saintship within ken,[6]
And, after that, none prayeth in the land.
Alas, this Italy has too long swept
Heroic ashes up for hour-glass sand;
Of her own past, impassioned nympholept![7]   190

---

1   "Se tu men bella fossi, Italia!"] "If only you were less beautiful, Italy!"—another
    allusion to Filicaja's sonnet (see above, ll. 25-26 and note), the fifth line of which
    begins, "deh, fossi tu men bella."

2   trammeled] hindered in activity or free movement.

3   ruth] regret, pity.

4   Angelo, Raffael, Pergolese] i.e., Michelangelo, the painter Raphael, and Giovanni
    Battista Pergolesi (1710-36), Italian composer, representing the highest cultural
    achievements of Italy's Renaissance.

5   chaplet] a string of beads used for counting prayers (similar to a rosary).

6   within ken] within knowledge or view.

7   nympholept] a person inspired by violent enthusiasm, especially for an ideal. EBB's use
    of this word led to a much cited exchange with the Victorian art and cultural critic, John
    Ruskin (1819-1900), who objected to it as an obscure Greek term. She replied, "Nympho-
    lepsy is no more a Greek word than epilepsy .... It's a word for a specific disease or mania
    among the ancients, that mystical passion for an invisible nymph common to a certain
    class of visionaries. Indeed, I am not the first in referring to it .... Lord Byron talks of 'The
    nympholepsy of a fond despair,' though he never was accused of being overridden by his
    Greek" (*LEBB* 2:201, referring to *Childe Harold's Pilgrimage* 4.115).

....

We do not serve the dead—the past is past!
God lives, and lifts his glorious mornings up
    Before the eyes of men, awake at last,
Who put away the meats they used to sup,   220
    And down upon the dust of earth outcast
The dregs remaining of the ancient cup,
    Then turn to wakeful prayer and worthy act.

....

 Shall I say
    What made my heart beat with exulting love,   445
A few weeks back?—
                 .... The day[1] was such a day
    As Florence owes the sun. The sky above,
Its weight upon the mountains seemed to lay,
    And palpitate in glory, like a dove
Who has flown too fast, full-hearted!—take away   450
    The image! for the heart of man beat higher
That day in Florence, flooding all her streets
    And piazzas with a tumult and desire.
The people, with accumulated heats,
    And faces turned one way, as if one fire   455
Both drew and flushed them, left their ancient beats,
    And went up toward the palace-Pitti wall,
To thank their Grand-duke,[2] who, not quite of course,
    Had graciously permitted, at their call,
The citizens to use their civic force[3]   460
    To guard their civic homes. So, one and all,

---

1   The day] 12 September 1847; see this poem's headnote on the momentous events in
    Florence on this day, also the first anniversary of the Brownings' marriage.

2   Grand-duke] Grand Duke Leopold II of Tuscany; see headnote.

3   civic force] alluding to the permission granted by Leopold II on 4 September 1847 for
    the Florentine people to form a Civic Guard in defiance of the will of the Austrian
    Empire.

The Tuscan cities[1] streamed up to the source
   Of this new good, at Florence, taking it
As good so far, presageful of more good,—
   The first torch of Italian freedom, lit   465
To toss in the next tiger's face who should
   Approach too near them in a greedy fit,—
The first pulse of an even flow of blood,
   To prove the level of Italian veins
Towards rights perceived and granted. How we gazed   470
   From Casa Guidi windows,[2] while, in trains
Of orderly procession—banners raised,
   And intermittent bursts of martial strains
Which died upon the shout, as if amazed
   By gladness beyond music—they passed on!   475
The Magistracy, with insignia, passed,—
   And all the people shouted in the sun,
And all the thousand windows which had cast
   A ripple of silks, in blue and scarlet, down,
(As if the houses overflowed at last,)   480
   Seemed growing larger with fair heads and eyes.
The Lawyers passed,—and still arose the shout,
   And hands broke from the windows to surprise
Those grave calm brows with bay-tree leaves thrown out.
   The Priesthood passed,—the friars with worldly-wise   485
Keen sidelong glances from their beards about
   The street to see who shouted! many a monk
Who takes a long rope in the waist,[3] was there!
   Whereat the popular exultation drunk

---

1   The Tuscan cities] the city-states of Tuscany such as Pisa, Siena, and Arezzo repre-
    sented in the procession described below in ll. 504-12.

2   From Casa Guidi windows] from windows in the palazzo facing the direction of the
    Pitti Palace, not from the Brownings' own apartment balcony and windows.

3   The Priesthood passed,-- the friars ... many a monk / Who takes a long rope in the
    waist] "The magistracy came first ... & then the priesthood ... I saw some brown monks
    there, with the rope girdle," EBB said in the letter describing this procession (see the
    headnote and *LTA* 1:130-38), alluding to the characteristic brown robe and rope girdle
    of the Franciscan monks. The friars were a more secular order than the cloistered
    monks. EBB's comments on both imply her skepticism of their professed asceticism.

With indrawn "vivas"[1] the whole sunny air,   490
    While, through the murmuring windows, rose and sunk
A cloud of kerchiefed hands,—"The church makes fair
    Her welcome in the new Pope's name."[2] Ensued
The black sign of the "Martyrs!" (name no name,
    But count the graves in silence). Next, were viewed   495
The Artists; next, the Trades; and after came
    The People,—flag and sign, and rights as good,—
And very loud the shout was for that same
    Motto, "Il popolo." IL POPOLO,[3]—
The word means dukedom, empire, majesty,   500
    And kings in such an hour might read it so.
And next, with banners, each in his degree,
    Deputed representatives a-row
Of every separate state of Tuscany.
    Siena's she-wolf, bristling on the fold   505
Of the first flag, preceded Pisa's hare,
    And Massa's lion floated calm in gold,
Pienza's following with his silver stare.
    Arezzo's steed pranced clear from bridle-hold,—
And well might shout our Florence, greeting there   510
    These, and more brethren. Last, the world had sent
The various children of her teeming flanks—
    Greeks, English, French—as if to a parliament
Of lovers of her Italy in ranks,
    Each bearing its land's symbol reverent.   515
At which the stones seemed breaking into thanks
    And rattling up the sky, such sounds in proof
Arose; the very house-walls seemed to bend;
    The very windows, up from door to roof,
Flashed out a rapture of bright heads, to mend   520
    With passionate looks, the gesture's whirling off

---

1   "vivas"] cheers ("long live!").

2   "... the new Pope's name."] Pius IX or Pio Nono, here probably an inscription on a
    banner.

3   IL POPOLO] the people; ll. 499-501 reflect the thought of Giuseppe Mazzini (see the
    headnote and Part II, below). A key slogan of Mazzini and his followers was "God and
    the people."

A hurricane of leaves. Three hours did end
    While all these passed; and ever in the crowd,
Rude men, unconscious of the tears that kept
    Their beards moist, shouted; some few laughed aloud,   525
And none asked any why they laughed and wept.
    Friends kissed each other's cheeks, and foes long vowed
More warmly did it,—two-months' babies leapt
    Right upward in their mother's arms, whose black,
Wide, glittering eyes looked elsewhere; lovers pressed   530
    Each before either, neither glancing back;
And peasant maidens, smoothly 'tired[1] and tressed,
    Forgot to finger on their throats the slack
Great pearl-strings; while old blind men would not rest,
    But pattered with their staves and slid their shoes   535
Along the stones, and smiled as if they saw.
    O heaven, I think that day had noble use
Among God's days. So near stood Right and Law,
    Both mutually forborne! Law would not bruise,
Nor Right deny, and each in reverent awe   540
    Honored the other. And if, ne'ertheless,
That good day's sun delivered to the vines
    No charta,[2] and the liberal Duke's excess
Did scarce exceed a Guelf's or Ghibelline's[3]
    In any special actual righteousness   545
Of what that day he granted,[4] still the signs
    Are good and full of promise, we must say,
When multitudes approach their kings with prayers
    And kings concede their people's right to pray,
    Both in one sunshine.

---

1 'tired] attired.

2 No charta] no charter of rights or constitution codifying the principles by which he
   would govern.

3 Guelf's or Ghibelline's] referring to rival political parties in late medieval Italy, whose
   conflicts marked the history of the period. The Guelphs were the papal and popular
   party, the Ghibellines the imperial and aristocratic party.

4 Of what that day he granted] The 1851 edition includes here a note by EBB that does
   not appear in the 1856 edition: "Since when the constitutional concessions have been
   complete in Tuscany, as all the world knows. The event breaks in upon the medita-
   tion, and is too fast for prophecy in these strange times."

....

Where guess ye that the living people met,
　　Kept tryst, formed ranks, chose leaders, first unrolled　　　580
Their banners?
　In the Loggia? where is set
Cellini's godlike Perseus,[1]....

　　　　　　　No, the people sought no wings[2]
　　From Perseus in the Loggia, nor implored
An inspiration in the place beside,[3]
　　From that dim bust of Brutus,[4] jagged and grand,　　　　590
Where Buonarroti[5] passionately tried
　　From out the close-clenched marble to demand
The head of Rome's sublimest homicide,—
　　Then dropt the quivering mallet from his hand,
Despairing he could find no model-stuff　　　　　　　　　　595
　　Of Brutus, in all Florence, where he found
The gods and gladiators thick enough.
　　Nor there! the people chose still holier ground!
The people, who are simple, blind, and rough,
　　Know their own angels, after looking round.　　　　　　　600
Whom chose they then? where met they?

　　　　　　　　　　On the stone
　　Called Dante's,[6]—a plain flat stone, scarce discerned
From others in the pavement,—whereupon
　　He used to bring his quiet chair out, turned
To Brunelleschi's church,[7] and pour alone　　　　　　　　605
　　The lava of his spirit when it burned.

1　Cellini's godlike Perseus] Benvenuto Cellini (1500–71), Italian artist and author, whose masterpiece, a bronze sculpture representing Perseus holding the head of the slain Medusa, stands in Florence's Loggia dei Lanzi.

2　wings] Perseus wore winged sandals.

3　the place beside] the Uffizi Gallery.

4　Brutus] Marcus Junius Brutus (85–42 BCE), Republican assassin of Julius Caesar.

5　Buonarroti] Michelangelo, whose bust of Brutus remained unfinished.

6　Dante's] Dante's stone on the Piazza del Duomo was thought to be the place where Dante habitually sat.

7　Brunelleschi's church] the Cathedral of Florence, Santa Maria del Fiore, whose dome was designed by the architect Filippo Brunelleschi (1377–1446).

....

And, mark ye, that the piercingest sweet smell   640
Of love's dear incense by the living sent
    To find the dead, is not accessible
To lazy livers! no narcotic,—not
    Swung in a censer[1] to a sleepy tune,—
But trod out in the morning air, by hot   645
    Quick spirits, who tread firm to ends foreshown,
And use the name of greatness unforgot,
    To meditate what greatness may be done.

....

And so with wide embrace, my England, seek
    To stifle the bad heat and flickerings
Of this world's false and nearly expended fire!
    Draw palpitating arrows to the wood,   710
And twang abroad thy high hopes, and thy higher
    Resolves, from that most virtuous altitude!
Till nations shall unconsciously aspire
    By looking up to thee, and learn that good
And glory are not different. Announce law   715
    By freedom; exalt chivalry by peace;
Instruct how clear calm eyes can overawe,
    And how pure hands, stretched simply to release
A bond-slave, will not need a sword to draw
    To be held dreadful. O my England, crease   720
Thy purple[2] with no alien agonies!
    No struggles toward encroachment, no vile war!
Disband thy captains, change thy victories,
    Be henceforth prosperous as the angels are,
Helping, not humbling.
....

---

1   censer] a vessel in which incense is burnt and used in Catholic religious rituals.
2   crease / Thy purple] The color purple is associated with royalty, especially royal
    mourning.

Meanwhile, in this same Italy we want   741
    Not popular passion, to arise and crush,
But popular conscience, which may covenant
    For what it knows.

    ....

    What ye want is light—indeed
Not sunlight—(ye may well look up surprised
    To those unfathomable heavens that feed   760
Your purple hills!)—but God's light organized
    In some high soul, crowned capable to lead
The conscious people, conscious and advised,—
    For if we lift a people like mere clay,
It falls the same. We want thee, O unfound   765
    And sovran teacher!—if thy beard be grey
Or black, we bid thee rise up from the ground
    And speak the word God giveth thee to say,
Inspiring into all this people round,
    Instead of passion, thought, which pioneers   770
All generous passion, purifies from sin,
    And strikes the hour for. Rise up teacher![1] here's
A crowd to make a nation!—best begin
    By making each a man, till all be peers
Of earth's true patriots and pure martyrs in   775
    Knowing and daring.

    ....

    This country-saving is a glorious thing,   860
And if a common man achieved it? well.
    Say, a rich man did? excellent. A king?
That grows sublime. A priest? improbable.
    A pope? Ah, there we stop, and cannot bring

---

1   Rise up teacher!] an apostrophe to a heroic leader, possibly made with Mazzini in mind
    (see headnote). Cf. the importance of leaders and heroes in the writings of Thomas
    Carlyle (1795-1881), especially his *On Heroes, Hero-Worship, and the Heroic in History*
    (1841). As an exile in London, Mazzini was a close personal friend of Carlyle's.

Our faith up to the leap, with history's bell   865
     So heavy round the neck of it—albeit
We fain would grant the possibility,
     For *thy* sake, Pio Nono!¹

....

Meanwhile, let all the far ends of the world
     Breathe back the deep breath of their old delight,
To swell the Italian banner just unfurled.
     Help, lands of Europe! for, if Austria fight,
The drums will bar your slumber. Had ye curled   1105
     The laurel for your thousand artists' brows,
If these Italian hands had planted none?
     Can any sit down idle in the house,
Nor hear appeals from Buonarroti's stone
     And Raffael's canvas, rousing and to rouse?   1110
Where's Poussin's² master? Gallic Avignon
     Bred Laura,³ and Vaucluse's fount⁴ has stirred
The heart of France too strongly, as it lets
     Its little stream out, (like a wizard's bird
Which bounds upon its emerald wing and wets   1115
     The rocks on each side) that she should not gird
Her loins with Charlemagne's⁵ sword when foes beset

---

1   Pio Nono] ll. 860-68 reflect hopes regarding Pope Pius IX that EBB shared with many
    others in Italy in 1847 (see headnote, *BC* 14:302, and Markus, *CGW*, xix-xxv), arising
    from Pio Nono's first official actions as Pope, which included granting an amnesty for
    political prisoners on 16 July 1846.

2   Poussin] Nicolas Poussin (1594-1665), the celebrated French painter, who spent much
    of his life in Italy.

3   Gallic Avignon / Bred Laura] Laura, the inspiration for Petrarch's love sonnets in the
    Canzoniere, was born in Avignon, within a region bordering Italy that was incorpo-
    rated into France in 1791.

4   Vaucluse's fount] a pool formed by a river gushing up from the earth near Avignon in
    Fontaine-de-Vaucluse, where Petrarch lived. On the Brownings' poetic "pilgrimage"
    to this site in 1846, see *BC* 14:23-24, 149.

5   Charlemagne's] Charles the Great or Charles I (742?-814), Carolingian king of the Franks from
    768 and emperor of the West from 800. Cf. the allusion to Charlemagne in *Aurora Leigh* 5:203.

The country of her Petrarch.[1] Spain may well
Be minded how from Italy she caught,
    To mingle with her tinkling Moorish bell,[2]   1120
A fuller cadence and a subtler thought.
    And even the New World, the receptacle
Of freemen, may send glad men, as it ought,
    To greet Vespucci Amerigo's[3] door.
While England claims, by trump of poetry,   1125
    Verona, Venice, the Ravenna-shore,[4]
And dearer holds John Milton's Fiesole[5]
    Than Langlande's Malvern[6] with the stars in flower.   1128

....

For Italy's the whole earth's treasury, piled   1165
    With reveries of gentle ladies, flung
Aside, like ravelled silk, from life's worn stuff;
    With coins of scholars' fancy, which, being rung
On work-day counter, still sound silver-proof;
    In short, with all the dreams of dreamers young,   1170
Before their heads have time for slipping off
    Hope's pillow to the ground. How oft, indeed,
We've sent our souls out from the rigid north,
    On bare white feet which would not print nor bleed,
To climb the Alpine passes and look forth,   1175

---

1   her Petrarch] the Italian Petrarch is deemed to belong to France in this gesture of
     cultural diplomacy.

2   Moorish bell] the Moorish bell towers of many Spanish cathedrals, here signify the
     influence on Spanish culture of the Moslem Berber and Arabic forces who conquered
     Spain in the eighth century.

3   Vespucci Amerigo's] Amerigo Vespucci (1451–1512), Florentine navigator and adven-
     turer, in whose honor America was named.

4   Verona, Venice, and Ravenna-shore] alluding to Shakespeare's use of Italy for his
     plays (e.g., Verona in *Romeo and Juliet*, Venice in *Othello*), as well as to Byron's period
     in Ravenna in 1819 to 1821, where he was visited by Shelley (in 1821).

5   Fiesole] Milton mentions Galileo in Fiesole (a hill town above Florence), in *Paradise
     Lost* (1667), 1:287–89.

6   Langlande's Malvern] William Langland (c.1332–c.1400), putative author of the
     allegorical poem *Piers Plowman*, set in the Malvern Hills, an area dear to EBB, close
     to her childhood home Hope End.

Where booming low the Lombard rivers lead
To gardens, vineyards, all a dream is worth,—
Sights, thou and I, Love, have seen afterward
From Tuscan Bellosguardo, wide awake,[1]
When, standing on the actual blessed sward   1180
Where Galileo stood at nights to take
The vision of the stars, we have found it hard,
Gazing upon the earth and heaven, to make
A choice of beauty.

Therefore let us all
Refreshed in England or in other land,   1085
By visions, with their fountain-rise and fall,
Of this earth's darling,—we, who understand
A little how the Tuscan musical
Vowels do round themselves as if they planned
Eternities of separate sweetness,—we,   1190
Who loved Sorrento vines[2] in picture-book,
Or ere in wine-cup we pledged faith or glee,—
Who loved Rome's wolf, with demi-gods at suck,[3]
Or ere we loved truth's own divinity,—
Who loved, in brief, the classic hill and brook,   1195
And Ovid's[4] dreaming tales, and Petrarch's song,
Or ere we loved Love's self even!—let us give
The blessing of our souls, (and wish them strong
To bear it to the height where prayers arrive,
When faithful spirits pray against a wrong,)   1200
To this great cause of southern men, who strive
In God's name for man's rights, and shall not fail!

---

1 Tuscan Bellosguardo, wide awake,] "Galileo's villa, close to Florence, is built on an
   eminence called Bellosguardo" [EBB's note]. The Brownings visited Galileo's villa,
   "where Milton visited him," in July 1847 (*BC* 14:246).

2 Sorrento's vines] Sorrento in southern Italy is known for its wines; cf. RB's sensuous
   description of Sorrento's landscapes in "The Englishman in Italy" (1845).

3 Rome's wolf, with demi-gods at suck] In Roman legend, Romulus and Remus, the sons
   of Mars and a vestal virgin, and the founders of Rome, were suckled by a she-wolf.

4 Ovid] Publius Ovidius Naso (43 BCE-18 CE), Roman poet, author of the *Metamorphoses*
   and other works.

Behold, they shall not fail. The shouts ascend
    Above the shrieks, in Naples,[1] and prevail.
Rows of shot corpses, waiting for the end   1205
    Of burial, seem to smile up straight and pale
Into the azure air and apprehend
    That final gun-flash from Palermo's coast
Which lightens their apocalypse of death.
    So let them die! The world shows nothing lost;   1210
Therefore, not blood. Above or underneath,
    What matter, brothers, if ye keep your post
On duty's side? As sword returns to sheath,
    So dust to grave, but souls find place in Heaven.
Heroic daring is the true success,   1215
    The eucharistic bread[2] requires no leaven;
And though your ends were hopeless, we should bless
    Your cause as holy. Strive—and, having striven,
Take, for God's recompense, that righteousness!

Part II

I wrote a meditation and a dream,
    Hearing a little child sing in the street.
I leant upon his music as a theme,
    Till it gave way beneath my heart's full beat,
Which tried at an exultant prophecy   5
    But dropped before the measure was complete—
Alas, for songs and hearts! O Tuscany,
    O Dante's Florence, is the type too plain?
Didst thou, too, only sing of liberty,
    As little children take up a high strain   10

---

1 The shouts ascend ... in Naples] ll. 1204-10 allude to popular insurrections within the
    Kingdom of the Two Sicilies in January 1848, beginning in Palermo, capital of Sicily, and
    spreading to Naples. On 29 January the ruler of the kingdom, Ferdinand II (1810-59),
    yielded to pressure and published a constitution based on the French Constitution of
    1830, leading to the formation of a Parliament. On 13 March 1849, Ferdinand suspended
    the new Parliament as reactionary forces and the Austrians regained control in Italy.
2 eucharistic bread] the bread used in the Communion service.

With unintentioned voices, and break off
　To sleep upon their mothers' knees again?
Could'st thou not watch one hour?[1] then, sleep enough—
　That sleep may hasten manhood, and sustain
The faint pale spirit with some muscular stuff. 　　　　　15

　But we, who cannot slumber as thou dost,
We thinkers, who have thought for thee and failed,
　We hopers, who have hoped for thee and lost,
We poets, wandered round by dreams,[2] who hailed
　From this Atrides' roof (with lintel-post 　　　　　20
Which still drips blood,[3] —the worse part hath prevailed)
　The fire-voice of the beacons, to declare
Troy taken, sorrow ended,—cozened[4] through
　A crimson sunset in a misty air,—
What now remains for such as we, to do? 　　　　　25
　God's judgments, peradventure,[5] will He bare
To the roots of thunder, if we kneel and sue?

　From Casa Guidi windows I looked forth,
And saw ten thousand eyes of Florentines

1　Could'st thou not watch one hour?] Christ's words to Peter at Gethsemane; see
　Matthew 26.40, Mark 14.37.

2　We poets, wandered round by dreams] "See the opening passage of the Agamemnon
　of Æschylus" [EBB's note]. In the opening scene of the *Agamemnon* (458 BCE) by
　the Greek dramatist Aeschylus (525-456 BCE), a watchman on the roof of King Ag-
　amemnon's palace scans the horizon for the fiery beacons that will signal the success
　of the king's battle against the Trojans. In keeping with the sombre subject here (the
　"tragedies" in l. 320, below), Aeschylus's drama portrays Agamemnon's murder, on his
　return from Troy, at the hands of his own wife Clytemnestra. On EBB's response to
　and translations of Aeschylus, see "A Vision of Poets," l. 301n. RB later translated the
　Agamemnon (pub. 1875).

3　with lintel-post / Which still drips blood] an allusion to Agamemnon's sacrifice of his
　own daughter Iphigenia (despite the protestations of her mother Clytemnestra) when
　the Greek ships were delayed by contrary winds in setting out for Troy. A "lintel" is
　the horizontal load-bearing piece of wood or stone over a doorway or window.

4　cozened] deceived or beguiled.

5　peradventure] perchance or perhaps.

Flash back the triumph of the Lombard north,[1]—   30
Saw fifty banners, freighted with the signs
    And exultations of the awakened earth,
Float on above the multitude in lines,
    Straight to the Pitti.[2] So, the vision went.
And so, between those populous rough hands   35
    Raised in the sun, Duke Leopold outleant,
And took the patriot's oath,[3] which henceforth stands
    Among the oaths of perjurers, eminent
To catch the lightnings ripened for these lands.
....

For me, I do repent me in this dust
Of towns and temples, which makes Italy,—
    I sigh amid the sighs which breathe a gust   60
Of dying century to century
    Around us on the uneven crater-crust
Of these old worlds,—I bow my soul and knee!
    Absolve me, patriots, of my woman's fault
That ever I believed the man was true![4] —   65
....

Forgive, that I forgot the mind which runs   91
    Through absolute races, too unsceptical!
I saw the man among his little sons,

---

1   the triumph of the Lombard north] the "Five Day" revolution in Milan beginning 18
    March 1848, which forced the Austrian army under Field Marshall Joseph Radetszky
    (1766-1858) to withdraw from the city—a triumph of civilian forces over professional
    troops that led volunteers from Tuscany and other regions to rush to aid the Lom-
    bards.

2   The Pitti] the Pitti Palace, Duke Leopold's residence, near Casa Guidi; see head-
    note.

3   the patriot's oath] after granting the liberal reforms described in Part I of the poem,
    Grand Duke Leopold II issued a proclamation on 5 April 1848, commending "the
    holy cause of Italian independence" and pointing out to Tuscan patriots that the cause
    would be "decided on the fields of Lombardy" (cited *LTA* 1:172n3).

4   my woman's fault ... true!] Since many men as well as women shared EBB's belief
    in the Grand Duke (see Markus, *CGW*, xxvi), the phrase "woman's fault" here has
    an ironic dimension. In the 1851 text, l. 64 reads, "And sigh and do repent me of my
    fault."

His lips were warm with kisses while he swore,—
And I, because I am a woman, I,   95
    Who felt my own child's coming life before
The prescience of my soul, and held faith high,—
    I could not bear to think, whoever bore,
That lips, so warmed, could shape so cold a lie.

    From Casa Guidi windows I looked out,   100
Again looked, and beheld a different sight.
    The Duke had fled[1] before the people's shout ...
....

    From Casa Guidi windows, gazing, then,   286
I saw and witness how the Duke came back.[2]
    The regular tramp of horse and tread of men
Did smite the silence like an anvil black
    And sparkless. With her wide eyes at full strain,   290
Our Tuscan nurse exclaimed, "Alack, alack,
    Signora! these shall be the Austrians." "Nay,
Be still," I answered, "do not wake the child!"
    —For so, my two-months' baby[3] sleeping lay
In milky dreams upon the bed and smiled,   295
    And I thought, "he shall sleep on, while he may,
Through the world's baseness. Not being yet defiled,
    Why should he be disturbed by what is done?"
Then, gazing, I beheld the long-drawn street
    Live out, from end to end, full in the sun,   300
With Austria's thousands. Sword and bayonet,
    Horse, foot, artillery,—cannons rolling on,

---

1   The Duke had fled] On 9 February 1849, shortly after a bill for a Constituent Assembly
    was passed in Florence—awaiting Grand Duke Leopold II's signature to complete
    it—he fled on the pretext of taking a drive while in Siena.

2   the Duke came back] In a letter to Henrietta of early May 1849, EBB describes the
    "hateful procession" of the Austrians—according to the Austrian General's proclama-
    tion to the Tuscans, "'Invited by your Grand Duke'" (*LTH* 107-08).

3   two-months' baby] Robert Wiedeman Barrett Browning, or "Pen," as he was later
    nicknamed, was born 9 March 1849; for RB's account of the birth and EBB's description
    of her "unspeakable rapture" on hearing the baby's "first cry," see *LTA* 1:234-35, 241.

Like blind slow storm-clouds gestant[1] with the heat
   Of undeveloped lightnings, each bestrode
By a single man, dust-white from head to heel,   305
   Indifferent as the dreadful thing he rode,
Like a sculptured Fate[2] serene and terrible.
   As some smooth river which has overflowed,
Will slow and silent down its current wheel
   A loosened forest, all the pines erect,—   310
So, swept, in mute significance of storm,
   The marshalled thousands,—not an eye deflect
To left or right, to catch a novel form
   Of Florence city adorned by architect
And carver, or of Beauties live and warm   315
   Scared at the casements!—all, straightforward eyes
And faces, held as stedfast as their swords,
   And cognisant of acts, not imageries.
The key, O Tuscans, too well fits the wards![3]
   Ye asked for mimes,—these bring you tragedies.   320
For purple,—these shall wear it as your lords.
   Ye played like children,—die like innocents.[4]
....

Meantime, from Casa Guidi windows, we   352
Beheld the armament of Austria flow
   Into the drowning heart of Tuscany.
And yet none wept, none cursed, or, if 'twas so,   355
   They wept and cursed in silence. Silently
Our noisy Tuscans watched the invading foe;
   They had learnt silence.[5] Pressed against the wall,

---

1   gestant] pregnant with (figurative); the *OED* cites this usage by EBB.

2   Like a sculptured Fate] cf. EBB's description of the soldiers like "dusty statues" (*LTH* 107).

3   wards] the ridges on the inside plate of a lock, corresponding to the incisions in the matching key; figuratively, several possible senses of "ward" may contribute to the wordplay here, including the action of guarding, a body of guards, places for guarding (in a fortress), and a person "in ward" or under the control of another.

4   die like innocents] an allusion to the biblical massacre of the innocents in Matthew 2.13-23.

5   Silently ... silence.] "The people shrank back to let them pass, in the deepest silence," EBB observed to Henrietta in early May (*LTH* 107); two months later, she similarly observed to Arabella, "Florence is in the shut hands of Austria—we dare'nt move or breathe" (*LTA* 1:249).

And grouped upon the church-steps opposite,
    A few pale men and women stared at all! 360
God knows what they were feeling, with their white
    Constrainèd faces, they, so prodigal
Of cry and gesture when the world goes right,
    Or wrong indeed. But here, was depth of wrong,
And here, still water; they were silent here; 365
    And through that sentient silence, struck along
That measured tramp from which it stood out clear,
    Distinct the sound and silence, like a gong
At midnight, each by the other awfuller,—
    While every soldier in his cap displayed 370
A leaf of olive. Dusty, bitter thing!
    Was such plucked at Novara,[1] is it said?

A cry is up in England, which doth ring
    The hollow world through, that for ends of trade
And virtue, and God's better worshipping, 375
    We henceforth should exalt the name of Peace,[2]
And leave those rusty wars that eat the soul,—
    Besides their clippings at our golden fleece.[3]
I, too, have loved peace, and from bole[4] to bole
    Of immemorial, undeciduous trees, 380
Would write, as lovers use, upon a scroll,
    The holy name of Peace, and set it high
Where none could pluck it down. On trees, I say,—

---

1 Novara] in Piedmont, site of the key battle in March 1849, in which the Austrians
    defeated the Italian forces under Charles Albert (1798-1849), King of Sardinia
    (1831-49), leading to his abdication. See the headnote.

2 A cry is up in England ... the name of Peace] an allusion to the movement for inter-
    national peace and non-intervention in European politics led by Richard Cobden
    (1804-65) and other members of the Manchester school of political and economic
    thought with which he was associated; Cobden was a British representative at the 1849
    Universal Peace Congress in Paris. See Appendix D for responses to EBB's critique in
    ll. 373-424. A similar critique appears in Tennyson's *Maud* (1855), Part I, I, vi-ix.

3 golden fleece] alluding to the fleece of a golden ram which, according to Greek my-
    thology, Jason and his Argonauts stole from the king of Colchis, aided by the sorceress
    Medea.

4 bole] tree-trunk.

Not upon gibbets![1] —With the greenery
Of dewy branches and the flowery May,   385
   Sweet mediation betwixt earth and sky
Providing, for the shepherd's holiday.
   Not upon gibbets!—though the vulture leaves
The bones to quiet, which he first picked bare.
   Not upon dungeons! though the wretch who grieves   390
And groans within, less stirs the outer air
   Than any little field-mouse stirs the sheaves.
Not upon chain-bolts! though the slave's despair
   Has dulled his helpless, miserable brain,
And left him blank beneath the freeman's whip,   395
   To sing and laugh out idiocies of pain.
Nor yet on starving homes! where many a lip
   Has sobbed itself asleep through curses vain.
I love no peace which is not fellowship,
   And which includes not mercy. I would have   400
Rather, the raking of the guns across
   The world, and shrieks against Heaven's architrave;[2]
Rather, the struggle in the slippery fosse[3]
   Of dying men and horses, and the wave
Blood-bubbling.... Enough said!—by Christ's own cross,   405
   And by this faint heart of my womanhood,
Such things are better than a Peace that sits
   Beside a hearth in self-commended mood,
And takes no thought how wind and rain by fits
   Are howling out of doors against the good   410
Of the poor wanderer. What! your peace admits
   Of outside anguish while it keeps at home?
I loathe to take its name upon my tongue.
   'Tis nowise peace. 'Tis treason, stiff with doom,—
'Tis gagged despair, and inarticulate wrong,   415
   Annihilated Poland, stifled Rome,

---

1 gibbets] gallows, particularly those on which criminals were suspended after
   execution.

2 architrave] in architecture, the lowest supporting part of the classical entablature (the
   part of a temple between the columns and the eaves), directly above the columns.

3 fosse] a ditch, moat, trench, or canal.

Dazed Naples, Hungary fainting[1] 'neath the thong,
  And Austria wearing a smooth olive-leaf
On her brute forehead, while her hoofs outpress
  The life from these Italian souls, in brief.   420
O Lord of Peace, who art Lord of Righteousness,
  Constrain the anguished worlds from sin and grief,
Pierce them with conscience, purge them with redress,
  And give us peace which is no counterfeit!

But wherefore should we look out any more   425
  From Casa Guidi windows? Shut them straight,
And let us sit down by the folded door,
  And veil our saddened faces, and, so, wait
What next the judgment-heavens make ready for.
  I have grown too weary of these windows. Sights   430
Come thick enough and clear enough in thought,
  Without the sunshine; souls have inner lights.
And since the Grand-duke has come back and brought
  This army of the North which thus requites
His filial South, we leave him to be taught.   435
  His South, too, has learnt something certainly,
Whereof the practice will bring profit soon;
  And peradventure other eyes may see,
From Casa Guidi windows, what is done
  Or undone. Whatsoever deeds they be,   440
Pope Pius will be glorified in none.[2]

---

1 Annihilated Poland, ... Hungary fainting] alluding to the repression of the European
   revolutionary uprisings of 1848: "[a]nnihilated Poland" because much of the country
   was brutally repressed by Russia, and the one remaining independent republic was
   occupied by Austria following the 1846 Krakow uprising; "stifled Rome" because
   the Republic established in February 1849 with Mazzini as one of the three trium-
   virs or rulers was overthrown with the help of Austria and France in June 1849, and
   Pope Pius IX was re-established as ruler; "[d]azed Naples"—see Part I, ll. 1204-05n;
   "Hungary fainting" because the revolutionary government established by Louis
   Kossuth (1802-94), influenced by the American Declaration of Independence, was
   suppressed by Austria and Russia when America and England refused to intervene
   in support of the Hungarians.

2 Pope Pius will be glorified in none] Pius IX was seen by many as a traitor to the cause
   of Italian nationalism for his role in calling upon the armies of Austria and France to
   reinstate his temporal power; see headnote.

Record that gain, Mazzini![1]—it shall top
Some heights of sorrow. Peter's rock,[2] so named,
    Shall lure no vessel any more to drop
Among the breakers. Peter's chair[3] is shamed   445
    Like any vulgar throne, the nations lop
To pieces for their firewood unreclaimed,—
    And, when it burns too, we shall see as well
In Italy as elsewhere. Let it burn.

    ....

Record that gain, Mazzini!—Yes, but first   526
Set down thy people's faults;[4]—set down the want
    Of soul-conviction; set down aims dispersed,
And incoherent means, and valour scant
    Because of scanty faith, and schisms accursed,   530
That wrench these brother-hearts from covenant
    With freedom and each other. Set down this,
And this, and see to overcome it when
    The seasons bring the fruits thou wilt not miss
If wary. Let no cry of patriot men   535
    Distract thee from the stern analysis
Of masses who cry only! keep thy ken
    Clear as thy soul is virtuous.
    ....

                        Let thy weft   565
Present one woof and warp,[5] Mazzini!—stand
With no man hankering for a dagger's heft,—

---

1 Mazzini] Giuseppe Mazzini; see headnote and Part I, l. 501n.
2 Peter's rock] the Roman Catholic Church.
3 Peter's chair] the Papal throne.
4 Set down thy people's faults] EBB's public advice here reflects her view in 1849
   that "though Mazzini is virtuous and heroic, he is indiscreet and mistakes the stuff
   of which the people is made, if he thinks to find a great nation in the heart of it"
   (*LTH* 101).
5 weft / Present one woof and warp] the weft refers to the horizontal threads interlaced
   through the twisted threads stretched vertically on a loom (the warp); "woof" is
   another term for "weft," or for a fabric's texture.

No, not for Italy!—nor stand apart,
No, not for the republic!—from those pure
   Brave men who hold the level of thy heart   570
In patriot truth, as lover and as doer,
   Albeit they will not follow where thou art
As extreme theorist. Trust and distrust fewer;
   And so bind strong and keep unstained the cause
Which (God's sign granted), war-trumps newly blown   575
   Shall yet annuntiate[1] to the world's applause.

But now, the world is busy; it has grown
   A Fair-going world.[2] Imperial England draws
The flowing ends of the earth, from Fez, Canton,
   Delhi and Stockholm, Athens and Madrid,   580
The Russias and the vast Americas,
   As if a queen drew in her robes amid
Her golden cincture,[3]—isles, peninsulas,
   Capes, continents, far inland countries hid
By jaspar-sands and hills of chrysopras,[4]   585
   All trailing in their splendours through the door
Of the gorgeous Crystal Palace. Every nation,
   To every other nation strange of yore,
Gives face to face the civic salutation,
   And holds up in a proud right hand before   590
That congress, the best work which she can fashion
   By her best means. "These corals, will you please
To match against your oaks? They grow as fast
   Within my wilderness of purple seas."—
"This diamond stared upon me as I passed   595

---

1   annuntiate] to proclaim or announce.

2   A Fair-going world] alluding to the Great Exhibition, a World's Fair that opened
   on 1 May 1851 at the new Crystal Palace in London. Initially, EBB's expectations of
   the Exhibition were more positive: "it must be deeply interesting, & suggestive, &
   worth much fatigue," she wrote in early June 1851 (*LTA* 1:382); earlier, in November
   1850, she expressed surprise at the negative view in some quarters in England of the
   Exhibition as "Prince Albert's 'folly'" (*LEBB* 1:466).

3   cincture] a belt or sash, especially one worn with an ecclesiastical vestment or the
   habit of a monk or nun.

4   chrysopras] a green variety of chalcedony (silica) used as a gemstone.

(As a live god's eye from a marble frieze[1])
Along a dark of diamonds. Is it classed?"—
    "I wove these stuffs so subtly that the gold
Swims to the surface of the silk like cream,
        And curdles to fair patterns. Ye behold!"—   600
"These delicatest muslins rather seem
        Than be, you think? Nay, touch them and be bold,
Though such veiled Chakhi's face in Hafiz' dream."[2]—
    "These carpets—you walk slow on them like kings,
Inaudible like spirits, while your foot   605
        Dips deep in velvet roses and such things."—
"Even Apollonius might commend this flute.[3]
        The music, winding through the stops, upsprings
To make the player very rich! compute."—
    "Here's goblet-glass, to take in with your wine   610
The very sun its grapes were ripened under!
        Drink light and juice together, and each fine."—
"This model of a steam-ship moves your wonder?
        You should behold it crushing down the brine,
Like a blind Jove, who feels his way with thunder."—   615
    "Here's sculpture! Ah, *we* live too! why not throw
Our life into our marbles? Art has place
        For other artists after Angelo."—
"I tried to paint out here a natural face;
        For nature includes Raffael, as we know,   620
Not Raffael nature. Will it help my case?"—
    "Methinks you will not match this steel of ours!"—

---

1   marble frieze] a "frieze" in architecture is a sculpted band of figures, usually beneath
    a cornice.

2   Chakhi's face in Hafiz' dream] Hafiz of Shiraz (Khwaja Shams ud-Din Hafiz-i Shirazi,
    c.1320 or 1325-c.1388/89), Persian lyric poet and master of the ghazal, an Eastern poetic
    lyric form with five to twelve couplets, all in the same rhyme. Many of his ghazals are
    addressed to the beautiful Shakh-e Nabat; he describes her face in a dream in Ghazal
    464. A ms variant of "Chaki's face in Hafiz's dream" is "Laura's face in Petrarch's
    dream" (Markus, *CGW*, 130).

3   Even Apollonius might commend this flute.] "Philostratus relates of Apollonius how
    he objected to the musical instrument of Linus the Rhodian, that it could not enrich
    or beautify. The history of music in our day, would satisfy the philosopher on one
    point at least" [EBB's note]. Flavius Philostratus (fl. c. 217 CE) wrote a *Life of
    Apollonius of Tyana*, on the first-century Greek philosopher.

"Nor you this porcelain! One might dream the clay
    Retained in it the larvæ of the flowers,
They bud so, round the cup, the old spring way."—   625
    "Nor you these carven woods, where birds in bowers
With twisting snakes and climbing cupids, play."

    O Magi of the east and of the west,[1]
Your incense, gold, and myrrh are excellent!—
    What gifts for Christ, then, bring ye with the rest?   630
Your hands have worked well. Is your courage spent
    In handwork only? Have you nothing best,
Which generous souls may perfect and present,
    And He shall thank the givers for? no light
Of teaching, liberal nations, for the poor,[2]   635
    Who sit in darkness when it is not night?
No cure for wicked children? Christ,—no cure!
    No help for women, sobbing out of sight
Because men made the laws? no brothel-lure[3]
    Burnt out by popular lightnings?—Hast thou found   640
No remedy, my England, for such woes?
    No outlet, Austria, for the scourged and bound,
No entrance for the exiled? no repose,
    Russia, for knouted[4] Poles worked underground,
And gentle ladies bleached among the snows?—   645
    No mercy for the slave, America?—

---

1 Magi of the east and of the west] The material display of imperial commodities at the
   Fair is compared to the gifts brought by the wise men to Christ in Matthew 2.11.

2 teaching ... for the poor] EBB's sister, Arabella, worked as a "Directress" in the
   Ragged Schools of London (schools for the poor) (*LTA* 1:xxiii, 110 n24). See EBB's
   "A Song for the Ragged Schools of London" (1854, 1862).

3 brothel-lure] cf. EBB's subsequent engagement with systemic prostitution in *Au-
   rora Leigh*: the "eighty thousand women" who "only smile at night beneath the gas"
   (8:414-15). See also *LEBB* 2:213, where EBB speaks of "the forty thousand wretched
   women" in London.

4 knouted] whipped with a knout, a scourge often fatal in its effects. In this and the next
   line, EBB alludes to the Siberian prisons to which Polish independence fighters were
   sent, often followed by their wives.

No hope for Rome, free France,[1] chivalric France?—
   Alas, great nations have great shames, I say.
No pity, O world, no tender utterance
   Of benediction, and prayers stretched this way   650
For poor Italia, baffled by mischance?—
   O gracious nations, give some ear to me![2]
You all go to your Fair, and I am one
   Who at the roadside of humanity
Beseech your alms,—God's justice to be done.   655
   So, prosper!

In the name of Italy,
Meantime, her patriot dead have benison.[3]
   They only have done well,—and, what they did
Being perfect, it shall triumph.   659
.....

   Ay, the least,   670
Dead for Italia, not in vain has died,
   Though many vainly, ere life's struggle ceased,
To mad dissimilar ends have swerved aside;
   Each grave her nationality has pieced[4]
By its own majestic breadth, and fortified   675
   And pinned it deeper to the soil. Forlorn
Of thanks, be, therefore, no one of these graves!
   Not Hers,—who, at her husband's side, in scorn,

---

1 No hope for Rome, free France] EBB repeatedly expressed hope that the Second
   Republic established in France in 1848, under Louis Napoleon (1808-73) as president,
   would intervene in support of the republican cause in Italy (see e.g., *LTH* 105-06);
   however, the French army that Louis Napoleon sent to Rome in 1849 acted to suppress
   the short-lived Roman republic and to restore the temporal power of Pope Pius IX,
   who immediately brought back the Inquisition, public floggings, and the guillotine.

2 give some ear to me] an echo of Mark Antony's famous speech, "Friends, Romans,
   countrymen, lend me your ears!," after the assassination of Caesar by Brutus in
   Shakespeare's play, *Julius Caesar*, act 3, scene 2, l. 76. On EBB's similar echo in
   addressing women of England in the unpublished "My sisters!" see Stone and Taylor
   2006.

3 benison] blessing or benediction.

4 pieced] mended or made whole by adding a piece; formed in one piece; figuratively,
   joined, united.

Outfaced the whistling shot and hissing waves,
    Until she felt her little babe unborn   680
Recoil, within her, from the violent staves[1]
    And bloodhounds of the world,—at which, her life
Dropt inwards from her eyes and followed it
    Beyond the hunters. Garibaldi's wife[2]
And child died so. And now, the sea-weeds fit   685
    Her body, like a proper shroud and coif,
And murmurously the ebbing waters grit
    The little pebbles while she lies interred
In the sea-sand. Perhaps, ere dying thus,
    She looked up in his face (which never stirred   690
From its clenched anguish) as to make excuse
    For leaving him for his, if so she erred.
He well remembers that she could not choose.
    A memorable grave! Another is
At Genoa. There, a king may fitly lie,[3]   695
    Who, bursting that heroic heart of his
At lost Novara, that he could not die,
    (Though thrice into the cannon's eyes for this
He plunged his shuddering steed, and felt the sky
    Reel back between the fire-shocks) stripped away   700
The ancestral ermine[4] ere the smoke had cleared,
    And, naked to the soul, that none might say
His kingship covered what was base and bleared
    With treason, went out straight an exile, yea,
An exiled patriot. Let him be revered.   705

---

1   staves] thin, narrow shaped pieces of wood used to form a cask; here, evidently with connotations of "stave" as a verb, to break to pieces or to beat with a staff or stave.

2   Garibaldi's wife] Anita Garibaldi (1821–49), see headnote. After the fall of the Roman Republic in July 1849, Garibaldi, Anita, and his volunteer army retreated towards Venice by sea. Pursued by the Austrians, they landed at Ravenna where Anita, six months pregnant and ill, died in Garibaldi's arms and had to be buried quickly in the shallow sand.

3   At Genoa. There, a king may fitly lie] Charles Albert (1798–1849), King of Sardinia (including Piedmont), who after the Italian defeat at the Battle of Novara (23 March 1849) abdicated in favor of his son, Victor Emmanuel, and died four months later in exile. "Heroic Charles Albert dead of a broken heart before the misfortunes of Italy," EBB commented (*LTA* 1:270).

4   ermine] a heraldic fur (white with black spots).

....

Still, graves, when Italy is talked upon.
Still, still, the patriot's tomb, the stranger's hate.   725
  Still Niobe![1] still fainting in the sun,
By whose most dazzling arrows violate
  Her beauteous offspring perished! has she won
Nothing but garlands for the graves, from Fate?
  Nothing but death-songs?—Yes, be it understood   730
Life throbs in noble Piedmont![2] while the feet
  Of Rome's clay image, dabbled soft in blood,
Grow flat with dissolution, and, as meet,
  Will soon be shovelled off like other mud,
To leave the passage free in church and street.   735
  And I, who first took hope up in this song,
Because a child was singing one ... behold,
  The hope and omen were not, haply, wrong!
Poets are soothsayers still, like those of old
  Who studied flights of doves,—and creatures young   740
And tender, mighty meanings, may unfold.

The sun strikes, through the windows, up the floor;
Stand out in it, my own young Florentine,
  Not two years old,[3] and let me see thee more!
It grows along thy amber curls, to shine   745
  Brighter than elsewhere. Now, look straight before,
And fix thy brave blue English eyes on mine,
  And from my soul, which fronts the future so,
With unabashed and unabated gaze,
  Teach me to hope for, what the angels know   750
When they smile clear as thou dost. Down God's ways

---

1 Niobe] The allusion to Niobe here echoes that in the poem's opening; see Part I, ll.
   32–48.

2 Life throbs in noble Piedmont] After the Italian defeat at Novara, EBB looked to
   Charles Albert's son of the House of Savoy, Victor Emmanuel, to provide leadership
   in the cause (see l. 227n, and l. 695n, above).

3 my own young Florentine, / Not two years old] the age of EBB's son, "Pen," de-
   scribed at two months of age in l. 294 above, indicates that almost two years have
   passed during the course of the poem.

With just alighted feet, between the snow
And snowdrops, where a little lamb may graze,
   Thou hast no fear, my lamb, about the road,
Albeit in our vain-glory we assume   755
   That, less than we have, thou hast learnt of God.
Stand out, my blue-eyed prophet!—thou, to whom
   The earliest world-day light that ever flowed,
Through Casa Guidi windows, chanced to come!
   Now shake the glittering nimbus[1] of thy hair,   760
And be God's witness that the elemental
   New springs of life are gushing everywhere
To cleanse the water-courses, and prevent all
   Concrete obstructions which infest the air!
That earth's alive, and gentle or ungentle   765
   Motions within her, signify but growth!—
The ground swells greenest o'er the labouring moles.

   Howe'er the uneasy world is vexed and wroth,
Young children, lifted high on parent souls,
   Look round them with a smile upon the mouth,   770
And take for music every bell that tolls;
   (WHO said we should be better if like these?)[2]
But *we* sit murmuring for the future though
   Posterity is smiling on our knees,
Convicting us of folly. Let us go—   775
   We will trust God. The blank interstices
Men take for ruins, He will build into
   With pillared marbles rare, or knit across
With generous arches, till the fane's[3] complete.
   This world has no perdition, if some loss.   780

---

1   nimbus] a cloudy radiance or mist said to surround a classical deity when on earth; a
    circle or halo about or over the head in the representation of a god, goddess, saint, or
    sacred person such as a king or an emperor.
2   (WHO ... like these?)] see Christ's words to the disciples, Matthew 18.2-5.
3   fane's] a fane is a temple or place of worship.

Such cheer I gather from thy smiling, Sweet!
    The self-same cherub-faces which emboss
The Vail,[1] lean inward to the Mercy-seat.

---

1   cherub-faces which emboss / The Vail] alluding to the wings of the cherubim in
    Exodus 37.9 that cover the "mercy seat," the top section of the Ark of the Covenant
    containing the ten commandments. In Hebrew, the "mercy-seat" signifies both a
    cover or lid and to pardon or atone for.

7. *From* Poems before Congress *(1860)*

Residing principally in Italy after her marriage in late 1846, EBB passionately supported the *Risorgimento*, the movement to unify Italy as an independent nation. After the 1848 uprisings failed (see the headnote to *Casa Guidi Windows* above), her hopes rekindled with the renewed political and military activities in the 1850s, which increasingly pressed to unite regions controlled as separate entities by various kings and dukes, the Austrian crown, the Spanish monarchy, and the Pope. In the war of 1859, *Risorgimento* forces claimed significant victories. Heartened by this momentum, EBB prepared this collection in anticipation of a meeting (congress) of Europe's major powers to negotiate Italy's destiny, planned for January 1859—but Austria eventually declined to participate and the gathering never took place.[1] Like *Casa Guidi Windows, Poems before Congress*—entitled *Napoleon III in Italy* in the American edition—records the dialectical process of high hope for Italian liberation transformed into disillusionment. In this case, the hope for Italian liberation, intensified by the military intervention of the French emperor Napoleon III on behalf of the Italian cause, rapidly yielded to dismay among many Italian patriots when Napoleon in 1859 abruptly made peace with Austria at Villafranca. In celebrating what EBB calls "the present triumph of great principles," *Poems before Congress* is nevertheless prophetic: although Italy's autonomy remained unachieved at her death in late June 1861, it came to fruition soon thereafter. In the preface to this collection EBB anticipates English reviewers' criticisms that she betrayed her Englishness by championing Napoleon III's intervention in Italy so vigorously, and she chides her homeland's government for parochialism in failing to support the Italian cause. Deaf to her call for transnational community, one reviewer in 1860 labeled her a "denationalized fanatic," writing "in a delirium of imbecile one-sidedness."[2] Hardly delirious, the preface and verses in *Poems before Congress* embody

---

1   Anticipating the congress in March 1859, EBB wrote: "I cant hope for much real good out of it, & I would rather have accepted it after a few battles.... I don't see, & nobody here sees very clearly, how it is possible to get on without war" (*LTA* 2:400).

2   *The Saturday Review*, no. 231 (31 March 1860): 402-4; cited Donaldson 1993a, 1860.10.

her claim that she was "a citizeness of the world now" (*LEBB* 2:13). Pleased that the poems were better received in America than in England, she expressed her unrepentance to Theodore Tilton, editor of the American periodical *The Independent*: "My book has had a very angry reception in my native country ..., but I shall be forgiven one day, and meanwhile, forgiven or unforgiven, it is satisfactory to one's own soul to have spoken the truth as one apprehends the Truth."[1]

Preface

These poems were written under the pressure of the events they indicate, after a residence in Italy of so many years, that the present triumph of great principles is heightened to the writer's feelings by the disastrous issue of the last movement, witnessed from "Casa Guidi windows" in 1849. Yet, if the verses should appear to English readers too pungently rendered to admit of a patriotic respect to the English sense of things, I will not excuse myself on such grounds, nor on the ground of my attachment to the Italian people, and my admiration of their heroic constancy and union. What I have written has simply been written because I love truth and justice *quand même*,[2]—"more than Plato" and Plato's country,[3] more than Dante and Dante's country,[4] more even than Shakespeare and Shakespeare's country.

And if patriotism means the flattery of one's nation in every case, then the patriot, take it as you please, is merely a courtier; which I am not, though I have written "Napoleon III. in Italy."[5]

---

1 Unpublished letter to Theodore Tilton (20 October 1860), at the Harry Ransom Humanities Research Center, University of Texas, Austin.

2 quand même] (French) really, even, still.

3 On EBB's long-held view of Greece as the cradle of democracy, see the Introduction.

4 See "A Vision of Poets" (1844) and Part 2 (ll. 598-606) of *CGW* (1851) for EBB's love of Dante as poet and patriot.

5 This poem, the first in *Poems before Congress*, celebrates the French emperor whom EBB saw as intervening in good faith against Austria to champion the Italian cause; "An August Voice," the fifth poem in the collection, presents a more conflicted and complex view of him.

It is time to limit the significance of certain terms, or to enlarge the significance of certain things. Nationality is excellent in its place; and the instinct of self-love is the root of a man, which will develop into sacrificial virtues. But all the virtues are means and uses; and, if we hinder their tendency to growth and expansion, we both destroy them as virtues, and degrade them to that rankest species of corruption reserved for the most noble organizations. For instance,—non-intervention in the affairs of neighboring states is a high political virtue; but non-intervention does not mean, passing by on the other side when your neighbor falls among thieves,—or Phariseeism would recover it from Christianity.[1] Freedom itself is virtue, as well as privilege; but freedom of the seas does not mean piracy, nor freedom of the land, brigandage;[2] nor freedom of the senate, freedom to cudgel a dissident member,[3] nor freedom of the press, freedom to calumniate and lie. So, if patriotism be a virtue indeed, it cannot mean an exclusive devotion to one's country's interests,—for that is only another form of devotion to personal interests, family interests, or provincial interests, all of which, if not driven past themselves, are vulgar and immoral objects. Let us put away the little Pedlingtonism[4] unworthy of a great nation, and too prevalent among us. If the man who does not look beyond this natural life is of a somewhat narrow order, what must be the man who does not look beyond his own frontier or his own sea?[5]

I confess that I dream of the day when an English statesman shall arise with a heart too large for England, having courage in the face

---

1   Alludes to Christ's parable of the Good Samaritan (Luke 29.30-37).

2   brigandage] banditry, robbery.

3   Alludes to an 1856 event in the American Senate. The abolitionist Senator Charles Sumner (1811-74) harshly criticized Senator Andrew Pickens Butler of South Carolina. Two days later, Butler's nephew Preston Smith Brooks, a member of the House of Representatives, caned Sumner so severely in the Senate chambers that he was incapacitated and absent from the Congress for several years. EBB's allusion here extends the range of reference in her collection to America as well as England, thus preparing for the final poem in the volume, "A Curse for a Nation."

4   little Pedlingtonism] in Little Pedlington and the Pedlingtonians (1839)—mentioned by EBB in BC 8:27, 9:174—John Poole (1786?-1872) satirized an imaginary village; "little Pedlingtonism" became synonymous with quackery, cant, and humbug.

5   EBB frequently complained that England's policies regarding the Italian question were "narrow," "selfish & cruel" (see, e.g., LTA 2:395, 400, 409-10).

of his countrymen to assert of some suggested policy,—"This is good for your trade; this is necessary for your domination; but it will vex a people hard by; it will hurt a people farther off; it will profit nothing to the general humanity: therefore, away with it!— it is not for you or for me." When a British minister dares speak so, and when a British public applauds him speaking, then shall the nation be so glorious, that her praise, instead of exploding from within, from loud civic mouths, shall come to her from without, as all worthy praise must, from the alliances she has fostered, and from the populations she has saved.

And poets who write of the events of that time, shall not need to justify themselves in prefaces, for ever so little jarring of the national sentiment, imputable to their rhymes.

Rome, *February,* 1860.

The Dance

In an incident witnessed by the Brownings in a wooded park where Florentine society congregated, aristocratic Florentine ladies in 1859 spontaneously honored French soldiers for supporting Italy's nationalist cause by asking them to dance. The women's act acquired added significance from the fact that for some time liberal, patriotic aristocrats had boycotted the Tuscan Grand Duke's formerly popular balls to protest his collaboration with the Austrians. Among the mixed reviews of *Poems before Congress*, in which this poem first appeared, the *Blackwood's* reviewer judged the poem's images baffling, while the reviewer for the *Critic* called it the best poem in the volume.[1] Criticism: Taylor 2003, Montwieler 2005.

---

1 W.E. Aytoun, "Poetic Aberrations," *Blackwood's* 87 (April 1860): 494 (excerpted in Appendix D.9); *Critic,* n.s. 20 (24 March 1860): 352, cited in Donaldson 1993a, 1860, 7.

I

You remember down at Florence our Cascine,[1]
Where the people on the feast-days walk and drive,
And, through the trees, long-drawn in many a green way,
O'er-roofing hum and murmur like a hive,
The river and the mountains look alive?   5

II

You remember the piazzone[2] there, the stand-place
Of carriages a-brim with Florence Beauties,
Who lean and melt to music as the band plays,
Or smile and chat with some one who a-foot is,
Or on horseback, in observance of male duties?   10

III

'Tis so pretty, in the afternoons of summer,
So many gracious faces brought together!
Call it rout, or call it concert, they have come here,
In the floating of the fan and of the feather,
To reciprocate with beauty the fine weather.   15

IV

While the flower-girls offer nosegays (because *they* too
Go with other sweets) at every carriage-door;
Here, by shake of a white finger, signed away to
Some next buyer, who sits buying score on score,
Piling roses upon roses evermore.   20

V

And last season, when the French camp had its station
In the meadow-ground, things quickened and grew gayer

---

1 Cascine] a wooded park, west of Florence along the Arno River, frequented by
fashionable society and often visited by EBB (see *BC* 14:207-8; *LTA* 1:88-89, 167,
2:88). She noted how Italian revolutionary politics registered in the park, where—in
contrast to the later event with French allies described in this poem—Italian nobles
"look at the Austrian officers," but "dont [sic] speak to them" (*LTA* 1:249, 270), and
where French troops camped in 1859 (*LTA* 2:408), as mentioned in ll. 21-22 below.

2 piazzone] (Italian) a large square.

Through the mingling of the liberating nation
      With this people; groups of Frenchmen everywhere,
      Strolling, gazing, judging lightly .. "who was fair."   25

VI

Then the noblest lady present[1] took upon her
      To speak nobly from her carriage for the rest;
"Pray these officers from France to do us honor
      By dancing with us straightway."—The request
      Was gravely apprehended as addressed.   30

VII

And the men of France bareheaded, bowing lowly,
      Led out each a proud signora[2] to the space
Which the startled crowd had rounded for them—slowly,
      Just a touch of still emotion in his face,
      Not presuming, through the symbol, on the grace.   35

VIII

There was silence in the people: some lips trembled,
      But none jested. Broke the music, at a glance:
And the daughters of our princes, thus assembled,
      Stepped the measure with the gallant sons of France.
      Hush! it might have been a Mass, and not a dance.   40

IX

And they danced there till the blue that overskied us
      Swooned with passion, though the footing seemed sedate;
And the mountains, heaving mighty hearts beside us,
      Sighed a rapture in a shadow, to dilate,
      And touch the holy stone where Dante sate.[3]   45

---

1   the noblest lady present] the Marchesa di Laiatico, wife of the Marquis de Laiatico, Prince Corsini (1805-59). They were both fervent patriots; he was a member of the Tuscan ministry that demanded abdication of the Tuscan Grand Duke who ruled as an Austrian puppet (see *LTA* 2:421n14).

2   signora] (Italian) lady.

3   stone where Dante sate] "Il Sasso di Dante," a stone near Florence's cathedral in the Piazza del Duomo, fabled to be the site where the poet Dante (1265-1321), author of *The Divine Comedy*, habitually sat; cf. *CGW*, 1:601-06.

X

Then the sons of France bareheaded, lowly bowing,
    Led the ladies back where kinsmen of the south
Stood, received them;—till, with burst of overflowing
        Feeling ... husbands, brothers, Florence's male youth,
        Turned, and kissed the martial strangers mouth to mouth.   50

XI

And a cry went up, a cry from all that people!
    —You have heard a people cheering, you suppose,
For the Member,[1] mayor .. with chorus from the steeple?
        This was different: scarce as loud perhaps, (who knows?)
        For we saw wet eyes around us ere the close.   55

XII

And we felt as if a nation, too long borne in
    By hard wrongers, comprehending in such attitude
That God had spoken somewhere since the morning,
        That men were somehow brothers, by no platitude,
        Cried exultant in great wonder and free gratitude.   60

A Curse for a Nation

One of EBB's most controversial works, this fiery poem was first
published in December 1855 as the lead poem in the 1856 issue of
the Boston anti-slavery annual *The Liberty Bell*—the same annual
for which EBB earlier wrote "The Runaway Slave at Pilgrim's
Point." The *Liberty Bell* context indicates that the poem was clearly
written as a denunciation of slavery in America, once again at the
request of EBB's anti-slavery contacts in Boston.[2] When the poem
was reprinted as the concluding work in *Poems before Congress* (1860),
however, its new context in a volume bitterly critical of England's
non-intervention in the Italian liberation struggle led some English

---

1   Member] Member of Parliament. This question specifically directs the poem to an
    English audience.
2   See EBB's letter to Edmund Ollier, dated 4 April 1860, now in the Wellesley College Library.

reviewers to interpret it as a curse directed not at America, but at their own country. More than one English reviewer suggested that the poem was the result not of an angel's inspiration, as the opening stanza maintains, but of more diabolical impulses. "To bless and not to curse is woman's function," the *Blackwood's* reviewer declared, observing that "for the peace and welfare of society ... women should not interfere with politics."[1] Henry Chorley's interpretation in the *Athenaeum* of "A Curse for a Nation" as an attack on England (see Appendix D.6) led EBB to write him a letter correcting his "mis-statement," which Chorley did not print in full (*LEBB* 2:367, 378). At the same time, she confessed to a close friend that "certain" of the stanzas in the poem "do 'fit' England 'as if they were made for her,' which they were *not* though" (*LEBB* 2:375). The revisions that EBB made in the *Liberty Bell* text of the poem before reprinting it in *Poems before Congress* suggest that, despite her public claims, she *did* adapt the poem to make it more applicable to England (see, in particular, the note to ll. 25-28).[2] She nonetheless observed, "In fact, I cursed neither England nor America.... the poem only pointed out how the curse was involved in the action of slave-holding" (*LEBB* 2:367). Criticism: Arishtein 1969, Gladish 1969, Stone 1986, Donaldson 1993b, Mermin 1989, Slinn 2002, and Woodworth 2006.

Prologue

I heard an angel speak last night,
    And he said "Write!
Write a Nation's curse for me,
And send it over the Western Sea."

I faltered, taking up the word: 5
    "Not so, my lord!
If curses must be, choose another
To send thy curse against my brother.

---

1   See the excerpt from W.E. Aytoun's review in Appendix D9.

2   There are numerous verbal variants between *The Liberty Bell* text (see the supplementary website) and the *Poems before Congress* text; we note only the stanza variants below.

"For I am bound by gratitude,
　　By love and blood,　　　　　　　　　　　　10
To brothers of mine across the sea,
Who stretch out kindly hands to me."

"Therefore," the voice said, "shalt thou write
　　My curse to-night.
From the summits of love a curse is driven,　　15
As lightning is from the tops of heaven."

"Not so," I answered. "Evermore
　　My heart is sore
For my own land's sins: for little feet
Of children bleeding along the street:[1]　　　20

"For parked-up honors that gainsay[2]
　　The right of way:
For almsgiving through a door that is
Not open enough for two friends to kiss:

"For love of freedom which abates　　　　　　25
　　Beyond the Straits:
For patriot virtue starved to vice on
Self-praise, self-interest, and suspicion:[3]

"For an oligarchic parliament,
　　And bribes well-meant.　　　　　　　　　30
What curse to another land assign,
When heavy-souled for the sins of mine?"

"Therefore," the voice said, "shalt thou write
　　My curse to-night.
Because thou hast strength to see and hate　　35
A foul thing done *within* thy gate."

1　Probably prompted by the work done by EBB's sister Arabella with homeless girls in London;
　　see "A Song for the Ragged Schools of London" (1854) on the supplementary website.

2　gainsay] deny, contradict.

3　This entire stanza (ll. 25-28) is not in *The Liberty Bell* text of the poem (hereafter, *LB*).

"Not so," I answered once again.
    "To curse, choose men.
For I, a woman, have only known
How the heart melts and the tears run down."   40

"Therefore," the voice said, "shalt thou write
    My curse to-night.
Some women weep and curse, I say
(And no one marvels,) night and day.

"And thou shalt take their part to-night,   45
    Weep and write.
A curse from the depths of womanhood
Is very salt, and bitter, and good."

So thus I wrote, and mourned indeed,
    What all may read.   50
And thus, as was enjoined on me,
I send it over the Western Sea.

The Curse

I
Because ye have broken your own chain
    With the strain
Of brave men climbing a Nation's height,   55
Yet thence bear down with brand and thong
On souls of others,—for this wrong
    This is the curse. Write.

Because yourselves are standing straight
    In the state   60
Of Freedom's foremost acolyte,
Yet keep calm footing all the time
On writhing bond-slaves,—for this crime
    This is the curse. Write.

Because ye prosper in God's name, 65
  With a claim
To honor in the old world's sight,
Yet do the fiend's work perfectly
 In strangling martyrs,—for this lie
   This is the curse. Write. 70

II
Ye shall watch while kings conspire
Round the people's smouldering fire,
  And, warm for your part,
Shall never dare—O shame!
To utter the thought into flame 75
  Which burns at your heart.
   This is the curse. Write.

Ye shall watch while nations strive
With the bloodhounds, die or survive,
  Drop faint from their jaws, 80
Or throttle them backward to death,
And only under your breath
  Shall favor the cause.
   This is the curse. Write.

Ye shall watch while strong men draw 85
The nets of feudal law
  To strangle the weak,
And, counting the sin for a sin,
Your soul shall be sadder within
  Than the word ye shall speak. 90
   This is the curse. Write.[1]

When good men are praying erect
That Christ may avenge his elect
  And deliver the earth,

---

1 In the *LB* text, between l. 91 and l. 92, appears another stanza not included in the
Poems Before Congress text.

The prayer in your ears, said low,   95
Shall sound like the tramp of a foe
   That's driving you forth.
      This is the curse. Write.

When wise men give you their praise,
They shall praise in the heat of the phrase,   100
   As if carried too far.
When ye boast your own charters kept true,
Ye shall blush;—for the thing which ye do
   Derides what ye are.
      This is the curse. Write.   105

When fools cast taunts at your gate,
Your scorn ye shall somewhat abate
   As ye look o'er the wall,
For your conscience, tradition, and name
Explode with a deadlier blame   110
   Than the worst of them all.
      This is the curse. Write.

Go, wherever ill deeds shall be done,
Go, plant your flag in the sun
   Beside the ill-doers!   115
And recoil from clenching the curse
Of God's witnessing Universe
   With a curse of yours.
      THIS is the curse. Write.

8. *From* Last Poems *(1862)*

Lord Walter's Wife[1]

As editor of the *Cornhill Magazine*, novelist William Makepeace Thackeray (1811-63) had asked EBB to contribute a poem. He declined to print "Lord Walter's Wife" (pub. 1862), however, because he judged its "account of unlawful passion" too bold for a family publication "written not only for men and women but for boys, girls, infants, sucklings almost." Expressing his respect for her "pure ethics" and "real modesty" together with his regard for her as "Browning's wife and Penini's mother,"[2] he "humbly" asked her pardon for his editorial decision (*LEBB* 2:444). In reply, EBB sent another poem, but defended her literary candor: "I don't like coarse subjects, or the coarse treatment of any subject. But I am deeply convinced that the corruption of our society requires not shut doors and windows, but light and air: and that it is exactly because pure and prosperous women choose to *ignore* vice, that miserable women suffer wrong by it everywhere. Has paterfamilias,[3] with his Oriental traditions and veiled female faces, very successfully dealt with a certain class of evil? What if materfamilias, with her quick sure instincts and honest innocent eyes, do more towards their expulsion by simply looking at them and calling them by their names?" (*LEBB* 2:445). Criticism: Stephenson 1989, Leighton 1992, Pollock 1996, Shires 2001, Slinn 2002, and Avery and Stott 2003.

I
"But why do you go?" said the lady, while both sate[4] under the yew,
And her eyes were alive in their depth, as the kraken[5] beneath
    the sea-blue.

---

1 A draft ms now in the Pierpont Morgan Library (*R* D489) is entitled "Lord Walter's Betrothed." In it, the girl Dora is the woman speaker's sister, not her daughter.

2 Penini's mother] EBB's son Robert Wiedeman Barrett Browning (1849-1912) was nicknamed Pen or Penini.

3 paterfamilias] (Latin) father of the family, protector and ruler of the household; the term implies the moral dimension of maintaining customary laws. *Materfamilias* is the counterpart for mother of the family.

4 sate] sat.

5 kraken] a huge mythical sea monster. Cf. Tennyson's 1830 poem "The Kraken."

II

"Because I fear you," he answered;—"because you are far too fair,
And able to strangle my soul in a mesh of your gold-colored hair."

III

"Oh that," she said, "is no reason! Such knots are quickly undone,   5
And too much beauty, I reckon, is nothing but too much sun."

IV

"Yet farewell so," he answered;—"the sun-stroke's fatal at times.
I value your husband, Lord Walter, whose gallop rings still from
     the limes."

V

"Oh that," she said, "is no reason. You smell a rose through a fence:
If two should smell it, what matter? who grumbles, and where's
     the pretence?"[1]   10

VI

"But I," he replied, "have promised another, when love was free,
To love her alone, alone, who alone and afar loves me."

VII

"Why, that," she said, "is no reason. Love's always free,[2] I am told.
Will you vow to be safe from the headache on Tuesday, and
     think it will hold?"

VIII

"But you," he replied, "have a daughter, a young little child,
     who was laid   15
In your lap to be pure; so I leave you: the angels would make
     me afraid."

---

1 pretence] carries the sense of claiming as well as feigning.
2 For mid-Victorians, the phrase "free love" conveyed immorality they especially
  associated with the French and with communist economics and communal living
  arrangements.

IX

"Oh, that," she said, "is no reason. The angels keep out of the way;
And Dora, the child, observes nothing, although you should
      please me and stay."

X

At which he rose up in his anger,—"Why, now, you no longer are fair!
Why, now, you no longer are fatal, but ugly and hateful, I swear." 20

XI

At which she laughed out in her scorn.—"These men! Oh, these
      men overnice,
Who are shocked if a color not virtuous, is frankly put on by a vice."

XII

Her eyes blazed upon him—"And *you!* You bring us your vices so near
That we smell them! You think in our presence a thought
      'twould defame us to hear!

XIII

"What reason had you, and what right,—I appeal to your soul
      from my life,—   25
To find me too fair as a woman? Why, sir, I am pure, and a wife.

XIV

"Is the day-star too fair up above you? It burns you not. Dare you imply
I brushed you more close than the star does, when Walter had set
      me as high?

XV

"If a man finds a woman too fair, he means simply adapted too much
To uses unlawful and fatal. The praise!—shall I thank you for such? 30

XVI

"Too fair?—not unless you misuse us! and surely if, once in a
      while,
You attain to it, straightway you call us no longer too fair, but
      too vile.

XVII

"A moment,—I pray your attention!—I have a poor word in my head
I must utter, though womanly custom would set it down better
      unsaid.

XVIII

"You grew, sir, pale to impertinence, once when I showed you a
      ring.   35
You kissed my fan when I dropped it. No matter!—I've broken
      the thing.

XIX

"You did me the honor, perhaps, to be moved at my side now and then
In the senses—a vice, I have heard, which is common to beasts
      and some men.

XX

"Love's a virtue for heroes!—as white as the snow on high hills,
And immortal as every great soul is that struggles, endures,
      and fulfils.   40

XXI

"I love my Walter profoundly,—you, Maude, though you faltered
      a week,
For the sake of .. what was it? an eyebrow? or, less still, a mole on
      a cheek?

XXII

"And since, when all's said, you're too noble to stoop to the
      frivolous cant
About crimes irresistible, virtues that swindle, betray and supplant,

XXIII

"I determined to prove to yourself that, whate'er you might
      dream or avow   45
By illusion, you wanted precisely no more of me than you have now.

XXIV

"There! Look me full in the face!—in the face. Understand, if you can,
That the eyes of such women as I am, are clean as the palm of a man.

XXV

"Drop his hand, you insult him. Avoid us for fear we should cost
      you a scar—
You take us for harlots, I tell you, and not for the women we are.   50

XXVI

"You wronged me: but then I considered ... there's Walter! And
      so at the end,
I vowed that he should not be mulcted,[1] by me, in the hand of a
      friend.

XXVII

"Have I hurt you indeed? We are quits then. Nay, friend of my
      Walter, be mine!
Come Dora, my darling, my angel, and help me to ask him to dine."

Bianca among the Nightingales[2]

The title and refrain link this poem both to John Keats's "Ode to a
Nightingale" (1819), with its emphasis on the emotional pain aris-
ing from the fleeting experience of sensuous pleasures in this world,
and to the classical myth of Philomela, a woman who was ravished,
rendered mute, and abandoned; she exacted terrible revenge and was
transformed into a nightingale that sings eternally of her wrongs.[3]
The poem is associated through manuscript evidence with the
composition of *Aurora Leigh* (1856).[4] Its rivalry between the Italian
speaker and an Englishwoman recalls Madame De Staël's novel

---

1   mulcted] penalized or punished.

2   The woman's name Bianca in Italian means "white."

3   The story is told in the *Metamorphoses* by Roman poet Ovid (43 BCE-18 AD).

4   See Margaret Reynolds, *AL* (Ohio), 109, 151-52n155.

Corinne (1807),[1] an important influence on *Aurora Leigh,* while the representation of fiery passion is evocative of Tennyson's "Fatima" (1832, 1842) and of Sappho's lyrics (an influence on "Fatima"). An example of EBB's adaptation of the ballad genre to achieve the psychological concentration of the dramatic monologue,[2] "Bianca among the Nightingales" was generally praised at the time of publication (1862; see Donaldson 1993a, 1862.4, 7, 32). One reviewer found it an example of "the writer's amazing command over language and metre, for interpreting passion, and interpenetrating words with passion," while another thought it "the most perfectly artistical" work in *Last Poems,* comparing it to the "mad rhymes" of Ophelia in *Hamlet,* Tennyson's "Mariana" (1830), and Margaret's pathetic songs in *Faust.*[3] The poem was translated into Italian in the early twentieth century (see Bisignano 1964, 218). Criticism: Mermin 1989, Stephenson 1989, Williams 1997.

I
The cypress[4] stood up like a church
  That night we felt our love would hold,
And saintly moonlight seemed to search
  And wash the whole world clean as gold;
The olives crystallized the vales'   5
  Broad slopes until the hills grew strong:
The fireflies and the nightingales
  Throbbed each to either, flame and song.
The nightingales, the nightingales.

---

1 EBB judged *Corinne* "immortal," deserving to be read "three score & ten times" (*BC* 3:25; see also 1:361).

2 For another dramatic monologue by EBB that similarly draws on ballad conventions to portray an embittered female speaker, see "Void in Law" (1862) on the supplementary website: www.ebbarchive.org.

3 "Mrs. Browning's *Last Poems,*" *Eclectic Review,* n.s. 2 (May 1862): 425; A. Wilson, "English Poets in Italy: Mrs. Browning's *Last Poems,*" *Macmillan's Magazine,* 6, 31 (May–October 1862): 85. *Faust* (Part I 1808, Part II 1832) is a dramatic poem by the German author, artist, and statesman Johann Wolfgang von Goethe (1749-1832). EBB translated a number of his poems in a notebook now at Wellesley College (*R* D1416, pocket notebook 1).

4 cypress] a coniferous tree plentiful in Italy and traditionally associated with death and mourning.

II

Upon the angle of its shade   10
     The cypress stood, self-balanced high;
Half up, half down, as double-made,
     Along the ground, against the sky.
And *we*, too! from such soul-height went
     Such leaps of blood, so blindly driven,   15
We scarce knew if our nature meant
     Most passionate earth or intense heaven.
The nightingales, the nightingales.

III

We paled with love, we shook with love,
     We kissed so close we could not vow;   20
Till Giulio whispered, "Sweet, above
     God's Ever guarantees this Now."
And through his words the nightingales
     Drove straight and full their long clear call,
Like arrows through heroic mails,[1]   25
     And love was awful in it all.
The nightingales, the nightingales.

IV

O cold white moonlight of the north,
     Refresh these pulses, quench this hell!
O coverture[2] of death drawn forth   30
     Across this garden-chamber .. well!
But what have nightingales to do
     In gloomy England, called the free ..
(Yes, free to die in! ..) when we two
     Are sundered, singing still to me?   35
And still they sing, the nightingales.

---

1 mails] coats of mail, flexible medieval armor made of a mesh of metal.

2 coverture] covering. The French word has specific resonance in Victorian marriage law, as Barbara Leigh Smith Bodichon explained in *A Brief Summary ... of the Most Important Laws Concerning Women* (1854): "A man and wife are one person in law; the wife loses all her rights as a single woman, and her existence is entirely absorbed in that of her husband. He is civilly responsible for her acts; she lives under his protection or cover, and her condition is called coverture."

V

I think I hear him, how he cried
      "My own soul's life" between their notes.
Each man has but one soul supplied,
      And that's immortal. Though his throat's   40
On fire with passion now, to *her*
      He can't say what to me he said!
And yet he moves her, they aver.
      The nightingales sing through my head,
The nightingales, the nightingales.   45

VI

He says to *her* what moves her most.
      He would not name his soul within
Her hearing,—rather pays her cost
      With praises to her lips and chin.
Man has but one soul, 'tis ordained,   50
      And each soul but one love, I add;
Yet souls are damned and love's profaned.
      These nightingales will sing me mad!
The nightingales, the nightingales.

VII

I marvel how the birds can sing.   55
      There's little difference, in their view,
Betwixt our Tuscan[1] trees that spring
      As vital flames into the blue,
And dull round blots of foliage meant
      Like saturated sponges here   60
To suck the fogs up. As content
      Is *he* too in this land, 'tis clear.
And still they sing, the nightingales.

VIII

My native Florence! dear, forgone!
      I see across the Alpine ridge   65

---

1   Florence, the Brownings' home in Italy, is in the region of Tuscany.

How the last feast-day of Saint John[1]
       Shot rockets from Carraia bridge.[2]
The luminous city, tall with fire,
       Trod deep down in that river of ours,
While many a boat with lamp and choir   70
       Skimmed birdlike over glittering towers.
I will not hear these nightingales.

IX
I seem to float, *we* seem to float
       Down Arno's stream in festive guise;
A boat strikes flame into our boat,   75
       And up that lady seems to rise
As then she rose. The shock had flashed
       A vision on us! What a head,
What leaping eyeballs!—beauty dashed
       To splendor by a sudden dread.   80
And still they sing, the nightingales.

X
Too bold to sin, too weak to die;
       Such women are so. As for me,
I would we had drowned there, he and I,
       That moment, loving perfectly.[3]   85
He had not caught her with her loosed
       Gold ringlets .. rarer in the south ..
Nor heard the "Grazie tanto"[4] bruised
       To sweetness by her English mouth.
And still they sing, the nightingales.   90

---

1   Commemoration of John's birthday, 24 June, one of two annual feast days for Saint
    John, blended with traditional (pagan) observances of Midsummer's Eve and Mid-
    summer Day to become one of the most popular festivals throughout much of Europe,
    one associated with romance.

2   One of four bridges spanning the Arno river (l. 74) in Florence.

3   Cf. RB's "By the Fireside," "Two in the Campagna," and "The Last Ride Together"
    (1855) for evocations of the concept of "the good minute," a fleeting moment of perfect
    love.

4   Grazie tanto] (Italian) thanks so much, many thanks.

XI

She had not reached him at my heart
      With her fine tongue, as snakes indeed
Kill flies; nor had I, for my part,
      Yearned after, in my desperate need,
And followed him as he did her   95
      To coasts left bitter by the tide,
Whose very nightingales, elsewhere
      Delighting, torture and deride!
For still they sing, the nightingales.

XII

A worthless woman! mere cold clay   100
      As all false things are! but so fair,
She takes the breath of men away
      Who gaze upon her unaware.
I would not play her larcenous tricks
      To have her looks! She lied and stole,   105
And spat into my love's pure pyx[1]
      The rank saliva of her soul.
And still they sing, the nightingales.

XIII

I would not for her white and pink,
      Though such he likes—her grace of limb,   110
Though such he has praised—nor yet, I think,
      For life itself, though spent with him,
Commit such sacrilege, affront
      God's nature which is love, intrude
'Twixt two affianced souls, and hunt   115
      Like spiders, in the altar's wood.
I cannot bear these nightingales.

---

1   pyx] a box or coffer; in the Church, the container that holds the consecrated bread for
    communion; historically, at the Royal Mint in London, a box in which gold and silver
    coins were deposited to be tested.

XIV

If she chose sin, some gentler guise
  She might have sinned in, so it seems:
She might have pricked out both my eyes,   120
  And I still seen him in my dreams!
—Or drugged me in my soup or wine,
  Nor left me angry afterward:
To die here with his hand in mine,
  His breath upon me, were not hard.   125
(Our Lady[1] hush these nightingales!)

XV

But set a springe for *him*, "mio ben,"[2]
  My only good, my first last love!—
Though Christ knows well what sin is, when
  He sees some things done they must move   130
Himself to wonder. Let her pass.
  I think of her by night and day.
Must *I* too join her . . out, alas! . .
  With Giulio, in each word I say?
And evermore the nightingales!   135

XVI

Giulio, my Giulio!—sing they so,
  And you be silent? Do I speak,
And you not hear? An arm you throw
  Round some one, and I feel so weak?
—Oh, owl-like birds! They sing for spite,   140
  They sing for hate, they sing for doom!
They'll sing through death who sing through night,
  They'll sing and stun me in the tomb—
The nightingales, the nightingales!

---

1 Our Lady] the Virgin Mary.

2 springe] a snare to trap small game; mio ben] (Italian) literally, "my good" (often in
  the sense of happiness, blessing, love); more colloquially, "sweetheart."

"THE GREAT GOD PAN."

Figure 4: Frederic Leighton's "The Great God Pan," from the *Cornhill Magazine*, July 1860.

A Musical Instrument

In April 1860 EBB sent this poem to the newly established *Cornhill Magazine* in response to a request for contributions from its editor, William Makepeace Thackeray (1811–63). She received "ten Guineas by return of post" (*LTA* 2:478), and Thackeray promptly published it—although he subsequently refused "Lord Walter's Wife" on moral grounds (see headnote to that poem). "A Musical Instrument" was "'meek as maid,'" according to EBB, but at least one anonymous reader of the *Cornhill* considered it "*immoral!*" (*LEBB* 2:377, 406). The illustration accompanying the poem in the *Cornhill* (see Figure 4), by Frederic Leighton,[1] may have contributed to its impact. In EBB's earlier poem "The Dead Pan" (1844), Pan represents the entire pantheon of pagan deities banished by the Christian dispensation: "*Pan* signifies *'all,'* besides his individual goat-godship," she explained in reference to that poem (*BC* 7:70).[2] In "A Musical Instrument," however, Pan appears as the individual goat-god, "half a beast" (l. 37), with a human form to the waist, and the lower body, ears, and horns of a goat, features that support a disturbing subtext of sexual violation in the poem, reinforced by its invocation of the classical story in which the nymph Syrinx escapes from Pan's lustful pursuit by transforming herself into a reed.[3] In some instances, the working draft of the poem (*R* D547) presents Pan's cruelty even more directly than the published poem (a few of these textual variants are noted below). The work (collected in *Last Poems*, 1862) is connected through its central metaphors to EBB's self-representation in "A Reed" (1850). With its concentrated expression of the human suffering that paradoxically yields the "sweet music" of the poet's song, "A Musical Instrument" has long been one of EBB's most anthologized and admired works. Criticism: Mermin 1989, Morlier 1990, Leighton 1992, and Chapman 2003b.

---

1   Frederic Leighton] (1830–96), prominent English painter and illustrator. A friend of the Brownings in Rome, in 1862 he designed the monument for EBB's grave in Florence.

2   See the supplementary website for the text of "The Dead Pan."

3   The story is told in the *Metamorphoses* by Roman poet Ovid (43 BCE–18 AD).

I

What was he doing, the great god Pan,
      Down in the reeds by the river?
Spreading ruin and scattering ban,[1]
Splashing and paddling with hoofs of a goat,
And breaking the golden lilies afloat   5
      With the dragon-fly on the river.

II

He tore out a reed, the great god Pan,
      From the deep cool bed of the river:
The limpid water turbidly ran,
And the broken lilies a-dying lay,   10
And the dragon-fly had fled away,
      Ere he brought it out of the river.

III

High on the shore sate[2] the great god Pan,
      While turbidly flowed the river;
And hacked and hewed as a great god can,   15
With his hard bleak steel at the patient reed,
Till there was not a sign of a leaf indeed
      To prove it fresh from the river.

IV

He cut it short, did the great god Pan,
      (How tall it stood in the river!)   20
Then drew the pith, like the heart of a man,
Steadily from the outside ring,
And notched the poor dry empty thing
      In holes, as he sate by the river.

---

1   ban] in this context, evil or harm.
2   sate] sat.

V

"This is the way," laughed the great god Pan,   25
      (Laughed while he sate by the river,)
"The only way, since gods began
To make sweet music, they could succeed."
Then, dropping his mouth to a hole in the reed,
      He blew in power by the river.   30

VI

Sweet, sweet, sweet, O Pan!
      Piercing sweet by the river!
Blinding sweet, O great god Pan!
The sun on the hill forgot to die,
And the lilies revived, and the dragon-fly   35
      Came back to dream on the river.

VII

Yet half a beast is the great god Pan,
      To laugh, as he sits by the river,
Making a poet out of a man:
The true gods sigh for the cost and pain,—   40
For the reed which grows nevermore again[1]
      As a reed with the reeds in the river.

Mother and Poet
Turin, After News from Gaeta, 1861[2]

The speaker of this dramatic monologue (first pub. in the New York *Independent*, 2 May 1861) is the Italian poet Olimpia Rossi

---

1 The true gods ... again] T.S. Eliot often quoted ll. 40-41, according to his wife (Mermin 1989, 278n35). On Eliot's knowledge of EBB's poetry, see Cuda 2004.

2 Turin ... Gaeta, 1861] Turin (Torino), the capital of Piedmont in the northeastern part of Italy, was the heart of the Italian movement for independence and unification. Gaeta, a city north of Naples on the west (Mediterranean) coast of Italy, in what was then the Kingdom of the Two Sicilies, was the site of a battle in January 1861 that represented the last effort by the Bourbon King Francis II of Naples (1836-94) to withstand the forces for a united Italy.

Savio, Baronessa di Bernstrel (1815–89).[1] Known in Turin for her literary salon, which she conceived to arouse patriotic fervor, she wrote poems promoting selfless devotion to the struggle for Italian unification and independence. Her two eldest sons, Alfredo and Emilio, died within four months of each other in late 1860 and early 1861 while fighting for the revolution as artillery officers. Ironically, both died in engagements that represented important victories for the Italian forces. Her tremendous loss gave her great stature at the parliament which soon thereafter convened in Turin, representing provinces in northern and central Italy which had established themselves as the core of an emerging unified nation. In this poem EBB develops the plight of a figure—the patriotic, bereaved mother—that she had recognized as early as her child-hood epic *The Battle of Marathon* (1820) in the Athenian matron who rallies the troops: "The mother wept, but 'twas the Patriot spoke" (l. 746). In the posthumous collection *Last Poems* (1862), following an order set out by EBB before her death, "Mother and Poet" immediately followed a companion poem also in five-line stanzas, "Parting Lovers," similarly treating war from a female perspective.[2] A review of *Last Poems* declared that this poem revealed EBB as "the politician, the woman, the poetess, and the mother combined."[3] Criticism: Cooper 1988, Donaldson 1980, Mermin 1989, Leighton 1992, Chapman 2003b, Kierstead 2005, and Taylor 2006.

I

Dead! One of them shot by the sea in the east,
  And one of them shot in the west by the sea.
Dead! both my boys! When you sit at the feast
  And are wanting a great song for Italy free,
    Let none look at *me*!   5

---

1 In *Last Poems*, the text of "Mother and Poet" is followed by the words, "This was Laura Savio, of Turin, a poetess and patriot, whose sons were killed at Ancona and Gaeta." For information on Savio, see Raffaello Ricci, *Memorie della Baronessa Olimpia Savio*, 2 vols. (Milan: Fratelli Treves, 1911). On Ancona, see l. 36, below.

2 See the supplementary website for the companion poem "Parting Lovers."

3 *Athenaeum*, no. 1796 (29 March 1862): 421–22; in Donaldson 1993a, 1862.2.

II

Yet I was a poetess only last year,
      And good at my art, for a woman, men said;[1]
But *this* woman, *this*, who is agonized here,
      —The east sea and west sea rhyme on in her head
          For ever instead.   10

III

What art can a woman be good at? Oh, vain!
      What art *is* she good at, but hurting her breast
With the milk-teeth of babes, and a smile at the pain?
      Ah boys, how you hurt! you were strong as you pressed,
          And I proud, by that test.   15

IV

What art's for a woman? To hold on her knees
      Both darlings! to feel all their arms round her throat,
Cling, strangle a little! to sew by degrees
      And 'broider the long-clothes and neat little coat;
          To dream and to doat.[2]   20

V

To teach them .. It stings there! *I* made them indeed
      Speak plain the word *country*. *I* taught them, no doubt,
That a country's a thing men should die for at need.
      I prated of liberty, rights, and about
          The tyrant cast out.   25

VI

And when their eyes flashed .. O my beautiful eyes! ..
      I exulted; nay, let them go forth at the wheels
Of the guns, and denied not. But then the surprise
      When one sits quite alone! Then one weeps, then one kneels!
          God, how the house feels!   30

---

1   See Appendices A and D for illustrations of the gender bias often manifest in Victorian literary criticism.

2   doat] dote, love extravagantly. This stanza encapsulates a continuing debate in Victorian culture: since motherhood is their "natural" role, should women pursue professions in writing or other arts?

VII

At first, happy news came, in gay letters moiled[1]
      With my kisses,—of camp-life and glory, and how
They both loved me; and, soon coming home to be spoiled,
         In return would fan off every fly from my brow
            With their green laurel-bough.[2]   35

VIII

Then was triumph at Turin: "Ancona was free!"[3]
      And some one came out of the cheers in the street,
With a face pale as stone, to say something to me.
      My Guido[4] was dead! I fell down at his feet,
         While they cheered in the street.   40

IX

I bore it; friends soothed me; my grief looked sublime
      As the ransom of Italy. One boy remained[5]
To be leant on and walked with, recalling the time
      When the first grew immortal, while both of us strained
         To the height he had gained.   45

X

And letters still came, shorter, sadder, more strong,
      Writ now but in one hand, "I was not to faint,—
One loved me for two—would be with me ere long:
      And *Viva l' Italia!*[6]—*he* died for, our saint,
         Who forbids our complaint."   50

---

1   moiled] moistened.

2   laurel-bough] In classical antiquity, both triumphant military leaders and prize-winning poets were crowned with wreaths made of laurel (bay) leaves.

3   Ancona] a city in the Papal States on the eastern (Adriatic) coast of central Italy, where troops for a united Italy finally seized the fortress they had long besieged. Savio's son Alfredo died at Ancona in September 1860.

4   Guido] nickname for her son Alfredo.

5   EBB apparently did not know that Savio's third, youngest son, Federico, remained at home with her. One ms draft of the poem (R D538) is entitled "The Childless Poetess."

6   Viva l'Italia!] (Italian) Long live Italy!

XI

My Nanni[1] would add, "he was safe, and aware
    Of a presence that turned off the balls,[2]—was imprest
It was Guido himself, who knew what I could bear,
    And how 'twas impossible, quite dispossessed,
        To live on for the rest."   55

XII

On which, without pause, up the telegraph-line
    Swept smoothly the next news from Gaeta: —*Shot.*
Tell his mother.[3] Ah, ah, "his," "their" mother,—not "mine,"
    No voice says "*My* mother" again to me. What!
        You think Guido forgot?   60

XIII

Are souls straight[4] so happy that, dizzy with Heaven,
    They drop earth's affections, conceive not of woe?
I think not. Themselves were too lately forgiven
    Through THAT Love and Sorrow which reconciled so
        The Above and Below.   65

XIV

O Christ of the five wounds,[5] who look'dst through the dark
    To the face of Thy mother![6] consider, I pray,
How we common mothers stand desolate, mark,
    Whose sons, not being Christs, die with eyes turned away,
        And no last word to say!   70

---

1   Nanni] nickname for her son Emilio.

2   balls] cannon and musket balls.

3   Savio received news of her second bereavement when her son Emilio died in the battle to liberate Gaeta.

4   straight] straightaway, immediately.

5   five wounds] the wounds Christ sustained at the Crucifixion: nail holes in his hands and feet, and a spear wound to the side.

6   Thy mother] alluding to the grief of Christ's mother Mary mourning her son's suffering at the foot of the Cross, an invocation of the figure of the *Mater dolorosa* (the grieving mother) earlier treated by EBB in "The Virgin Mary to the Child Jesus" (1838) and "Stabat Mater," her modernization of a medieval ballad (see *LEBB* 2:80-81).

XV

Both boys dead? but that's out of nature. We all
      Have been patriots, yet each house must always keep one.
'Twere imbecile, hewing out roads to a wall;
      And, when Italy's made, for what end is it done
          If we have not a son?   75

XVI

Ah, ah, ah! when Gaeta's taken, what then?
      When the fair wicked queen[1] sits no more at her sport
Of the fire-balls of death crashing souls out of men?
      When the guns of Cavalli[2] with final retort
          Have cut the game short?   80

XVII

When Venice and Rome keep their new jubilee,
      When your flag takes all heaven for its white, green and red,[3]
When *you* have your country from mountain to sea,
      When King Victor[4] has Italy's crown on his head,
          (And *I* have my Dead)—   85

XVIII

What then? Do not mock me. Ah, ring your bells low,
      And burn your lights faintly! *My* country is *there*,
Above the star pricked by the last peak of snow:
      My Italy's THERE, with my brave civic Pair,
          To disfranchise despair!   90

---

1 fair wicked queen] Maria Sofia Amelia (1841-1925), Queen Consort of Francis II of
   Naples (King of the Two Sicilies), whose reign was ended by the revolutionaries'
   success at Gaeta, where he had taken refuge. As EBB reported in a letter, her young
   son Pen in April 1861 saw the queen and described her as "so very pretty! .... So fair!
   such golden hair! & looking so melancholy" (*LTA* 2:531n11).
2 Cavalli] Italian general Giovanni Cavalli (1801-79).
3 white, green and red] the tricolor flag representing a newly unified Italy.
4 King Victor] Victor Emmanuel II (1820-78), King of Piedmont, was proclaimed king
   of a united Italy in March 1861.

XIX

Forgive me. Some women bear children in strength,
　　And bite back the cry of their pain in self-scorn;
But the birth-pangs of nations will wring us at length
　　Into wail such as this—and we sit on forlorn
　　　　When the man-child is born.　　　　　　　　95

XX

Dead! One of them shot by the sea in the east,
　　And one of them shot in the west by the sea.
Both! both my boys! If in keeping the feast
　　You want a great song for your Italy free,
　　　　Let none look at *me!*　　　　　　　　100

Appendix A: *Views, Reviews of collected* Poems, and Criticism[1]

1. From William Michael Rossetti, *Some Reminiscences of William Michael Rossetti* (London: Brown Langham, 1906), 1:232[2]

Towards 1845, or even 1844, the poems of Miss Elizabeth Barrett Barrett first caught the attention of my brother [poet and painter Dante Gabriel Rossetti] and myself. We revelled in them with profuse delight. Our perceptions of poetry were not then of the totally uncritical order, and we found some things which we thought faulty, both in excess and in defect; but in the main our pleasure was unalloyed. *The Drama of Exile, The Rhyme of the Duchess May, The Lost Bower, Lady Geraldine's Courtship, A Vision of Poets,* and numerous other pieces, held us spellbound. In the course of two or three years we must have read some of these more than half-a-hundred times over; and either of us (but more especially Dante Gabriel, who was much the better at verbal memory) could repeat them with great exactness.

2. From Edgar Allan Poe, a review of EBB's 1844 *Poems,* in the *Broadway Journal* (New York) 1, #1 & #2 (4 and 11 January 1845): 4-8, 17-20[3]

Now of all the friends of the fair author, we doubt whether one exists, with more profound—with more enthusiastic reverence and

---

1 For additional excerpts from reviews and commentaries, and for poems written in tribute to EBB, see the supplementary website to this edition. For most reviews prior to 1847, see the appendices to vols. 1-15 of *BC.*

2 Repr. New York: AMS Press, 1970, 232. W.M. Rossetti (1829-1919), a founder of the Pre-Raphaelite Brotherhood of artists with his brother D.G. Rossetti, became an influential art critic and literary editor. The PRB included EBB in their "List of the Immortals," compiled in 1848, ranking her with Tennyson; see W[illiam] Holman Hunt, *Pre-Raphaelitism and the Pre-Raphaelite Brotherhood,* 2 vols. (London: Macmillan, 1905), 1: 159.

3 Facsimile repr. in *Collected Writings of Edgar Allan Poe,* vol. 3, *Writings in the Broadway Journal,* ed. Burton R. Pollin (New York: Gordian, 1986), 1-15 (the text and pagination followed here). Poe (1809-49) dedicated his 1845 volume *The Raven and Other Poems* to EBB.

admiration of her genius, than the writer of these words. And it is for this very reason, beyond all others, that he intends to speak of her *the truth* (2).

....[W]e are not to look in Miss Barrett's works for any examples of what has been occasionally termed "sustained effort;" for neither are there, in any of her poems, any long commendable paragraphs, nor are there any individual compositions which will bear the slightest examination as consistent Art-products. Her wild and magnificent genius seems to have contented itself with points—to have exhausted itself in flashes;—but it is the profusion—the un-paralleled number and close propinquity of these points and flashes which render her book *one flame*, and justify us in calling her, unhesitatingly, the greatest—the most glorious of her sex (5-6).

.... "The Cry of the Children," ... is full of a nervous unflinch-ing energy—a horror sublime in its simplicity—of which a far greater than Dante might have been proud. "Bertha in the Lane," a rich ballad, very singularly excepted from the wholesale com-mendation of the "Democratic Review," as "perhaps not one of the best," and designated by Blackwood, on the contrary, as "decidedly the finest poem of the collection," is *not* the *very* best, we think, only because mere pathos, however exquisite, cannot be ranked with the loftiest exhibitions of the ideal.... With the exception of Tennyson's "Locksley Hall," we have never perused a poem combining so much of the fiercest passion with so much of the most ethereal fancy, as the "Lady Geraldine's Courtship," of Miss Barrett. We are forced to admit, however, that the lat-ter work *is* a very palpable imitation of the former, which it surpasses in plot or rather in thesis, as much as it falls below it in artistical management, and a certain calm energy—lustrous and indomitable—such as we might imagine in a broad river of molten gold (8).

Her affectations are unquestionably many, and generally inex-cusable. ... what can be well said in defence of the unnecessary nonsense of "'ware" for "aware"—of "'bide," for "abide" ...? .... Although we grant, too, that the poetess is very usually Homeric in her compounds, there is no intelligibility of construction, and therefore no force of meaning in "dew-pallid," "pale-passioned," and "silver-solemn" (10).

In her inattention to rhythm, Miss Barrett is guilty of an error that might have been fatal to her fame—that *would* have been fatal to any reputation less solidly founded than her own. We do not allude, so particularly, to her multiplicity of inadmissible rhymes. We would wish, to be sure, that she had not thought proper to couple Eden and succeeding—glories and floorwise—burning and morning—thither and æther—enclose me and across me—misdoers and flowers—centre and winter—guerdon and pardon—conquer and anchor—desert and unmeasured—atoms and fathoms—opal and people—glory and doorway—trumpet and accompted—taming and overcame him—coming and woman—is and trees—off and sun-proof—eagles and vigils—nature and satire—poems and interflowings—certes and virtues—pardon and burden—thereat and great—children and bewildering—mortal and turtle—moonshine and sunshine. It would have been better, we say, if such apologies for rhymes as these had been rejected. But deficiencies of *rhythm* are more serious. In some cases it is nearly impossible to determine what metre is intended. "The Cry of the Children" cannot be scanned.... (12).[1]

With this extract we make an end of our fault-finding— and *now*, shall we speak, equally in detail, of the *beauties* of this book? Alas! here, indeed, do we feel the impotence of the pen. We have already said that the supreme excellence of the poetess whose works we review, is made up of the multitudinous sums of a world of lofty merits. It is the multiplicity—it is the *aggregation*—which excites our most profound enthusiasm, and enforces our most earnest respect. But unless we had space to extract three fourths of the volumes, how could we convey this aggregation by specimens? (13).

That Miss Barrett has done more, in poetry, than any woman, living or dead, will scarcely be questioned:—that she has surpassed all her poetical contemporaries of either sex (with a single exception) is our deliberate opinion—not idly entertained, we think, nor founded on any visionary basis (14).

---

1   On EBB's deliberate experimentation with rhyme and meter see the Introduction, pp. 45–46; Smith 1939; and Morlier 1999.

3. From Frederick Rowton, *The Female Poets of Great Britain* (London, 1853)[1]

ELIZABETH BARRETT BROWNING

It may be a question ... whether an intense devotion to scholastic learning is not rather injurious than beneficial to the female mind. It cannot be pretended, of course, that schoolcraft, and the philosophy of art, science, and reason, ought to be altogether overlooked and unstudied by woman:—the proposition would be monstrous. But it may perhaps be fairly argued that, as woman's faculties are rather perceptive than investigative, and as her knowledge of truth is rather intuitive than acquired, there is a possibility of her understanding being injured by over-cultivation. Just as some flowers lose their native beauty when forced by horticultural art, may the female mind be spoiled by excess of intellectual culture.

Far as we should carry female education, we should, I think, take especial care not to found it on the same studies as appear necessary to man's. The acquirements of the sexes must be kept *unlike*, or man will find in woman, not a help meet, but a rival. Harmony results not from similarity, but from difference....

Further, the spheres of the sexes are different and require different faculties, and different education. The man—"for contemplation formed"—should learn by study, and reflection, and comparison, and investigation; the woman—"for softness formed and sweet attractive grace"[2]—should acquire knowledge mainly through her rapid instincts, her wide-spreading sympathies, and her quick instantaneous perceptions.

The male and female minds arrive at truth by different roads. Man reaches it by proof; woman, by faith. Man knows it; woman feels it. Man demonstrates it; woman believes it....

---

1   Republished in the United States as *Cyclopædia of Female Poets* (Philadelphia: J.B. Lippincott, n.d.), the edition and pagination followed here. See the supplementary website www.ebbarchive.org for George Bethune's similar views in *The British Female Poets* (Philadelphia: Lindsay & Blakiston, 1852): "The prominent fault of female poetical writers is an unwillingness to apply the pruning-knife and the pumice-stone. They write from impulse, and rapidly as they think" (viii).

2   The quoted phrases allude to John Milton's contrast between men and women in *Paradise Lost* 4.297-98.

In proof of these remarks I think I can fairly say that learned poetesses, however great their genius, have rarely been so effective and popular as less cultivated writers, possessed of even smaller natural powers.... (500-01).

4. From "Elizabeth Barrett Browning," *English Woman's Journal* 7, #42 (7 August 1861): 369-75[1]

There are few homes in England where the announcement of the death of Elizabeth Barrett Browning will not have roused a feeling of regret for the departed....

Many will look back with grateful remembrance to the lessons she has taught, the comfort she has given, and the aspirations which she has led away from the false beacon lights of this world, and guided towards the holy and steadfast shining of the purest faith and the loftiest resolve. Many who never looked upon her face will feel that a friend and counsellor has been taken from them. For she was indeed faithful to the true poetic mission. She was called, as every real poet is called, to be prophet, philosopher, and priest....

There has been no woman in this country—we think we may say in any country—who has possessed, not only the poetic faculty, but the true poetic consecration, so fully and so entirely as Elizabeth Barrett Browning (369-70).

We may be pardoned if we make a special reference to the courage which led her, for at that time it needed courage, to sign the petition which was sent up with regard to the property of married women.[2] Her name came with ... an added weight just because of the happy home where no shield of law or justice was needed, and where "division of interest" could not be....

---

1   The *English Woman's Journal* (1858-64) was established primarily to promote women's professional opportunities by feminist activists Bessie Raynor Parkes and Barbara Leigh Smith Bodichon, with whom EBB in 1856 supported reform of property laws for married women (see the following note).

2   "Presented by Lord Brougham and Sir Erskine Perry to the House of Lords and Commons respectively in 1856" [author's note]. EBB supported this effort to alter existing property law, under which a married woman's possessions—even her clothing and personal effects—belonged to her husband. The 1856 effort failed; the law was not modified until 1870 and was more fully reformed in 1882.

Her enthusiasm for liberty burns through her later volumes with an intense fire; so absorbing was her faith in a glorious future of freedom for Italy, that leading her to "believe all things," it let her place a crown of splendour and of truth upon a name which she chose to look upon as the herald and harbinger of her hopes... (374-75).

5. From [William Stigand], "The Works of Elizabeth Barrett Browning," *Edinburgh Review* 114 (July-October 1861): 512-34

.... The gifted person, whose recent death calls forth this notice from us, was in truth more fortunate than might be expected from the nature of her publications (513).

.... She was unquestionably a woman of rare genius, if that term can with propriety be applied to an excess of ardent irregular power. She had also learning and power of thought; but she was entirely deficient in the highest gifts of her own art. She had neither simplicity, taste, or [sic] good sense. Her style was always inflated; and her fame would be ten times as great and as deserved as it is, if she had left us a single lucid and finished performance, instead of a crowd of incoherent thoughts and extravagant images.

For these errors of spirit also affected most seriously the form of Mrs. Browning's verse.... She is often more quaint than Quarles in her imagery, more grotesque than Cowley or Donne in her ideas, more eccentric in her rhymes than the author of "Hudibras," and often more coarsely masculine than any known female writer....[1]

Due allowance, therefore, being made for these strange defects, it stands beyond doubt that much as Mrs. Browning sank at times below the commonest demands of harmony and expression, yet that no woman has ever handled the English tongue with greater force and spirit when she is at her best (524-25).

---

1   Francis Quarles (1592-1644), author of *Emblems* (1635), devotional poems illustrated by engravings; Abraham Cowley (1618-67), associated with the "metaphysical" school of John Donne (1572-1631), poets noted for their startling and witty "conceits" or metaphors; "Hudibras" (1663) by Samuel Butler (1612-80), a satire famous for its outrageously comical rhymes. For EBB's views of these poets, see her essay "The Book of the Poets" (*CW* 6:240-311).

.... Considering the great capabilities she possessed, her career may be accepted as some proof of the impossibility that woman can ever attain to the first rank in imaginative composition. Such a combination of the finest genius and the choicest results of cultivation and wide-ranging studies has never been seen before in any woman, nor is the world likely soon to see the same again (533).

6. From [Gerald Massey],[1] untitled review, *The North British Review* 36 (February–May 1862): 513–34

In his Essay upon Joan of Arc, De Quincey thus addresses Woman,[2] not as the general mother, but as the general sister: "Woman, sister—there are some things which you do not execute as well as your brother, Man; no, nor ever will. Pardon me, if I doubt whether you will ever produce a great poet from your choirs, or a Mozart, or a Phidias, or a Michel Angelo,[3] or a great philosopher, or a great scholar." With perfect fairness might our sister retort that there are many things she can execute better than her brother. She might also urge something more to the point, in the fact that woman has done very great things both in art and literature since De Quincey's words were written—the greatest things probably she has ever done. She has not yet produced her Shakspeare [sic], her Newton, her Bacon, her Handel; and most likely never will. But what she has done during the last twenty years is quite sufficient to make man look down on her from his intellectual throne with less of the smile of superiority. In more than one department of literature, she has almost run abreast of her brother in the race....

.... Since De Quincey wrote his words, we have seen Rosa Bonheur[4] handling her palette and pencil with manly mastery,—

---

1 Gerald Massey (1828-1907) was a radical poet and essayist associated with the Chartist movement.

2 Thomas De Quincey (1785-1859), Romantic essayist, whose address to women is echoed in Romney's statement to Aurora in *Aurora Leigh* (2.224-25) and frequently cited or refuted in treatments of EBB.

3 Citing figures acclaimed among the greatest artists in music, classical sculpture, and painting.

4 Rosa Bonheur (1822-99), French realist painter and sculptor.

.... We have had fiery little Charlotte Brontë emerging from those lonely Yorkshire wolds, with the wild Celtic blood working weirdly in her English veins .... We have seen George Eliot lay hold of life with a large hand, look at it with a large eye, feel it with a large heart.... De Quincey himself would have admitted that in Mrs. Browning we have woman's nearest approach to a great poet. We call her the greatest woman-poet of whom we have any record. Not a complete and perfect poet by any means; but great in virtue of her noble fire of passion, her inspired rush of energy, which vitalizes wherever it moves, and the good, true, loving heart that beats through all her works—... (514-16).

Before writing "Aurora Leigh," Mrs. Browning had done far more in poetry than any other woman living or dead... (528-29).

7. From Peter Bayne, *Two Great Englishwomen: Mrs. Browning and Charlotte Brontë; with an Essay on Poetry, Illustrated from Wordsworth, Burns, and Byron* (London: James Clarke, 1881)[1]

.... In no poet whatever was the lyrical glow more authentically fervid and genuine.... Had she done as much for men as she did for women—had man's work, passion, character been delineated on a scale, and with a truth and power correspondent to those with which, in the world of her art, she embodied woman's—I scarce know what place among the throned ones would have been too high for her.... But Mrs. Browning is not so great in the delineation of men as in that of women... (lxxvi-lxxvii).

If Mrs. Browning's intelligent readers were asked to name her most characteristic poem, they would probably fix upon Lady Geraldine's Courtship....

Lady Geraldine's Courtship belongs to the same class of poems as Locksley Hall. It is a story of love, and its love-story is delineated in connection with certain social truths or doctrines which the

---

1 One of the most extended Victorian analyses of EBB's poetry, this study by Bayne revises and expands on material earlier published in 1857; see Donaldson 1993a, 1857:30; 1879:1; 1881:1. For additional comments by Bayne on EBB, see Appendix B.I.5 and the supplementary website.

poet intends to teach.... Lady Geraldine's Courtship and Locksley Hall are profoundly democratic in spirit. They belong to the period when the atmosphere of our island was still tingling with the Reform Bill[1] agitation; when the hope and aspiration of ardent spirits were stirred with visions of class reconciled to class; of high and low, rich and poor, warming towards each other in the glow of common brotherhood; of all distinctions being effaced except those between honest men and knaves, between base men and honorable... (60-61).

8. From Edmund Gosse,[2] *Critical Kit-Kats* (New York: Dodd, Mead, 1896)

It was in the second or 1850 edition of the *Poems in two volumes* that the *Sonnets from the Portuguese* were first given to the public. The circumstances attending their composition have never been clearly related. Mr. Browning, however, eight years before his death, made a statement to a friend, with the understanding that at some future date, after his own decease, the story might be more widely told. The time seems to have arrived when there can be no possible indiscretion in recording a very pretty episode of literary history.[3]

During the months of their brief courtship, closing, as all the world knows, in the clandestine flight and romantic wedding of September 12, 1846, neither poet showed any verses to the other.[4] Mr. Browning, in particular, had not the smallest notion that the circumstances of their betrothal had led Miss Barrett into any

---

1   The First Reform Bill (1832) increased the political power of the middle classes.

2   Sir Edmund Gosse (1849-1928), linguist, literary scholar, and lecturer at Cambridge University.

3   Gosse's widely cited story of this "pretty episode" illustrates the myths that long have surrounded EBB's works. For the poet's own account of presenting the sonnets to RB, see *LTA* 1:368-69; for RB's account, see *Robert Browning and Julia Wedgwood: A Broken Friendship as Revealed by Their Letters*, ed. Richard Curle (New York: Frederick A. Stokes, 1937), 99-100.

4   Contrary to Gosse's assertion, in the courtship letters both EBB and RB refer to seeing each other's work-in-progress; see, e.g., *BC* 11:375-401, Appendix IV: "EBB's Notes on RB's Poems, 1845-1846."

artistic expression of feeling. As little did he suspect it during their honeymoon in Paris, or during their first crowded weeks in Italy. They settled, at length, in Pisa; and ... the young couple took up each his or her separate literary work.

Their custom was, Mr. Browning said, to write alone, and not to show each other what they had written. This was a rule which he sometimes broke through, but she never.[1] He had the habit of working in a downstairs room, where their meals were spread, while Mrs. Browning studied in a room on the floor above. One day, early in 1847,[2] their breakfast being over, Mrs. Browning went upstairs, while her husband stood at the window watching the street till the table should be cleared. He was presently aware of some one behind him, although the servant was gone. It was Mrs. Browning, who held him by the shoulder to prevent his turning to look at her, and at the same time pushed a packet of papers into the pocket of his coat. She told him to read that, and to tear it up if he did not like it; and then she fled again to her own room.

Mr. Browning seated himself at the table, and unfolded the parcel. It contained the series of sonnets which have now become so illustrious. As he read, his emotion and delight may be conceived.[3] Before he had finished it was impossible for him to restrain himself, and, regardless of his promise, he rushed upstairs, and stormed that guarded citadel. He was early conscious that these were treasures not to be kept from the world; "I dared not reserve to myself," he said, "the finest sonnets written in any language since Shakespeare's." But Mrs. Browning was very loth indeed to consent to the publication of what had been the very notes and chronicle of her betrothal. At length she was persuaded to permit her friend, Miss Mary Russell Mitford, to whom they had originally been sent in manuscript, to pass them through the press, although she absolutely declined to accede to Miss Mitford's suggestion that they should appear in one of the fashionable annuals of the day.

---

1   A manuscript draft of EBB's "The Runaway Slave at Pilgrim's Point" (*R* D802) with RB's marginal comments in pencil demonstrates Gosse's further inaccuracy here.

2   EBB actually did not show RB the sonnets until summer 1849; see *LTA* 1:371n14.

3   RB reported mixed emotions, describing the sequence as "a strange, heavy crown, that wreath of Sonnets" (Curle 99).

Accordingly, an octavo of 47 pages was printed, entitled *Sonnets/ by/ E.B.B./ Reading/ Not for Publication/* 1847.[1]

When it was determined to publish the sonnets in the volumes of 1850, the question of a title arose. The name which was ultimately chosen, *Sonnets from the Portuguese*, was invented by Mr. Browning, as an ingenious device to veil the true authorship, and yet to suggest kinship with that beautiful lyric, called *Catarina to Camoens*, in which so similar a passion had been expressed. Long before he ever heard of these poems, Mr. Browning called his wife his "own little Portuguese," and so, when she proposed "Sonnets translated from the Bosnian," he, catching at the happy thought of "translated," replied, "No, not Bosnian—that means nothing—but from the Portuguese! They are Catarina's sonnets!"[2] And so, in half a joke, half a conceit, the famous title was invented... (1-3).

9. From G.K. Chesterton, *The Victorian Age in Literature* (London: Thornton Butterworth, 1913)

Before leaving [Robert Browning] it should be added that he was fitted to deepen the Victorian mind, but not to broaden it. With all his Italian sympathies and Italian residence, he was not the man to get Victorian England out of its provincial rut.... His celebrated wife was wider and wiser than he in this sense; for she was, however one-sidedly, involved in the emotions of central European politics. She defended Louis Napoleon and Victor Emmanuel;[3] and intelligently, as one conscious of the case against them both.... These old political poems of hers are too little read to-day; they are amongst the most

---

1   There is no evidence in the abundant extant correspondence with Mitford to suggest that she played a role in the sonnets' publication. Moreover, the "1847 Reading pamphlet" to which Gosse refers here was a forgery by collector and bibliophile Thomas J. Wise. Scholars have debated whether or not Gosse was an accomplice of Wise, using this reference to authenticate the forged pamphlet, or simply a dupe of Wise. See the headnote to *Sonnets from the Portuguese* and Richard D. Altick, *The Scholar Adventurers* (Columbus: Ohio State UP, 1950, rpt. 1987): 58-59.

2   Gosse is the only source suggesting that EBB thought to name the poems "Sonnets ... from the Bosnian." EBB explains the association with "Catarina to Camoens" (*LTA* 1:368-69).

3   Two men EBB celebrated as heroes for resisting Austrian domination of Italy.

sincere documents on the history of the times, and many modern blunders could be corrected by the reading of them. And Elizabeth Barrett had a strength really rare among women poets; the strength of the phrase. She excelled in her sex, in epigram, almost as much as Voltaire in his. Pointed phrases like: "Martyrs by the pang without the palm"[1]... came quite freshly and spontaneously to her quite modern mind. But the first fact is this, that these epigrams of hers were never so true as when they turned on one of the two or three pivots on which contemporary Europe was really turning. She is by far the most European of all the English poets of that age; all of them, even her own much greater husband, look local beside her. Tennyson and the rest are nowhere.... But her case was, in one sense, extreme. She exaggerated both ways. She was too strong and too weak, or (as a false sex philosophy would express it), too masculine and too feminine.... Yet the question, as asked, does her a heavy historical injustice; we remember all the lines in her work which were weak enough to be called "womanly," we forget the multitude of strong lines that are strong enough to be called "manly".... She had one of the peculiar talents of true rhetoric, that of a powerful concentration. As to the critic who thinks her poetry owed anything to the great poet who was her husband, he can go and live in the same hotel with the man who can believe that George Eliot owed anything to the extravagant imagination of Mr. George Henry Lewes[2] (176-81).

10. From Virginia Woolf, "Aurora Leigh" (1931), *The Second Common Reader*, ed. Andrew McNeillie (New York: Harcourt Brace Jovanovich, 1986), 202-03[3]

.... nobody can deny the power of the Brownings to excite our sympathy and rouse our interest. "Lady Geraldine's Courtship" is glanced at perhaps by two professors in American universities once

---

1   "The Cry of the Children," l. 144.

2   Though G.H. Lewes (1817-78), prolific essayist, critic, biographer, and dramatist, was immensely supportive of the writing career of his common law wife Mary Anne Evans, novelist George Eliot (1819-80), her artistic talent unquestionably dwarfed his.

3   First published in slightly different form in the *Yale Review* (June 1931): 677-90, and reprinted with slight variations in the *Times Literary Supplement* (2 July 1931): 517-18.

a year; but we all know how Miss Barrett lay on her sofa; how she escaped from the dark house in Wimpole Street one September morning; how she met health and happiness, freedom, and Robert Browning in the church round the corner.

But fate has not been kind to Mrs Browning as a writer. Nobody reads her, nobody discusses her, nobody troubles to put her in her place. One has only to compare her reputation with Christina Rossetti's to trace her decline. Christina Rossetti[1] mounts irresistibly to the first place among English women poets. Elizabeth, so much more loudly applauded during her lifetime, falls farther and farther behind. The primers dismiss her with contumely. Her importance, they say, "has now become merely historical. Neither education nor association with her husband ever succeeded in teaching her the value of words and a sense of form." In short, the only place in the mansion of literature that is assigned her is downstairs in the servants' quarters, where, in company with Mrs Hemans, Eliza Cook, Jean Ingelow, Alexander Smith, Edwin Arnold, and Robert Montgomery,[2] she bangs the crockery about and eats vast handfuls of peas on the point of her knife.

---

1   Christina Rossetti (1830-94), who acknowledged EBB's influence. For a contrary view of EBB in relation to Rossetti, see Oscar Wilde's "English Poetesses," *Queen* (8 December 1888): 742-43, excerpted on the supplementary website: www.ebbarchive.org..

2   On Hemans, see the Introduction and EBB's poem "Felicia Hemans"; Eliza Cook (1818-89) was the author of popular sentimental poems and editor of *Eliza Cook's Journal* (1849-54); Jean Ingelow (1820-97) was a popular poet and author of children's stories; Alexander Smith (1830-67) was a minor poet of the Spasmodic school; and Sir Edwin Arnold (1832-1904) wrote "The Light of Asia ...," a poem about Buddha. The religious poet Robert Montgomery (1807-55) enjoyed great popularity among Low Church readers but was viewed satirically by EBB (see Stone 2005, 19-21).

Appendix B: Religion and Factory Reform

I. Religion

1. From "Reviews," *The Guardian* (22 January 1851): 55-56

.... Every where the artist is conspicuous, and generally, we must say, the deeply-feeling and religious lady.

Religious, our reader must remember, after her own kind, which is not exactly our kind, nor a kind that we feel at all disposed to substitute for our own. Mr. Carlyle, Mr. Tennyson, and her husband, Mr. Browning, are her intellectual idols, as the two latter are, to some extent, the models for her poetry.[1] Her own good sense, and instinctive right feeling, preserve her, however, from most of that irreverence on such matters which is at times disagreeable in Mr. Browning, and constantly so offensive in Mr. Carlyle; and it is rather from what is conveyed in a chance expression, than from any very definite or expanded statement, that we gather how far we should probably differ, if we came to a regular discussion upon religious subjects. But, in the present state of religious discord and confusion, we may regret it, but it would be dishonest to be severe upon her because she differs from teaching of which she has most likely never heard, and is deficient in doctrine which she has had no opportunity to supply.

2. From Samuel B. Holcombe, "Death of Mrs. Browning," *Southern Literary Messenger* 33 (December 1861): 412-17

.... In the entire range of female poetry, there is absolutely nothing which deserves to be compared for a moment with the marvelous effusions of this poetess. She is truly the Shakespeare among her sex; and yet, no woman has written in a spirit of such genuine, intense, and pathetic *womanliness*... (414).

---

1 On relationships between EBB's work and that of Thomas Carlyle, Alfred Tennyson, and Robert Browning, see the Introduction.

.... We rejoice to be able to assert, most distinctly, that Mrs. Browning, though no sectarian, is eminently a Christian poetess. Her poetry is not religious in the sense of Watts or Montgomery,[1] or the common generation of hymn writers. But, like Alfred Tennyson, the greatest living poet, Mrs. Browning adhered zealously to the great central truths of the Christian Religion. Like Tennyson, she was perfectly familiar with all that the most modern science has to teach; had gone through all that German speculation[2] has to offer; had pondered the deep controversies of the age; and yet, in her fearless strains, the eternal divinity and paramount power of Christianity is reverentially confessed.... The recognition of a Divine Creator of all things, a Being of perfect love and wisdom, who is to each and all of His numberless creatures really and truly a Heavenly Father and personal protector, broods like an ever present spirit over the pages of Mrs. Browning (415-16).

3. From [Hannah Lawrance], "Mrs. Browning's Poetry," *The British Quarterly Review* 42 (October 1865): 359-84

.... Mrs. Browning has also exercised the higher faculties of the poet, in giving life to the mere abstractions of history. The Virgin Mary is to many of us little more than a name, or perchance a half-angelic face looking down from some beautiful Italian picture. We seldom think of her even as she is represented in Scripture, as one for virtue and goodness highly favoured among women. From this dim unreal existence Mrs. Browning has called her into life. In the "Virgin Mary and the Infant Jesus" we see her maiden face as she walks in lonely thought among the midnight hills of Galilee; and watch the workings of her heart as she presses the Holy Child to her bosom with mingled reverence, adoration, and deep maternal

---

1 Isaac Watts (1674-1748), a Nonconformist remembered for his many popular hymns; Robert Montgomery (1807-55), a prolific author of popular religious poems. In 1832, EBB's father presented her with a copy of the third edition of Montgomery's *The Messiah. A Poem in Six Books*, but she later mocked its author as "no more a poet than" her dog Flush (*BC* 6:167, 184); see *R* A1635 and Stone 2005.

2 German speculation] refers to the German "Higher Criticism," which analyzed the Bible as a compilation of texts rather than as sacred infallible "truth."

love. How little had we before considered the large share of agony that mother bore in sympathy with the pains which wrought the redemption of the world, or that consciousness, stronger than in any other human being, that the Saviour was really of the same flesh with her! (378-79).

4. From *The True Mary: Being Mrs. Browning's Poem: "The Virgin Mary to the Child Jesus," with Comments and Notes* (1868)[1]

It is charged by those who pay divine homage to the blessed Virgin, that they who religiously refrain from it, fail to render her any extraordinary reverence, and leave her but a common place among the saints. This may be partially true. From the tendency of one extreme to beget another, some in recoiling from anything like a deification of Mary, fear to elevate her humanity,—to guard against adoring her, they almost discourage honoring her, as the highly favored of the Lord. But this is not common. There are few Protestants who do not cherish the deepest feeling of pious veneration for the mother of our Lord. Though not hailing her regnant in Heaven, they esteem her a queenly saint, yet originally partaking of their sinful mortality. An exemplification of the true Protestant feeling on this point, we have in the poem on the following pages. None but a Protestant could have written it; and who, whether Protestant or Catholic, we venture to ask, has ever written more worthily of Mary, with profounder or more delicate and lovely thoughts of her as the mother of the Holy Child? No notions of an immaculate conception invest her with such genuine purity and grace, as this exquisite effort of the imagination, rich in fancy, yet sound in theology and entirely warranted by Holy Writ. For a Madonna, give us Mrs. Browning's before a Raphael's or a

---

1   Edited by W.A. Muhlenberg, "Preface" and "Comment and Notes" by A.A. (New York: Thomas Whittaker, 1868). This pamphlet (2nd ed. 1870), reprinting EBB's poem on the Virgin Mary with notes and commentary, reflects her poem's role in Protestant responses to the dogma of Mary's Immaculate Conception—i.e., the doctrine that Mary was born free of any stain of original sin—which was pronounced by Pope Pius IX in 1854.

Correggio's,[1] for hers is the portraiture of Mary's soul, such as in material lineaments no art could express.

A.A., "PREFACE," 7-8.[2]

The following, while among the shortest of Mrs. Browning's poems, is, in many respects, one of the most perfect, and strikingly characteristic. The skill with which the transcendent dignity of the subject is maintained throughout, yet interpenetrated all along with the deepest yearnings of the mother's heart is all her own. We do not think any other pen could achieve the same.

But beyond the artistic merits of this piece, or more properly the perfection of them, is its crystalline embodiment of Christian truth. This high Christmas ode, this Divine Lullaby of the Virgin Mother to the Word made Flesh is both a magnificent enunciation of the doctrine of the Incarnation, and a forcible repudiating of the false worship of her whose true title is "blessedest of women."

In these days when the prime articles of our holy faith are so often found overlaid if not quite obscured by the glitter of sickly sentiment or puerile æsthetic fancies, it is something to light upon a pure gem of heavenly truth in a right royal setting—the jewel itself intact, clear, and luminous; its glory heightened and held to view, not covered by the golden rim which holds it. And a gem of this sort we esteem the poem before us, though hitherto but slightly noticed among the varied productions of its author.

5. From Peter Bayne, *Two Great Englishwomen: Mrs. Browning and Charlotte Brontë; with an Essay on Poetry, Illustrated from Wordsworth, Burns, and Byron* (London: James Clarke, 1881)[3]

The first poems by which Mrs. Browning chose to be permanently represented have as their subject that tale of sin and redemption which occupied the mature genius and veteran skill of Milton....

1   Comparing the poem to the many paintings of Madonna and Child by famous Italian artists.

2   A.A. is identified as "the principal of the Sisters [Protestant nurses] in charge of St. Luke's Hospital."

3   For additional extracts from Bayne, see Appendix A.7.

As works of literary art, the performance of Mrs. Browning cannot enter into rivalry with those of Milton. In constructive power, in sustained strength and severe beauty of language, in majestic harmony and subtle modulation of music, organ, harp, and flute, *Paradise Lost* and *Paradise Regained* surpass *A Drama of Exile* and *The Seraphim*....

On the other hand, Mrs. Browning is in some respects—and these important—more successful in the treatment of the subject than Milton. She throws a finer tenderness into her portraiture of Adam and Eve, especially of the latter.

.... All who have carefully considered *Paradise Lost* and *Paradise Regained* as the parts of one great poem of sin and salvation, must have been struck by the fact that Milton has almost ignored the death of Christ. In *Paradise Lost* he was not required to say much of it, but he almost wholly omits it also from *Paradise Regained*.... Additional books seem to be wanted for the treatment of the rest of Christ's life and of His death.... It is well known that Milton in the latter portion of his life held Arian opinions;[1] and the only way in which I can account for the virtual omission of the crucifixion from *Paradise Regained* is by supposing that, when he wrote the poem, he had ceased to accept the Catholic view of Christ's death as a propitiatory sacrifice. Be this, however, as it may, Mrs. Browning, in *The Seraphim*, presents to us the victory of Christ over evil as consummated on the cross. Both in that poem and in the *Drama of Exile,* she seeks to penetrate into the spiritual meanings of the death of Christ, into the mystery of sorrow shared by Divinity, into love that, through death, conquers death and hell. If the feeling of Christendom, sanctioned by the opinion of such men as Lessing, Goethe, and Hegel,[2] is right in apprehending atonement as distinctive of Christianity, then Mrs. Browning must be allowed to be more comprehensive than Milton in her treatment of their common theme... (7-10).

---

1 Arians, condemned as heretics in 325, maintained that God and Christ are distinct beings, that the Son was not equal to the Father, and that the Messiah was not a real man but a divine being in a veil of flesh.

2 Gotthold Ephraim Lessing (1729-81), German critic and dramatist; Johann Wolfgang von Goethe (1749-1832), German novelist, scientist, and dramatist; Georg Wilhelm Friedrich Hegel (1770-1831), German philosopher.

1. From Frances Trollope, *The Life and Adventures of Michael Armstrong, The Factory Boy* (London: Henry Colburn, 1844; serial publication, 1840)[1]

The party entered the building, whence—as all know who have done the like—every sight, every sound, every scent that kind nature has fitted to the organs of children, so as to render the mere unfettered use of them a delight, are banished for ever and ever. The ceaseless whirring of a million hissing wheels, seizes on the tortured ear; and while threatening to destroy the delicate sense, seems bent on proving first, with a sort of mocking mercy, of how much suffering it can be the cause. The scents that reek around, from oil, tainted water, and human filth, with that last worst nausea, arising from the hot refuse of atmospheric air, left by some hundred pairs of labouring lungs, render the act of breathing a process of difficulty, disgust, and pain. All this is terrible. But what the eye brings home to the heart of those, who look round upon the horrid early hell, is enough to make it all forgotten; for who can think of villainous smells, or heed the suffering of the ear-racking sounds, while they look upon hundreds of helpless children, divested of every trace of health, of joyousness, and even of youth! Assuredly there is no exaggeration in this; for except only in their diminutive size, these suffering infants have no trace of it. Lean and distorted limbs—sallow and sunken cheeks—dim hollow eyes, that speak unrest and most unnatural carefulness, give to each tiny, trembling, unelastic form, a look of hideous premature old age.

But in the room they entered, the dirty, ragged, miserable crew, were all in active performance of their various tasks; the overlookers, strap in hand, on the alert; the whirling spindles urging the little slaves who waited on them, to movements unceasing as their own .:..

.... [A] little girl about seven years old, whose office as "*scavenger*," was to collect incessantly from the machinery and from the floor,

---

1 First published in 1840 in monthly parts; EBB refers to it in January of that year (*BC* 4:232).

the flying fragments of cotton that might impede the work. In the performance of this duty, the child was obliged, from time to time, to stretch itself with sudden quickness on the ground, while the hissing machinery passed over her; and when this is skillfully done, and the head, body, and outstretched limbs carefully glued to the floor, the steady-moving, but threatening mass, may pass and repass over the dizzy head and trembling body without touching it. But accidents frequently occur... (79-81).

2. From *On the Employment of Children and Young Persons in the Iron Trades and other Manufactures ... and on the actual State, Condition, and Treatment of such Children and Young Persons* (1841)[1]

No. 54. March 19. *Eliza Field*, age "going a[2] 10":
Works at pressing washers; works with an iron machine; has never caught her fingers. Has worked at Mr. Glover's a good time; don't know how long. Never any accidents since she has been there; thinks she has worked there nearly a year. Gets a shilling a week; is paid by the master's wife. Goes at six in the morning and leaves at seven at night; has two hours allowed for meals in the course of the day; is well treated, she thinks; gets a box[3] sometimes because she don't just do her work; does not feel it very hard; does not feel it for an hour; is stinted; works piece-work;[4] if she loses any time she does not get so much as a shilling a-week—sometimes only 10*d.*, or 9*d.*, or 11*d.*[5] Cannot spell her own name; does not know

---

1   From the Irish University Press Series of British Parliamentary Papers, vol. 11, *Industrial Revolution, Children's Employment*, 13-14 (generously provided by Tricia Lootens). These excerpts come from reports assembled in 1841 by EBB's correspondent and collaborator R.H. Horne (1802?-84) for a Parliamentary commission studying child labor in factories and mines. EBB's reading of the reports influenced her "The Cry of the Children" (1843; see the poem's headnote and *BC* 7:274).

2   going a] going on.

3   gets a box] receives a blow or slap.

4   is stinted] has deductions from her pay (perhaps for inattention); works piece-work] is paid by the number of pieces she produces rather than by the hour (piece work was usually the poorest paid labor).

5   10*d.*] 10 pence or pennies.

her letters. Used to go to school before she came to this town, but now she don't. Comes from Kidderminster; went to school there at a day-school, and a Sunday-school[1] besides; cannot sew; cannot use a needle at all; says her prayers; does not know the Lord's Prayer. When she says her prayers she says "Our Father"—no more; knows no more. Has never heard of Heaven; nor of Jesus Christ; thinks she has heard of the name of our Saviour; never goes to church, or chapel, or school; has no things to go in; has heard of ... Jack Sheppard;[2] they were a talking about him, saying what a rum'un[3] he was.

A little object with a round face; apparently in good health. Her clothing was a mass of rags, excessively dirty.

No. 55. March 19. *Mary Field,* age "going of 11":
Works at washers.... Never heard of another world, nor of heaven, nor of another life; has looked up at the stars very often; thinks there's a good many on'em; that's all she ever thought looking at 'em.

This witness was a sister of the foregoing; her experience and her ignorance were just of the same kind; she looked unhealthy, was very badly grown, and still more filthily dirty.

No. 56. March 19. *Sarah Field,* age "going a 14":
Works at pressing washers.... Feels tired after her work at night sometimes when she has worked over-hours, but that does not often happen; feels no pains now. Her second sister, Mary, is very ailing. Thinks it is not the work makes her sister ill, who has always been very ailing. Haven't enough to eat at home; her mother has no work, and another younger child to keep; the three that work keep the family, and the soup they have three times a-week from the old workhouse.[4] Wishes she could go to school; but she

---

1   Sunday-schools were organized to educate working children on their one free day.

2   Jack Sheppard] a notorious eighteenth-century thief whose daring escape from Newgate Prison and subsequent hanging became the subject of countless popular songs, pamphlets, pantomimes, plays, and books.

3   rum'un] rum one; i.e., good or great.

4   workhouse] an asylum where the destitute performed menial labor in exchange for their keep.

has nothing to go in; not a shoe to her foot, but rags; hasn't a bit of toes in 'em.

This was the eldest of the three sisters Field; she was very small for her age, not the least appearance of approaching womanhood—quite a child. Her health seemed very good; not so dirty in her person as her sisters, but her clothes were dirty rags.

No. 57. March 20. *Edward Haling Coleman,* Esq., surgeon:
Has practiced 10 years in Wolverhampton; extensively among the working classes.... Many children are burnt to death, particularly in the winter, by their parents going out to work and leaving them alone all day. Godfrey's cordial[1] is much given by the mothers to infants to quiet them. Has known many infants die from its effects. Considers that children and young persons are worst treated by the small masters among the locksmiths, key-makers, and bolt makers, who are themselves generally poor. Accidents sometimes happen at the edge-tool makers: they very often happen in the pits, and also at the nail and tip manufactories, particularly at Hemingsley and Co.'s. Only yesterday a boy was killed, another had both legs fractured, and several were injured....

No. 58. March 21. ★★★ ★★★, aged 19:
Works at tip-punching at Mr. Hemingsley's. Gets 4*s.* a-week. Was at work at Hemingsley's on Friday night last, when the accident happened. Part of the floor, where she was working, fell. A boy, who worked at the nail-cutting below, was killed on the spot by the weight of the tips that fell upon him; another boy had both his thighs broken and one arm, another boy had his knee hurt, another his arm, and one hurt his back. Attributes the accident to the rottenness of the floor and the weight of the tips. Great weights were constantly laid upon the floor, and the floor was in a broken shattered condition nearly all over; it had been propped up very much, two or three times. You could see from one floor down into the other through the holes. Cannot read or write. Was at a Sunday-school at ★★★★ about two years. The teachers came

---

1 Godfrey's cordial] a patent medicine containing opium that was widely used to quiet babies; often used by working mothers forced to leave their children unattended or with harried or neglectful keepers.

one Sunday and not another—very neglectful. Was taken away at 10 years of age to go to work; has never been able to go to school since; would be very glad if she could.

Appendix C: Trans-Atlantic Abolitionism and Responses to EBB's Anti-Slavery Poems

I. FROM *THE LIBERTY BELL*

The items that follow—abolitionist poems and prose excerpts focused on slave mothers, the lure of freedom in the North, and the American Union—all appeared in issues of the Boston Anti-Slavery Bazaar's annual *The Liberty Bell* in the 1840s, prior to the publication of EBB's "The Runaway Slave at Pilgrim's Point" in the 1848 volume (published in late 1847; see the poem's headnote). EBB was sent presentation copies of the 1844 and 1845 volumes of *The Liberty Bell* (most probably at the time she was first invited to submit a contribution), as well as a copy of the 1856 volume in which she first published "A Curse for a Nation."[1] Through their connections and contrasts to EBB's anti-slavery poems, *The Liberty Bell* selections both reveal how she drew on the conventions of abolitionist writing and accentuate the relatively radical nature of her contributions.[2] On EBB's own slave-holding ancestry, see the Introduction. For additional materials see the supplementary website: www.ebbarchive.org.

1. From George S. Burleigh, "The Worth of the Union," *The Liberty Bell* (1845): 52-59[3]

Brave heart of granite firmness,
     That to our Northland gives
The bounding tide of valor's blood,—
     The pulse whereon she lives;—
Why beats that pulse so feebly

---

1   A copy of the 1858 volume of *The Liberty Bell* was also in the Brownings' library at RB's death; see *R* A619, A620, A621, A622.

2   On *The Liberty Bell* contexts of "The Runaway Slave at Pilgrim's Point," see Stone 2003 and Slinn 2003.

3   George Shepard Burleigh (1821-1903) lectured on abolition and in 1846-47 edited a Connecticut newspaper in its support.

That was wont to leap so high?
Why bend so low, thou stubborn neck.
To the Southron's chivalry?

Sons of the brave New England!
Ye are plundered, ye are whipt,
Ye are shot, and hanged, and fettered;
Yet how dumb and lily-lipped
Are your brothers, are your fathers.
Are the rulers of your land,—
Nay, linking with the murderer's
Their own heart and their hand.
....

Calmly ye saw your symbol Bird
On another's dove-cote stoop,
And bear away his fluttering prey,
At one destroying swoop;
Ye saw him tear the Baby
From the shrieking Mother's breast,
Fleshing his beak in its soft cheek;
And still, your hands could rest.
Now his impartial hunger
Demands another prey,
And from your own warm hearth-fires
He plucks your sons away.
....

Now speak! —or, dumb forever,
Trail on your clanking chain,
And give your white cheek to the brand,
And creep around your plundered land
On pliant knee and coward hand,
In Slavery's spaniel-train!
Put on your ancient valor,
And rise, if yet ye can,
Till the haughty Tyrant trembles
Before the upright MAN;

And from Canadian forests
    O'er all our rugged hills,
On to Virginia's mountains
    One voice like thunder thrills, —
"Down with the bloody Union!
    Mighty alone to spoil!
Wrench off its anaconda-folds
    Or perish in their coil!
Pluck down that fustian banner,
    Whose stars gleam redly there
Like demon-eyes, wide-blighting all
    Beneath their savage glare;
And rend its streaks of crimson,
    Types of the hungry lash
That ploughs its livid furrows deep
    On Woman's naked flesh!
'NO UNION WITH THE SLAVEHOLDER!'
    Down with the blood-streaked flag!
Trample that gore-writ Compact
    With Slavery's wrinkled hag!
We snap the bond which held us;
    And to remotest time
Stand severed from the robber-land,
    Where mercy is a crime!"

2. Martha Hempstead, "The Fugitive," *The Liberty Bell* (1845): 209-14[1]

She is weeping, bitterly weeping,
    Far away in the tangled wild;
And in her arms, all sweetly sleeping,
    Is clasped a fair young child.

---

1   This poem's conventional scenario of a master's seducing a slave contrasts with EBB's relatively radical depiction of rape; in *The Liberty Bell*, the rape of slave women by their masters was sometimes acknowledged, but generally referred to indirectly through terms such as "pollution."

Why thus does she flee away
From the cheerful haunts of men?
Why hides she thus from the face of day,
In the dark and noisome fen?

Oh! hers is a common fate;
And there's none to give it heed,
There is none to care for the desolate,
In her hour of bitter need.

But the father of that babe,
Which hath his azure eye
And his sunny hair, hath he betrayed
And left them there to die?

No! that were far more kind;
But it is not even so!
With his hunting train he is close behind;
She hath heard their loud hollo.

Oh! hers is a tale of wrong,
Too grievous to be spoken,
If the voice that utters be not strong,
And the heart that prompts unbroken.

She hath been his paramour,
And still his wretched Slave;
And long had the light of her life's dim hour
Been but the smile he gave.

But he turned from her tears away,
Away from her earnest prayer.
To the free, far North his journey lay,
And warm was his greeting there.

Long, weary nights and days
She hid herself, for sadness;
There was no word her hope to raise,
There was no smile of gladness.

But when, in anguish lone,
For the first time she pressed
Her infant, newly born—her own—
Upon her throbbing breast;

One momentary gleam,
One thought, one vision bright,
O'er her spirit passed, and then the dream
Was gone, and she woke in night.

Long, weary hours she hearkened,
If his well-known step was nigh,
But a strange mistrust had her spirit darkened,
And she asked—she knew not why—

"Oh! will he love the child?
Will he name it as his own?
Will he smile on me, as once he smiled,
And speak in the same soft tone?"

Ah! little did she know
Of his treachery, foul and deep,
As she breathed his name, in accents low,
O'er her infant's quiet sleep.

At length to the household came
A message from abroad;
And 'twas delivered in his name—
The name of their absent lord.

He bade them to array
His mansion in its pride,
For he should come, on such a day,
From the North, with his fair young bride.

And he also bade that she,
Who his favorite Slave had been,
Should, to the highest bidder, be
Struck off, ere he came again.

ELIZABETH BARRETT BROWNING   335

From his sight she must be sold,
    Nor longer there remain;
He had need, beside, of all the gold
    Which her beauty would obtain.

Her ear the tidings heard;
    She had sorrowed much and long,
But now were the depths of her spirit stirred,
    And she grew, in her madness, strong.

They sought her, to obey
    Their master's bidding then,
But found her not, and by night and day
    They searched through field and fen.

Meanwhile, with his gentle bride,
    He came, all smiles and grace:—
At the morrow's dawn he left her side,
    To join in the eager chase.

They are on the track, at last!
    They are swiftly gaining ground!
She hath heard the shout—the bugle blast—
    Her hiding-place is found!

3. Maria Lowell, "The Slave-mother," *The Liberty Bell* (1846): 250-52[1]

Her new-born child she holdeth, but feels within her heart
It is not her's, but his who can outbid her in the mart;
And, through the gloomy midnight, her prayer goes up on high,—
"God grant my little helpless one in helplessness may die!

---

1   Maria Lowell (1821-53), an American abolitionist, Transcendentalist, and poet of some
    note, was married to the better known poet James Russell Lowell (1819-91), who initi-
    ated a correspondence with EBB in 1842; EBB sent "The Runaway Slave at Pilgrim's
    Point" to him for inclusion in *The Liberty Bell* in December 1846 (*BC* 5:298, 14:86-87).
    EBB met Lowell and "his interesting wife" in London in 1852 (*LTM* 3:385).

If she must live to womanhood, oh may she never know,
Uncheered by mother's happiness, the depth of mother's woe;
And may I lie within my grave, before that day I see,
When she sits, as I am sitting, with a slave-child on her knee!"

The little arms steal upward, and then upon her breast
She feels the brown and velvet hands that never are at rest;
No sense of joy they waken, but thrills of bitter pain,—
She thinks of him who counteth o'er the gold those hands shall gain.

Then on her face she looketh, but not as mother proud,
And seeth how her features, as from out a dusky cloud,
Are tenderly unfolding, far softer than her own,
And how, upon the rounded cheek, a fairer light is thrown;

And she trembles in her agony, and on her prophet heart
There drops a gloomy shadow down, that never will depart;
She cannot look upon that face, where, in the child's pure bloom,
Is writ with such dread certainty the woman's loathsome doom.

She cannot bear to know her child must be as she hath been,
Yet she sees but one deliverance from infamy and sin,
And so she cries at midnight, with exceeding bitter cry,
"God grant my little helpless one in helplessness may die!"

4. From William Lloyd Garrison,[1] "The American Union," *The Liberty Bell* (1845): 230–38

Tyrants of the old world! contemners of the lights of man! disbelievers in human freedom and equality! enemies of mankind! console not yourselves with the delusion that REPUBLICANISM and the AMERICAN UNION are synonymous terms—or that the downfall of the latter will be the extinction of the former, and, consequently, a proof of the incapacity of the people for self-government, and a

---

1   William Lloyd Garrison (1805–79), founder of the abolitionist newspaper *The Liberator* and of the American Anti-Slavery Society, was a leading figure among the Boston abolitionists who produced *The Liberty Bell*.

confirmation of your own despotic claims! Your thrones must crumble to dust; your sceptre of dominion drop from your powerless hands; your rod of oppression be broken; yourselves so vilely abased, that there shall be "none so poor to do you reverence." The will of God, the beneficent Creator of the human family, cannot always be frustrated.... Humanity, covered with gore, cries with a voice that pierces the heavens, "His will be done!" Justice, discrowned by the hand of violence, exclaims in tones of deep solemnity, "His WILL BE DONE!" Liberty, burdened with chains, and driven into exile, in thunder-tones responds, "HIS WILL BE DONE!"....

Tyrants! confident of its overthrow, proclaim not to your vassals that the AMERICAN UNION is an experiment of freedom, which, if it fail, will forever demonstrate the necessity of whips for the backs, and chains for the limbs of the people. Know that its subversion is essential to the triumph of justice, the deliverance of the oppressed, the vindication of the BROTHERHOOD OF THE RACE. It was conceived in sin, and brought forth in iniquity; and its career has been marked by unparalleled hypocrisy, by high-handed tyranny, by a bold defiance of the omniscience and omnipotence of God. Freedom indignantly disowns it, and calls for its extinction; for within its borders are three millions of Slaves, whose blood constitutes its cement, whose flesh forms a large and flourishing branch of its commerce, and who are ranked with four-footed beasts and creeping things. To secure the adoption of the Constitution of the United States, it was agreed, first, that the African Slave-trade,—till that time, a feeble, isolated colonial traffic,—should for at least twenty years be prosecuted as a national interest under the American flag, and protected by the national arm;—secondly, that a Slave-holding oligarchy, created by allowing three-fifths of the Slave population to be represented by their taskmasters, should be allowed a permanent seat in Congress;—thirdly, that the Slave system should be secured against internal revolt and external invasion, by the united physical force of the country;—fourthly, that not a foot of national territory should be granted, on which the panting fugitive from Slavery might stand, and be safe from his pursuers—thus making every citizen a Slave-hunter and Slave-catcher. To say that this "covenant with death" shall not be annulled—that this "agreement with hell" shall continue to stand—that this "refuge of lies" shall not be swept away—is to hurl defiance at the eternal throne, and to give the lie to Him who sits thereon. It is an attempt, alike monstrous and impracticable, to blend the light of heaven with the darkness of the bottomless pit, to unite the living with the dead, to associate the Son of God with the prince of evil.

Accursed be the AMERICAN UNION, as a stupendous republican imposture!

Accursed be it, as the most frightful despotism, with regard to three millions of the people, ever exercised over any portion of the human family!

Accursed be it, as the most subtle and atrocious compromise ever made to gratify power and selfishness!

Accursed be it, as a libel on Democracy, and a bold assault on Christianity!

Accursed be it, as stained with human blood, and supported by human sacrifices!

Accursed be it, for the terrible evils it has inflicted on Africa, by burning her villages, ravaging her coast, and kidnapping her children, at an enormous expense of human life, and for a diabolical purpose!

Accursed be it, for all the crimes it has committed at home—for seeking the utter extermination of the red men of its wildernesses, and for enslaving one-sixth part of its teeming population!

Accursed be it, for its hypocrisy, its falsehood, its impudence, its lust, its cruelty, its oppression!

Accursed be it, as a mighty obstacle in the way of universal freedom and equality!

Accursed be it, from the foundation to the roof, and may there soon not be left one stone upon another, that shall not be thrown down!

Henceforth, the watchword of every uncompromising Abolitionist, of every friend of God and liberty, must be, both in a religious and political sense—"NO UNION WITH SLAVE-HOLDERS!"

II. THE ORIGINAL OPENING OF "THE RUNAWAY SLAVE AT PILGRIM'S POINT"

The draft ms of "The Runaway Slave at Pilgrim's Point"[1] opens with the uncancelled passage transcribed here, featuring a male slave as the dramatic speaker, comforted by a female slave who declares her love for him. This opening section is followed, on a new leaf, by identifiable stanzas of the finished poem, numbered in pencil in EBB's hand, with check marks beside each, beginning with stanzas 4-8; in these stanzas in the ms, it is still not clear that the decision has been made to switch to a female slave as speaker. This change becomes apparent only in Stanza 16 of the ms, "I am black. I am black / I wear a child upon my breast," which follows number 8 in the Wellesley ms. For discussion of the stanza sequence in the convoluted Wellesley draft, and the hypothesis that the abandoned opening reflects the influence of the *Narrative of the Life of Frederick Douglass, An American Slave* (1845) by Frederick Douglass (1818-95), the American abolitionist, orator, author and statesman, see Stone 2003 and 2005.

I am a slave. I will not say so much
As that I am a man. And if indeed
God as the priests tell, ever made me such
I think he looked round after, taking heed,
And smiled to all his angels that He God
Had used such base black clay to make a man
Then threw it bushward with a scorn & ban
Below His better creatures .. to be trod.

I had a dream once in my ignorance
I dreamed I was a man. One noon by chance
I sate as slaves do stupid in the sun
And wished that as the ripened gourds have done
I might fall heavily from the weary world ..

---

1   *R* D799, now in the English Poetry Collection of Wellesley College Library. The untitled ms (a title written in pencil at the top of the ms first page is not in EBB's hand) begins neatly, but in the second stanza EBB began crossing out lines and phrases, drafting anew as she proceeded.

When [a] some friend of my colour [with] unfurled[1]
Wide wings below to catch me. Suddenly
A live melodious laugh brake over me
And dew dropped upon my eyelids in a kiss[2]
Which when it passed, the world was changed to bliss.
And in between & my Tyrants stood
A smile that made me smile as if for good
Though thinking of this evil. Then began
That dream in which [I][3] dreamed I was a man

She looked into my black face with her own[4]
As might the fair white angels each to each
And said I love thee .. love thee .. thee alone
I sing thy name instead of songs & reach
The best notes with it! When the drivers drive
I sing it low for comfort, sing it low—
Backward & forward as the wind will go
The women cannot guess it though they strive[5]
The girls can never guess it
And I said to her — O my single bird
The silent woods have one & I have thee
And all my silence round is softly stirred.[6]

---

1 This line is much reworked; we present a reading of it here, marking words in square brackets that meter and sense suggest would have been deleted.

2 This line is inserted above the uncancelled line, "And left a kiss upon my folded eyes."

3 "I," required for the sense here, is omitted, probably accidentally, in the ms.

4 Above this line, EBB first wrote, "For I loved—loved —."

5 Above this line are inserted the words, "& some guess it to be cursing" followed by an illegible word.

6 This uncancelled opening section of the draft is followed (on the same leaf) by EBB's partially illegible jotted translation of some unrelated Italian verses RB had mentioned to her in a letter, 8 February 1846 (*BC* 12:50). On a new leaf, EBB continues with identifiable stanzas of the finished poem, beginning with Stanza 4 of the published version. On the convoluted stanza sequence of the ms, see Stone 2003. The opening stanza of the poem as published was written relatively late in the compositional process.

III. RESPONSES TO "THE RUNAWAY SLAVE AT PILGRIM'S POINT" AND "HIRAM POWERS' GREEK SLAVE"[1]

1. *The Literary World* on "Hiram Powers' Greek Slave" and "The Runaway Slave at Pilgrim's Point" (1851)[2]

We cannot omit, among the new poems (not to be found in the Francis edition),[3] a tribute to our country .... [quotes all of "Hiram Powers' Greek Slave"].

While this is grateful to our national pride, there is another American poem in the collection, which we cannot receive without dissent. With all respect and acknowledgement of the pure and elevated impulses which prompt her in all her utter-ances, as well of thought as feeling, we must plainly assure Mrs. Browning that she has erred in her poem of "The Runaway Slave," in as far as it is directed against our American Union. With slavery, whether it be regarded with loathing, liking, or indifference, the Union has nothing to do; the American is not responsible for it; it is purely a local institution: if there is any complaint to utter it should be addressed, respectively, to the citizens where slavery exists; and in the individual States—which are in many, if not most respects, independent communities—you must seek audience and relief. The plan of the American Federation, which hereby proves itself essentially original, seems difficult of apprehension to the foreign mind; and statesmen and practical men have committed the confusion in which our respected poet is involved (85).

---

1 For responses to "A Curse for a Nation," see the reviews of *Poems before Congress* in Appendix D.

2 "Elizabeth Barrett Browning's Poems," *The Literary World* 8, 209 (1851): 85-86.

3 A pirated edition by Charles Stephen Francis (1805-87) of *Prometheus Bound, and Other Poems; Including Sonnets from the Portuguese, Casa Guidi Windows, etc.* (New York: C.S. Francis, 1851); for EBB's comments on Francis's pirated editions, see *LTA* 1:429.

2. Charlotte Forten on "The Runaway Slave at Pilgrim's Point" (1854)[1]

Tuesday, May 30. [1854] Rose very early and was busy until nine o-clock; then, at Mrs. Putnam's urgent request, went to keep store for her while she went to Boston to attend the Anti-Slavery Convention. I was very anxious to go, and will certainly do so to-morrow; the arrest of the alleged fugitive[2] will give additional interest to the meetings, I should think. His trial is still going on and I can scarcely think of anything else; read again to-day as most suitable to my feelings and to the times, "The Run-away Slave at Pilgrim's Point," by Elizabeth B. Browning; how powerfully it is written! how earnestly and touchingly does the writer portray the bitter anguish of the poor fugitive as she thinks over all the wrongs and sufferings that she has endured, and of the sin to which tyrants have driven her but which they alone must answer for! It seems as if no one could read this poem without having his sympathies roused to the utmost in behalf of the oppressed.—

---

1   From *The Journal of Charlotte Forten: A Free Negro in the Slave Era*, ed. Ray Allen Billington (New York: W.W. Norton, 1981), 44-45. From a prominent African American Philadelphia family, Forten (1837-1914) was an educator, poet, and abolitionist.

2   A fugitive slave named Burns was tried under the Fugitive Slave Law of 1850, which required citizens in Northern States, under penalty of fines and imprisonment, to help catch runaway slaves. The slaves were denied the rights to testify and to a trial by jury.

Appendix D: The Italian Question, Reviews of Casa Guidi Windows, and Reviews of Poems Before Congress[1]

1. From [Giuseppe Mazzini], "Europe: Its Conditions and Prospects," *Westminster Review* (April 1852): 236-50[2]

The literature of the Continent during the last few years has been essentially political, revolutionary, and warlike. Out of ten historical works, seven at least speak to us from a favorable point of view or otherwise, of a revolution now extinct; out of ten polemical, political, economical, or other works, seven at least proclaim or combat a revolution about to take place.... The pen seems as it were, sword-shaped; all the world thinks and writes as if it felt itself on the eve of a battle (236)....

Europe—we might say the world, for Europe is the lever of the world—no longer believes in the sanctity of royal races .... She has invented the political axiom, "Kings reign without governing;" wherever they govern and govern badly, she overthrows them....

Now look at the organization of Europe—is it not altogether based upon privilege, by whatever name it may be known? How then can one wonder at the struggle which is engendered within it?

Let it, then, be openly declared by every honest man, that this struggle is sacred, sacred as liberty, sacred as the human soul. It is the struggle which has for its symbol, since the commencement of the historical world, the great type of Prometheus; which has for its altar, in the midst of the march of the human race, the cross of Jesus; which has for its apostles almost all the men of genius, the thousand

---

1 Most studies have assumed that *Casa Guidi Windows* prompted mainly negative reviews and that *Poems before Congress* launched an avalanche of hostile reviews. However, the response was in fact more mixed, as these extracts show, with notable differences between English and American reviews. For additional materials on the Italian question, see the supplementary website: www.ebbarchive.org.

2 On Mazzini and the European revolutions he refers to here, see the headnote to *CGW*.

pillars of humanity.... Yesterday we worshipped the priest, the lord, the soldier, the master; to-day we worship MAN, his liberty, his dignity, his immortality, his labor, his progressive tendency, all that constitutes him a creature made in the image of God,—not his color, his birth, his fortune—all that is accidental and transitory in him.... We believe in the sacredness of individual conscience, in the right of every man to the utmost self-development compatible with the equal right of his fellows; and hence we hold that whatever denies or shackles liberty is impious, and ought to be overthrown, and as soon as possible destroyed. This it is which is at the bottom of the ever-recurring struggle in Europe ... (238-39).

.... Wherever nations have risen to organize themselves in a manner more suitable to their present belief and interest, Prussian, Austrian, or French despotism has employed its brute force upon each isolated people; England has not even protested upon the tombs of Rome and Hungary.[1]....

If England persist in maintaining this neutral, passive, selfish part, she must expiate it. European transformation is inevitable; when it shall take place, when the struggle shall burst forth at twenty places at once, when the old combat between fact and right is decided, people will remember that England has stood by an inert, immovable, skeptical witness of their sufferings and efforts... (249).

2. From a review of *Casa Guidi Windows*, *The Athenaeum* 1232 (7 June 1851): 597-98

It is not only as regards its local and historical interest that Italy is presented in the pages before us. Though fraught with the spirit of English strength and insight, they are Italian in their style. Fervid, unrestrained, and imaginative, they might have been delivered by an *improvisatore*[2] in a Florentine thoroughfare to an audience of his countrymen. Nor are they, it must be said, free from those defects which belong to such *impromptu* inspirations. Diffuseness, rugged-

---

1   See the note to *CGW* 2.416-17.

2   An Italian poet who composes and recites verses extemporaneously. Mme de Staël's *Corinne* (1807) furnished an example to English literature, echoed in Letitia Landon's *The Improvisatrice* (1824).

ness, *concetti*,[1] and at times colloquialisms, impair and disfigure much that is noble in this poem both as regards its conception and its forms. We are aware that this loose mode of poetic utterance has its disciples,—and that Mrs. Browning's errors are likely to be commended by those who can emulate them more easily than they can her genius....

Our readers will agree with us that poetry like this is somewhat too loose and colloquial in its manner:—and we think they will see also in it, that Mrs. Browning has, consciously or unconsciously, caught the tone of her husband. Ere this grows on her, we desire to warn her that her own poetical mantle was of too good stuff and pattern for her not to be a loser by borrowing any other.

The second part of the poem resumes the tale of Florence after the Duke has broken his pledge and fled from his subjects....

The Duke is brought back to subjugated Florence by the aid of Austria. His return is told in words which are as defined and glowing as the forms and colours by which painting appeals to the eye. In dealing with these "modern instances," Mrs. Browning has invested them with a tone of ideal grandeur which gives them in point of poetic effect all the remoteness of antiquity....

Deeply as Mrs. Browning venerates peace, she is no party to that one-sided tranquillity which is built on the sacrifice of the weak. True peace she holds to be the recognition of mutual rights by the component classes of a State. The apathy of a nation prostrate beneath tyranny she thinks to be a worse evil than the horrors of popular insurrection. We know few things in modern poetry more passionate, vigorous, or true than her protest against that hushing of human claims which means not the silence of a people contented, but that of a people stifled. Her protest, it is almost needless to say, is not directed against those noble teachers who, abhorring recourse to the sword, would base national peace upon national justice,—but against the despotic who in the lust of power would crush the soul, and the sordid who would postpone its demands to the convenience of traffic. [cites 2.379-420 critiquing the peace movement cause led by Richard Cobden and the Manchester School]

---

1   *concetti*] an Italian term (literally meaning *concepts*) referring to ingenious metaphors (in English, conceits), which are intellectually clever rather than emotional conceptions often expressed in elaborate analogies between strikingly different things.

Notwithstanding the ostensible failure of the Italian struggle, Mrs. Browning believes that it has already subserved the interests of freedom. It has shattered the last link that knit the affections of the people to Papal domination. It has prepared the mind of Italy for the reception of religious freedom. It has emancipated human hearts from those superstitions which make intolerance easy. In expressing these hopes, the poetess renders a worthy and judicious tribute to Mazzini,—and makes touching reference to the patriotic impulse of Charles Albert,[1] to his interval of weakness, and to its final expiation....

3. From "Mrs. Browning's New Poem," *The Leader* (14 June 1851): 560-61

That Mrs. Browning is gifted with the special faculty which demarcates poets from verse writers—singers from speakers—we have already in these columns emphatically declared; the great deficiency in her writings we found to be a want of experience, an imperfect grasp of life, a certain unsubstantiality, which made the arabesques upon her Temples more important than the Temples themselves. In her *Casa Guidi Windows* we notice an immense improvement. The subject is grave with sad memories and disappointed hopes, and although vast in its scope, and somewhat abstract in its treatment, is animated by the lifeblood of reality. Out of reality it grew: direct to reality it appeals. She was there in Florence—not there in bodily presence merely—but there in spirit, in sympathy, in hope, in gladness and in sadness; and the actual *experience* of the things she utters in musical creativeness has given a graver and more touching tone to the rhythm of her thoughts, such as transcends all excellence of imagery and chastened expression (560)....

Noble writing some of this [various passages in Part I]; but the whole of the first part is inferior, we think to the second, written three years afterwards, in 1851, when all the hopes of Italy had been frustrated, when it seemed as if Italy did—[cites 2.9-12]....

---

1 On Mazzini, see the headnote to *CGW*, 1.499n, and the poet's addresses to Mazzini in 2.442, 526, 566; on Charles Albert, see 2.695-723.

... And in another strain how fine is this outburst upon that penny trade sophism—spawned by the Manchester School[1] upon a real though misguided philanthropy—the Peace Agitation:— [cites 2.373-424] (561).

4. From "Casa Guidi Windows," *The Spectator* 24, 1200 (28 June 1851): 616-17

The subjective mode of treatment, by which the theme has been fitted to a woman's hand, and by which it acquires the unity of a work of art and at the same time dispenses with the detail of continuous narrative, enables the writer to diverge at pleasure from her direct course, and, without causing any feeling of interruption, to introduce a variety of topic and allusion. Foremost among such discursions is a magnificent description of the treasures of the Crystal Palace [see *CGW* 2:577-627], and a fervent appeal on behalf of "poor Italia baffled by mischance," [*CGW* 2.651] to the nations on their way to the World's Fair, "O gracious nations," cries the poetess, [cites 2:652-56]. But of these episodical passages there is one so stirring in its fervid enthusiasm and righteous indignation, as to be not unworthy of standing side by side with Milton's noblest sonnet, "Avenge, O Lord, thy slaughtered saints!" and which as coming from a woman's heart is a tenfold more impressive protest against a phase of philanthropy of which we have heard much of late years, and under which is very apt to lurk, unsuspected by itself, an epicurean love of ease and an immoral lust of gain. A Joan of Arc might have uttered it in her loftiest moments, in the fervent prayer which strengthened her arm and moved her heart for some heroic action of great enterprise. [cites 2.373-424, critiquing the peace movement cause led by Richard Cobden and the Manchester school]....

Well said Wordsworth, "Wisdom doth live with children round her knees";[2] and had he been living, even he, with all his indifference

---

1 An allusion to the movement for international peace and non-intervention in European politics led by Richard Cobden and other members of the Manchester school of political and economic thought.

2 From the sonnet, "I grieved for Buonaparte," l. 9 (1807).

to contemporary poetry, would scarcely have failed to recognize this passage as a genuine inspiration caught, where poets too seldom seek it, at their own hearths. And to those who think that women and politics should be wide as the poles asunder, we recommend it, as a proof of the feminine warmth of heart that may coexist with a vivid sympathy with the public affairs of nations, and of the deeper human interest those affairs themselves assume when thus viewed in relation to family life and from the centre of the natural affections....

5. From *"Casa Guidi Windows. A Poem,"* Eclectic Review, 5th ser. 2 (September 1851): 306-17

.... "Casa Guidi Windows" is the natural product of the contemplation of the events which have passed in Italy since the great European outbreak of 1848, by a mind of deep observation and high and generous feeling. Mrs. Browning did not escape the delusive contagion of a popular movement which promised so much, only again to disappoint us.... [T]ens of thousands kindled into astonished hurrahs at the first movements of Pio Nono in Rome; and as many of us were still ready to believe with spasms of delirious delight in the third French convulsion of 1848 .... In her short preface, Mrs. Browning makes *her* confession of weakness, under such circumstances, with praiseworthy candor and amiableness ... (306-07).

.... It was a woful story, ending, as all such stories must end, where the aim, however excellent, has to be carried out by mere noise and bravado, against the steady, unwavering, implacable myrmidons[1] of a despotism, which has no feeling beyond its grand instinct of ruling, and crushing to rule.

Yet, even in the midst of this striking fact, we are surprised at Mrs. Browning, even, while in most eloquent terms, she is taking shame to herself for having hoped success from such materials, lowering the tone of her own philosophy, and becoming an advocate, and a most energetic and dangerous one, for war. In her first book, in the midst of her genuine aspiration, and before experience had shown

---

1   myrmidons] followers or supporters (often in a derogatory sense).

her how frail were the reeds on which she leaned, she eulogized, and most beautifully, the philosophy of peace. [cites 1.685-725]

This is glorious poetry—glorious in its intellectual strength, in its lofty eloquence, and glorious in the divinity of a resplendent truth, which the world is slowly learning from the oracles of all truth, from the words of Christ, uttered nearly two thousand years ago on the hills of Judea. It would be difficult to find, in all the treasured wealth of English literature, words which more completely describe the policy which the people of England have adopted, and to which they are every day giving a more zealous adhesion, than are contained in the concluding lines of this passage. The cry is for "no war!" to "disband our captains, change our victories;" and "henceforth be prosperous, as the angels are—helping, not humbling" [alluding to ll. 722-25 of the above passage from *CGW*]. That, if we understand anything, is precisely the doctrine of Mr. Cobden, and the policy of the Peace Society.[1] How astounding, therefore, is it to find the same mouth which had been so eloquent for this pacific policy, in the very same volume, and in the very part of it where one should have expected that the woful experiments of physical force would have confirmed inconceivably that great belief in the omnipotency of gentleness—crying so coldly and cruelly for war! [cites 2.373-424, critiquing "the cry" in England for "Peace"] (311-16).

6. From [Henry Fothergill Chorley], "*Poems before Congress*," *The Athenaeum* 1690 (17 March 1860): 371-72

Mrs. Browning is in this book authoritatively dithyrambic,[2] blessing or banning as suits an anointed priestess. She is more political than poetical, expressing her blind faith in Napoleon the Third as the hope of Italy, and flinging out a malediction against England ....

How shall we give an idea of this pamphlet of sixty pages? It must first be remarked that Mrs. Browning's Art suffers from the violence of her temper. Choosing to scold, she forgets how to sing....

---

1 See Section 3, p. 349, note 1, above, and the note to *CGW* 2.376.

2 dithyrambic] wildly enthusiastic, impassioned; also wildly irregular in form.

.... Her present pamphlet opens with a pæan to the Emperor of the French, and ends with a curse to England, whereof the following is the copy:— [cites ll. 53-119 of "A Curse for a Nation"].

The terrible assumption of vain-glory, that those whom the poetess curses must be accursed, seems to be lost in the blaze of her own infallibility as regards Italian men and affairs,—French relations,—English abominations, and every grave, intricate question which makes men weigh, wait and suspend the sledge-hammer or—the curse. For all this, Mrs. Browning is here, as before, a real poetess—one of the few among the few,—one who has written, in her time, better than the best of English poetesses...—and proves the same on this occasion, by taking to its extremity the right of "insane prophet" to lose his head,—and to loose his tongue.

7. From [Henry Fothergill Chorley], "Our Weekly Gossip," *The Athenaeum* 1693 (7 April 1860): 477[1]

Mrs. E.B. Browning wishes us to state that the verses in her "Poems before Congress," entitled "A Curse for a Nation," are leveled— not against England, as is generally thought—but against the United States; not on account, she now tells us, of any remissness on the Italian Question, but on account of the Negro Question. Every English reader of Mrs. Browning will rejoice in this assurance. We may be allowed to ask, in extenuation of our own hasty and incorrect inference,—why a rhyme on Negro slavery should appear among "Poems before Congress"?[2]

8. From "Mrs. Browning's New Poems," *The Atlas* (24 March 1860): 231-33

The tumultuous hopes and longings newly born, or rather revivified, by the Italian war of last year, have found a noble utterance in these

---

1 On EBB's protest against Chorley's first notice of the volume (Section 7 above) and this rejoinder from him, see the headnote to "A Curse for a Nation."

2 For EBB's reactions to Chorley's remarks, see *LEBB* 2:367, 378.

rough, yet in some sort harmonious, verses by the greatest poetess our language has yet produced—a writer who unites the strength of a man's intellect to the largeness of a woman's heart. We know perfectly well beforehand what will be said of them by those who hate the cause they glorify—by deniers of popular rights, lovers of Austrian "order," scorners of sentiment, worshippers of aristocratical exclusiveness and petty international jealousies. They will assert that these songs of freedom are harsh and rugged, for they will make no account of that exaltation of soul which may well cause a verse to stagger now and then, as it causes the human voice to break and fail when it would speak. They will talk of eccentricity and obscurity; and they will raise the cuckoo cry which every one whose sympathies are wider than the limits of his own land has to meet—the foolish cry that the authoress is anti-English simply because she is cosmopolitan. This last objection Mrs. Browning herself anticipated and replied to in her Preface .... (231).

...The concluding poem—"A Curse for a Nation"—is worthy of the rest; but the form is injudicious. Mrs. Browning tells us on seraphic authority, that—

A curse from the depths of womanhood
Is very salt, and bitter, and good

Nevertheless, it is unpleasant to hear a lady even "making believe" to curse her own country. It is nothing more than "make believe"; for this so-called "curse" is simply a sorrowful rebuke to England for not extending her sympathies to other lands. The objectors to Mrs. Browning's book will probably make much of this little indiscretion; but nothing will blot from the hearts of generous men and women, or remove from the sphere of their gratitude, a series of poems which will remain as an abiding contribution to an immortal cause (233).

9. From [William Edmondstoune Aytoun], "Poetic Aberrations," *Blackwood's Edinburgh Magazine* 87, 534 (April 1860): 490-94

We are strongly of opinion that, for the peace and welfare of society, it is a good and wholesome rule that women should not interfere with politics. We love the fair sex too well, to desire that they should be withdrawn from their own sphere, which is that of adorning the domestic circle, and tempering by their gentleness the asperities of our ruder nature, to figure in the public arena, or involve themselves in party contests.... We have a tender side for ladies who delight in enveloping their pretty ancles in azure.[1] Whether, inspired by verse, they warble like larks in the firmament, or dole like doves in a coppice, or coo like pigeons in spring—whether, in less ambitious prose, they conduct hero and heroine through a love-story ... or whether they apply themselves to the exposition of the finer arts, or the collection of culinary maxims—we listen, read, comment, perpend, and approve without the slightest feeling that they have in any degree overstepped the pale of propriety. And when we see them engaged in deeds of true charity—in visiting the sick, relieving the distressed, providing food for the hungry and clothing for the naked, or praying at the lonely deathbed, —we acknowledge that it is no vain figure of poetry, no fanciful association of thought, that likens women to the angels!

But very different is the case when women addict themselves to politics. Then they resemble, to our shuddering fancy, in spite of all their charms, not angels, but so many *tricoteuses*[2] in the gallery of the National Convention. Of all imaginable inflictions and torments, defend us from a domestic female partisan! Belinda on the ballot, Sophia on suffrage, Robina on reform, Barbara on the budget, Isabella on Italy, Henrietta on Hungary, Maggie on Mazzini, Gatty on Garibaldi, and Polly on the Poles—what unhappy male creature could hope to preserve his senses in the midst of so conflicting a concert? To reason they will not listen; to argument they are utterly impervious....

The case is worse when women of real talent take part in political affray. Patriotism in woman we honor. If the integrity of our own

---

1 Invoking the nineteenth-century gender ideology that men and women are designed to inhabit "separate spheres," Aytoun here refers to "bluestockings," women disparaged as unfeminine because they had more intellectual accomplishment than was usual for their gender.

2 *tricoteuses*] knitters (French), alluding to women active in the French Revolution; Dickens had portrayed one such woman (the fictional character Madame Defarge) as particularly bloodthirsty in his popular novel *A Tale of Two Cities*, serialized in *All the Year Round* in 1859.

country were assailed, or the sanctity threatened of our shores, we know that thousands of our women, overcoming mere feminine instinct, would with their own hands array their lovers, husbands, brothers, for the fight, and love them better than they did before if they fell upon the field of glory. But cosmopolitanism is quite another thing, and so is identification with foreign nationalities....

We have not made those remarks without an appropriate text. We have just received a thin volume of verses—for we cannot call them poems—by one who we are proud otherwise to style as a real poetess, and to whose high merit we have before now borne most willing testimony—Elizabeth Barrett Browning; and very sincerely do we regret, for her sake, that she has fallen into the error of publishing anything so ineffably bad, if we regard it as poetical composition—so strangely blind, if we look upon it as a political confession of faith—or so utterly unfair to England and English feeling, as has been penned by one of England's most gifted daughters. Long residence in Italy, especially in Florence, has evidently given Mrs. Browning strong Italian tendencies towards the reconstitution, or rather formation, of a nationality.... (490-91).

.... We need not advert to several other pieces, which are utterly devoid of merit, but turn to the last, which is called "A Curse for a Nation."

Mrs. Browning avers that she heard an angel speak, and he said, Write!—

"Write a nation's curse for me,
And send it over the Western Sea."

We are always sorry to be under the necessity of contradicting a lady, but we are decidedly of opinion that no angel desired the gifted authoress to do anything of the kind. The communication came directly from a pernicious little imp who had been turned out of Pandemonium[1] for profanity. Angels, we firmly believe, have a decided objection to all kinds of cursing and swearing; and had Mrs. Browning's good angel been beside her when she penned this

---

1   Pandemonium] In Milton's *Paradise Lost*, the capital of Hell built by the rebel angels after they were cast out of Heaven.

very objectionable production, we do think he would have entered his most solemn protest against its publication. For what nation the curse was intended by the diabolical instigating Balak,[1] we do not clearly understand; but from the mention of the Western Sea, we suppose that it applies to America, though what America has to do with European Congresses or the settlement of the affairs of Italy, we cannot comprehend. We have a strong suspicion, however, that it originally had another application....

.... But let us ask Mrs. Browning in all seriousness whether she considers it her duty to curse any one? To bless and not to curse is woman's function; and if Mrs. Browning, in her calmer moments, will but contrast the spirit which has prompted her to such melancholy aberrations with that which animated Florence Nightingale,[2] she can hardly fail to derive a profitable lesson for the future... (494).

10. Translation of the Italian inscription, composed by the Italian poet Niccolò Tommaseo (1802-74), on the tablet affixed to the Browning's home Casa Guidi by the city of Florence after EBB's death

HERE WROTE AND DIED

ELIZABETH BARRETT BROWNING

WHO IN THE HEART OF A WOMAN RECONCILED

A SCHOLAR'S LEARNING AND A POET'S SPIRIT

AND MADE OF HER VERSE A GOLDEN RING

BETWEEN ITALY AND ENGLAND

GRATEFUL FLORENCE

SETS THIS MEMORIAL

1861[3]

---

1 Balak] a pagan god in the Bible.

2 While honoring Florence Nightingale, EBB remarked that "I do not consider the best use to which we can put a gifted and accomplished woman is to make her a hospital nurse. If it is, why then woe to us all who are artists! The woman's question is at an end" (*LEBB* 2:188-89); in an earlier description of meeting Nightingale, EBB nonetheless describes her as "acting greatly" (*LTH* 207-08).

3 "Qui scrisse e morì / Elisabetta Barrett Browning / che in cuore di donna conciliava / scienza di dotto e spirito di poeta / e fece del suo verso aureo anello / Fra Italia e Inghilterra. / Pone questa memoria / Firenze grata / 1861."

Select Bibliography

For collections of EBB's poetry and correspondence, see the "Abbreviations, Primary Sources, and Website," pp. XI-XII. See also the "Note on Citation Practices," p. XIII.[1]

Agajanian, Shaakeh. 1985. *"Sonnets from the Portuguese" and the Love Sonnet Tradition*. New York: Philosophical Library.

Alaya, Flavia. 1978. "The Ring, the Rescue, and the *Risorgimento*: Reunifying the Brownings' Italy." *Browning Institute Studies* 6: 1-41. Rpt. in Donaldson 1999.

Arishtein, Leonid M. 1969. "'A Curse for a Nation': A Controversial Episode in Elizabeth Barrett Browning's Political Poetry." *Review of English Studies*, n.s. 20: 33-42.

Armstrong, Isobel. 1993. *Victorian Poetry: Poetry, Poetics and Politics*. London: Routledge.

——. 2003. "*Casa Guidi Windows*: Spectacle and Politics in 1851." In Chapman and Stabler 2003. 51-69.

Avery, Simon. 2004. *The Brownings*. Lives of Victorian Literary Figures II. London: Pickering & Chatto.

——. 2006. "Telling it Slant: Promethean, Whig, and Dissenting Politics in Elizabeth Barrett's Poetry of the 1830s." *VP* 44: 405-24.

Avery, Simon, and Rebecca Stott. 2003. *Elizabeth Barrett Browning*. London: Pearson Education.

Barker, Nicholas. 2003. "A Note on *Two Poems*." In *Form and Meaning in the History of the Book: Selected Essays*. London: The British Library. 353-63.

Barnes, Warner. 1967. *A Bibliography of Elizabeth Barrett Browning*. Austen: Humanities Research Center, University of Texas & Armstrong Browning Library, Baylor University.

---

1 This is a Select Bibliography of criticism on EBB's works aside from *Aurora Leigh*. For additional secondary sources, see the supplementary website to this edition, www.ebbarchive.org; the annual overviews of criticism on EBB in *VP* by Mermin (up to 2000) and by Stone (2001-); and Donaldson's annotated bibliography of materials up to 1990 (in this bibliography). See also Donaldson's comprehensive bibliographical lists in *Victorian Literature and Culture* up to 2001 (covering materials published through 1998), a continuation of annual bibliographies earlier appearing from 1973 to 1990 in *Browning Institute Studies*.

Barrett, R.A. 2000. *The Barretts of Jamaica: The Family of Elizabeth Barrett Browning.* Waco, TX: Wedgestone Press.

Battles, Elizabeth H. 1991. "Slavery through the Eyes of a Mother: 'The Runaway Slave at Pilgrim's Point.'" *SBHC* 19: 93-100.

Bayne, Peter. 1881. *Two Great Englishwomen: Mrs. Browning and Charlotte Brontë; with an Essay on Poetry, Illustrated from Wordsworth, Burns, and Byron.* London: James Clarke.

Benson, Arthur Christopher. 1896 "Elizabeth Barrett Browning." In *Essays*. London: Heineman.

Billone, Amy. 2001. "'In Silence Like to Death': Elizabeth Barrett's Sonnet Turn." *VP* 39: 533-50.

Bisignano, Dominic James. 1964. "The Brownings and Their Italian Critics." Ph.D. dissertation. New York University.

Blake, Kathleen. 1986. "Elizabeth Barrett Browning and Wordsworth: The Romantic Poet as a Woman." *VP* 24: 387-98.

Bristow, Joseph. 2004. "Whether 'Victorian' Poetry: A Genre and Its Period." *VP* 42: 81-109.

Brophy, Sarah. 1998. "Elizabeth Barrett Browning's 'The Runaway Slave at Pilgrim's Point' and the Politics of Interpretation." *VP* 36: 273-88.

Brown, Susan. 1995. "'Black and White Slave': Discourses of Race and Victorian Feminism." In *Gender and Colonialism*, ed. Timonthy P. Foley, Lionel Pilkington, Sean Ryder and Elizabeth Tilley. Galway: Galway University Press. 124-38.

Byrd, Deborah. 1987. "Combating an Alien Tyranny: Elizabeth Barrett Browning's Evolution as a Feminist Poet." *Browning Institute Studies* 15: 23-41. Rpt. in Donaldson 1999.

Byron, Glennis [Stephenson]. 2003. "Rethinking the Dramatic Monologue; Victorian Women Poets and Social Critique." In Chapman 2003d. 79-88.

Campbell, Wanda. 1991. "Isabella Valency Crawford and Elizabeth Barrett Browning." *Canadian Poetry*: 25-37.

Chapman, Alison. 1998. "Mesmerism and Agency in the Courtship of Elizabeth Barrett Browning and Robert Browning." *Victorian Literature and Culture* 26: 303-19.

——. 1999. "Uncanny Epiphanies in the Nineteenth-Century Sonnet Tradition." In *Moments of Moment: Aspects of the Literary Epiphany*, ed. Wim Tigges. Amsterdam: Rodopoi. 115-35.

——. 2001a. "'All that I have dreamed and more': Elizabeth Barrett Browning's Florence." *Journal of Anglo-Italian Studies* 6: 127-37.

——. 2001b. "Elizabeth Barrett Browning and Sophia Eckley: A Note on the End of the Affair." *Notes & Queries* 48: 144-45.

——. 2002. "Sonnet and Sonnet Sequences." In Cronin, Chapman, and Harrison 2002. 99-114.

——. 2003a. "The Expatriate Poetess: Nationhood, Poetics and Politics." In Chapman 2003d. 57-77.

——. 2003b. "'In our own blood drenched the pen': Italy and Sensibility in Elizabeth Barrett Browning's *Last Poems* (1862)." *Women's Writing: The Elizabethan to the Victorian Period* 10: 269-86.

——. 2003c. "*Risorgimento*: Spiritualism, Politics and Elizabeth Barrett Browning." In Chapman and Stabler 2003. 70-89.

——, ed. 2003d. *Victorian Women Poets.* Suffolk: Boydell and Brewer.

Chapman, Alison, and Jane Stabler, eds. 2003. *Unfolding the South: Nineteenth-Century British Women Writers and Artists in Italy.* Manchester: Manchester UP.

Chevasco, Berry. 2003. "'Naughty Books': Elizabeth Barrett Browning's Response to Eugène Sue." *Browning Society Notes* 28: 7-17.

Cooper, Helen. 1988. *Elizabeth Barrett Browning: Woman and Artist.* Chapel Hill: U of North Carolina P.

Cronin, Richard. 2002. "Civilizing Romanticism." In *Romantic Victorians: English Literature, 1824-1840.* Basingstoke and New York: Palgrave Macmillan. Ch. 5.

——. 2003. "*Casa Guidi Windows*: Elizabeth Barrett Browning, Italy and the Poetry of Citizenship." In Chapman and Stabler 2003. 35-50.

Cronin, Richard, Alison Chapman, and Antony H. Harrison, eds. 2002. *A Companion to Victorian Poetry.* Oxford: Blackwell.

Cuda, Antony J. 2004. "Eliot's Quotation from Elizabeth Barrett Browning's 'Shadows for My Company.'" *Notes & Queries* 51: 164-65.

David, Deirdre. 1987. *Intellectual Women and Victorian Patriarchy: Harriet Martineau, Elizabeth Barrett Browning, George Eliot.* Ithaca, NY: Cornell UP.

Davies, Corinne. 2006. "Two of Elizabeth Barrett Browning's Pan Poems and Their After-Life in Robert Browning's 'Pan and Luna.'" *VP* 44: 561-70.

Davies, Corinne, and Marjorie Stone. 2006. "'Singing Song for Song': The Brownings in the Poetic Relation." In *Literary Couplings: Writing Couples, Collaborators, and the Construction of Authorship*, ed. Marjorie Stone and Judith Thompson. Madison: Wisconsin UP. 150-74.

Dillon, Steve. 2001. "Barrett Browning's Poetic Vocation: Crying, Singing, Breathing." *VP* 39: 509-32.

Dillon, Steve, and Katherine Frank. 1997. "Defenestrations of the Eye: Flow, Fire, and Sacrifice in *Casa Guidi Windows*." *VP* 35: 471-92.

Donaldson, Sandra. 1980. "'Motherhood's Advent into Power': Elizabeth Barrett Browning's Poems about Motherhood." *VP* 18: 151-60.

——. 1993a. *Elizabeth Barrett Browning: An Annotated Bibliography of the Commentary and Criticism, 1826-1990*. New York: G.K. Hall.

——. 1993b. "'For Nothing Was Simply One Thing': The Reception of Elizabeth Barrett Browning's 'A Curse for a Nation.'" *SBHC* 20: 137-44.

——. 1997. "Elizabeth Barrett's Two Sonnets to George Sand." *SBHC* 5: 19-22. Rpt. in Donaldson 1999.

——, ed. 1999. *Critical Essays on Elizabeth Barrett Browning*. New York: G.K. Hall.

——. 2002. "Versions of a Text: 'A Drama of Exile' as a Test Case for a New Edition of Elizabeth Barrett Browning's Collected Poems." *The Papers of the Bibliographical Society of America* 96: 49-58.

Dow, Miroslava Wein. 1980. *A Variorum Edition of Elizabeth Barrett Browning's* Sonnets from the Portuguese. Troy, NY: Whitston.

Fish, Laura. 2006. "*Strange Music*: Engaging Imaginatively with the Family of Elizabeth Barrett Browning from a Creole and Black Woman's Perspective." *VP* 44: 507-24.

Forster, Margaret. 1988. *Elizabeth Barrett Browning: A Biography*. London: Chatto & Windus.

Furr, Derek. 2002. "Sentimental Confrontations: Hemans, Landon, and Elizabeth Barrett Browning." *English Language Notes* 40: 29-47.

Gaja, Katerine. 2003. "White Silence: Body and Soul in the Letters of Elizabeth Barrett Browning and Hiram Powers." *Times Literary Supplement* 229 (26 June): 16-17.

Garrett, Martin. 2002. *Elizabeth Barrett Browning and Robert Browning: Interviews and Recollections.* New York: Palgrave.

Gladish, Robert W. 1969. "Mrs. Browning's 'A Curse for a Nation': Some Further Comments." *VP* 7: 275-80.

Gray, Erik. 2002. "Sonnet Kisses: Sidney to Barrett Browning." *Essays in Criticism* 52: 126-42.

Groth, Helen. 2000. "A Different Look—Visual Technologies and the Making of History in Elizabeth Barrett Browning's *Casa Guidi Windows.*" *Textual Practice* 14: 31-52.

Harris, Leigh Coral. 2000. "From Mythos to Logos: Political Aesthetics and Liminal Poetics in Elizabeth Barrett Browning's *Casa Guidi Windows.*" *Victorian Literature and Culture* 28: 109-31.

Harrison, Antony H. Harrison. 1990. *Victorian Poets and Romantic Poems: Intertextuality and Ideology.* Charlottesville: UP of Virginia.

——. 1998. *Victorian Poets and the Politics of Culture: Discourse and Ideology.* Charlottesville: UP of Virginia.

Hayter, Alethea. 1962. *Mrs. Browning: A Poet's Work and its Setting.* London: Faber and Faber.

Hickok, Kathleen. 1984. *Representations of Women: Nineteenth-Century British Women's Poetry.* Westport, CT: Greenwood.

Hoagwood, Terence Allan. 2004. "Biblical Criticism and Secular Sex: Elizabeth Barrett's *A Drama of Exile* and Jean Ingelow's *A Story of Doom.*" *VP* 42: 165-80.

Homans, Margaret. 1998. *Royal Representations: Queen Victoria and British Culture, 1837-1876.* Chicago: U of Chicago P.

Houston, Natalie M. 2002. "Affecting Authenticity: *Sonnets from the Portuguese* and *Modern Love.*" *Studies in the Literary Imagination* 35: 99-121.

Hurst, Isobel. 2006. *Victorian Women Writers and the Classics: The Feminine of Homer.* Oxford: Oxford UP.

Johnson, Stephanie L. 2006. "*Aurora Leigh's* Radical Youth": Derridean *Parergon* and the Narrative Frame in 'A Vision of Poets.'" *VP* 44: 425-44.

Jones, Christine Kenyon. 2002. "'Some World's-Wonder in Chapel or Crypt': Elizabeth Barrett Browning and Disability." *Nineteenth Century Studies* 16: 21-35.

Kaplan, Cora. 1978. "Introduction." *Aurora Leigh with Other Poems.* London: Women's P.

Karlin, Daniel. 1985. *The Courtship of Robert Browning and Elizabeth Barrett.* Oxford: Clarendon.

——. 1997. "The Discourse of Power in Elizabeth Barrett Browning's Criticism." *SBHC* 20: 30-38. Rpt. in Donaldson 1999.

Kennedy, Richard S. 2000. "Disposing of a New Myth: A Close Look at Julia Markus' Theory about the Brownings' Ancestry." *Browning Society Notes* 26: 21-47.

Keirstead, Christopher M. 2005. "A 'Bad Patriot'?: Elizabeth Barrett Browning and Cosmopolitanism." *Victorians Institute Journal* 33: 69-95.

Kimery, Millard. 1993. "A Sense of Place in Elizabeth Barrett Browning's 'A Drama of Exile.'" *SBHC* 20: 17-23.

Leighton, Angela. 1986. *Elizabeth Barrett Browning.* Brighton: Harvester.

——. 1988. "Stirring a Dust of Figures: Elizabeth Barrett Browning and Love." *Browning Society Notes* 17: 11-24. Rpt. in Donaldson 1999.

——. 1992. *Victorian Women Poets: Writing Against the Heart.* Charlottesville: UP of Virginia.

Levine, Caroline. 2006. "Strategic Formalism: Toward a New Method in Cultural Studies." *Victorian Studies* 48: 625-57.

Lewis, Linda M. 1998. *Elizabeth Barrett Browning's Spiritual Progress: Face to Face with God.* Columbia: U of Missouri P.

——. 2003. *Germaine de Staël, George Sand, and the Victorian Woman Artist.* Columbia: U of Missouri P.

Lewis, Scott, ed. 2002. *The Letters of Elizabeth Barrett Browning to Her Sister Arabella.* 2 vols. Waco, TX: Wedgestone Press.

Lines, Richard. 2004. "Swedenborgian Ideas in the Poetry of Elizabeth Barrett Browning and Robert Browning." In *In Search of the Absolute: Essays on Swedenborg and Literature,* ed. Stephen McNeilly. *Journal of the Swedenborg Society* 3: 23-43.

Lootens, Tricia. 1996. *Lost Saints: Silence, Gender, and Victorian Literary Canonization.* Charlottesville: UP of Virginia.

——. 2006. "Publishing and Reading 'Our EBB': Editorial Pedagogy, Contemporary Culture, and 'The Runaway Slave at Pilgrim's Point.'" *VP* 44: 487–506.

Marks, Jeanette. 1938. *The Family of the Barrett: A Colonial Romance.* New York: Macmillan.

Markus, Julia. 1977. "Introduction." *Casa Guidi Windows.* New York: The Browning Institute.

——. 1995. *Dared and Done: The Marriage of Elizabeth Barrett and Robert Browning.* New York: Alfred Knopf.

Marshall, Gail. 2006. "Elizabeth Barrett Browning and Shakespeare: Translating the Language of Intimacy." *VP* 44: 467–86.

Matthews, Samantha. 2001. "Entombing the Woman Poet: Tributes to Elizabeth Barrett Browning." *SBHC* 24: 31–53.

Mazzaro, Jerome. 1991. "Mapping Sublimity: Elizabeth Barrett Browning's *Sonnets from the Portuguese*." *Essays in Literature* 18: 166–79. Rpt. in Donaldson 1999.

Melnyk, Julie. 2003. "'Mighty Victims': Women Writers and the Feminization of Christ." *Victorian Literature and Culture* 31: 131–57.

Merivale, Patricia. 1965. "The Pan Figure in Victorian Poetry: Landor to Meredith." *Philological Quarterly* 44: 258–77.

Mermin, Dorothy. 1981. "The Female Poet and the Embarrassed Reader: Elizabeth Barrett Browning's *Sonnets from the Portuguese*." *ELH* 48: 351–67.

——. 1986. "The Damsel, the Knight, and the Victorian Woman Poet." *Critical Inquiry* 13: 64–80.

——. 1989. *Elizabeth Barrett Browning: The Origins of a New Poetry.* Chicago: U of Chicago P.

Monteiro, George. 1980. "On First Looking into Strangford's Camões: Elizabeth Barrett Browning's 'Catarina to Camoëns.'" *SBHC* 8: 7–19.

Montwieler, Katherine. 2005. "Domestic Politics: Gender, Protest, and Elizabeth Barrett Browning's *Poems before Congress*." *Tulsa Studies in Women's Literature* 24: 291–318.

Moore, Mary B. 2000. *Desiring Voices: Women Sonneteers and Petrarchism.* Carbondale and Edwardsville: Southern Illinois UP.

Morlier, Margaret M. 1990. "The Death of Pan: Elizabeth Barrett Browning and the Romantic Ego." *Browning Institute Studies* 18: 131–55. Rpt. in Donaldson 1999.

——. 1993. "Elizabeth Barrett Browning and Felicia Hemans: The 'Poetess' Problem." *SBHC* 20: 70-79.

——. 1999. "*Sonnets from the Portuguese* and the Politics of Rhyme." *Victorian Literature and Culture* 27: 97-112.

——. 2003. "The Hero and the Sage: Elizabeth Barrett's Sonnets 'To George Sand' in Victorian Context." *VP* 41: 319-32.

Moser, Kay. 1984. "Elizabeth Barrett Browning's Youthful Feminism: 'Fragment of an Essay on Woman.'" *SBHC* 12: 13-26.

Neri, Barbara. 2000. "A Lineage of Love: The Literary Bloodlines of Elizabeth Barrett Browning's *Sonnets from the Portuguese*." *SBHC* 23: 50-69.

——. 2003. "The Consolation of Poetry: A Performance by Barbara Neri." *The Drama Review* 47: 45-77.

——. 2005. "'Sonnet I' and 'Sonnet II' of Elizabeth Barrett Browning's *Sonnets from the Portuguese*: Setting the Stage for Divine Reunification." *SBHC* 26: 40-52.

——. 2006. "*Cobridme de flores*: (Un)Covering Flowers of Portuguse and Spanish Poets in *Sonnets from the Portuguese*." *VP* 44: 571-84.

Parry, Ann. 1988. "Sexual Exploitation and Freedom: Religion, Race, and Gender in Elizabeth Barrett Browning's *The Runaway Slave at Pilgrim's Point*." *SBHC* 16: 114-26.

Paul, Sarah. 1989. "Strategic Self-Centering and the Female Narrator: Elizabeth Barrett Browning's *Sonnets from the Portuguese*." *Browning Institute Studies* 17: 75-91.

Petrioli, Piergiacomo. 2001. "The Brownings and Their Sienese Circle." *SBHC* 24: 78-109.

Phelan, Joseph. 1993. "Elizabeth Barrett Browning's *Casa Guidi Windows,* Arthur Hugh Clough's *Amours de Voyage,* and the Italian National Uprisings of 1847-49." *Journal of Anglo-Italian Studies* 3: 137-52.

——. 2003. "Ethnology and Biography: The Case of the Brownings." *Biography* 26: 261-82.

Pollock, Mary Sanders. 1996. "The Anti-Canonical Realism of Elizabeth Barrett Browning's 'Lord Walter's Wife.'" *Studies in the Literary Imagination* 29: 43-53.

——. 2003. *Elizabeth Barrett and Robert Browning: A Creative Partnership.* Aldershot: Ashgate Publishing.

Porter, Katherine. 1972. *Through a Glass Darkly: Spiritualism in the Browning Circle*. New York: Octagon Books.

Prins, Yopie. 1991. "Elizabeth Barrett, Robert Browning, and the *Différance* of Translation." *VP* 29: 435-51.

Radley, Virginia L. 1972. *Elizabeth Barrett Browning*. Boston: Twayne.

Raymond, Meredith. 1981. "Elizabeth Barrett Browning's Poetics, 1845-1846: 'The Ascending Gyre.'" *Browning Society Notes* 11: 1-11.

Reynolds, Margaret. 1997. "Love's Measurement in Elizabeth Barrett Browning's *Sonnets from the Portuguese*." *SBHC* 21: 53-65.

Reynolds, Margaret, and Barbara Rosenbaum. 1997. "'Aeschylus' Soliloquy' by Elizabeth Barrett Browning." *VP* 35: 329-48.

Reynolds, Matthew. 2001. *The Realms of Verse, 1830-1870: English Poetry in a Time of Nation Building*. Oxford: Oxford UP.

Riede, David G. 1999. "Elizabeth Barrett Browning's Poetry of Exile: Difficulties of a Female Christian Romanticism." *Victorians Institute Journal* 27: 91-112.

——. 2005. *Allegories of One's Own Mind: Melancholy in Victorian Poetry*. Columbus: Ohio State UP.

Rosenblum, Dolores. 1985. "*Casa Guidi Windows* and *Aurora Leigh*: The Genesis of Elizabeth Barrett Browning's Visionary Aesthetic." *Tulsa Studies in Women's Literature* 4: 61-68.

Sadenwasser, Tim. 1999. "Rhyme, Form, and Sound in Elizabeth Barrett Browning's 'The Dead Pan.'" *VP* 37: 521-37.

Saunders, Clare Broome. 2006. "'Judge no more what ladies do': Elizabeth Barrett Browning's Active Medievalism, the Female Troubadour, and Joan of Arc." *VP* 44: 585-99.

Scheinberg, Cynthia. 2002. *Women's Poetry and Religion in Victorian England: Jewish Identity and Christian Culture*. Cambridge: Cambridge UP.

Schor, Esther. 1998. "The Poetics of Politics: Barrett Browning's *Casa Guidi Windows*." *Tulsa Studies in Women's Literature* 17: 305-24.

Shires, Linda. 2001. "Elizabeth Barrett Browning: Cross-Dwelling and the Reworking of Female Poetic Authority." *Victorian Literature and Culture* 30: 326-43.

Simonsen, Pauline. 1997. "Elizabeth Barrett Browning's Redundant Women." *VP* 35: 509-32.

Slinn, E. Warwick. 2002. "Elizabeth Barrett Browning and the Problem of Female Agency." In *Tradition and the Poetics of Self in Nineteenth-Century Women's Poetry*, ed. Barbara Garlick. Amsterdam: Rodopi. 43-55.

——. 2003. *Victorian Poetry as Cultural Critique: The Politics of Performative Language.* Charlottesville: UP of Virginia.

Smith, Fred Manning. 1939. "Mrs. Browning's Rhymes." *PMLA* 54: 829-34.

Stauffer, Andrew. 1997. "Elizabeth Barrett Browning's (Re)visions of Slavery." *English Language Notes* 34, 4: 29-48.

Stephenson, Glennis. 1989. *Elizabeth Barrett Browning and the Poetry of Love.* Ann Arbor: UMI Press.

Stephenson, Will, and Mimosa Stephenson. 1993. "Adam's Farewell and the Poet's Farewell: New Poetry by Elizabeth Barrett Browning." *SBHC* 20: 7-16.

Stone, Marjorie. 1986. "Cursing as One of the Fine Arts: Elizabeth Barrett Browning's Political Poems." *Dalhousie Review* 66: 155-73. Rpt. in Donaldson 1999.

——. 1993. "A Cinderella Among the Muses: Elizabeth Barrett Browning and the Ballad Tradion." *Victorian Literature and Culture* 21: 233–68.

——. 1994. "Sisters in Art: Christina Rossetti and Elizabeth Barrett Browning." *VP* 32: 339-64.

——. 1995. *Elizabeth Barrett Browning.* Basingstoke and New York: Palgrave Macmillan.

——. 1997. "Editing Elizabeth Barrett Browning: *Aurora Leigh*, Recent Editions of 'Selected Poems,' and the Case for a Comprehensive Critical Edition." *SBHC* 21: 132-52.

——. 1998. "Bile and the Brownings: A New Poem by Browning, Barrett Browning's 'My Heart and I,' and New Questions about the Brownings' Marriage." In *Robert Browning in Contexts*, ed. John Woolford. Winfield, KS: Wedgestone P. 213-32.

——. 1999. "*Monna Innominata* and *Sonnets from the Portuguese.*" In *The Culture of Christina Rossetti: New Essays on Christina Rossetti*, ed. Mary Arseneau, Antony H. Harrison, and Lorraine Janzen Kooistra. Athens: Ohio UP. 46-74.

——. 2002. "Between Ethics and Anguish: Feminist Ethics, Feminist Aesthetics, and Representations of Infanticide in 'The Runaway

Slave at Pilgrim's Point' and *Beloved*." In *Between Ethics and Aesthetics: Crossing the Boundaries*, ed. Dorota Glowacka and Stephen Boos. Albany: SUNY Press. 131–58.

——. 2003a. "Elizabeth Barrett Browning and the Garrisonians: 'The Runaway Slave at Pilgrim's Point,' The Boston Female Anti-Slavery Society, and Abolitionist Discourse in the *Liberty Bell*." In Chapman 2003d. 33–55.

——. 2003b. "The Search for a Lost Atlantis: Feminist Paradigms, Narratives of Nation, and Genealogies of Victorian Women's Poetry and Anti-Slavery Writing." In *Women and Literary History*, ed. Katherine Binhammer and Jeanne Wood. Newark, DE: U of Delaware P. 119–51.

——. 2004. "Elizabeth Barrett Browning." *New Dictionary of National Biography*, ed. H.C.G. Matthew and Brian Harrison, 60 vols. Oxford: Oxford UP. Vol. 8, 233–42.

——. 2005. "A Heretic Believer: Victorian Religious Doubt and New Contexts for Elizabeth Barrett Browning's 'A Drama of Exile,' 'The Virgin Mary to the Child Jesus,' and 'The Runaway Slave at Pilgrim's Point.'" *SBHC* 26: 6–39.

Stone, Marjorie, and Beverly Taylor. 2006. "'Confirm my voice': 'My sisters,' Poetic Audiences, and the Published Voices of EBB." *VP* 44: 391–403.

Straight, Julie. 2000. "'Neither keeping either under': Gender and Voice in Elizabeth Barrett's *The Seraphim*." *VP* 38: 269–88.

Sullivan, Mary Rose. 1987. "'Some Interchange of Grace': 'Saul' and *Sonnets from the Portuguese*." *Browning Institute Studies* 15: 55–68. Rpt. in Donaldson 1999.

Swyderski, Ann. 2000. "Dickinson and 'that Foreign Lady—.'" *Symbiosis* 4: 51–65.

——. 2003. "Dickinson's Enchantment: The Barrett Browning Fascicles." *Symbiosis* 7: 75–98.

Taplin, Gardiner B. 1957. *The Life of Elizabeth Barrett Browning*. New Haven: Yale UP.

Taylor, Beverly. 1993. "Elizabeth Barrett Browning's Subversion of the Gift Book Model." *SBHC* 20: 62–69.

——. 1999. "Elizabeth Barrett Browning." In *Dictionary of Literary Biography*, Vol. 199, *Victorian Women Poets*, ed. William B. Thesing. Detroit: Gale Research. 79–99.

——. 2003. "A Date for an Undated Letter and an Unpublished Reminiscence of the Brownings." *Browning Society Notes* 28: 67-72.

——. 2005a. "Childhood Writings of Elizabeth Barrett Browning: 'At four I first mounted Pegasus.'" In *The Child Writer from Jane Austen to Virginia Woolf*, ed. Christine Alexander and Juliet McMaster. Cambridge: Cambridge UP. 138-53.

——. 2005b. "Elizabeth Barrett Browning's Political-Aesthetic Philosophy: The Poetics of Engagement." *SBHC* 26: 94-104.

Taylor, Olivia Gatti. 2006. "Written in Blood: The Art of Mothering Epic in the Poetry of Elizabeth Barrett Browning." *VP* 44: 153-64.

Tucker, Herbert F. 2006a. "An Ebbigrammar of Motives; or, Ba for Short." *VP* 44: 445-66.

——. 2006b. "Tactical Formalism: A Response to Caroline Levine." *Victorian Studies* 49: 85-93.

Waddington, Patrick. 1997. "Russian Variations on an English Theme: The Crying Children of Elizabeth Barrett Browning." *SBHC* 21: 94-131.

Williams, Jeni. 1997. *Interpreting Nightingales: Gender, Class and Histories.* Sheffield: Sheffield Academic P. 169-225.

Woodworth, Elizabeth. 2006. "Elizabeth Barrett Browning, Conventry Patmore, and Alfred Tennyson on Napoloeon III: The Hero-Poet and Carlylean Heroics." *VP* 44: 543-61.

Woolford, John. 1979. "EBB: 'Woman and Poet.'" *Browning Society Notes* 9: 3-5.

——. 1993. "Elizabeth Barrett and William Wordsworth." *SBHC* 20: 48-61.

——. 1995. "Elizabeth Barrett and the Wordsworthian Sublime." *Essays in Criticism* 45: 36-56.

——. 2001. "The Romantic Brownings." *SBHC* 24: 7-30.

Woolf, Virginia. 1986. "Aurora Leigh" (first pub. 1931). In *The Second Common Reader*, ed. Andrew McNeillie. New York: Harcourt Brace Jovanovich. 202-13.

Wörn, Alexandra M.B. 2004. "'Poetry is where God is': The Importance of Christian Faith and Theology in Elizabeth Barrett Browning's Life and Work." In *Victorian Religious Discourse: New Directions in Criticism*, ed. Jude V. Nixon. New York: Palgrave. 235-52.